ELEMENTARY READING

A Comprehensive Approach

ELEMENTARY READING

A Comprehensive Approach

John N. Mangieri
University of South Carolina

Lois A. Bader
Michigan State University

James E. Walker
Northern Illinois University

McGraw-Hill Book Company

*New York   St. Louis   San Francisco   Auckland   Bogotá   Hamburg
Johannesburg   London   Madrid   Mexico   Montreal   New Delhi
Panama   Paris   São Paulo   Singapore   Sydney   Tokyo   Toronto*

ELEMENTARY READING

A Comprehensive Approach

1 2 3 4 5 6 7 8 9 0 DODO 8 9 8 7 6 5 4 3 2 1

ISBN 0-07-039886-0

This book was set in Baskerville by Better Graphics.
The editors were Phillip A. Butcher and James R. Belser;
the designer was Janice Noto;
the production supervisor was Leroy A. Young.
The photo editor was Inge King;
the cover photograph was taken by Ken Karp.
The drawings were done by Danmark & Michaels, Inc.
R. R. Donnelley & Sons Company was printer and binder.

Library of Congress Cataloging in Publication Data

Mangieri, John N.
    Elementary reading.

    Includes bibliographies and index.
    1. Reading (Elementary)   I. Bader, Lois A.
II. Walker, James E. (James Eugene), date
III. Title.
LB1573.M326   372.4   81-12317
ISBN 0-07-039886-0   AACR2

To teachers and other individuals
who work tirelessly toward
giving children a most precious gift—LITERACY
and to the memory of
Dr. Mary J. Heimberger

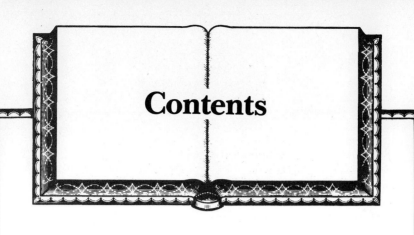

Contents

Foreword   xvii
Preface   xix

Chapter One

THE EFFECTIVE TEACHER OF
ELEMENTARY READING   1

Overview   1
Definition of Terms   1
On Teaching Reading   2
A Tale of Two Teachers   3
  Linda   3
  Rose   5
  Analysis and Explanation   7
    Analysis of Linda • Explanation of Linda •
    Analysis of Rose • Explanation of Rose
  Evaluation   18
Activities Related to the Chapter   18
Bibliography and References   18

Chapter Two

READINESS TO READ   21

Overview   21
Definition of Terms   21

Readiness and Chronological Age   22
Readiness and Maturity   23
Sex Differences and Maturity   23
Is Maturity a Factor?   23
Social and Psychological Factors   25
Cultural Factors   25
Predicting Reading Success or Failure   26
Readiness Tests   27
Readiness Checklists   28
Readiness Programs versus Readiness for the Task   29
Reading to Children and Readiness   30
Prereading Activities   30
Readiness at Later Levels   36
Summary   36
Activities Related to the Chapter   37
Bibliography and References   37

Chapter Three

VOCABULARY: THE KEYSTONE OF READING   41

Overview   41
Definition of Terms   41
Vocabulary Defined   42
Learners   43
Types of Vocabularies   43
Reading Vocabulary   44
  Sight Vocabulary   44
  Delayed Recall   46
    Phonics • Configuration • Structural
    Analysis • Context • Dictionary Usage
  Summary   52
Vocabulary Acquisition and Retention   52
Vocabulary Activities   54
Summary   59
Activities Related to the Chapter   60
Bibliography and References   60

Chapter Four

COMPREHENSION: THE CORE OF READING 63

Overview 63
Definition of Terms 63
Literal Comprehension 66
 Literal Reading Skills 66
 Activities for Literal Reading 68
Interpretive Comprehension 69
 Interpretive Readings Skills 70
 Activities for Interpretive Reading 71
Critical Reading 72
 Critical Reading Skills 72
 Activities for Critical Reading 74
Creative Reading 75
 Creative Reading Skills 75
 Activities for Creative Reading 76
Limitations to Comprehension 77
Summary 78
Activities Related to the Chapter 78
Bibliography and References 79

Chapter Five

READING APPROACHES AND MATERIALS 81

Overview 81
Definition of Terms 81
The Language-Experience Approach 82
 Background 82
 Rationale 82
 Characteristics 83
 Objectives 84
 Advantages 84
 Disadvantages 85
Basal Reading Programs 85
 Rationale 85
 Characteristics 86

Recent Developments   87
Objectives   88
Advantages   88
Disadvantages   88
Individualized Reading Programs   89
  Background   89
  Rationale   89
  Characteristics   90
  Objectives   90
  Advantages   91
  Disadvantages   91
  Motivational Activities   92
    Storytelling • Sustained Silent Reading
Content Reading Materials   93
  Readability Formulas   94
  Other Concerns   98
Teacher-Made Reading Materials   98
Supplementary Reading Materials   100
  High-Interest, Low-Vocabulary Books   101
  Games and Teaching Devices   101
Summary   101
Activities Related to the Chapter   101
Bibliography and References   102

Chapter Six

INTEGRATING INSTRUCTIONAL APPROACHES 105

Overview   105
Definition of Terms   105
The Language-Experience Approach   106
  Organic Reading   106
  Language-Experience Stories   107
Guided Reading Techniques   109
  The Directed Reading Activity   110
    Preparation • Silent Reading • Developing Com-
    prehension • Oral Reading • Developing Word
    Power • Evaluation
  The Directed Reading-Thinking Activity   119

Content-Area Reading Procedures   121
    Content-Area Guidelines   121
    Strategies for Reading Content Materials   123
    Content-Area Vocabulary   124
    Content-Area Comprehension   124
Content-Area Study Skills   125
Summary   126
Activities Related to the Chapter   126
Bibliography and References   127

Chapter Seven

SKILLS RELATED TO READING

SKILLS RELATED TO READING   129

Overview   129
Definition of Terms   129
Oral Expression   130
    Objectives   130
    Primary-Grade Activities   130
    Intermediate-Grade Activities   131
Written Expression   132
    Objectives   132
    Primary-Grade Activities   133
    Intermediate-Grade Activities   133
Handwriting   134
    Objectives   135
    Readiness   135
    The Handwriting Lesson   136
    Manuscript and Cursive Writing   136
    Left-handedness   137
Spelling   138
    Objectives   138
    Readiness   138
    The Content of Spelling   139
    The Spelling Lesson   139
    Spelling Rules   140
    Spelling Demons   140
    Spelling and Reading   141
Fluency and Flexibility in Reading   141
    Improving Reading Rates   142

The Purposes of Reading   143
Flexibility   144
Activities for Improving Reading Rates   144
Study Skills   145
  Readiness   145
  What Are Study Skills?   146
  Teaching Study Skills   147
    Activities for Teaching Study Skills   147
Summary   148
Activities Related to the Chapter   148
Bibliography and References   149

Chapter Eight

ASSESSMENT OF READING AND
READING-RELATED ABILITIES

                                                           151

Overview   151
Definition of Terms   151
Formal and Informal Assessment   152
  Formal Assessment   152
  Informal Assessment   154
Assessment of Reading-Related Abilities   155
  Language Development   155
    Receptive and Expressive Vocabulary • Oral
    Reading • Hearing Speech Sounds • Speech
    Difficulties • Oral Language Expression •
    Written Language Expression
  Conceptual Background   159
    Language Concepts Related to Reading • Concepts
    Related to School Tasks • Conceptual Background
    Related to the Comprehension of Information
Assessment of Specific Reading Abilities   162
  Determining Levels of Reading Abilities   162
  Procedures for Tentative Placement   163
    Alternate Oral Reading • Cloze Testing •
    Word-List Testing
  The Informal Reading Inventory   164
    Directions for Preparing and Administering the
    Informal Reading Inventory   166

Summary   168
Activities Related to the Chapter   168
Bibliography and References   168

Chapter Nine

INTEGRATING LANGUAGE, LITERATURE, AND READING FOR ENJOYMENT   171

Overview   171
Definition of Terms   171
Values of Literature   172
Children's Interests   173
  Assessing Children's Interests   173
  Children's Reading Interests and Their Attitudes
  toward Reading   175
Locating and Selecting Reading Materials   177
  Criteria for Book Selection—Fiction   177
  Criteria for Book Selection—Nonfiction   177
  Some Other Materials for Children   179
Getting Materials into the Classroom   180
A Classroom Library and Reading Center   182
Literature in the Elementary Curriculum   182
  Oral Reading   183
  Storytelling   183
  The Teaching of Poetry   183
  Using Media   184
  Other Techniques for Motivating Pupils   184
Which Books for Which Pupils   186
Bibliotherapy   186
Activities That Help Children Share What They Read   186
  Activities Emphasizing Written Language   187
  Activities Emphasizing Oral Language   188
  Activities Emphasizing Arts and Crafts   189
  Miscellaneous Activities   189
  Book Day: An Integrating Activity That
  Emphasizes Literature   190
Summary   190

Activities Related to the Chapter 190
Bibliography and References 191

Chapter Ten

CLASSROOM MANAGEMENT 195

Overview 195
Definition of Terms 195
Interclass Grouping 196
Independent Learning 198
  Teacher-Directed Approaches 198
  Student-Directed Approaches 199
Classroom Organization for Instruction 200
  Achievement-Level Grouping 200
  Skill-Needs Grouping 201
  Special-Interest Grouping 202
  Scheduling 203
Effective Management 203
  Establishing Work Routines 204
A Plan for Reading-Materials Management for Group
and Individual Learning 206
  Completing the Grade-Levels Charts 206
  Completing the Group and Individual Plans 214
Summary 215
Activities Related to the Chapter 215
Bibliography and References 216

Chapter Eleven

CHILDREN WITH SPECIAL NEEDS 219

Overview 219
Definition of Terms 219
Learning Disabilities 220
  Definition 221
  Implications 222
  Instruction 223

Slow Learning Rates   226
  Reading   226
  Instruction   227
Linguistic and Cultural Diversity   228
  Instruction   229
Gifted Children   230
  Characteristics   231
  Instruction   231
Children with Physical Limitations   233
  Vision   233
    Assessment and Accommodation   234
  Hearing   238
    Assessment and Accommodation   238
Summary   240
Activities Related to the Chapter   240
Bibliography and References   240

Chapter Twelve

PROGRAM DEVELOPMENT AND IMPROVEMENT

PROGRAM DEVELOPMENT
AND IMPROVEMENT   245

Overview   245
Definition of Terms   245
Program Evaluation   246
  Testing   246
    Grade Placement • Potential
  Programmatic Objectives   249
  Checklists and Questionnaires   250
Program Improvement   255
Additional Resources   257
  Special Services   257
    Reading Specialist • Guidance Counselor • Librarian
  Administrators   260
  Parents   262
Summary   264
Activities Related to the Chapter   264
Bibliography and References   265

APPENDIXES

A Materials and Procedures for Classroom
   Reading Instruction 269
B Recreational and Supplemental Reading 301
C Informal Techniques for Assessing Readability 395
D Assessing Reading Interests 399
E Published Tests 405
F Organizations and References for Reading
   Professionals 413
G Materials and Suggestions for Dealing with Parents   417
H Names and Addresses of Publishers 423

Index 431

Foreword

This book can serve as a valuable resource for individuals preparing to become teachers of reading as well as for those currently in service in the field. The authors have done a fine job in providing a straightforward explanation of reading instruction within the confines of the elementary school. The book's inclusion of time-tested techniques, sound theoretical content, and unique ideas can give a teacher an excellent knowledge base from which to provide exemplary reading instruction in the 1980s.

Three aspects of this book are particularly noteworthy. First, the authors not only endorse the concept of individual differences in children, but also provide strategies for effectively dealing with these divergencies. The authors do not want all children to become similar in reading ability; rather, they advocate that students read in accordance with their potential. Abundant ideas for making this occur are offered by the authors.

Second, the book presents several strategies for equipping children with the skills necessary to become proficient in reading. Since the three authors are all former classroom teachers, they have pinpointed the crucial facets of the teaching-learning act, and they discuss how a teacher can provide children with quality reading instruction.

Third, the *human* element of elementary reading instruction is given its proper importance in this book. Techniques, materials, curricular designs, and instructional strategies are indeed important, but it must be remembered that children are the ones who are to be served. The students, regardless of ability, interest, or any other factor, should be the most important of an elementary teacher's priorities.

Elementary Reading: A Comprehensive Approach has many additional positive features which I will not enumerate at this time but which I found professionally stimulating. While individuals may disagree with some of the authors' ideas, it is my opinion that the book is informative and will help its readers to grow in their understanding of elementary reading instruction. And as we know, when we as professionals become more knowledgeable, the children whom we teach are the beneficiaries.

Paul C. Berg
John E. Swearingen Chair
Professor of Education
University of South Carolina

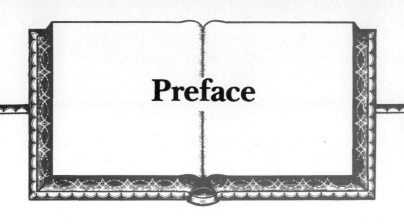

Preface

When we first began to plan this work, we sought to write a practical and useful textbook which describes and explains how reading should be taught in an elementary school. The degree to which this goal was realized will ultimately be determined by you, the reader.

In this book, we discuss the key ideas necessary to understand fully how reading should be taught to children. The book is divided into separate chapters, but one should not infer that reading is composed of isolated skills and acts. As the title of the book indicates, we believe reading is a comprehensive act. Proficient readers are able to integrate many elements concurrently, and the effective teacher helps make this possible.

The format of the chapters may also require some explanation. Each chapter begins with an overview and definitions of the key terms used. These sections are intended to aid in understanding the chapter. At each chapter's conclusion, we present several activities which afford opportunities for applying the material in the chapter to real-life situations.

The writing of this book was truly a shared venture. In our desire to produce a textbook of high quality, we sought and received professional assistance from many persons. We would like to thank the colleagues, students, teachers, and administrators who have shared their thoughts and expertise with us. Acknowledgment is given to the authors, publishers, and organizations who permitted us to reproduce portions of prior publications; to the late Dr. Mary Heimberger, of the University of

South Carolina, the author of Chapter 9; to Dr. Margaret Corboy, for compiling the book's appendixes; to Richard C. Ingram, for technical assistance; and to Renee Welch, for typing the manuscript.

We also thank Dr. L. Jerold Miller, of Westminster College, Dr. Ezra L. Stieglitz, of Rhode Island College, and Dr. Margaret Corboy, of the University of South Carolina, for suggesting ways in which to improve the book and for serving as reviewers for it. Heartfelt thanks are extended to Phillip A. Butcher, education editor at McGraw-Hill, for his patience, his editorial expertise, and the strong support he gave us during the writing of the book.

Finally, we thank the members of our families. They sacrificed much to permit the completion of this textbook.

John N. Mangieri
Lois A. Bader
James E. Walker

ELEMENTARY READING

A Comprehensive Approach

The Effective Teacher of Elementary Reading

Overview

This chapter responds to the question: What is an effective teacher of elementary reading? Descriptions of two reading teachers are presented in the chapter, and through an analysis of their practices, traits perceived as representing an effective teacher of elementary reading are identified, and explanatory comments about each are offered.

Definition of Terms

1. *Reading inventory*—an instrument for assessing a student's proficiency in such areas as word recognition, phonics, comprehension, listening, and spelling.
2. *Checklist*—a comprehensive and sequential arrangement of reading skills which can be used for classroom diagnosis and evaluation.
3. *Conference*—a meeting during which a teacher discusses with a child material which the child is reading.
4. *Diagnosis*—the act of identifying a child's proficiencies and deficiencies in the area of reading.
5. *Heterogeneous grouping*—bringing together students of differing ability into a single unit for instructional purposes.
6. *Homogeneous grouping*—bringing together students with similar ability in one or more areas into a single unit for instructional purposes.
7. *Kinesthetic approach*—an approach to reading instruction wherein a student traces letters, words, or geometric patterns.
8. *Readability*—a measure of the ease or difficulty of printed material.
9. *Seatwork*—the reading activities engaged in by students when not working directly with a teacher.
10. *Self-evaluation*—an assessment by a teacher of how well she or he taught a particular lesson to students.

Your ability to read the words contained in this textbook is the result of a teacher's effort. Regardless of the materials and methods employed to teach you how to read, the teacher was the key factor in your acquisition of reading proficiency. If you doubt the accuracy of this statement, refer to the National First and Second Grade Studies (12). These investigations and many subsequent ones have suggested that the teacher is the key in determining whether or not children read at a level commensurate with their ability. Put in another way, children will learn to read better with good teaching than with inferior instruction.

We are not suggesting that the teacher is the only factor in determining how well a child learns to read. This textbook will describe the complexity of the reading act. Success in reading is predicated not only upon the skill of the teacher but also upon the way in which intellectual, physical, emotional, social, and environmental factors interact in an individual.

Many people do not realize how difficult learning to read can be. Our profession has been severely criticized because some students cannot read well. The criticisms of Flesch (8) and Copperman (6) are representative of statements made about reading instruction in America's elementary schools. Flesch says: "Are you worrying about your child's education? You should be. Chances are about three to one that your Johnny or Mary will never learn to read properly." Copperman contends: "Our problem is a nationwide deterioration in basic academic skills and knowledge. Students do not read, write, or compute as well as they did ten years ago."

We believe that while criticism of *some* teachers of reading may be justified, fortunately such criticism is not applicable to the majority of teachers. For most children, elementary school educators are doing a fine job of teaching reading. In fact, as Farr reports (7): "Today's children read as well as and probably better than students their age thirty years ago."

ON TEACHING READING

We should not have a false sense of complacency because our profession as a whole is successful in teaching children to read. For one thing, we must recognize that teaching reading is difficult. It demands the refinement of a teacher's skills through training and experience.

Also, while many children do become proficient in reading, we know that a large number of students do not. In 1971, the United States Office of Education reported that over 8 million school-age children were not learning to read adequately (9). Clearly, it is essential that every effort be made to reduce this number.

Finally, in recent years there has been an explosion of knowledge in the field of reading. As a result, new teaching materials, pedagogical techniques and strategies, and curricular designs have emerged. Teaching is a profession, and it is the obligation of the professional to become knowledgeable about new developments. This will not happen through a process of osmosis; it requires study, and study is seldom easy or uncomplicated.

Contrary to those who say, "I'm just a teacher," we feel teachers of reading play a very significant role in our society. The level at which students read will have a key impact on their school success and subsequent economic well-being. Reading can also give a child innumerable hours of joy through the vicarious experiences offered by books and other printed materials. When one considers the importance of reading to a child's future, it is easy to understand why we hold good teachers of reading in high esteem.

Wanting to be a good reading teacher is undeniably important. Studies have consistently shown that motivation has an impact upon one's performance. A person who wants to do something is more likely to accomplish it than is a person of comparable competence who is ambivalent about the task or who does not want to perform it.

However, in teaching reading, the desire to perform the task will carry one only so far. Clearly, one must also possess a certain degree of knowledge about or innate ability in the teaching of reading. The effective teacher of reading not only has the *desire* to perform the job in an exemplary manner but also has *knowledge* of the practices which best promote growth in reading for every child in the class.

At this juncture, you may be wondering about the degree of knowledge which you possess relative to the teaching of reading. Instruments such as *Inventory of Teacher Knowledge of Reading*, by Artley and Hardin (1), are available, and an individual's score on such a measure provides one means of judging that individual's grasp of content in the area of teaching reading. Although these measures undoubtedly perform a significant function, we will not employ any of them in this textbook. Instead, in order to aid you in assessing your grasp of effective teaching of reading, we have devised a rather unconventional "test."

A TALE OF TWO TEACHERS

The following descriptions are of two real-life teachers, Linda and Rose. Please read each, and then on a separate sheet of paper discuss the practices of the two teachers which you think characterize the effective teaching of reading at the elementary school level. Try to be as thorough as possible in your analysis of the two teachers described.

A format such as the one shown on the following page may aid you in completing this task.

Linda

Linda was a second-grade teacher in a poor, rural school district. There were twenty-six children in her class.

A group achievement reading test showed that Linda's students

Linda	Effective Practice(s)	Reason(s) Why
1.		
2.		
3.		
.		
.		
.		
.		
.		

Rose	Effective Practice(s)	Reason(s) Why
1.		
2.		
3.		
.		
.		
.		
.		
.		

ranged in ability from nonreaders to slightly above grade level. These test scores were supplemented by a diagnosis conducted by Linda at the beginning of the school year. She administered an informal reading inventory to those class members who were the lowest achievers, as well as to the children with a significant difference between their reading expectancy or potential and their reading achievement scores. This diagnosis revealed the reading proficiencies and deficiencies of each child.

Linda had an old classroom. The walls were in dire need of paint, but on them were book jackets from the children's favorite reading selections, experience stories by class members, and a mural depicting a vivid incident in a book which Linda was then reading to the class.

Linda used a basal reader and had her class divided into three ability groups for reading instruction. She worked with one group at a time, asking each group a variety of comprehension questions, some of which should be answerable by simply remembering what was directly said in the reading, while others should require the drawing of inferences. At the conclusion of her work with a group, she wrote comments about specific children in the group. Linda made these notes because she "did not trust her memory" to retain detailed information about particular students.

With a second group, Linda adapted her instruction to the abilities of the members. This group was not as capable as the preceding one; nevertheless, Linda's questioning was once again comprehensive in nature.

While Linda was instructing the third group, we had the opportunity to view the seatwork she assigned the other two groups. Our observation was in line with Linda's statement: "Seatwork shouldn't be busywork. It should help to develop a student's reading power and reinforce the important reading skills already learned, or be an informal way to diagnose a child's understanding of an aspect of reading."

Linda gave a great deal of encouragement to all her students. She urged the class to work hard at assigned tasks. She complimented children for completing assignments and sought to help her students develop favorable attitudes toward reading. Linda tried hard to give each of her students a positive self-concept.

At the end of the school day, Linda conferred with her principal. She was concerned about one of her students, Tommy, whom she suspected of having a hearing problem. Linda mentioned the traits she had observed, and she asked about the procedure for having auditory testing conducted on Tommy. Linda requested a referral, and said that until the testing was completed, she would do at least three things: Tommy's seat would be moved so he would be directly in front, where Linda usually taught. Directions and instructions would be repeated when necessary. Alternative modes of instruction—that is, visual and kinesthetic—would be used to supplement phonic and auditory teaching.

Prior to planning the next day's instruction, Linda evaluated the present day's teaching of reading. She judged whether all, a portion, or none of the instruction provided had been effective. In instances where she "blew it," Linda asked, "How could I have better taught the material?" The results of this self-evaluation were incorporated into her next day's instruction.

Friday of each week was Linda's "big-picture" day. Linda would assess her effectiveness in teaching reading during the past week, particularly with specific children. She also planned what she wanted to accomplish the following week in reading. Big-picture day, which gave her an opportunity both to review how the past week's instruction had gone and to plan for the next week, helped her relate her goals in reading for that week to her goals for the entire year.

Rose

Rose was a fifth-grade teacher in an inner-city school. She had twenty-one children in her class.

At the beginning of the present academic year, standardized test results showed that Rose's students ranged in reading ability from grade level 1.5 to grade level 6.6. Rose believed in conducting a diagnosis after instruction. She used standardized diagnostic instruments, informal measures, and teacher observation in order to determine the reading skills which her students possessed, as well as those in which they were deficient.

Rose used an individualized approach to the teaching of reading. She did so because she believed that the "only true group is a group of one." Although Rose employed individualized instruction, it should not be inferred that she never taught more than a single child at a time. When several children needed to acquire the same skill, Rose used group instruction with them, since this was an expeditious way of teaching.

Two key elements in Rose's instruction were checklists and conferences. Rose had a folder for each child in her class. Each folder contained a list of essential skills which she believed every child must acquire. She arranged these skills on a checklist that paralleled the scope and sequence lists which accompany most basal reading series.

The checklist and Rose's anecdotal comments gave her a profile of each child's reading proficiencies and deficiencies. Rose said the checklist form of record keeping gave her "a sense of direction, so I'll know what to teach each child tomorrow and after."

Anyone familiar with the individualized approach to the teaching of reading knows the importance of conferences with the student. In observing Rose's conferences with her students, it was obvious she was an excellent teacher. She conveyed a genuine interest in what the students were reading. She asked each child questions relating to what that child was reading, and she managed her time well, spending neither too much nor too little time with any one student.

Rose said she wanted all her students "to love reading as much as I do." She provided many opportunities for the children to have pleasurable experiences with books. Her class had a daily quiet time for reading. She initiated a weekly fun-with-reading activity, and she regularly read aloud a story or a portion of a book to her class. Rose was an avid reader, and she shared what she read with her students.

When not engaged in direct instruction, Rose walked around the classroom while her students were involved in reading-related tasks. She observed students, helped them, listened to their concerns and ideas, and encouraged each child "to be the best possible reader."

Rose and the school's librarian conferred regularly about books. Rose tried very hard to find out about and have available books appropriate in interest and difficulty to her students. One student, Leon, had a keen interest in submarines. Rose and the librarian discussed which books dealing with submarines might be written at a level that Leon could comprehend. In time, Leon made his own choices of books.

Once each week, Rose and the school's other intermediate-grade teachers met to talk about reading. At these sessions, the reading needs of particular children were talked about, and strategies for teaching these children were discussed. In addition, teachers sometimes discussed professional articles or instructional materials which were of interest to other teachers.

Analysis and Explanation

Having read about Linda and Rose, you are now ready to take our test. Skim through one or both descriptions if you wish. You may also refer to the descriptions as you write your "answers."

Remember the task is to identify, on a separate sheet of paper, the practices of Linda and Rose which you feel are part of the effective teaching of reading at the elementary school level.

After you have taken this test, read the rest of this chapter. You will see our responses, and you will have an opportunity to judge how you have done.

In the following sections the descriptions of Linda and Rose are reprinted with certain passages underlined. In the section "Analysis of Linda," twelve passages are underlined. In the section "Analysis of Rose," nine passages are underlined. Each underlined passage is followed by a number.

Immediately following each analysis, an explanation is made as to why those particular passages were underlined. For easy reference, the numbers in the analyses correspond to the numbers in the explanations following.

It should be stated that the twenty-one items noted do not represent the only correct responses to our test. Depending upon one's perspective, other teaching practices of Linda and Rose may be seen as characterizing an effective teacher of elementary reading.

Analysis of Linda

Linda was a second-grade teacher in a poor, rural school district. There were twenty-six children in her class.

A group achievement reading test showed that Linda's students ranged in ability from nonreaders to slightly above grade level. These test scores were supplemented by a diagnosis conducted by Linda at the beginning of the school year.[1] She administered an informal reading inventory to those class members who were the lowest achievers, as well as to the children with a significant difference between their reading expectancy or potential and their reading achievement scores.[2] This diagnosis revealed the reading proficiencies and deficiencies of each child.

Linda had an old classroom. The walls were in dire need of paint, but on them were book jackets from the children's favorite reading selections, experience stories by class members, and a mural depicting a vivid incident in a book which Linda was then reading to the class.[3]

Linda used a basal reader and had her class divided into three ability groups for reading instruction. She worked with one group at a time, asking each group a variety of comprehension questions,[4] some of which should be answerable by simply remembering what was directly said in the reading, while others should require the drawing of inferences. At the conclusion of her work with a group, she wrote comments about specific children in the group.[5] Linda made these notes because she "did not trust her memory" to retain detailed information about particular students.

With a second group, Linda adapted her instruction to the abilities of the members.[6] This group was not as capable as the preceding one; nevertheless, Linda's questioning was once again comprehensive in nature.[7]

While Linda was instructing the third group, we had the opportunity to view the seatwork she assigned the other two groups. Our observation was in line of Linda's statement: "Seatwork shouldn't be busywork.[8] It should help to develop a student's reading power and reinforce the important reading skills already learned, or be an informal way to diagnose a child's understanding of an aspect of reading."

Linda gave a great deal of encouragement to all her students.[9] She urged the class to work hard at assigned tasks. She complimented children for completing assignments and sought to help her students develop favorable attitudes toward reading. Linda tried hard to give each of her students a positive self-concept.

At the end of the school day, Linda conferred with her principal. She was concerned about one of her students, Tommy, whom she suspected of having a hearing problem.[10] Linda mentioned the traits she had observed, and she asked about the procedure for having auditory testing conducted on Tommy. Linda requested a referral, and said that until the testing was completed, she would do at least three things: Tommy's seat would be moved so he would be directly in front, where Linda usually taught. Directions and instructions would be repeated when necessary. Alternative modes of instruction—that is, visual and kinesthetic—would be used to supplement phonic and auditory teaching.

Prior to planning the next day's instruction, Linda evaluated the present day's teaching of reading.[11] She judged whether all, a portion, or none of the instruction provided had been effective. In instances where she "blew it," Linda asked, "How could I have better taught the material?" The results of this self-evaluation were incorporated into her next day's instruction.

Friday of each week was Linda's "big-picture" day.[12] Linda would assess her effectiveness in teaching reading during the past week, particularly with specific children. She also planned what she wanted to accomplish the following week in reading. Big-picture day, which gave her an opportunity both to review how the past week's instruction had gone and to plan for the next week, helped her relate her goals in reading for that week to her goals for the entire year.

Explanation of Linda

In the preceding description of Linda's classroom, twelve aspects of her teaching of reading were identified as being particularly noteworthy. An explanation of each positive practice follows:

1. Classroom diagnosis is a prelude to optimally effective reading instruction. In order to conduct this diagnosis, a teacher may use the following devices: a standardized diagnostic test, an informal reading-assessment measure, and teacher observation. Through the correct use of one or more of these, a teacher can determine the reading proficiencies and deficiencies of children. Subsequent reading instruction can then be planned and carried out with this information in mind.

   Although classroom diagnosis can make a significant contribution to the teaching-learning situation within an elementary classroom, it is not often used by teachers. Some educators erroneously equate group achievement testing with diagnosis. The two, of course, are not the same. Reading achievement tests yield a score which indicates the approximate level at which a child is performing. The results show the teacher and the school administration the amount of progress that a child has made since the time at which the tests were last administered.

   One reason often given by teachers for not using diagnosis involves the time which it takes to complete it. We have frequently heard teachers insist: "I'm just too busy to diagnose." Such attitudes are unfortunate since they convey a lack of understanding about diagnosis. First, diagnosis is not something extra, nor is it a luxury. It must be perceived for what it is—an *essential* aspect of the teaching of reading. Second, classroom diagnosis, unlike clinical diagnosis, does not require great expenditures of teacher or student time.

2. It is well documented that students have different capacities for learning. In reading, formulas for determining a child's potential or expectancy—that is, the level at which the child is capable of reading—have been designed by Bond, Tinker, and Wasson (4), Cleland (5), and other reading authorities. In some school settings, where intelligence testing is prohibited or discouraged, an estimate of students' reading potential is made on the basis of their scores on a computation test or a listening comprehension test.

   Whether using a reading expectancy formula, a computation test, or a listening comprehension test, a teacher should make some type of estimate of each child's reading potential. By comparing this estimate with the student's score on a reading achievement test, a teacher can determine whether or not a child's performance in reading is commensurate with the child's potential. If it is, then a teacher may conclude that the student is making satisfactory progress in reading.

   For children in grades 1 to 3, a difference of approximately half a year or more between a child's potential and achievement is generally considered significant. In grades 4 to 6, a discrepancy of one year or more is significant. In either case, a diagnosis assessment should be conducted in order to determine *why* the discrepancy exists.

3. Learning to read is a difficult process, requiring a great deal of work

on the part of teacher and pupil. But learning to read is not just the acquisition of a skill. Reading is an act which can afford an individual countless hours of pleasure. Reading should not be an all work–no enjoyment task. It should not be all diphthongs, workbook sheets, and the schwa sound. We support a philosophy that reading can be *fun*. Activities such as storytelling, games, and creative dramatics should be an integral part of an elementary school classroom's *modus operandi*. These activities afford children an opportunity to apply the reading skills which they have acquired. Equally important, they can foster a love of reading in children.

4.   Over the years, professionals such as Barrett (3), Herber (11), and Harker (10) have attempted to classify or analyze reading comprehension skills. Which skills are most important is a matter of conjecture. Most authorities seem to agree that children of all abilities should be exposed to the full range of comprehension questions in even the earliest stages of reading. This means that children should be asked questions demanding factual answers (who? what? when?) and questions requiring judgments (why? what if?) in conjunction with their reading assignments.

   Despite the acceptance of this premise among reading authorities, it has not gained general acceptance in elementary classrooms. Some teachers feel primary-grade children should not be given questions requiring judgments because they will become confused by the possibility of multiple correct answers. Teachers often cite a similar reason for not asking such questions of their less able readers. However, we believe that these viewpoints contradict sound pedagogical practices in reading.

5.   We encourage writing comments about specific children immediately after instruction occurs for at least three reasons. First, pertinent comments about specific children are likely to be forgotten by a teacher if they are not written down. A teacher is a busy professional during the course of a school day. It is rare that a teacher can recall all, or even most, of the incidents which occurred during reading instruction.

   Second, writing comments can serve as a form of record keeping. A thorough system of record keeping is a must in an elementary school classroom. A classroom system of record keeping should not be confused with a school's permanent records. In reading, record keeping entails systematically collecting information about each child's performance. Included in the records kept by a teacher may be such things as reading test results, the teacher's anecdotal comments, a checklist of the proficiencies and deficiencies of each child, and related information.

   Third, by getting into the habit of writing comments, a teacher becomes more oriented to diagnosis. Writing comments about each child makes the teacher more observant and analytical during reading instruction and better able to ascertain the degree to which the children have acquired specific reading skills.

6. Regardless of the instructional approach used to teach reading, the teacher will be faced with the task of providing reading instruction to children of varying ability. By their own admission, some teachers like to teach children of a particular ability range or are more competent doing so. Some teachers, excellent with children of limited reading ability, are perhaps mediocre with students proficient in reading. Other teachers may excel with average readers but have little success with children of poor reading ability.

    We have often urged teachers to analyze their own teaching in terms of their ability to provide instruction to excellent, average, and poor readers. We have asked such questions as: With which groups of readers are you most effective and least effective? To what extent do you change your style of teaching according to the ability of the students? With which group(s) of children have test results shown you to be most effective and least effective?

7. We underlined this statement for the reasons cited in number 4. Note that Linda asked a full range of comprehension questions even though this group was not as capable in reading as the preceding one.

8. Seatwork, the activities engaged in by students when not working directly with a teacher, should be an extremely important part of reading instruction. Since a teacher cannot work individually with all children simultaneously, reading instruction must be provided in alternative ways. Used properly, seatwork can be very valuable.

    The teacher can use seatwork to reinforce previously acquired reading skills, to develop additional skills, or for enrichment or recreation. In some instances, seatwork can be used for diagnostic purposes, giving a teacher an opportunity to assess a child's competence in a particular aspect of reading.

    Seatwork should not be merely a way of keeping children busy with hastily conceived activities. Poorly planned seatwork is likely to serve little or no real instructional purpose. We urge teachers of reading to plan seatwork carefully; it should assist in making children more proficient readers.

9. In these days of behavioral objectives, minimal competency testing, and accountability, teachers of reading face great pressures. They know that their efforts to teach children to read are being closely scrutinized. If reading test results are even a little below expectations, they are likely to face the questions of parents and of the school administration. As a result, some teachers have become more content-oriented than previously and perceive the human needs of children to be of lesser importance.

    We do believe in teaching reading skills to children. However, we would like to remind educators of the importance of the affective domain with regard to children. As teachers, we should not become so preoccupied with teaching skills that we forget it is our job to teach *children*. We have observed that teachers who are especially effective in teaching students to read are concerned with the human element in youngsters. The teacher seeks to help children develop positive attitudes about themselves and about reading, school, and society in general. In addition, the teacher discerns the specific interests of the children in the class and whenever possible gives the children opportunities to develop these interests further.

10. Anyone who has analyzed the teaching-learning process in reading is well aware that reading is not solely an intellectual act. For instruction in and acquisition of reading to take place a child must have satisfactory vision and hearing and be in good health. When a child's lack in one or more of these qualities is undetected, the child will be likely to experience difficulty in learning to read.

   Most elementary schools periodically conduct medical examinations to determine the children's physical condition, but such testing is generally less than adequate, for the reasons described in Chapter 11. We urge teachers to monitor the physical status of the children in their classes. If a student appears to need attention in some area, the teacher should recommend that the child be referred for proper medical evaluation. The referral process will entail following a school's established procedure(s) for medical assessment.

11. Teachers often say that they spend a great deal of time planning and teaching reading lessons. We do not doubt this statement. Anyone who has ever taught reading to children knows that it is a complex and time-consuming process.

   We feel, however, that self-evaluation in the teaching of reading is often neglected. Teachers plan a lesson, teach, and then begin planning the next day's lesson. Rarely does a teacher systematically evaluate how well or poorly a particular lesson was taught. For example, how does the teacher know that the content was grasped by the children? How could the lesson have been taught better? Is there a need to reteach parts of it to one or more of the children? Should seatwork be assigned tomorrow to reinforce today's content?

   We are suggesting that the process of planning and teaching should include self-evaluation. By carefully and honestly scrutinizing your present day's efforts, you will be better able to provide the next day's instruction.

12. "Can't see the forest for the trees." Over the years, how often have we heard this adage? And yet, in many instances, our actions are perfectly described by this saying.

   A teacher's day is an extremely busy one. Often, a teacher is so busy teaching the current day's lesson and planning subsequent lessons that he has little or no opportunity for long-term planning. We encourage teachers to establish a set time each week for long-term planning, in order to determine what was accomplished, to decide upon the objectives of the next week's instruction, and perhaps most importantly, to determine how the next week's instruction will relate to the entire year's reading goals.

Analysis of Rose

Rose was a fifth-grade teacher in an inner-city school. She had twenty-one children in her class.

At the beginning of the present academic year, standardized test results showed that Rose's students ranged in reading ability from grade level 1.5 to grade level 6.6. Rose believed in conducting a diagnosis after instruction. She used standardized diagnostic instruments, informal measures, and teacher observation in order to determine the reading skills which her students possessed, as well as those in which they were deficient.[1]

Rose used an individualized approach to the teaching of reading. She did so because she believed that the "only true group is a group of one."[2] Although Rose employed individualized instruction, it should not be inferred that she never taught more than a single child at a time. When several children needed to acquire the same skill, Rose used group instruction with them, since this was an expeditious way of teaching.

Two key elements in Rose's instruction were checklists and conferences. Rose had a folder for each child in her class. Each folder contained a list of essential skills which she believed every child must acquire. She arranged these skills on a checklist that paralleled the scope and sequence lists which accompany most basal reading series.

The checklist and Rose's anecdotal comments gave her a profile of each child's reading proficiencies and deficiencies.[3] Rose said the checklist form of record keeping gave her "a sense of direction so I'll know what to teach each child tomorrow and after."

Anyone familiar with the individualized approach to the teaching of reading knows the importance of conferences[4] with the student. In observing Rose's conferences with her students, it was obvious she was an excellent teacher. She conveyed a genuine interest in what the students were reading. She asked each child questions relating to what that child was reading, and she managed her time well, spending neither too much nor too little time with any one student.

Rose said she wanted all her students "to love reading as much as I do." She provided many opportunities for the children to have pleasurable experiences with books.[5] Her class had a daily quiet time for reading. She initiated a weekly fun-with-reading activity, and she regularly read aloud a story or a portion of a book to her class. Rose was an avid reader, and she shared what she read with her students.[6]

When not engaged in direct instruction, Rose walked around the classroom while her students were involved in reading-related tasks. She observed students, helped them, listened to their concerns and ideas, and encouraged each child "to be the best possible reader."[7]

Rose and the school's librarian conferred regularly about books. Rose tried very hard to find out about and have available books appropriate in interest and difficulty to her students.[8] One student, Leon, had a keen interest in submarines. Rose and the librarian discussed which books dealing with submarines might be written at a level that Leon could comprehend. In time, Leon made his own choices of books.

Once each week, Rose and the school's other intermediate-grade teachers met to talk about reading.[9] At these sessions, the reading needs of particular children were talked about, and strategies for teaching these children were discussed. In addition, teachers sometimes discussed professional articles or instructional materials which were of interest to other teachers.

Explanation of Rose

1. As we stated previously, classroom diagnosis makes the effective teaching of reading a more attainable goal. Some teachers, such as Linda, conduct a diagnosis at the beginning of the school year, before instruction takes place in earnest. Other teachers, like Rose, observe students while they are reading and then perform an appropriate diagnosis.

    There are advantages and disadvantages to diagnosis before or after instruction. When conducted before instruction, a specific segment of the class—for example, the lowest achievers—are administered one or more diagnostic measures. The strengths and weaknesses of the children can be determined from the results, and appropriate instruction can then follow. The disadvantage of this form of diagnosis is that needless testing frequently occurs. Since the teacher is not aware of the nature of each child's reading skills, tests of little or no relevance to a student are often administered.

    Diagnosis after classroom instruction allows the teacher to identify possible reading deficiencies. Appropriate assessments can then be made in order to determine whether or not the teacher's perceptions about a particular child are accurate. Thus, assessment is kept to a minimum, being done only in those reading areas where it seems warranted. A possible drawback of diagnosis after instruction is that the teaching that occurs prior to the diagnosis may not be relevant to certain children.

    Regardless of which form of diagnosis a teacher chooses to use, instruction can be substantially improved. Diagnosis should have a place in every elementary classroom.
2. There are two basic forms of ability grouping used in most elementary

schools, heterogeneous and homogeneous. In heterogeneous grouping, students of varying reading abilities are placed together in a group and receive instruction simultaneously from a teacher. In homogeneous grouping, students who are presumed to be approximately equal in reading ability, on the basis of a measure such as a reading achievement test score, are placed together for instructional purposes.

Teachers who use grouping, particularly homogeneous grouping, often feel that the children in the group are all the same. This belief has been disproven by research and by the experience of teachers. The children in a group may have similar scores on a test, but they will probably greatly differ physically, emotionally, and intellectually. They may also differ in their specific proficiencies and needs.

We are not advocating the abolition of grouping in elementary schools. Rather, we are suggesting that teachers who use grouping be aware of some of its limitations.

3. Learning to read is basically a sequential process. There is an interdependence among certain of the skills which must be acquired by children if subsequent reading instruction is to be successful.

Most forms of developmental reading instruction make provision for the sequential nature of learning to read. They present material logically and hierarchically in progressively more difficult lessons.

However, it cannot be inferred that students in a particular grade have all mastered the same skills. First, children have different capacities for learning, and it must be recognized that some children are more able readers than others. Second, our society is a mobile one, and as a result, many children change schools from one year to another or even within the same year. Such children often come from a school where the reading materials and the approach were different from those used at their present school. The sequence in which reading skills were taught to the child (and, one hopes, acquired) might also differ. Third, it must be recognized that some children may be confronted with material of a difficulty for which they are ill prepared. This may be due to a school's policy of so-called social promotion, to administrative mandates, or to one of many other reasons.

As the preceding implies, teachers cannot assume that all their students have the same reading skills. Within a particular grade level, the children are likely to vary greatly in competence in reading.

In reading, a checklist typically includes a comprehensive and sequential arrangement of skills. Its composition may duplicate, or be very similar to, the scope and sequence lists which accompany basal reading series. Some teachers use checklists developed by such reading authorities as Barbe (2) and Guszak (9), while others utilize either their own or one developed by the school system.

Regardless of the checklist a teacher uses, if its content accurately reflects the reading process, it can serve as a valuable device in reading instruction. By indicating on the checklist the skills which a child has acquired and those he has not, the teacher will have a record of the child's reading proficiencies and deficiencies. This information will make subsequent instruction more relevant to the child's reading needs.

4. The conference is an indispensable component of individualized reading. It is the time when a teacher meets individually with a child, usually to discuss a book which the child is reading. Questions are asked by the teacher in order to judge how well the student is grasping the book's content and how much progress the child is making and to show the student that the teacher is interested in the book.

We recommend the use of pupil conferences even by a teacher who does not use an individualized approach. Conferences could provide the teacher with excellent opportunities to acquire detailed information about individual children. In addition, a conference can be an excellent motivator, showing a child that the teacher is personally interested in him or her.

5. We cannot overemphasize the importance of children's developing positive attitudes toward reading. If students are successful at reading, they are likely to view it as a pleasurable activity.

Rose wanted all of her students to love reading as much as she did. We heartily endorse this goal, and we favor activities which make children realize that reading can be pleasurable. Reading for enjoyment, storytelling, creative dramatics, stories read to the class by a teacher, or any other activity designed to make reading fun has a place in the classroom.

Some teachers contend that they do not have enough time to permit their students to have fun with reading. It is our belief that they should analyze how they are presently using their classroom instructional time. Perhaps they could figure out how to provide sufficient time for allowing children to have fun with reading. After all, what purpose is served when children have the *skill* to read but not the *will* to read?

6. It often is not enough for students to be told that a teacher enjoys reading. Children must be shown that a teacher does not just teach reading but is also a reader.

We urge teachers who read books that are suitable for elementary school children to share an incident from a book or a quick summary of it with the class. This usually will delight the youngsters and, perhaps more importantly, will illustrate that the teacher is not engaging in a "do as I say, not as I do" form of behavior regarding reading.

7. This statement closely parallels number 9 in the analysis of Linda. The human aspect of reading should not be overlooked by a teacher. Contrary to what some teachers may feel or have heard, children do look

up to teachers. They generally seek to please the teacher and to be recognized and praised.

Children want to see that teachers are genuinely concerned about them, their well-being, and their interests. Teachers should not only verbally convey this concern but also reflect it in their actions.

8. Getting the right book into the right student's hands is a desirable but difficult goal. Teachers are more likely to succeed in this if they use books that are written at a level of difficulty within their students' comprehension range and that deal with subjects consistent with their students' reading interests. Many elementary teachers fail to consider these two factors when aiding students in the selection of recreational reading materials.

The difficulty of a book can be determined through either formal or informal measures. The principal formal measure available to educators is the readability formula. This is a mathematical method of determining the grade level at which a particular book is written. Many formulas, differing in complexity and accuracy, have been developed over the years. We will treat readability formulas useful with elementary reading materials in Chapter 5.

In order to determine the interests of children, a teacher can converse with students and have conferences with them and/or administer a reading interest inventory. (See Appendix D for a sample interest inventory.)

Matching children to books can greatly aid a teacher's instructional efforts in reading. More importantly, perhaps, it can help the children develop a love for reading.

9. We favor the notion of collaboration among reading teachers in an elementary school. Meetings may be structured (for example, all primary teachers or the third-grade staff) or informal (for example, two or three teachers who confer once or twice a week, regardless of grade level). The exact format is relatively unimportant, as long as it permits the free flow of information and ideas among the participants.

Collaboration among teachers can help to overcome the "Lone Ranger syndrome." By getting together to discuss reading, teachers can achieve positive results. Ideas can be exchanged, strategies for dealing with the reading needs of specific children can be formulated, and new reading materials can be shown.

Collaboration can also afford reading teachers an opportunity to further their professional growth. Interesting articles and books can be presented, and teachers can be made cognizant of reading workshops and meetings held locally. The meetings can also serve as forums for discussing other activities which will enhance teachers' competence in teaching reading.

Evaluation

You have now had a chance to take our test and to see how your responses compare with ours. Your performance may or may not have surprised you.

Regardless of how you did on the test, we hope it served at least two purposes: to give you a general indication of your ability to recognize effective teaching practices and to make you aware of why we view these practices positively.

In subsequent chapters of this textbook, the majority of the points made in this chapter will be discussed in depth. Each topic will be presented separately, for the convenience of this textbook's readers, but we hope you keep in mind that the topics are interrelated. We believe that the effective teaching of reading at the elementary school level should be perceived as a comprehensive process. The items discussed in the chapters are not isolated. Rather, the effective teacher of reading seeks to blend them together in the classroom.

ACTIVITIES RELATED TO THE CHAPTER

1. Visit several elementary classrooms. Do the teachers primarily conduct diagnosis before instruction, diagnosis after instruction, or no discernible form of diagnosis at all? What is the teacher's rationale for using a particular form of diagnosis or for not conducting any diagnosis?
2. Compile a list of books which can be used for enjoyment purposes in an elementary classroom. They must be appropriate in difficulty to the reading levels of the students and in line with their reading interests.
3. Observe the seatwork done by a class during reading time. Are the purposes of the activities readily apparent to you? Do the children know why they are doing the designated tasks? Of which facets of the seatwork do you approve? Which do you perceive negatively?
4. Gather several reading checklists used by elementary teachers. How do these compare to each other? Which checklist is the best in your opinion? Why? Which is of least merit in your view? Why?
5. Sit in on a meeting in which teachers discuss the teaching of reading. What do the teachers see as the chief value of these meetings? What do they view as the drawbacks of such meetings? What are *your* feelings about such meetings?
6. Write a description of how you would teach reading. Use the Rose and Linda descriptions as models. What parts of your description are particularly noteworthy?

BIBLIOGRAPHY AND REFERENCES

1. Artley, A. Sterl, and Veralee B. Hardin: *Inventory of Teacher Knowledge of Reading*, Lucas Brothers, Columbia, Missouri, 1975.
2. Barbe, Walter B.: *Personalized Reading Instruction*, Prentice-Hall, Englewood Cliffs, 1961.

3. Barrett, Thomas: "The Barrett Taxonomy of Cognitive and Affective Dimensions of Reading Comprehension," in Clymer, Theodore. "What Is 'Reading'? Some Current Concepts," *67th Yearbook of the National Society for the Study of Education*, The University of Chicago Press, Chicago, 1968, pp. 7–29.
4. Bond, Guy L., Miles A. Tinker, and Barbara B. Wasson: *Reading Difficulties: Their Diagnosis and Correction*, 4th ed., Prentice-Hall, Englewood Cliffs, 1979, pp. 62–63.
5. Cleland, Donald L: "Clinical Materials for Appraising Disabilities in Reading," *The Reading Teacher*, **17**:428 (1964).
6. Copperman, Paul: *The Literacy Hoax*, Morrow, New York, 1978, p. 185.
7. Farr, Roger: Testimony before Senator Thomas F. Eagleton's hearing on the teaching and learning of basic academic skills in schools, for the Senate Subcommittee on Education, Arts, and Humanities (April 9, 1979).
8. Flesch, Rudolf: "Why Johnny Still Can't Read," *Family Circle*, **92**(15):26 (1979).
9. Guszak, Frank J: *Diagnostic Reading Instruction in the Elementary School*, Harper & Row, New York, 1972, pp. 1, 141–154.
10. Harker, W. John: "Teaching Comprehension: A Task Analysis Approach," *Journal of Reading*, **16**:379–382 (1973).
11. Herber, Harold L. *Teaching Reading in Content Areas*, 2d ed., Prentice-Hall, Englewood Cliffs, 1978, chap. 3.
12. *The Reading Teacher*, May 1966, October 1966, May 1967, and October 1967.

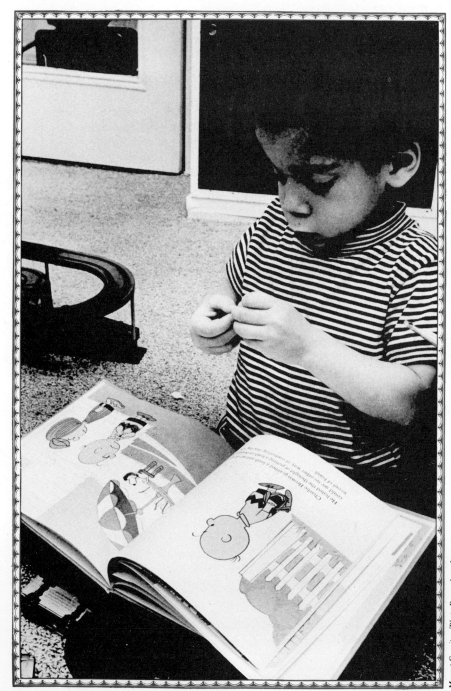

Readiness to Read

2

Overview

In this chapter, we will explore critically some traditional theories regarding readiness to read and examine the validity of considering maturity, sex differences, and language and cultural factors as determiners of readiness. In addition, we will look at predictors of reading success or failure and various readiness tests and activities which may help the beginning teacher assess children's preparedness for reading instruction.

Definition of Terms

1. *Auditory acuity*—the ability to hear; certain hearing difficulties may be alleviated by hearing aids or surgery.
2. *Auditory discrimination*—the ability to distinguish individual sounds; it is necessary for attending to sound-letter associations.
3. *Cultural factors*—factors which may affect achievement in reading by children whose primary language is not standard English and/or whose ethnic-cultural background is dissimilar to the white middle-class norms commonly manifested in reading materials.
4. *Prereading activities*—activities designed to develop the abilities which make a child ready for formal reading instruction.
5. *Reading readiness*—a child's preparedness for beginning formal reading instruction, based on physical, psychological, and social maturity.
6. *Social and psychological factors*—factors behind problems in such areas as social adjustment, concentration, and ability to work independently; such problems are among those which inhibit reading development.
7. *Visual acuity*—the clarity of one's visual focus.
8. *Visual discrimination*—the ability of a child to see likenesses and differences.

any teachers are justifiably concerned about reading readiness. They want to help children begin to read, yet they worry about the effects of failure. We suggest that teachers learn to assess each pupil's readiness for specific reading tasks rather than try to determine readiness for a set of materials or a program. The approach to instruction, as well as maturity and environment, affects readiness to read.

READINESS AND CHRONOLOGICAL AGE

For many years the question of when children should be taught to read has engaged the attention of prominent psychologists and educators. Edmund Burke Huey (7), in 1908, suggested that *formal* instruction in reading should be secondary to other experiences in school until the age of 10. He stated that children before this age are "motor-oriented" and have difficulty passively attending to formal instruction. Huey quoted John Dewey as suggesting that before the age of 8 the teaching of reading and writing should be incidental. However, many of Dewey's ideas were based on his objections to the methods then used. He decried the use of drill that "benumbs" and deplored the "utter triviality" of the content of the primers. In schools subscribing to Dewey's ideas on the need for learning through meaningful experiences, children were taught to read through the method we refer to today as the *language-experience approach* (see Chapter 5).

Many eminently sensible discussions about the nature of reading and the teaching of reading published at the turn of the century seem to have been disregarded by educators of the 1920s and 1930s who subscribed to a "scientific" approach based on measurements. In his 1978 article on the impact of research on education (14), Singer describes "research that made a difference but shouldn't have." One of the studies he mentions is that of Morphett and Washburne (10), who are still cited today as having proven that children with a mental age of 6 years and 6 months are ready for beginning reading instruction, despite much evidence to the contrary.

Over the years, popular literature expressing contradictory ideas has added to the confusion. Some authors warn parents not to teach their preschoolers to read; others describe how to teach babies to read (16).

Durkin points out that the question of when children should learn to read is complicated (4). Some children may be reading before they enter school, while others entering first grade not only may not be reading, but may not be ready to begin.

The need then is to assess a child's preparedness for reading. This common-sense notion is followed by many parents and educators, but others feel that social and psychological pressures to conform often stifle children who read early and hurry children who need more time. This can be harmful to the children and frustrating for parents and teachers.

Children signal their readiness for beginning reading in several ways: They learn to recognize some common words. They copy words and letters with reasonable accuracy. They ask for the names and/or the sounds of letters. They ask to have words read to them or written down for them. They pretend to read a passage they have committed to memory. They express a need to read, for reasons important to them.

READINESS AND MATURITY

In his study of nonpromoted first-grade children (11), Pottorff collected comments made by teachers about why they had recommended that certain children be retained. The reasons most frequently given were immaturity and lack of readiness. Real evidence for these assertions was rarely mentioned. The results of the study indicated that, in contrast to promoted children, nonpromoted children often:

1. were members of a minority race
2. were part of a large family
3. had mothers with lower educational levels
4. had parents who were either separated or divorced
5. were low in reading
6. were low in mathematics

Also, the first four factors are likely to be related to economic level.

Teachers usually suggest that a child who reads well should be promoted, regardless of immaturity. Also, poor readers who behave well are usually promoted. Girls are seldom retained unless they are disruptive.

SEX DIFFERENCES AND MATURITY

In the United States, boys tend to score lower than girls on reading tests. More boys than girls are referred in the earlier grades for remedial reading services. A key reason that has been given for these differences is that boys mature more slowly than girls, especially with regard to the abilities required to begin reading during the primary grades. Yet, while sex-related differences exist, they are not so great as to account entirely for the significant differences in achievement. In his review of research on sex differences related to reading (3), Downing reports that in several countries boys clearly have the advantage. When reading is considered an important masculine activity, boys are more likely to achieve. Thus, sex differences in reading achievement appear to relate more to cultural expectations than to maturity.

IS MATURITY A FACTOR?

In the preceding sections the vague use of the word *immaturity* and its questionable use in analyzing sex differences in achievement may well lead one to wonder whether maturity is a factor in achievement. The answer is that physical factors can play a part in a child's learning to read under certain instructional conditions.

For example, the eyes of some children in first grade may not have matured sufficiently for them to make the near-point discriminations necessary to beginning reading. Spache and Spache state that the visual skills of the young child are among the most significant factors in early reading success (16). Yet, many schools do not make binocular screening a priority. Commercial vision-screening batteries are readily available and fairly simple to administer. Spache and Spache have recommended the following usual screening patterns:

1. *Keystone Visual Survey Tests;* Keystone View Company, Meadville, Pennsylvania.
2. *Orthorater;* Bausch and Lomb Optical Company, Rochester, New York.
3. *Professional Vision Tester;* Titmus Optical Company, Petersburg, Virginia.
4. *Spache Binocular Reading Test;* Keystone View Company, Meadville, Pennsylvania.
5. *Stereotests;* Titmus Optical Company, Petersburg, Virginia.

Children capable of making the necessary visual discriminations for reading at far-point can be instructed with the use of charts and the chalk board until they are ready for near-point work. All beginning readers should be given materials with large print. Mature readers can determine at a glance that words with a similar appearance, such as *horse* and *house*, are different. Beginning readers need to look at words more closely. Even the context does not always help. For example: "Mary was happy. She said, 'We have a new _____ .'" Either *horse* or *house* would fit. Fine discriminations are easier to make in large print.

The part played by auditory development is less clear. However, auditory abilities seem to be related more closely to instructional approaches than are visual abilities. For example, if the beginning reading approach is highly dependent upon single letter-sound associations, success would be related to the child's ability to hear fine sound differences. Wallach and Wallach's research focused on teaching young children from low socioeconomic backgrounds how to recognize and manipulate letter sounds (phonemes) (18). They believe that helping children perceive phonemes and blend them into words contributes significantly to the children's success in beginning reading. They also believe that teaching children to read by emphasizing a whole-word approach may be less dependent upon the ability to make fine sound discriminations.

Finally, any physical condition that interferes with a child's ability to attend to instruction is likely to hinder learning. Physical problems should always be ruled out before considering psychological problems or falling back on a vague term such as *immaturity*.

SOCIAL AND PSYCHOLOGICAL FACTORS

The social and emotional adjustment of the child needs to be considered in the context of the classroom setting. As a member of a group a child must take turns, share, follow directions, concentrate in the presence of distractions, work independently, and follow classroom routines. Some children have difficulty in these areas. As a result, they appear to be lost most of the day and are seldom working on their assigned tasks. Those who are especially hungry for adult attention quickly learn that needing help can bring the warmth of one-to-one support, and such children are reluctant to learn to be independent.

What should be done with a child who appears to be unable to work in a classroom setting? Should he or she be retained in the hope that another year will make a difference? We suggest that waiting is not the best approach. Rather, children should be placed with teachers whose style of classroom management is best suited to their needs. A child who needs a great deal of structure should be placed with a teacher who uses carefully worked out, step-by-step procedures, which make some children feel secure. Children who need a lot of freedom to move and explore their environment require a teacher who provides such opportunities and tolerates deviations from routine. Neither teachers nor children should be forced into a mode of behavior.

In addition, children having unusual difficulty in adjusting to the classroom setting should be observed carefully to discover the conditions that best promote their adjustment. Teachers are usually involved with many children and may not be able to chart the behavior of every child day after day. A supervisor, student teacher, or trained aide can unobtrusively observe children who are having problems and can often make helpful suggestions. For example, a child whose teacher said, "She never pays close attention to her work," was observed to work carefully when the teacher or an aide was nearby. A child who used misbehavior to get attention changed when the teacher began to ignore the misbehavior and instead to express approval, verbally and nonverbally, when the child worked well.

Thus, we endorse both helping children to adjust to the classroom and matching children with teachers in terms of their various classroom procedures, rather than depending on time to cure the ills that arise from difficulties in adjustment. If such attempts fail and if an honest appraisal of the school environment does not suggest practicable changes, children with social or emotional difficulties will require further professional help, and this should not be delayed.

CULTURAL FACTORS

Generally, the content of beginning reading materials is familiar to children—simple stories about everyday events. At one time, these stories dealt almost exclusively with white middle-class families. During the past few years, efforts have been made to correct this situation. Some states do not permit materials with a sexual, racial, or cultural bias to be used in the schools. Also, handicapped individuals have been included in reading materials. It is hoped that all students will feel that they are represented in a positive way and as contributing members of our society. Some materials continue to fall short of the ideal, but, overall, materials are much improved. This aspect of reading materials is a subtle factor that can strongly influence children's ability to view themselves as competent, achieving individuals.

Rosenthal and Jacobson use the term *self-fulfilling prophecy* to describe their finding that expecting children to learn increases the likelihood of their doing so (12). For example, a teacher's appearing to feel that a child's language is unacceptable may contribute more to the student's lack of achievement than do the differences between the pupil's language and the standard language. For generations, many people in the United States have entered school speaking little or no English, but when teachers have been confident in the newcomers' ability to achieve and fully accepted them, they were able to learn. It is this spirit of acceptance that the children of minorities need.

Successful programs have been reported in which the standard language has been learned by black children from lower socioeconomic levels. Strickland describes a study in which kindergarten children participated in such oral-language activities as creative dramatics, imitation and repetition of language patterns, engaging in active dialogue, and listening to children's books. These activities helped expand the language repertoire of linguistically different black five-year-olds.

It is well to note that school children from all social classes and races may lack language readiness. The causes of this lack vary and can include physical abnormalities (such as auditory dysfunctions), inadequate language at home (for example, baby talk), rigid parental discipline, or a failure by one or both parents or another primary caretaker to spend time at home with the child in a meaningful way or to properly encourage the child or nurture the child intellectually. Children develop their language through experience with language. If children's experience with language is inadequate, their language development will be inadequate.

Ruddell's research suggests that children's comprehension of materials written according to their speech patterns is better than their comprehension of materials written using a standard language (13). Perhaps children who use a nonstandard English would do better if they began by reading their own dictated passages (a language-experience approach), at least for part of their formal instruction.

PREDICTING READING SUCCESS OR FAILURE

Efforts have been made for many years to discover ways of predicting which children will succeed in reading most easily. One of the best predictors of future ability to read well has been the ability to name letters at the end of first grade. Monroe (9), Durrell (5), Bond and Dykstra (1), and Jansky and de Hirsch (8), among others, have concurred in this finding.

This information is useful, for instance, when children are being selected for early reading programs, but it is a mistake to assume that a direct cause-and-effect relationship exists. Education, like other professions, has not escaped problems caused by faulty inferences. A well-known example of faulty reasoning is found in a story told by researchers about studies that have found a strong, positive relationship between the number of churches in a town and the amount of alcohol that is consumed in the town. Those who assume a cause-and-effect relationship might argue that attending church causes drinking or that drinking causes people to go to church. The underlying factor, of course, is the size of the population.

So it is with a factor such as the ability to name letters. It is a mistake to reason that children must be taught to name letters before they can learn to read. This is not to say, however, that it is not useful to know letter names. We need to examine the underlying factor or factors, as we did in our humorous example. In order to learn to name letters, children need to be able to:

1. visually discriminate one letter from another
2. hear the differences between the names of the letters
3. associate letter names with letter forms
4. attend closely to instruction
5. intend to remember
6. practice until letter forms are easily recalled

Some studies have found that being able to recognize words (including one's name) and to match short letter sequences and words, as well as having a large vocabulary can be predictive of later success in reading. However, these abilities, too, depend on underlying factors that may be interrelated and that need to be carefully analyzed to see why they are predictive in some cases.

Perhaps children who come to school knowing letter names have supportive people at home who expect these children to succeed and who encourage them, provide printed materials, and are willing to answer questions about words and letters.

READINESS TESTS

Reading readiness tests, though widely used, have some serious limitations and should not alone determine children's placement in a program. Care should also be taken that test results do not become part of a self-fulfilling prophecy, a notion described earlier in this chapter.

First, one of the major difficulties associated with readiness tests is that young children are tested in large groups, where their inattention, confusion about directions, or unwillingness to do their best may not be easily detected by the examiner.

Second, children from low socioeconomic or culturally different backgrounds tend to score low on these tests regardless of their intelligence, which indicates a cultural bias.

Third, the tasks required by some subtests may be more closely related to intelligence than to beginning reading abilities.

Fourth, many of the subtests may really be testing reading rather than readiness to read.

Fifth, reading readiness tests vary a great deal in what they do and do not test.

These tests are of varying validity and reliability. Those who use readiness tests should analyze them carefully and consult authoritative reviews in sources such as Buros (2).

Some widely used reading readiness tests are: *Clymer Barrett Prereading Battery; Harrison-Stroud Reading Readiness Profiles; Murphy-Durrell Reading Readiness Analysis; Gates-MacGinitie Readiness Skills Test; Metropolitan Readiness Tests; and Macmillan Reading Readiness Test.* (See Appendix E.)

READINESS CHECKLISTS

Reading readiness tests reflect a sample of children's behavior under timed, controlled conditions; therefore, it is important that they be supplemented by observations made by teachers who work with the children daily over a period of time. A checklist can help teachers keep track of their observations and the test results of a group of children. A sample checklist is shown in Figure 2-1.

FIGURE 2-1
A Reading Readiness Checklist

VISION

———— Passes binocular test of near-point and far-point vision
———— Exhibits no signs of visual discomfort
———— Discriminates among letter and word forms that are alike and different
———— Moves entire head while reading
———— Squints eyes
———— Rubs eyes frequently or has eyes that water excessively
———— Turns head to one side to favor one eye
———— Recognizes own name in print

HEARING

———— Passes audiometric hearing test
———— Exhibits no signs of poor hearing
———— Identifies rhyming words
———— Turns head to one side to favor one ear

_____ Exhibits difficulty hearing when there is background noise
_____ Watches face of speaker closely
_____ Follows spoken directions inconsistently

ORAL LANGUAGE DEVELOPMENT

_____ Communicates ideas clearly
_____ Uses language patterns suitable to age and background
_____ Articulates words clearly
_____ Uses standard dialect
_____ Listens to and recalls details from a short paragraph or short story

GENERAL HEALTH

_____ Physical condition does not interfere with ability to learn

FINE MOTOR COORDINATION

_____ Copies letters

CLASSROOM ADJUSTMENT

_____ Shares appropriately
_____ Takes turns
_____ Follows simple directions
_____ Works independently

ATTITUDE TOWARD READING

_____ Enjoys listening to stories
_____ Expresses interest in learning to read
_____ Appears confident in ability to learn to read

CONCEPT DEVELOPMENT

_____ Understands position words, such as *up*, *down*, *under*, *over*, *through*, and *by*
_____ Understands opposites, such as *hot-cold*, *in-out*, and *hard-soft*

OTHER

_____ Identifies body parts
_____ Identifies colors
_____ Identifies letters

READINESS PROGRAMS VERSUS READINESS FOR THE TASK

On the basis of teacher judgments, readiness tests, and, occasionally, psychological evaluations, some children are judged not ready for reading at the end of kindergarten or at the beginning of first grade. These children may be given "extended readiness" or may repeat the kindergarten program. Routinely, many children go through a readiness program whether they are reading or not at the beginning of kindergarten.

When readiness is conceived in general terms as a vague constellation of abilities to be developed in a program, rather than as specific abilities required for particular tasks, one finds that readiness programs do little to bring out the individual qualities of children. For example, some children may be asked to complete dozens of ditto sheets where they must find all the *n*'s in a line containing several different letters and then circle them, when they can easily recognize, name, and write all the letters of the alphabet!

Rather than having the children complete a readiness program in unison, we suggest individualizing as much as possible by analyzing each task in relation to the capabilities of each child and by planning instruction that will help individual children master the task. Let us look at an example. Some readiness programs have attempted to help children discriminate visual forms by having them trace, match, draw, and name circles, triangles, and squares. As you might imagine, this activity helped children identify circles, triangles, and squares, but it did not help them discriminate or recognize letters and words. This is not to say that many activities in readiness programs lack value, but that the activities may have little or no relation to *reading* readiness. Thus, direct instruction, paced to fit the capability of each child and specific in content, results in more learning than mere exposure to activities that are supposed somehow to have an influence on reading at the beginning level.

READING TO CHILDREN AND READINESS

Reading to children is extremely important in developing readiness for reading instruction. Reading stories to children can help them develop a positive attitude toward reading by creating a desire in them to read on their own and cultivating in them an awareness that printed material can be a source of entertainment and information.

In addition, reading aloud to children can help them develop an ability to discriminate among sounds, especially in rhymes. They also become able to recognize the characteristic rhythms of various sentence patterns. Further, reading to children can aid in developing their ability to remember stories and to recognize in their own reading such elements as setting, sequence, reactions, and consequences.

PREREADING ACTIVITIES

Not all children need the activities listed here, and children vary in the amount of practice they need. The following prereading activities, grouped into categories, are listed for teachers working with children who may be in the prereading stage and some of whom may benefit from these activities.

ORAL LANGUAGE DEVELOPMENT

Purpose:
Useful in expressive and receptive language development.

Activity:
Play "Policeman Find My Child." One child plays the role of a policeman and another that of a parent who has become separated from the child. The parent asks the policeman for help and describes the child—the color and type of clothing and some physical characteristics. The policeman has to decide which child in the class has been described and bring that child to the front of the class.

FOLLOWING DIRECTIONS

Purpose:
Useful in responding to common sentence forms.

Activity:
Play "Simon Says."

CATEGORIZING

Purpose:
Useful in helping children organize ideas and concepts.

Activities:

1. Play "Put It Right." Make a large pocket board and a number of word cards or pictures to fit in the pockets. The words or pictures should suggest two or three such categories as people, animals, weather, transportation, and so on. Next have children put cards together to form categories.
2. Classify items in the room. Select various kinds of items according to function, and place them all together on a large table. For example, writing implements, things to write on, art supplies, books, and other categories of objects. Have children place like items together. The more categories on the table, the more difficult the task.

SEQUENCING

Purpose:
Useful in helping children see the order of events.

Activities:

1. Cut out cartoon frames, and have a child arrange them in the order in which the child believes the actions depicted occur.
2. The teacher names several activities such as those listed below. The child is to arrange the activities in the order in which they are performed.

    I get up out of bed.
    I eat breakfast.

I wash my hands and face.

I brush my teeth.

I go to school.

I work hard in school.

I come home from school.

I play with my friends.

I eat dinner.

I go to bed.

DIRECTIONALITY

Purpose:
Useful in teaching the concept of left-to-right order, a prerequisite to understanding sound-letter relationships.

Activities:

1. Have each child select an object that is easy to hold. Tell children where you want them to place their object ("*over* your head," "*under* your table," "*between* your hands" and so on). This activity helps children learn directional concepts.
2. Have children name the objects from left to right in a series of pictures.
3. Help children make a calendar by having them trace over dotted numerals, progressing of course from left to right.

LETTER MATCHING

Purpose:
Useful in helping children to recognize the differences among the letter forms.

Activities:

1. Draw a large tree. To each side of the tree draw leaves with lowercase letters on them. On the tree draw uppercase letters. Have children draw lines between matching letters.
2. Make six lotto cards, each with twenty 1-inch squares. Choose five letters of the alphabet for each card. Repeat each letter four times on the card, using lowercase letters. For each card, make twenty one-inch squares with the corresponding five capital letters each on four squares. Each card and its set of matching squares should be of one color so that they can be kept together easily.

a	f	r	a	d
r	d	f	d	t
t	a	t	f	r
f	r	d	t	a

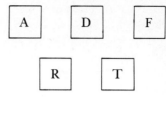

Show or call out a letter, and have each player who has that letter on his or her card place a matching square on it. The winner is the first to cover a card with squares. By changing the number of squares to 16 or 25, you can develop a bingo game using the same materials.

LETTER NAMES

Purpose:
Useful in talking about letters and to some extent helpful in learning letter sounds.

Activities:

1. Draw a large car on the chalk board, and print letters of the alphabet all over it. Children take turns finding a given letter, saying it, then erasing it. The object is to wash the car clean.
2. Play "Cross the River." Draw a river on the chalk board and place several letters on the left side of it. Children say the name of a letter, erase it, and place it on the right side of the river. Caution them about the alligators in the river who will eat any letters which fall in.
3. Play "Which Hand?" Use a box of plastic letters. One child takes a letter from the box and holds it in one hand, with both hands behind his back. The other children take turns guessing which hand is holding the letter. A child who guesses the correct hand and can name the letter, gets a turn to hide a letter.
4. The traditional alphabet song is an excellent means of teaching letter names. Sing it slowly with the children, and point to the letters as you go along.

BEGINNING SOUNDS

Purpose:
Useful in teaching children to hear the differences between phonemes and in introducing the concept of sound order.

Activities:

1. If children recognize their own names when written down, use two or more names which begin with the same letter and sound. Have the children listen for the beginning sound as the names are spoken. Write the letter on the board, and have the children practice the sound. Do this with several different letter combinations. (You may encounter such sound-letter variations as *Gary-George* and *Cathy-Cecilia*.) Be ready to explain the hard-soft sounds, and reinforce that explanation with other examples, immediately and later.
2. Children who have mastered several sounds can be asked to call out the names of objects in the room which begin with sounds you specify (*t* is for *table*, *d* is for *desk*, and so on).
3. Ask children to cut out words beginning with the "sound(s) of the week" from old magazines and newspapers.

LABELING

Purpose:
Useful in teaching the concept that a printed word can represent the name of a person, place, or thing and in building a stock of sight words.

Activities:

1. Ask children to name objects found in their homes. Write the names on the board, and have children make up simple sentences using these words, such as, "I like to stay in *bed*."
2. Have the class make scrapbooks of items found in a grocery store. Use pictures from magazines and have children print the names of the objects below the pictures.
3. Make a word card for each word a child is learning. The child can use these cards for review and for a class activity such as word-recognition baseball. Individual differences are accounted for by allowing each child to use his or her personalized stock of cards.

SIMPLE SENTENCES (Dictation and Reading)

Purpose:
Useful in teaching the concept of reading as talk that is written down.

Activities:

1. Have the children tell a story as a group. One child makes up a short sentence. Write it on the chalk board, and have the next child continue the story with another sentence, and so forth. A variation would be to have the group write just one sentence, with each child contributing

just one word (for small groups). Or have one row of the class make up a sentence, and then let the next row continue the story.

2. Use five columns of words as follows:

Determiner	Noun	Verb	Determiner	Noun
The	boy	saw	a	bird
A	dog	bit	the	tree
	girl	carried		dog
	horse	walked		cat
		asked		man

Have children construct sentences from left to right. Allow silly sentences; humor is a good memory aide. Vary this game as you go along, perhaps dropping a determiner, adding adjectives, and so forth.

RHYMING WORDS

Purpose:
Useful in developing the enjoyment of language and the ability to discriminate vowel sounds and common phonograms.

Activities:
1. Using the sound family approach, have children call out words as you write them *(fit, pit, bit)*. Change the ending *(fin, pin, bin)*. Change the vowel *(fun, pun, bun)*.

   Once children catch on, have them make changes at the middle or end to make new series of rhyming words.
2. Make up a simple class poem, similar to the following:

   > It's always such fun.
   > To play in the sun.
   > We run and we run.
   > It's always such fun.

   Have children dictate verse, including rhyming words. Help them only if they get stuck. They are likely to tackle more difficult words in rhymes, and they have a great deal of fun with hilarious wording.

CONCEPTS USED IN INSTRUCTION

Purpose:
Useful in teaching the meanings of such words as *beginning*, *last*, *circle*, *cross out*, *underline*, *more*, *most*, *under*, and *from*.

Activities:

Before proceeding with readiness activities, be certain children understand the concepts they will be using. At the beginning of each activity demonstrate such instructions as those listed above. Let children practice concepts before testing children with them.

READINESS AT LATER LEVELS

At the beginning of this chapter, we mentioned that most children do not have difficulty comprehending the simple stories in their beginning reading materials, since the content usually reflects their experiences. However, when reading materials begin to take in more subject areas, many students lack the background of experiences and concepts necessary to comprehend their reading assignments.

Readiness for reading is crucial at all levels. If we accept the idea that we bring our experiences to the printed page, then we must conclude that the richer and the more extensive those experiences are, the greater will be our ability to comprehend written material.

Teachers must analyze material that they plan to assign in order to identify enabling concepts that may need explanation. Teachers may also need to give students appropriate firsthand experiences. Many children in the intermediate and secondary grades have difficulty with the brief explanation in their American-history books of the electoral college, but when teachers build students' readiness with appropriate experiences, their comprehension is greatly increased. For example, a teacher might show the children two different ways of voting about when to hold a party. In the first way, each child votes, and the teacher collects the ballots and tallies them. In the second way, the children vote first for one person in each row or at each table to represent them, and then these representatives vote. The teacher collects these ballots and tallies them. The teacher then announces the results of the two ways of voting, and the children compare the two procedures in a discussion. Prereading experiences such as these will help them understand abstract concepts.

Readiness has been emphasized at the prereading and beginning reading levels, but it needs to be considered and dealt with at all levels.

SUMMARY

Many of the so-called readiness factors which have been used traditionally to predict children's preparedness for formal reading instruction should be reexamined. We tend to discount theories that chronological age and sex differences by themselves are of any great significance, and we question whether it is proper to blame language and/or cultural factors for reading difficulties. The idea of the self-fulfilling prophecy appears to be of paramount importance with regard to teachers' expectations of ethnic and racial minorities, of boys, and of the younger children in their classes.

Developmental factors which do affect readiness are physical abilities to make visual and auditory discriminations. In addition, children must make certain social and psychological adjustments if they are to learn in group situations.

We have recommended several commercial readiness tests which we feel are of good quality, but we caution that all tests should be used carefully because of their limitations. A reading readiness checklist may be used for more accurate, individualized assessment. Finally, readiness activities that focus on direct instruction on letters, words, and sentence construction seem more germane to the reading process than activities that involve spending time on such questionably related readiness drills as discriminating geometric shapes.

ACTIVITIES RELATED TO THE CHAPTER

1. Visit a nursery school to observe the school's activity. Talk with the teacher about the goals of the nursery school. Judge whether children from this school are likely to be prepared for kindergarten. In what area of the nursery school program do you find strengths in developing readiness skills? What is the weakest area?
2. Look at the reading readiness checklist (Figure 2-1). Visit an elementary classroom to see if the activities and materials meet the needs listed in the checklist.
3. Watch a one-hour segment of *Sesame Street*. Make a list of the readiness skills addressed in the program.
4. Select two kindergarten children. Using the concepts and activities presented in this chapter, determine whether or not each child is ready to read. What led you to reach your conclusions?
5. Choose three standardized readiness tests. Analyze the strengths and weaknesses of each in terms of your concept of readiness.

BIBLIOGRAPHY AND REFERENCES

1. Bond, Guy L., and Robert Dykstra: "The Cooperative Research Program in First-Grade Reading Instruction," *Reading Research Quarterly*, **11**(4) (1967).
2. Buros, Oscar K. (ed.): *The Eighth Mental Measurement Yearbook*, 2 vols. Gryphon, Highland Park, NJ, 1978.
3. Downing, John: "Cultural Expectations," in Downing, John, *Comparative Reading*, Macmillan, New York, 1973.
4. Durkin, Dolores: "When Should Children Learn to Read," in Robinson, Helen M., "Innovation and Change in Reading Instruction," *67th Yearbook of the National Society for the Study of Education*, 1968.
5. Durrell, Donald D: *Improvement of Basic Reading Abilities*, World, Yonkers, 1940.

6. Forgan, Harry W: *The Reading Corner: Ideas, Games, and Activities for Individualized Reading*, Goodyear Santa Monica, CA, 1977.

7. Huey, Edmund Burke: *The Psychology and Pedagogy of Reading*, Macmillan, New York, 1908.

8. Jansky, Jeanette, and Katrina de Hirsch: *Preventing Reading Failure: Prediction, Diagnosis, Intervention*, Harper & Row, New York, 1972.

9. Monroe, Marion: *Children Who Cannot Read*, University of Chicago Press, Chicago, 1932.

10. Morphett, Mabel V., and Carleton Washburne: "When Should Children Begin to Read?" *Elementary School Journal*, 31:496–563 (1931).

11. Pottorff, Donald: "Profile of the Salient Characteristics of Non-Promoted First-Grade Children," unpublished Ph.D. dissertation, Michigan State University, 1978.

12. Rosenthal, Robert, and Lenore Jacobson: *Pygmalion in the Classroom*, Holt, New York, 1968.

13. Ruddell, Robert B.: "The Effect of Oral and Written Patterns of Language Structure on Reading Comprehension," *The Reading Teacher*, 18:270–275 (1965).
14. Singer, Harry: "Research in Reading That Should Make a Difference in Classroom Instruction," in Samuels, S. Jay, *What Research Has to Say about Reading Instruction*, International Reading Association, Newark, DE, 1978.
15. Spache, Evelyn B: *Reading Activities for Child Involvement*, 2nd ed., Allyn and Bacon, Boston, 1978.
16. Spache, George D., and Evelyn B. Spache: *Reading in the Elementary School*, 4th ed., Allyn and Bacon, Boston, 1978.
17. Strickland, Dorothy S.: "A Program for Linguistically Different Black Children," *Research in the Teaching of English*, 7(1):79–86 (1973).
18. Wallach, Michael, and Lise Wallach: *Teaching All Children to Read*, University of Chicago Press, Chicago, 1976.

Vocabulary: The Keystone of Reading

3

Overview

Vocabulary development is one of the most crucial aspects of a child's learning to read. In this chapter, the various components of vocabulary are discussed, and information is given regarding how students can acquire and retain a satisfactory reading vocabulary. The chapter also includes discussions of a variety of activities which can help children develop their vocabulary.

Definition of Terms

1. *Configuration*—a method of identifying a word according to its shape.
2. *Context*—the use of familiar surrounding words or sentences in an attempt to determine the meaning of a word or words.
3. *Hearing (or listening) vocabulary*—the words understood by a child when spoken by another person.
4. *Phonics*—a system for teaching the recognition of words in print through sound-symbol relationships.
5. *Reading vocabulary*—the printed words for which a child can derive the correct meaning.
6. *Sight vocabulary*—the words known instantaneously by a child; words which appear frequently in reading materials.
7. *Speaking vocabulary*—the words used by a child when talking.
8. *Structural analysis*—the breaking up of an unfamiliar word into its component parts as a possible way of identifying it.
9. *Writing vocabulary*—the words employed by a child when presenting information in a written format.

he importance of vocabulary in the reading process is so obvious that it sometimes is overlooked. If this statement sounds contradictory, it was meant to.

Among the basics of reading, vocabulary is probably one of the most essential. One who cannot associate meanings with words, cannot read with comprehension. Competence in phonics, structural analysis, or configuration does not alter this condition dramatically.

Despite the obvious importance of vocabulary in the reading process, it is frequently underemphasized by teachers in their classrooms. It is also a facet of reading about which some teachers have many misconceptions. This chapter represents our attempt to delineate the significant role which vocabulary plays in reading. In addition, after reading this chapter, we hope that you are able to answer the following questions: What is vocabulary? What is known about how children acquire and retain reading vocabulary? What activities are conducive to increased proficiency in vocabulary?

VOCABULARY DEFINED

Ralful hamet bextil premaces fompart silkness minther. No, what you have just read is not a typographical error. The words are printed precisely as we wrote them. Now, please read the first sentence again. Do your best to read it and derive meaning from it.

How did you do this time? Were you able to comprehend the sentence's meaning? Chances are that your responses to both of these questions indicate a lack of success. This is in spite of the fact that you were probably able to pronounce every word in the sentence and that you recognized the prefixes and suffixes. Also, even if you possess competence in the skills of configuration, structural analysis, and dictionary usage, you still were unable to get the sentence's meaning.

The sentence is composed of nonsense words that were simply invented. Each word's meaning, and therefore the sentence's meaning, is a mystery to you.

This exercise is not unlike one faced daily by many elementary students. Numerous words are as unfamiliar to these children as our words were to you. They may be able to say words and read them fluently while their comprehension of the words is virtually nonexistent. The students are unable to attach *meanings* to printed words.

Therefore, when we think of a vocabulary in reading, let us remember that it encompasses not only a child's ability to know how to correctly say a word or recognize it instantaneously in print but also to know the meaning associated with the word in context. Karlin is among those who hold a comparable view (12). He states: "Regardless of the way in which words are presented to him, the ultimate goal of instruction is the development of his ability to know words without having to analyze them."

42

A discussion of vocabulary would be remiss if the human element were not described. Let us now turn our attention to this part of the vocabulary development process.

LEARNERS

Few educators would argue with the concept that every child is a unique person. If each child were studied, differences would be found to exist among children relative to age, intelligence, interests, motivation, experiences, and so on.

These differences in children relate to the area of vocabulary as well. Dale says: "If you are going to plan a systematic program of vocabulary development grade by grade, you must realize that vocabulary development will be influenced by age, by sex, by income, by native ability, by social status, by locale" (2). Dale's statement lays the foundation for the effective teaching of vocabulary to children. It is a reminder that students, even in the same grade, vary greatly in terms of the reading vocabulary which they possess. In addition to their differences in *achievement*, the children have greatly varying *capabilities* for vocabulary development. Dale reminds us that there is a "very close relationship between vocabulary and mental ability." Therefore, it can be generally concluded that the more intelligent students have a greater capability for vocabulary development than students of lesser intelligence.

TYPES OF VOCABULARIES

Some people perceive vocabulary as a single thing. This is incorrect; we do, in fact, possess several vocabularies. By the time children have reached the intermediate grades, they should be developing four vocabularies: (1) hearing (or listening)—the words understood by a child when spoken by another person; (2) reading—the printed words for which a child can derive the correct meaning; (3) speaking—the words used by a child when talking; and (4) writing—the words employed by a child when presenting information in a written format. In mature readers, the listening vocabulary is the most extensive, followed in size by the reading, speaking, and writing vocabularies.

The relationships among these four types of vocabularies are a source of confusion to some. The four vocabularies overlap. Words in one vocabulary may also be found in the other vocabularies. However, a word's appearance in one of the vocabularies of a child is no assurance that the word will occur in any of the other vocabularies.

When we speak of vocabulary development, then, we are not simply equating it with word recognition. Word recognition is the basis of the reading vocabulary, but efforts designed to develop a child's four vocabularies concurrently have a definite place in the elementary school classroom. Petty and Jensen give support to this viewpoint (21). They state that "the best evidence indicates that teachers need to recognize that vocabulary growth occurs as children develop their ability to use language."

READING VOCABULARY

Reading vocabulary breaks down into two primary classifications: *sight vocabulary* and words identified on a *delayed recall* basis. An explanation of each of these follows.

Sight Vocabulary

There are two somewhat divergent schools of thought about how to define sight vocabulary. The first is based upon the concept of *acquisition*, and the second is based upon *utilization*. Hill offers a definition of sight vocabulary consistent with the acquisition position (9). He says: "The reader's sight vocabulary consists of that reservoir of graphic words with which he can associate the appropriate referential and/or linguistic meaning in one-third to one-fifth of a second." Others speak of sight words in terms of their *utilization*. According to Johnson and Pearson (11), sight words may refer "to one or another of the compilations of high-frequency words which are essential to fluent reading."

It is our view that the effective teacher of reading will perceive sight vocabulary according to *both* definitions. Inherent in the acquisition view of sight words is the element of spontaneity. A child is able to identify and attach meaning to such words almost as soon as they have been seen. No time-consuming word analysis (for instance, phonics or structural analysis) is employed. The words are so familiar to the child that such an analysis is unnecessary.

What words should constitute a child's sight vocabulary? It is here that the utilization factor comes into play. While many words could conceivably be part of a student's sight vocabulary, a child should *at least* possess words which appear frequently in print. This does not mean that a student should learn only these words. We are recommending that high-frequency words be part of a child's sight vocabulary because they are potentially so useful to the student.

There are currently numerous sight-word compilations available to educators. Rinsland (22), Otto and Chester (20), Moe (19), and Kucera and Francis (14) are among those who have compiled word lists.

Although the lists offered by these individuals are all excellent, it is our view that the Dolch list of 220 basic sight words is still the most frequently used of the word lists (4). This list was originally compiled in 1936, and according to Dolch it is composed of a short and useful core of basic vocabulary words. Some have disputed the value of the Dolch list, but in a 1978 study by Mangieri its relevance was reaffirmed (17). This study sought to determine how often Dolch's words appeared in four of the most popular American basal reading series. It was found that "the Dolch List still is quite relevant in terms of contemporary reading series. These words accounted for 76% of the sample drawn from primer and first-level readers, 69% of the second-level words, and 62% of the sample derived from the third-level readers of the four designated series. In terms of the total sample, Dolch words represented 69% of all of the words drawn from grades primer to third of the four series."

Therefore, Dolch's list of 220 basic sight words is extremely useful to teachers of reading. The list is presented in Figure 3-1.

FIGURE 3-1
The Dolch Basic Sight Vocabulary*

a	call	full	jump	on	sing	under
about	came	funny	just	once	sit	up
after	can			one	six	upon
again	carry	gave	keep	only	sleep	us
all	clean	get	kind	open	small	use
always	cold	give	know	or	so	
am	come	go		our	some	very
an	could	goes	laugh	out	soon	
and	cut	going	let	over	start	walk
any		good	light	own	stop	want
are	did	got	like			warm
around	do	green	little	pick	take	was
as	does	grow	live	play	tell	wash
ask	done		long	please	ten	we
at	don't	had	look	pretty	thank	well
ate	down	has		pull	that	went
away	draw	have	made	put	the	were
	drink	he	make		their	what
be		help	many	ran	them	when
because	eat	her	may	read	then	where
been	eight	here	me	red	there	which
before	every	him	much	ride	these	white
best	fall	his	must	right	they	who
better	far	hold	my	round	think	why
big	fast	hot	myself	run	this	will
black	find	how			those	wish
blue	first	hurt	never	said	three	with
both	five		new	saw	to	work
bring	fly	I	no	say	today	would
brown	for	if	not	see	together	write
but	found	in	now	seven	too	
buy	four	into	of	shall	try	yellow
by	from	is	off	she	two	yes
		it	old	show		you
		its				your

* "Dolch Basic Sight Vocabulary" by E. W. Dolch. Available in card form from Garrard Publishing Co., Champaign, Illinois 61820.

Dolch's list is the most popular one among educators; however, we would like to call an additional list to your attention. Hillerich's 190 starred starter words represent an attempt "to identify a basic list that would be a representative reading and writing vocabulary used by children and adults" (10). There are two premises underlying the development of Hillerich's list: (1) that words for a recognition vocabulary ought to be selected on the basis of frequency of use in *natural* language (as opposed to the controlled vocabularies of basals) and (2) that the length of the list should be limited, since teachers quickly reach a point of diminishing returns when merely teaching extensive lists of words. The list is presented in Figure 3-2.

Lists such as Dolch's and Hillerich's can serve two basic purposes. First, a teacher can show the words on a list to a child and ask the child to identify each word. This will reveal how many of the words are known by the child, enabling the teacher to make judgments about the student's sight vocabulary. Second, such a list can also be used for instruction. The words can be given increased emphasis by a teacher in the hope that, as a result of their high incidence, students will subsequently be able to spontaneously recognize each of these words in print.

Delayed Recall

A perfect reader, if one could ever be created, would be someone who would instantaneously know the meaning of every word appearing in print. However, anyone who has read an erudite editorial is aware that it is impossible for a person to recognize instantly every word encountered.

In situations where a word is not recognized immediately by an individual there are various procedures available which might aid in determining its meaning. These procedures, termed *word-recognition* measures, include (1) phonics, (2) configuration, (3) structural analysis, (4) context, and (5) dictionary usage.

Phonics

Phonics is a system for associating specific sounds with letters. By doing so, a child is able to say words orally or silently, provided they are *regular*. A word is regular when it looks the way it sounds (that is, sounds in accordance with the letters contained in it). For example, *cat* is a regular word. By using phonics correctly, a child could properly pronounce the previously unknown word. Phonics can be an invaluable word-recognition device to a teacher who is aware of its strengths and its limitations. Unfortunately, some teachers either embrace phonics as a panacea or reject it completely. Clearly, we do not hold either of these opinions.

The principle strength of phonics as a word-recognition device is that it can help children cope with words which are not part of their sight vocabulary. In sounding out words through phonics, students hear them-

FIGURE 3-2
The 190 Starred Starter Words
(in order of frequency of use)

the	from	down	only	last
and	up	back	much	away
a	will	just	us	each
to	do	year	take	never
of	said	little	name	while
in	then	make	here	took
it	what	who	say	men
is	like	after	got	next
was	her	people	around	may
I	go	come	any	Mr.
he	them	no	use	give
you	time	because	place	show
that	if	first	put	once
for	some	more	boy	something
on	about	many	water	room
they	by	know	also	must
with	him	made	before	didn't
have	or	thing	off	always
are	can	went	through	car
had	me	man	right	told
we	your	want	ask	why
be	an	way	most	small
one	day	work	should	children
but	their	which	don't	still
at	other	good	than	head
when	very	well	three	left
all	could	came	found	white
this	has	new	these	let
she	look	school	saw	world
there	get	too	find	under
not	now	been	tell	same
his	see	think	help	kind
as	our	home	every	keep
were	two	house	again	am
would	into	play	another	best
so	did	old	big	batter
my	over	long	night	soon
out	how	where	thought	four

There is a copyright on this list. Hillerich, however, has given permission for teachers to use the list—and reproduce it for their use—in schools.

selves say the words and may recognize them as being part of their listening vocabulary. This is not rare, provided that the words are regular, that the children possess competence in phonics, and that their listening vocabulary is appreciably larger than their reading vocabulary.

There are three limitations on the use of phonics as a vocabulary device. First, it must be remembered that many of the words encountered by a child are not regular. The child who phonically attempts to sound out *pneumonia*, for example, is likely to experience little success.

Another difficulty with phonics is that some teachers fail to perceive it simply as a support in teaching vocabulary. When a word is recognized instantaneously by a student, it is absurd to insist that the child sound it out anyway. It should be noted that a child's memorization of phonic rules does not insure that the child will use these rules while reading. Rather than encouraging rote memorization of these rules, a teacher would do well to develop the rules inductively with children.

Configuration

Configuration has become somewhat of a time-honored device used principally by kindergarten, primary, and remedial teachers. According to Lapp and Flood (15), it is "an aid in word recognition that makes use of the shape and pattern of the letters in a particular word. It relies mainly on the presence of ascending and descending letters."

Boxes are usually drawn around a word in order to point out its graphic appearance. Advocates of configuration feel that children who are made aware of the shape of a word and its contrast to other words will subsequently remember the word. For example, the configurations of *tale* and *jello* are shown below. You can note their dissimilar shapes.

We cannot, however, endorse the view that configuration is a legitimate word-recognition skill. Despite its relative popularity in classrooms, the technique is of dubious value. For one thing, different words can have the same configuration. As an example, *tall*, *ball*, and *bell* all have identical configurations, even though the words are different.

In addition, we have seen little evidence that the technique does help a child "unlock" an unfamiliar word. Because of the limitations of the strategy, drawing boxes around unknown words does not aid students in getting the meaning of these words. Rather, configuration becomes an exercise to be done with familiar words, and why should a child have to draw a box around a familiar word?

Structural Analysis

Johnson and Pearson differentiate the roles of phonics and structural analysis in terms of vocabulary (11). They state: "Unlike phonics, whose purpose is to help children pronounce unfamiliar printed words, the purpose of structural analysis is to help children analyze unfamiliar printed words by picking out already known meaningful parts of words." Although there is some difference among reading authorities as to what structural analysis encompasses, the following seem to be included within the term's application: compound words, variants of words, root words, and affixes (that is, prefixes and suffixes).

Compound words. Durkin delineates the conditions under which a word is classified as being compound (5): "Introducing a child to compound words is introducing him to the fact that roots can combine to form words in which the pronunciation of the roots is maintained and in which the roots have a connected meaning." The elements of *pronunciation* and *connected meaning* are often a source of confusion to children. For example, words such as *snowstorm*, *playground*, and *outside* meet both criteria. The words *nothing* and *breakfast* are not compound words.

If children understand the fundamentals of identifying compound words, then the defining of words by connected meanings (for instance, *after-noon*) may be helpful. The limitation of this system becomes apparent when a student attempts to analyze words as compounds which do not fit this categorization.

Variants of words. The addition of *y, ly, ed, ing*, and other such endings often presents difficulty to students. A word which is in a student's sight vocabulary, may suddenly become unrecognizable when a particular ending is attached to it. When the child is able to recognize that *sleeping* is merely *sleep* with an *ing* added to it, then *sleeping* is no longer unknown, provided the student knows the word *sleep*.

Obviously, we feel that students must become competent at recognizing the variants of words. Instruction in this area can be beneficial to the development of the student's vocabulary. However, this form of structural analysis is of limited value to the child who knows few words.

Root words. Harris and Smith define a root word as "a word base that is not compounded or modified by a prefix, suffix, or inflectional ending and that remains unchanged through such modifications" (8). Examples of root words would be *four* in *fourth*, *swift* in *swiftest*, and *strong* in *stronger*.

Children confronted with modified forms of known words are occasionally unable to derive any meaning from these new words. Children taught to seek out base words in the larger word actually use root words to deal with troublesome vocabulary. For example, a student might be able to discern that *quickly* is merely *quick* with *ly* added to it. Thus, the word would mean *in a quick manner*. Proficiency in searching for root words can be helpful to children in dealing with words. However, structural analysis is of no real value to a child who does not know the meanings of the root words. Most poor readers are in this position.

Prefixes and suffixes. Prefixes and suffixes are what we refer to as *affixes*, parts which are *fixed to* or *added to* words. Affixes should be used to help children determine the meaning of initially unknown words. The student who is able to recognize a prefix or a suffix in a word, as well as its associated definition, is able to discern at least part of the word's meaning.

Only fifteen prefixes account for 80 percent of the 5,000 words having prefixes. These fifteen prefixes and their associated meanings are

ab- (from)	*dis-* (apart)	*pre-* (before)
ad- (to)	*en-* (in)	*pro-* (in front of)
be- (by)	*ex-* (out)	*re-* (back)
com- (with)	*in-* (into)	*sub-* (under)
de- (from)	*in-* (not)	*un-* (not)

Some words, of course, also contain suffixes. Guszak reports (6): "In a study of the most common features of the words in children's reading, Thorndike found the following suffixes to be most common: *-ion, -tion, -ation, -er, -y, -al, -ent, -ful, -ity, -ure, -ous*."

Clearly children should be taught these suffixes, as well as the ways in which they affect the words to which they are affixed (for example, *taller* is the word *tall* with the suffix *er* added to it). We are not recommending that numerous hours be devoted to the study of prefixes and suffixes, since many words do not contain them. Also, as previous comments indicate, only a relatively small number of prefixes and suffixes appear with any real degree of frequency. Obviously, it would not be wise in classroom instruction to spend considerable time on infrequently used affixes.

Context

Context is the use by a reader of familiar surrounding words or sentences in an attempt to determine the meaning of a word or words. Effective readers generally possess the ability to utilize context in searching for the meaning of unknown words.

There are two main forms of context usage. The first entails the use of *picture clues*. In this, a child analyzes the objects and actions portrayed in a picture in an effort to determine the meaning of its accompanying text.

The second form of context involves using what Tinker and McCullough term *verbal-context clues* (25). Numerous different types of contextual-analysis skills could be looked at in this way. In terms of frequency of appearance, four of the context aids analyzed by McCullough seem to be particularly pertinent (18):

1.   *Comparison or context clue*—uses the reader's knowledge of one word to provide comparison or contrast with an unknown word: "Ed is *big* and Jeffrey is *little*."
2.   *Synonym clue*—occurs when a sentence calls for a repetition of the same word, and a synonym is given: "Susan was *mad* and *angry* with Helen."
3.   *Summary clue*—the unknown word is a summary of several ideas that have been, or are to be, presented: "The house had been *ransacked*. Drawers were opened. Things were broken; other items were missing. Clothing and papers were thrown on the floor."
4.   *Definition clue*—unknown word is defined in the surrounding context. "An *island* is a body of land surrounded by water."

A certain controversy exists as to the merits of context usage. Some have made the term a catch-all, standing for numerous vague reading strategies and skills. This has caused some educators to downplay the significance of this word-identification skill. Also, context sometimes is of little or no value to a reader. Robinson cites three instances when the use of context does not unlock meaning (23): "When the reader's experience is not matched to that of the writer, when a piece of writing is poorly organized, and/or when the writing lacks much redundancy."

Dictionary Usage

When teachers think of strategies for identifying unknown words, the dictionary often is forgotten. This is regrettable, since the dictionary can help a child become an independent reader. Students must be taught a variety of skills in order to make proper use of a dictionary.

A teacher cannot assume that a child knows how to use a dictionary. If you doubt this, construct a test dealing with dictionary usage and administer it to your students. The results will confirm our point: most elementary students do not know how to use a dictionary properly.

Students must be taught not only *how* to use a dictionary but also *when* to use one. Although the dictionary can unlock the meaning of an unknown word for a child, dictionary usage is the most time-consuming of the word-recognition techniques. Therefore, it should be considered a last resort.

Teachers who want students to use dictionaries must make them available. A child will not generally get up from his seat at school in order to determine a single word's meaning in a dictionary. This parallels our own behavior. After a full day's work, how often do you leave your easy chair while reading a book or newspaper in order to look up an unknown word in a dictionary? If dictionaries are to be used by children, each child must have a personal copy, or a sufficient number of copies must be available in a classroom to insure that one is readily within each student's grasp. Many fine dictionaries for students exist. A list of these books is presented in Appendix A.

Summary

In this section, we have discussed various strategies through which a student can identify words. The larger the number of words in a child's sight vocabulary, the better, since the child recognizes these words instantaneously. Delayed recall is important, since it can enable students to recognize many words. However, delayed recall requires more time than does sight-word identification and, in some instances, does not appreciably aid children in discerning the meaning of a particular word.

VOCABULARY ACQUISITION AND RETENTION

Did you study a foreign language in high school? Are you as proficient in that language today as you were then? If you are like most individuals, your response is yes to our first question and no to the second. You thus support the point that the acquisition of a word does not insure its retention by a student.

The very nature of basal reading series insures that a controlled vocabulary is presented to a child one step at a time. By a controlled vocabulary we mean the words in these readers, which are taught to students and which they are expected to learn. Most series also provide for a certain degree of repetition and practice to insure reinforcement of a child's learning of these words. For numerous elementary students, this form of vocabulary instruction proves adequate.

It must be recognized, however, that despite the efforts of publishers to produce perfect basal reading series, some children's vocabularies are extremely deficient. Among the reasons for this condition are the following:

1. These days, people move about more, and a child might not remain at a single elementary school from kindergarten through sixth grade. As a result, one or more different series might be used to teach him to read. The vocabularies of these series undoubtedly differ in composition and in the sequence in which the words are presented.
2. Words initially acquired by students may be forgotten if not adequately reinforced.
3. Some children, especially those in low-achievement groups, may never have been taught certain words. These words were perhaps in a section of a reader not used or only superficially covered by a teacher. Undoubtedly, then, these children would not acquire and retain these vocabulary words.

If children are to become proficient readers, they must possess an adequate reading vocabulary as well as the word-recognition techniques necessary for becoming independent in reading. A teacher cannot assume that a basal reading series automatically gives these things to every child. Beginning reading programs generally do an excellent job of introducing new words to children. Through their stories and associated materials, they enable many students to acquire numerous words and skills important to success in reading. However, the use of these basic readers alone does not insure the development of an adequate reading vocabulary by every child. The reading series should be perceived as a prime resource in a vocabulary-development effort. The series should not make up the entire program; in many schools, though, this is the case.

In elementary classrooms, teachers must begin to think about how they can provide children with the experiences necessary for acquiring and retaining words. This entails careful planning, as well as an understanding of vocabulary development on a teacher's part. Teachers should consider the following:

1. Children are likely to be successful in reading if they possess a sizable vocabulary. Of perhaps equal importance is the ability of students to *use* the words they have acquired. Proficient readers know several meanings for a word, and they are able to determine which meaning is appropriate in the context of a given sentence.

2. The English language encompasses numerous types of words. Some words refer to concrete objects, such as *chalk* or *book*. Others convey an abstract idea, such as *freedom*. The style of presentation of an effective teacher will be in accord with the nature of the word to be acquired.

3. Learning and retaining words should be stimulating for children. Techniques and activities which foster a high level of student motivation should be used by a teacher. Vocabulary instruction which is dull and mechanical customarily produces little tangible success.

4. A word may appear often in print, but it should not be assumed that children therefore know the word. They may be able to say the word but lack a sense of its meaning. If you desire proof of this statement, ask students to tell you the meanings of words which they pronounce correctly.

5. In a previous section of this chapter, we stated that children possess four vocabularies: listening, reading, speaking, and writing. The words in one of these vocabularies may or may not exist in the others, but all the vocabularies are used in communication. The effective teacher seeks to use as many communication skills as possible when teaching vocabulary words to children. Listening, writing, and speaking are excellent ways of not only teaching new words to pupils but also reinforcing words, and reinforcement makes retention possible.

6. School is not the only place where vocabulary development occurs. School may be the only place where vocabulary is formally taught, but

children have ample opportunities to acquire and use language elsewhere. Effective teachers both instill in pupils the desire to learn new words and provide proper reinforcement for their acquisition of new words.

The nonschool environment is an excellent arena for children to *use* the language they have acquired in school. Through reading, writing and speaking, students are afforded ample opportunities to use words, which also helps them to retain words.

7. "If you can't beat 'em, join 'em" is a popular saying that applies to multimedia techniques of vocabulary development. Today's elementary student is a product of television. Instead of fighting the media, teachers should use them when possible in vocabulary instruction. Audiovisual aids are precisely that—*aids* to teaching vocabulary to children.

8. Regardless of which way you teach vocabulary to children, differences in the abilities of pupils still matter. The wise teacher recognizes individual differences in children, rather than seeking to make all children perform similarly.

VOCABULARY ACTIVITIES

The title of this chapter is "Vocabulary: The Keystone of Reading." By now, the significance of this title should be obvious to you. Vocabulary is one of the most basic elements of reading. Good readers know and use many words; poor readers do not.

We are not alone in recognizing the importance of vocabulary in elementary reading. Basal reading series devote numerous exercises to the development of children's vocabulary. As previously pointed out, this does not insure that students have an adequate reading vocabulary. Many professional articles, research investigations, portions of books, and entire textbooks have dealt with vocabulary development. Books written by Deighton (3), Lewis (16), Burmeister (1), and Johnson and Pearson (11) are particularly helpful.

It is our hope that at this point you have come to at least two realizations: (1) the use of basic readers must be supplemented with regard to vocabulary, and (2) ample resources exist for aiding you in this effort.

There are many techniques and activities which can be used to help children develop a reading vocabulary. We will describe some activities which we have found to be particularly popular with and useful to teachers. These activities are pedagogically sound but should not be perceived as rigid prescriptions. They are offered as resources which reading teachers may wish to modify for use in their classrooms.

Personal Experiences. Going places, seeing things, and meeting people give children fine opportunities to learn words. Personally experiencing the events associated with certain words gives students a real interest in the words. Examples of activities that offer personal experiences are a trip to the zoo, a walk around the block, or the bringing of certain objects into the classroom for the students to see. The teacher makes note of the words employed during the experience and teaches them to the children. Personal experience is one of the key ingredients in the language-experience approach to reading.

Indirect Experiences. Indirect experiences involve the use of pictures, film strips, movies, and other audiovisual aids with children. The objects, events, or activities presented are noted. Teachers are afforded opportunities to present and explain new words and reinforce previously taught ones. Children's literature contributes greatly to these vicarious experiences.

Notecards. Notecards can be very flexible in helping students acquire and retain vocabulary. Essential words (that is, words from the Dolch list, from basal series, and so on) are written individually on notecards. These words are then used with individuals, small groups, or the entire class.

The notecards can be utilized in several different ways, depending on a teacher's goal. For example, ten words might be shown to children and they could be asked to say them (sight-word recognition), define them (word meaning), provide a word similar to each one (synonym), supply a word opposite in meaning (antonym), or use the word in a sentence (context usage).

If the notecards are kept in a convenient location, the teacher can use them whenever an opportune moment presents itself. The notecards can serve the teacher as a word bank of essential vocabulary.

TABA Lesson. In this activity (24), the children say all of the words they know regarding a certain topic. Some examples of topics are (1) everything that pertains to Christmas or Thanksgiving, (2) everything that comes in a can or a bottle, (3) everything in a house or a kitchen, (4) words beginning with the letter *b*, and so forth. Other topics may, of course, be used. Any words offered by the children are acceptable. At this time, the teacher should not overtly, even nonverbally (for example, through facial expression), express a judgment as to the merits of a child's response. After each pupil has had an opportunity to contribute a few words, the teacher stops this part of the activity. This is done by saying, for instance, "I'll take two more answers."

The children then read over the words; the teacher may have to read certain words to the younger children. The students suggest which words they would like to keep (it is recommended that there be five to seven words kept). The teacher should call on individual children to pick words; after saying them, the teacher asks the children why they selected those particular words. Finally, the students can be requested to give their word-groups titles, which could also be shared with the teacher.

The lists developed in a TABA activity can be posted in the classroom and can form word banks for future vocabulary development. TABA activities also give the teacher an opportunity to observe how individual children organize ideas.

Reading. Materials can be read by students or be read to them. Both activities are excellent for vocabulary development.

We have previously stressed that children should be afforded many opportunities to read materials of their own choice. This serves a motivational purpose, and it implies that essential reading skills can be developed. In reading many and varied materials, in addition to those required in the classroom, the child encounters numerous new words and diverse language patterns and styles of writing. Wide reading develops a student's vocabulary as well. Thorndike recommends such reading "as the best solution to the problem of vocabulary building, providing pupils with a wide variety of interesting books that are easy enough so that the new words and ideas can be learned from the context" (7).

These experiences also present opportunities for a student to engage in related writing, speaking, and listening activities.

Reading such materials as short stories or pleasurable books to children, furthers vocabulary development in basically the same way as when children read materials themselves. When a teacher reads to students, she also can emphasize key words to children. The meanings of these words may be discussed, as well as how the words are used to create a certain tone or atmosphere in the materials being read.

Word Analogies. Word-analogy activities can be used with individuals, small groups of students, or an entire class. An analogy focuses on how two or more objects relate or are similar to one another.

Although students are frequently tested on word relationships, they are rarely given an opportunity to develop their ability in this area. Also, contrary to the viewpoint of some, when analogies are suited to the abilities of children, they can be a source of fun for students.

Two forms of analogies are customarily used. In the first kind (for example, "A fish is to _____ as a bird is to air") no answers are provided. Children must supply what they believe to be an appropriate answer for the blank. In the second type of analogy, two or more possible answers are provided, and the child must select the best of these choices. An example of this would be "Feet are to humans as _____ are to car," with the possible answers (A) roofs, (B) horns, (C) tires, and (D) windshields.

The Teacher's Cat. "The Teacher's Cat" is another enjoyable activity. In this vocabulary activity, primarily adjectives are used. The Teacher's Cat may be used with an individual child, a small group of children, or an entire class. The teacher supplies the participants with the sentence "The teacher has a(n) ——— cat." The first letter of the word to be put in the blank is determined by the teacher. For example, if the teacher says *b*, the children are to supply such words as *brown*, *big*, and *beautiful*.

After each round among the participants, a different letter is given to the children by the teacher. When a child gives a correct response, the child is awarded a point. The individual or team with the most points wins the game.

Scrambles. In "Scrambles," the letters of a word are mixed up, and children are asked to identify the scrambled word. The teacher supplies the students with scrambled words as *ifx*, *eutr*, *uby*, *lewl*, and *ocem*. These represent the words, *fix*, *true*, *buy*, *well*, and *come*, respectively. Both the level of difficulty of the words and their number vary in accordance with the maturity of the children.

Word Speed. "Word Speed" is another activity designed to allow children to have fun while using language. The teacher places the students into groups of two. In each group, one child says as many words as he or she can in a minute. The other student listens to the first child and counts how many words were said. The two then change roles. One minute per role is the maximum time recommended for elementary students. For remedial children or very young pupils, less time is suggested. The teacher times the activity. The teacher may wish to discuss with the children how they decided upon the words they said. Did categories (that is, states, colors, things in the classroom, or other classifications) serve as the stimulus for the words said, or were the words randomly chosen? Some of the words said by the children may also be placed into the class word bank.

Three and Two. "Three and Two" is a comparison and contrast activity. Students are given a list of five words. Three of them belong in one group, and two belong in another group. The children are asked to decide which words go in which group. Two such lists are shown below.

A	B
blue	over
car	under
brown	run
green	walk
bus	in

In list A, *blue*, *brown*, and *green* are the group of three; *car* and *bus* are the other group. In list B, *over*, *under*, and *in* are one group; *run* and *walk* are the other.

After the children give their answers, the teacher attempts to determine why they selected certain words as belonging to a particular group. This will reveal not only whether or not the children performed the exercise correctly but also the degree of understanding the pupils have of specific words. It is recommended that words of significance in reading, such as some of the Dolch basic sight words, be used in this exercise. The differences between the two groups of words may be either very minimal or great depending upon the teacher's intent and the students' ability.

Word Builders. In "Word Builders," the teacher gives the children a sentence with a portion of it missing. It is the responsibility of the students to supply one or more words appropriate for completing the missing section of the sentence. Word Builders can be employed to develop students' proficiency with all kinds of words and phrases—adjectives, verbs, adverbs, prepositional phrases, and so on. Here is an example of a Word Builders activity.

A.   The wind _____ .
     (Children may supply such words as *howled*, *whistled*, *screamed*, or *blew*)

B.   The _____ wind blew.
     (The teacher would ask children for words which describe what kind of wind it was—*horrible*, *killer*, *fierce*, and so on.)

C.   The wind blew _____ .
     (Students would give words which describe where the wind blew—*in our yard*, *into my bones*, *down the chimney*, *through the school*, and so on.)

D.   The wind blew _____ .
     (The teacher would ask children for words which tell when the wind blew—*after I went to sleep*, *today*, *on Tuesday*, *in the blackness of night*, and so on.)

In "Word Builder's" the students offer many words in response to each exercise. This gives them a chance to use language. The teacher may wish to write down some of these words or phrases and to call particular attention to them, especially to those words which are essential to children's reading. The sentences used in the preceding example are illustrative of the types which can be used in Word Builders. For motivational purposes, of course, the sentences should be varied. Care should be taken that a sentence's difficulty does not appreciably exceed the ability level of the students.

Pictures. Students are shown a photo or a picture from a magazine or some other comparable source. The children are then asked to write all of the words which describe or explain the picture to someone.

The teacher may wish to compare the responses of the various children in a group or in the classroom. Words of special significance can be noted and used for subsequent vocabulary development.

Crossword Puzzles. Crossword puzzles can serve to develop a child's reading vocabulary, provided that the puzzles are of a level of difficulty congruent with the student's achievement level. Care should also be taken to insure that the content of the puzzles is varied. If the puzzles are too similar, the children may become bored with them. After the pupils have completed a puzzle, the teacher may wish to discuss the correct answers with the students. The teacher may also wish to have the pupils define the answer words and, jointly with the children, may suggest other words which could have been employed in the crossword puzzle.

Rewriting Sentences. The teacher supplies a group or the entire class with a list of sentences. These sentences should be well written and should describe people, places, and things. The students rewrite each sentence in one or more ways. The sentences written by the students should be compared, and the meaning of significant words contained in them should be emphasized by the teacher.

How Many? "How Many?" is an excellent activity for reinforcing words previously learned by children. It can also serve as a device by which other members of the group or class learn new words.

The children are asked "How many _____ can you name?" The categories to which the missing portion of the sentence might belong include states, colors, foods, vehicles, games, musical instruments, and kinds of tools.

As we stated at the beginning of this section, many activities in addition to the fifteen just described could be discussed. We have attempted to present activities which demonstrate the types of classroom instruction capable of supplementing vocabulary growth in children. The descriptions of these activities need not be rigidly followed; rather, teachers should feel free to modify these activities or to use comparable ones so that the activities best serve the students in their classrooms.

SUMMARY

In this chapter, we sought to answer three basic questions: What is vocabulary? What is known about a child's acquisition and retention of a reading vocabulary? What activities are conducive to the development of a child's vocabulary?

We hope that having read the preceding pages you are now aware of our views on these questions and that you now have a conceptual framework within which to think about them.

Vocabulary is the keystone of a child's reading. A child who can read and understand many words is a child who is successful in reading. Students with a deficient vocabulary are generally poor readers.

We have emphasized that children do not necessarily become adept with words on their own. Good teachers can make this happen by remembering that vocabulary development entails not only the acquisition of words but also their retention. Retention occurs when children are given many diverse opportunities to use words in reading, writing, speaking, and listening.

The teacher must recognize that effective teaching of vocabulary is a blend of direct instruction and incidental methods. Kennedy contends: "Direct instruction makes it possible for pupils to utilize to the greatest advantage the experiences they have" (13). Through direct instruction, a teacher presents new words to children, reinforces previously acquired vocabulary, and develops children's proficiency in the use of techniques for determining a word's meaning on a delayed recall basis. Of incidental learning with regard to vocabulary development, Kennedy says: "The vast majority of new words and meanings is learned incidentally or indirectly by students through personal experiences, listening to others talk, and reading independently."

Developing a child's reading vocabulary is difficult and time-consuming. Effective teachers of reading recognize that it is a crucial part of their job. As a result, they devote the time and effort necessary to help *each* child develop optimally in this area.

ACTIVITIES RELATED TO THE CHAPTER

1. Examine the word lists compiled by Dolch, Hillerich, Rinsland, Moe, Otto and Chester, and Kucera and Francis. Which of these lists do you like best? Why?
2. Prepare a test to determine how well children are able to use a dictionary. Administer the test to several students or to an entire class. Analyze the results. What do they tell you about the students?
3. Visit an elementary school. Have personnel at the school describe how vocabulary growth is promoted in ways other than through the basic reading program. How does the school's approach compare with the approach presented in this chapter?
4. Analyze the vocabulary subsections of three standardized reading tests. What type of competence relative to vocabulary—comprehension, word recognition, synonym usage, and so on—do they use? Which subtests do you like best and least? Why?
5. In this chapter, we· have presented fifteen vocabulary activities. Now design three original activities. For each, describe not only the procedures involved, but also the objective(s).

BIBLIOGRAPHY AND REFERENCES

1. Burmeister, Lou E.: *Words—from Print to Meaning*, Addison-Wesley, Reading, MA, 1975.

2. Dale, Edgar: "The Development of Vocabulary," paper presented at the Reading Conference at the University of Pittsburgh, Pittsburgh, PA, 1962.
3. Deighton, Lee C.: *Vocabulary Development in the Classroom*, Columbia University Press, New York, 1959.
4. "Dolch Basic Sight Vocabulary" by E. W. Dolch. Available in card form from Garrard Publishing Co., Champaign, Illinois 61820.
5. Durkin, Dolores: *Teaching Them to Read*, 2nd ed., Allyn and Bacon, Boston: 1974, p. 328.
6. Guszak, Frank J.: *Diagnostic Reading Instruction in the Elementary School*, Harper & Row, New York, 1972, p. 45.
7. Harris, Albert J., and Edward R. Sipay: *How to Increase Reading Ability*, 6th ed., McKay, New York, 1975, p. 441.
8. Harris, Larry A., and Carl B. Smith: *Reading Instruction through Diagnostic Teaching*, Holt, New York, 1972, p. 212.
9. Hill, Walter R.: *Secondary School Reading: Process, Program, Procedure*, Allyn and Bacon, Boston, 1979, p. 247.
10. Hillerich, Robert L.: "The 190 Starred Starter Words," in *Analysis of Words Used in Creative Writing, Grades 1-6*, unpublished study, Glenview, IL, 1966.
11. Johnson, Dale D., and P. David Pearson: *Teaching Reading Vocabulary*, Holt, New York, 1978, pp. 4-7.
12. Karlin, Robert: *Teaching Reading in High School*, Bobbs-Merrill, Indianapolis, 1972, p. 119.
13. Kennedy, Eddie C.: *Methods in Teaching Developmental Reading*, F. E. Peacock, Itasca, IL, 1974, p. 224.
14. Kucera, Henry, and W. Nelson Francis: *Computational Analysis of Present-Day American English*, Brown University Press, Providence, RI, 1967.
15. Lapp, Diane, and James Flood: *Teaching Reading to Every Child*, Macmillan, New York, 1978, p. 761.
16. Lewis, Norman: *Word Power Made Easy*, Pocket Books, New York, 1976.
17. Mangieri, John N.: "Dolch List Revisited," *Reading World*, 18(1):91-95 (1978).
18. McCullough, Constance M.: "Context Aids in Reading," *The Reading Teacher*, 11:225-229 (1958).
19. Moe, Alden J.: "Word Lists for Beginning Reading," *Reading Improvement*, 10(2):11-15 (1973).
20. Otto, Wayne, and Robert Chester: "Sight Words for Beginning Readers," *The Journal of Educational Research*, 65:435-443 (1972).
21. Petty, Walter T., and Julie M. Jensen: *Developing Children's Language*, Allyn and Bacon, Boston, 1980, p. 66.
22. Rinsland, Henry: *A Basic Vocabulary of Elementary School Children*, Macmillan, New York, 1945.
23. Robinson, H. Alan: *Teaching Reading and Study Strategies*, Allyn and Bacon, Boston, 1975, p. 59.
24. Taba, Hilda: *Teacher's Handbook for Elementary Social Studies*, Addison-Wesley, Reading, MA, 1967.
25. Tinker, Miles A., and Constance M. McCullough: *Teaching Elementary Reading*, Appleton-Century-Crofts, New York, 1962, p. 145.

Compre-hension: The Core of Reading

4

Overview

There have been many attempts to clarify what reading is and as many attempts to suggest what comprehension is. This chapter focuses on the efforts made to analyze and explain what comprehension is and what classroom teachers can do to develop the understanding of their readers. Since reading is intended to be an active process, the part which critical reading in particular should have in a reading program is also discussed in detail. Many instructional suggestions are offered throughout the chapter.

Definition of Terms

1. *Creative comprehension*—comprehension based on prior literal, interpretive, and critical comprehension; it involves asking how a reader can apply information. New situations are considered apart from the reader's own experience in an attempt to solve problems and to appreciate the reading more fully.
2. *Critical comprehension*—comprehension based on an evaluation of the language and the overall effect of the material. The reader makes judgments by looking at the materials in the light of suitable criteria.
3. *Interpretive comprehension*—comprehension based on reader's summarizing, inferring, drawing generalizations and reaching conclusions, and predicting outcomes. The reader also judges what prompted the writing of the selection.
4. *Literal comprehension*—comprehension based on an understanding of the author's words and ideas; it deals with the fairly simple thought processes of the author.

here is a true story of a teacher who proudly said that he had developed many questions to ask about the novel *Lord of the Flies*. In fact, for the twelve chapters of the book there were no less than 528 questions. That is an average of forty-four questions per chapter. The reason for mentioning this is to point out that there are many different ways to look at the topic of comprehension. It was at one time quite fashionable in educational circles to pay attention to teachers' questioning strategies. The idea was that the more questions you had and the better they were, the better your students would comprehend what they read. Therefore, it was considered appropriate to drill teachers in the art of questioning.

Another approach to the topic of comprehension involved the development of lengthy lists and taxonomies. It was fashionable for educators to be very well versed in Bloom's taxonomy (2). In time, however, it came to be felt that even a thorough knowledge of this schema did not translate easily into classroom teaching practices. There was, then, another significant effort to simplify matters by using a text such as *Classroom Questions: What Kinds?* (13). It was hoped that with this handy manual, teachers and prospective teachers would write questions that would better direct their students' thinking to higher cognitive levels. In time, this hope too appeared futile.

Using the idea of a broad taxonomy, some educators then began to consider comprehension in relation to lengthy lists of necessary reading skills. One such list contained 95 skills under the category of comprehension. This was yet another point of view as to what comprehension was all about (9).

In a very well known study (3), Davis tried to isolate those factors which should be thought of as relating to comprehension. He concluded that there were nine such factors.

1. Knowledge of word meanings.
2. Ability to select the appropriate meaning for a word or phrase according to its context.
3. Ability to follow the organization of a passage and to identify antecedents and references in it.
4. Ability to select the main thought of a passage.
5. Ability to answer questions that are directly answered in a passage.
6. Ability to answer questions that are answered in a passage, but not in the words in which the questions are asked.
7. Ability to draw inferences from a passage about its content.
8. Ability to recognize literary devices used in a passage and to get its tone and mood.
9. Ability to determine a writer's purpose, intent, and point of view—that is, to draw inferences about a writer.

One thing that can be said in favor of Davis's explanation of what goes into comprehension is that such a list allows teachers to deal with a manageable number of skill areas in looking at what they are currently doing. This is certainly preferable to having to use a list of 95 items.

Do not read too much into our comments on lists and taxonomies. In fact, researchers who have compiled such lists have helped us immensely in trying to understand the complex nature of comprehension. Program developers and writers of materials would do well to become familiar with this research in an attempt to insure that learners have opportunities to practice all kinds of needed skills—whether comprehension, vocabulary, or study skills—at all grade levels.

In Chapter 1 we indicated the overall conclusion of the First Grade Studies: it is the teacher who makes the difference in determining whether children become effective readers or not. Therefore, we turn now to a consideration of other efforts which have been made to untangle the comprehension web so that in an everyday and eminently practical way teachers may develop the comprehension abilities of their pupils.

In the last decade, Herber in particular has spent a great deal of time working with teachers in developing comprehension abilities on three levels (7). His efforts have made the idea of looking at comprehension on three levels quite popular. His ideas along these lines are well explicated in his revised text (8). Others have spoken in the same general manner of dealing with levels of comprehension. We prefer this approach in dealing further in this chapter with comprehension. Perhaps a way to view levels of comprehension is through a table such as the following:

AUTHOR	LEVEL I	LEVEL II	LEVEL III	LEVEL IV
Barrett	Literal	Inferential	Evaluation	Appreciation
Durkin	Literal	Interpretive	Critical	
Herber	Literal	Interpretive	Applied	
Taba	Concepts	Interpretation	Application	

Over twenty years ago, Russell offered another variation of levels when he suggested there are four overlapping comprehension levels (12): (1) Word identification; (2) Casual skimming; (3) Reading for exact, literal meanings; and (4) Creative reading for (a) implied and inferred meanings, (b) appreciative reactions, and (c) critical evaluations. The first three are usually considered to be under the category *literal*. The fourth includes levels II and III of the four authors listed in the table. We prefer to consider comprehension, as did Smith (14), under the labels of *literal*, *interpretive*, *critical*, and *creative*. In a democracy such as ours, it is especially crucial to train children to go beyond the superficial level of simple fact. The manifold claims made by corporations and politicians make it necessary that all readers be able to weigh evidence carefully. There have been sad times in our country when the public has been lied to and abused by people in power. To protect our freedoms and privileges, we need to be informed intelligently. For this reason, we proceed now to consider in turn each of the levels of comprehension. The components of and activities suited to each level will be discussed as appropriate.

LITERAL COMPREHENSION

The literal level of comprehension is that level in relation to which many teacher-initiated questions are asked to which children respond; the result is little more than a facts-oriented reading class. Guszak's famous study of the questions asked by elementary teachers presents an interesting picture of this phenomenon (6). His conclusions verify that what you ask for is what you get. Children fed a steady diet of factual questions learn quickly to expect such questions from the teacher. We have all heard of the classroom variable called *teacher expectation*, but there is also the variable *child expectation*. The children anticipate that their teacher will ask certain types of questions repeatedly.

We are not suggesting that the literal level be ignored. It is the logical point of departure for the far more intriguing higher levels of comprehension for learners of all abilities, not only for the more intelligent children. There are a number of components of literal comprehension. What follows is by no means an exhaustive discussion. However, it should guide a teacher of reading toward an understanding of which abilities are significant and should be developed in this first level of comprehension.

Literal Reading Skills

Some of the more obvious skills to be developed under this category can be thought of in the following ways:

1. You will recall from the previous chapter some of the major techniques teachers can use to help children enlarge their vocabularies. Learning the meanings of words is a process which never ends; it continues throughout the school years. A reader who has enough words to be able to read must also be able to get the important details in what is being read. Some details are interesting in themselves but not highly significant, and children need to see the difference.
2. When children have some details with which to work, they can be taught to state the main idea of a selection in a sentence that summarizes the meaning of the selection. Keep in mind that at times, depending on the difficulty of the passage and other factors, stating the main idea may require thinking at the next level, that of interpretation. It is difficult to understand why high school students still work at the literal level in workbooks, trying to determine the main idea in ten

one-paragraph exercises. The suggestions at the end of this section may help to alert teachers to some ways in which this skill can be developed in the elementary grades.

3.   We would like to point out that often children seem not to understand the function of *signal words*, terms which provide clues as to how an author has organized the writing in a selection. The following lists give signal words under their related patterns of organization:

Simple Listing	Sequence
the following	first
in addition	second
another	third
likewise	subsequently
as well as	next
several	afterward

Cause and Effect	Comparison and Contrast
since	even though
therefore	otherwise
because	on the other hand
consequently	similarly
accordingly	in spite of
it follows that	conversely

We too often assume that everyone understands the meanings and functions of such words and phrases, but this is simply not so. Key transitions in paragraphs and stories hinge on the use of such expressions, and children often miss the transition because they were never taught the expressions. Signal words can help children recall important details in their reading, particularly with regard to the sequence of ideas. This recall obviously reflects a more advanced skill than does a simple recitation of details. It is a slightly more complex task to recall a related sequence of details.

4.   In addition to being able to recall details in their proper sequence, readers need to be able to see relationships among ideas. For example, consider the sentence *Since it was raining so hard, my hair got wet*. This obviously expresses a cause-and-effect relationship, and children need to be able to identify such relationships, especially in reading for content. Cause-and-effect relationships can also be found at the more complex level of interpretation, but it should be pointed out that basic action-and-reaction situations can be understood by children early on. Making simple topical lists of information is a suitable activity for developing literal comprehension. Lists of animals, people, towns, fruits, books, or teams can help children to categorize concepts.

5. The ability to follow directions is necessary if children are to progress properly not only in reading instruction, but also in language arts in general. For this reason, it is urged that careful attention be paid to instruction in several of the language arts so that children learn to see how these interrelate in the everyday world.

Activities for Literal Reading

Here are a few suggestions on how to start some significant activities in the elementary reading class in order to develop children's abilities on the literal level of comprehension.

1. When children stop in their reading and seem to want the teacher to assist them, gently prompt them to read to the end of the sentence. Often, they will be able to overcome obstacles by using the contextual assistance they receive from completing the sentence.
2. Give children a fairly long list of similar words, such as the names of animals or foods, and have them classify the words. One word in the list should name the category to which the rest belong. This one word is the main idea. This activity should later be extended to the details in stories by listing the details on cards for children to classify.
3. Read aloud some short paragraphs with one wrong word which is intended to destroy comprehension. Children have to listen carefully, pick out the wrong word, and correct it.
4. Describe a room in a public building. Children have to pay careful attention to details and see which ones are significant before they can state the main idea.
5. Provide the class with a list of many details, and have them decide which ones were included in a story they read recently.
6. Pair paragraphs and, later, stories with suitable titles by having these items prepared and kept in envelopes for quick distribution and collection. This is a good activity to help children review favorite stories.
7. After a reasonable period of time has elapsed, ask children to list the characters of stories they have read. The ability to recall this kind of information must be fostered from the very beginning of school life.
8. From time to time, have children close their eyes as you read part of a story. Have them tell what they see in their minds. Closing their eyes helps them avoid distractions and focus their lively imaginations on what they are hearing.
9. Older students often are led to believe that the first sentence of a selection always contains the main idea. This is an erroneous notion stemming from poor instruction. Show children paragraphs where the main idea is in the first sentence, the last sentence, in the middle of the passage, at the beginning and again at the end, and interspersed throughout in a general way. Helping children to see

clearly that the first sentence does not always contain the main idea can be important to their understanding when they read and write.

10. Give directions one step at a time, before proceeding to two-step directions. Use one- and two-step directions repeatedly before moving to three-step directions. Continue in this manner, trying to find familiar materials with which to begin these activities but gradually introducing unfamiliar materials to make sure that the children can understand the several steps required of them. Real-life situations frequently call for understanding directions of this complexity.

11. Read riddles to the class. Riddles require careful listening by children, and they are quite entertaining.

12. Have children circle the transition and signal words and phrases in a paragraph or story. Analyze the functions of these words and phrases.

13. Make two contrasting columns of traits for two characters in stories the children have already read. This helps students to recall and to think about relationships of comparison and contrast in literature.

14. Read a recipe for a type of food children like, and have them write down the ingredients from memory. At a higher level, have the students verbalize the procedures required by the recipe.

15. Show the children a series of pictures or cartoons in scrambled order. Have the children arrange them in proper sequence and give a title to the sequence.

INTERPRETIVE COMPREHENSION

The accumulation of certain basic information from a selection or story does not always give a reader the essence of the author's ideas. Something has to be done mentally with the literal information to come to a fuller understanding of the author's message. This requires what is termed *interpretation*. Teachers and students know how comfortably they can all survive in a classroom if the teacher is dealing only with "safe" information. It is a lot easier to stay at the literal level of understanding. At this level not too much thinking is occurring which has any degree of significance. Exciting discussion and greater understanding of a passage happen when we focus on the interpretive level.

Ask some children to tell you a story that they have seen on television. You will find that certain children seem never to miss a detail. Ask them to interpret this information, however, and they are frequently stymied. They simply are at a loss to do anything with what they see or read except to repeat the factual details.

Some class discussions would be more lively if this didn't often mean noise. In so many schools noise is to be avoided, and so, too, is thinking. It seems at times that noisy discussion is bothersome to the teacher, the authority figure in the classroom. Original forms of thinking are not encouraged, so the class is back to the literal level. We think of this as the safe level.

Ask ten factual questions, and pupils will get the majority of them correct. This allows teachers to consider themselves good. It is all too painful to see such happenings in classrooms.

We now consider some of the skills related to helping children become proficient in interpreting what they read.

Interpretive Reading Skills

Once readers have determined the facts in a passage or story, they can, with instruction, develop the more elevated skills discussed in the following paragraphs:

1. Determining some of the characteristics of the writer of a story can sometimes be routine, but at other times many different views may be presented. All learners can profit from hearing the opinions of others and then judging the merits of the various positions.
2. There is no question that one of the most troublesome aspects of reading is understanding figures of speech. Comparisons, exaggerations, sarcastic statements, and personifications need to be interpreted. We cannot let young readers believe that all such statements are to be taken literally. These figures of speech demand explanation and clarification.
3. Reading for facts is often quite boring. Reading for the interpretation of facts is a lot more interesting. In order to understand what the author had in mind, we make inferences from what was suggested or hinted at. Inferences can be made from simple pictures, brief character sketches, and descriptions of places. Readers can also infer things from conversations between characters and about characters. Combining inferences with what is already known from the literal level makes for exciting reading. Reaching this level, however, is not always easy for teachers or children, because this is the level of uncertainty. Here is where different judgments can be made, and therein lies the interest. Learners invest something of themselves in an interpretation when they commit themselves in some way in a discussion. For example, if we hear of an animal wandering through a field without any other animals in sight, we might make some inferences. Perhaps we shall never know for sure if a particular inference is totally "correct." However, this should not dissuade us from making inferences, especially when reading. Not everything we experience is in blueprint form; we have to put information and hints together and infer what they all mean.
4. After a reader has made some tentative interpretations, the next step is to make a generalization. This is more than simply stating a main idea, about which we have previously spoken. The difference between the two is that the generalization gives greater clarification and understanding because of the inferences previously made.

5. Readers who have arrived at a greater understanding than can be gotten from the literal level and who have attempted some generalizations are ready for exercising one of the most rewarding of the interpretive skills. We refer to predicting outcomes. Bringing readers along in a story to a point where they have a certain amount of information allows them to suggest what will happen next in the story. Readers do not always agree. Again, this is a point where reading becomes interesting. It becomes a healthy challenge to suggest an outcome, support the suggestion, and then forge ahead to see what really happens.

6. Akin to predicting outcomes is reaching conclusions. Both skills require a lot more than facts. There is greater involvement on the reader's part than in merely repeating the story. Reaching conclusions entails working with all the inferences, the generalizations, and the predicted outcomes.

Activities for Interpretive Reading

Interpretive reading, which is far more interesting than literal reading, requires careful and consistent attention. We feel that time spent on activities designed to stimulate the development of interpretive skills is more than justified by the responses of pupils. The following paragraphs discuss some of these activities:

1. To help children learn to summarize quickly, so that they can move to the interpretive level, ask the questions Who? Where? What? When? Why? and How? This activity might also help pupils to see the difference between the important and the insignificant details in a reading selection.

2. Read a story from *Aesop's Fables* to younger children. Have them select from a list the moral of the story.

3. Paraphrasing is not the easiest skill to deal with, and for this reason many teachers avoid teaching it. Paraphrasing can be a true test of a reader's comprehension. Looking at some good paraphrases of stories the teacher has used before will enable children to see what a paraphrase is and how one generally is written.

4. When teaching the earlier grades, list several reasons why an author may have written a story. This serves as a way to initiate a discussion about the author's purpose. In the upper grades, this technique either is not used at all or is used for a shorter time than with younger readers.

5. Develop a list of incomplete sentences and have children complete them. Do the same with short paragraphs and then with brief stories.

6. Show the children a series of cartoon frames in proper sequence, and ask the class to predict the content of the final frame.

7. Have the children apply their skills in other areas. Bring in maps and graphs suited to their level, and ask them to interpret the information provided. Write down this information in a form that allows the class to refer to it.
8. Schedule several "Let's Pretend" activities. Have cards ready on which children can read a description of some action or character. One child then pantomimes what a card says, and the rest of the class or a small group guesses what is taking place.

CRITICAL READING

We have seen that the interpretive level concerns mainly figuring out the author's meaning. Interpretation often requires making accurate inferences from statements which suggest ideas indirectly. We now consider another level, that of critical reading. At this level, a reader typically uses some criteria or standards for making judgments about what the author has said. This requires more analysis and evaluation, as we shall see.

Critical reading almost seems to be regarded as an instructional luxury. We get the impression that students and teachers are so intent on getting and interpreting the facts that they have little time for anything else. Perhaps the rigidity of class schedules seldom allows us to spend any appreciable time analyzing what we read.

Another explanation for the lack of attention to this level of reading is the idea that critical reading is reserved for the more sophisticated readers. We do not subscribe to this position. Instead, we endorse the notion expressed by the title of the publication *Critical Reading Develops Early* (11). Not only should critical reading find its rightful place in the very early grades, but it also deserves attention with all types of learners. We know that children are too often disillusioned with their schooling. The popularity of Encyclopedia Brown and other mystery solvers and the way children relate to these types of activities can certainly make us feel comfortable in saying that "turned off" learners are simply crying out for resourceful and energetic teachers. It is precisely at the level of critical reading that many stimulating activities for children can be introduced, as you will see later in this section.

How do we bring children to this level of reading? To begin, we will consider some of the major aspects of critical reading.

Critical Reading Skills

When readers have understood materials at the literal and interpretive levels of comprehension, they would do well to evaluate those same materials. They might consider the strengths of the author, such as the author's qualifications. Such considerations can often be informal means of working on research and study skills using important reference sources. The date of writing of many materials is quite significant because of the knowledge explosion taking place today. The ways in which children assess the validity of statements can often be related to their television viewing habits.

Materials must be evaluated for their validity; readers need to know when and what they can believe in print. There is no place in our democratic society for readers to argue that because they read something in a book it is true. There are too many stories reported in the media of cases where so-called facts are simply not credible. In the lower grades, there are many enjoyable activities that can be used to help children distinguish fact from fantasy. With older learners the emphasis shifts to fact versus opinion. The area of critical reading that consists of techniques for analyzing propaganda is a valuable study for those who are trying to learn how to earn a livelihood. What reader of this paragraph has not at some time believed an advertisement or somebody's glowing claims for a service, only to find out that something is lacking? We know much about the effects of opinion polls, particularly in elections. Often, the results of such a poll seem to depend on who commissioned the poll in the first place. People appreciate being taught how to analyze information intelligently, and this is where critical reading comes to the fore. The propaganda techniques most commonly discussed are

1. *Name Calling*—*Red*, *illiterates*, *wrong side of the tracks*, and *dunces* are examples of words and phrases which are used to conjure up in the reader's or listener's mind an impression which, typically, is a stereotype.
2. *Glad Names and Bad Names*—The general tone of printed materials is manifested in the language used to create impressions. Such language can consist of positive or negative terms.
3. *Testimonials*—Testimonials usually try to relate a notable person to an event, a product, or another person, as when Hollywood stars endorse political candidates. In some cases, commercial products are promoted by persons who never use the products.
4. *Plain Folks*—A writer or speaker can claim to be "plain folks" in order to appear to be on the same level as the average person, in the hope of being readily accepted.
5. *Bandwagon*—The bandwagon technique banks on causing a "snowball" effect so that many people will buy a product or support an issue or a candidate for public office. The technique is based on the idea that everybody likes to be on the winning side.
6. *Transfer*—The general idea of transfer is to suggest that a noted symbol, such as a flag or an anthem, applies to an unrelated situation. For example, "let's fly the flag so that we will be a united people dedicated to certain causes." The prestige of a religion might also be used for transfer.

7. *Card Stacking*—Card stacking involves using information and arguments which are heavily weighted in favor of, or against, an issue and ignoring contrary arguments.

The information gained and insights had by readers typically relate to judgments made on the basis of their own experiences. Just as the directed reading-thinking activity (see Chapter 6) relies so much on prior experiences, so, too, is making sound judgments related to readers' past experiences.

Readers who have examined and made judgments about what they have read, are frequently ready to begin criticism. This term needs to be clarified, for, unfortunately, many learners go through all their years of schooling with the erroneous idea that criticism means finding fault, either with people or, in this instance, with the materials they have read. Criticism, or making a critique, stresses both the good and the bad points in what is read. Criticism insists on stating the positive and the negative. Again, this is not a skill which is inherited or arrived at by intuition. It is taught. Becoming even a fair critic is a complex process that cannot be mastered in a few weeks. The skills involved in making a proper critique are developed over many years.

In most cases, critical reading involves working with a set of criteria for making judgments. Again, such criteria are not established in a single class period. Also, opportunities for using study and research skills arise when we are trying to teach children how to establish criteria for critical analysis.

Activities for Critical Reading

There are many invaluable ways to help younger readers grow in their critical evaluation skills.

1. Children need to distinguish between *objective* and *subjective*. Learners at the secondary level often do not know the difference when these terms are used in reference to types of examinations. Objective facts can be verified, and they do not change with the person stating them. Subjective opinions vary. Stressing the differences between fact and fantasy, between the real and unreal, helps children develop the ability to make these distinctions.
2. Have each reader select a book and then read the exact words with which each story begins. Make a compilation of these beginning expressions and discuss with the children what they expect will follow in the stories.
3. Especially in children's literature a teacher can find incidents which are suited to the question, "Could this have happened in real life?" Find such situations in books, and have children discuss their realism or lack of it.

4. Have children take a science book written in the early 1960s and another one written in the early 1980s. By comparing the tables of contents and the indexes, have children draw conclusions about developments in this subject in the past two decades. What does this suggest about outdated resource materials when doing research?

5. Collect some samples of writing in which you have circled the "glad" words and the "bad" words. Discuss how these words set the general tone of the materials. Allow children time to circle such words in other materials. Have them read these circled words aloud so they can sense the general mood which is created.

6. Read Lamkin (10), and discuss in your reading-education class the impact of the book *"Why Johnny Can't Read"* and the developments in the field recently. What implications do you draw about being an analytical reader?

CREATIVE READING

We have consciously separated the level of creative reading from the preceding three because it too often goes unrecognized, subsumed in some other category. Yet, when we consider the possibilities of creative reading, we are convinced that readers would enjoy instruction in this area if they saw beforehand the rewards to be gained.

Creative reading essentially refers to the use which readers make of what is learned from the first three levels. Having read, interpreted, and critiqued material, what remains? How can the learning that has taken place be used to enhance future learning? Good literature is meant to be appreciated. That it is difficult to define *appreciation*, and even harder to measure it, does not mean we are free to ignore it. Rather than tackle the academic questions dealing with this term, we prefer to talk about ways to develop readers' appreciation of what they read and to show them ways to put their learning and appreciation to use.

Creative Reading Skills

How many times have you heard the expression—in jest, one hopes—"I liked the story because it was interesting"? What does that statement tell you? As a teacher, what would you infer if a child said that after completing a storybook? It is at times painful for teachers to try to help pupils express what they really want to say about their reading. It is not something that comes easily to most students. Early has identified three stages in the development of appreciation (5).

1. *Unconscious enjoyment*—the reader knows what he likes but does not know why he enjoys his own or the teacher's reading of rhymes or of stories with plot and humor.

2. *Self-conscious appreciation*—the reader both enjoys the material and makes an effort to look at the logical development of character and to ask "Why?"
3. *Conscious delight*—the reader responds with pleasure, knows why he does, and relies on his own judgments about aesthetic qualities.

Appreciation does not come easily. Later, we will discuss some activities for developing this skill.

So many times teachers complain that children cannot think. This complaint is often a reflection not so much on the children as on the type of schooling they have had. We wrote earlier that the types of questions teachers ask will determine the types of thinking that will go on in their classes. This idea extends to the role which problem solving will have in a classroom. Children will never learn to solve problems if they are never given an opportunity to think. Not every day need provide a major problem-solving situation; such opportunities usually demand careful planning on the part of the teacher. Stimulating children to take their new learnings and apply them to problems about which they have previously thought little is in itself challenging and creative. Taking generalizations and conclusions and applying them to new settings is an important part of learning.

We like to incorporate formal and informal study skills development whenever possible. In teaching creative reading, there are natural places for raising questions which require further study after reading. Literature has great significance and many applications at this level. Pure enjoyment is a major reason for reading literature. In the process of enjoying good literature, however, we also find much deliberate and incidental learning taking place. These forms of learning are important purposes for reading.

Activities for Creative Reading

The following activities can help children appreciate what they have read and apply what they have learned in new settings:

1. Discuss with children the significance of a character in a story. What role did the character play? How might the character be changed? Would this hurt or help the story? What if this character were omitted entirely?
2. Ask how famous people who children have learned about would have acted in a present-day context. How would Columbus have acted had he been the first man on the moon? How would Martha Washington have acted if offered a consultant's position on the filming of her husband's life? Of her own life?
3. When children have finished reading a story, have them write a story which could have occurred before the one they have just finished.

4. Have children suggest a new ending to a story they have finished. If this is done individually, they could then compare endings to see which ones seem most reasonable.
5. Have children use characters from stories they have read or historical persons they have studied to make up conversations for skits to be performed at holiday times during the year.

One day while visiting a classroom, one of us asked a student teacher why the children were all doing a set of exercises in the workbook. The reply was that the exercises followed from a skill-development exercise related to a story just completed. It was asked whether all children were to do the entire page, and the answer was affirmative. We raise the point only to ask the question: Must all the children always do all the exercises? Allowing children to work individually encourages them to appreciate more what they read and to read more. The comprehension and creativity which can be fostered at this level will help teachers and children learn that reading can be its own reward.

LIMITATIONS TO COMPREHENSION

In this chapter, we have already referred to certain practices which do not develop comprehension sufficiently in children. We prefer not to dwell on negative elements, but feel obligated to mention some others which are regarded as deterrents to the understanding of printed materials.

Chapter 9, speaks about children's interests in reading. Obviously, if readers are not interested in the material, there will be a problem in how well they will comprehend. However, it is not solely a matter of children's reading only what they like. As one pupil said after completing the comprehension portion of a standardized reading test, "I did not like what I read."

Interests are to be taken into consideration, but a lack of purpose for reading can also typically hinder comprehension. At first, teachers can establish the purpose, but in time, children should be taught to decide on their own purposes. When learners are on their own, what do they do if they have come to depend on the teacher's setting the purpose?

Another factor which often hinders adequate comprehension is an overreliance on word-analysis skills. We are not opposed to word analysis; we are opposed to belaboring the point. Too much word-recognition drill can effectively destroy the interests children possess when they come to school.

Related to the problem of too much word analysis is that of too much oral reading. Oral reading needs to be used for its rightful purpose: at times to entertain, at times for diagnosis, at times to inform. However, this does not mean five days a week. Too much oral reading or too much word analysis produces children who are great word callers but who subsequently hate to read. If this is the outcome, then why stress these practices? What is needed, of course, is balance. We are not against phonics; we are not opposed to oral reading, either. We are opposed to abuse of these practices. So many new approaches to reading are being proposed by experts, but we wonder how these experts themselves learned to read. We are convinced that they learned in a balanced program which fostered comprehension, including appreciation and enjoyment. Also, four levels of comprehension are supported by the vocabulary skills discussed in Chapter 3.

SUMMARY

In this chapter, we have looked at various approaches to the topic of comprehension. These have included elaborate lists of skills and taxonomies developed through the years. What seems most needed, however, is a manageable schema of comprehension.

Use of the literal, interpretive, critical, and creative levels of comprehension appears to be highly practical, especially for busy teachers. Many of the skills suited to each level were discussed, and activities applicable to each level were described.

The discussion was concluded by citing a few of the more salient obstacles to developing adequate comprehension.

ACTIVITIES RELATED TO THE CHAPTER

1. In small groups, brainstorm topics and draw up multiple lists of related words for children to categorize. If possible, cut up the word groups and place them in individual envelopes for use with children who have problems seeing the relationships between main ideas and supporting details.
2. Analyze two or three stories in the manuals which accompany basal series or systems programs. Assign the categories *literal*, *interpretive*, *critical*, and *creative* to the various activities suggested. Report your findings in your reading course.
3. In an actual classroom, attend to the types and numbers of questions related to the four levels discussed in this chapter. What conclusions can you draw about the improvement of children's comprehension?
4. Using a few stories in a basal reader or children's literature book, circle or list the transition words. What conclusions can you draw about the need to teach the functions of these words?
5. For a grade level in which you are interested, browse through at least a dozen books and make a list of story beginnings, such as "Once upon a time" or "In the faraway land of Spain, there was a queen . . . ." These story starters can be used to help children make predictions.
6. With small groups of children, discuss the characteristics you would need in order to be a consultant on the filming of the life of, for example, a U.S. Olympic medalist, a Russian Olympic medalist, the originator of the Muppets television series, or the first woman American President. What levels of comprehension skills are required for this activity?

BIBLIOGRAPHY AND REFERENCES

1. Barrett, Thomas C.: *A Taxonomy of Reading Comprehension*, Ginn, Lexington, MA, 1972.

2. Bloom, Benjamin S. (ed.): *Taxonomy of Educational Objectives*, McKay, New York, 1956.

3. Davis, Frederick B.: "Two New Measures of Reading Ability," *The Journal of Educational Psychology*, 33:365–372 (1942).

4. Durkin, Dolores D.: *Teaching Them to Read*, 3rd ed., Allyn and Bacon, Boston, 1978.

5. Early, Margaret J.: "Stages of Growth in Literary Appreciation," *English Journal*, 49:161–167 (1960).

6. Guszak, Frank J.: "Questioning Strategies of Elementary Teachers in Relation to Comprehension," in Figurel, J. Allen (ed.), *Reading and Realism*, International Reading Association, 1969, Newark, DE, pp. 110–116.

7. Herber, Harold L.: *Teaching Reading in Content Areas*, Prentice-Hall, Englewood Cliffs, NJ, 1970.

8. —————— : *Teaching Reading in Content Areas*, (2nd edition). Prentice-Hall, Englewood Cliffs, NJ, 1978.

9. Johnson, Terry D.: "Must It Always Be *The Three Little Pigs*?" *The Reading Teacher*, 23:209–210 (1970).

10. Lamkin, F. Duane: "An Analysis of Propaganda Techniques Used in *Why Johnny Can't Read*," *The Reading Teacher*, 9:107–117(1955).

11. Lee, Dorris, Alma Bingham, and Sue Woelfel: *Critical Reading Develops Early*, International Reading Association, Newark, DE, 1968.

12. Russell, David H.: *Children Learn to Read*, 2nd ed., Ginn, Boston, 1961, pp. 455–458.

13. Sanders, Norris: *Classroom Questions: What Kinds?* Harper & Row, New York, 1966.

14. Smith, Nila Banton: *Reading Instruction for Today's Children*, 2nd ed., Prentice-Hall, Englewood Cliffs, NJ, 1980.

15. Taba, Hilda: "The Teaching of Thinking," *Elementary English*, 42:534–542 (1965).

Reading Approaches and Materials

5

Overview

The materials which a teacher has available in a classroom often influence the approach to reading used by that teacher. In other words, materials often become the plan or curriculum for reading. This should not be the case; materials should not dictate the philosophy for the teaching of reading in a school. Rather, a well-grounded philosophy of reading instruction should determine the choice of materials.

In this chapter, you will be introduced to the major approaches to reading instruction: the language-experience approach, basal reading programs, and individualized reading programs. We will also include a discussion on reading in the content areas.

Definition of Terms

1. *Basal reading program*—a systematic instructional plan for teaching basic reading skills using a series of readers.
2. *Basal readers*—a set of materials including readers, workbooks, filmstrips, manuals, and games for use in a developmental reading class.
3. *Developmental reading program*—an instructional plan designed for learners who are reading at a level commensurate with their overall capacity.
4. *Experience background*—the accumulated firsthand or vicarious experiences which a learner has had with objects, people, places, and ideas. These experiences help the child to form concepts which are the basis for new learning.
5. *Individualized reading program*—a method of teaching reading by using trade books. Seeking, self-selection of, and self-pacing with these materials are characteristics of this approach, as are teacher-student conferences on the materials read.

6. *Language-experience approach*—a method of teaching reading by using materials reflecting the experiences of the learner.
7. *Supplementary materials*—trade books, games, and storybooks that reinforce skills or provide enjoyment; filmstrips and recordings; and practice materials.

he major reading approaches today are language experience, basal reading, and individualized reading. Many of the materials used in the teaching of reading are created by children; others are elaborate, commercially developed programs. Teacher-made materials and readability factors are also considered in this chapter.

The first approach to reading that we discuss is one that stems from the children themselves.

THE LANGUAGE-EXPERIENCE APPROACH

Background

Methods of teaching reading seem to come to the fore and recede in cycles. This is probably a reflection of our unrest when we do not see immediate and dramatic results from our instructional practices. The clamor of the general public is another reason for constant change in education. Most teaching practices today are not new. Some are merely reinventions, while others—like the language-experience approach—are new versions of methods which have long shown their merits in our classrooms.

It is natural for human beings to want to express their thoughts by speaking in some form. In the history of the race, there came a time when individuals had the need to express thoughts to persons not immediately present. The need to tell our story has always been part of the human experience. The way in which this story is conveyed is through language. It takes much longer to master language in its written or printed forms than in speech. Nevertheless, using language to convey thoughts to others is natural to us. It is precisely because this is a natural process that the language-experience approach is a popular method for giving youngsters their initial reading experiences.

Rationale

There are certain principles which form the basis of the language-experience approach. A summary of the principles of Lee and Allen would include some key factors (4).

1. What children think about, they can talk about.
2. What they can talk about can be expressed in written or some other form.
3. Anything children write can be read.
4. Children can read what they write and what other people write.
5. Some words are used over and over in our language, while others are not used very often.
6. What children have to say and write is as important to them as what others have written for them to read.
7. Most of the words that children use are the same as the words used by other people who write for them to read.

Children know that there is something of themselves embodied in the stories they write. The stories, based upon children's actual experiences, are meaningful because they emanate from the learner's own background. Language-experience stories are, therefore, relevant to children. In contrast, in many stories in books which are supposed to help children learn to read, the interest factor, the personal involvement, simply is not there.

Characteristics

When children are trying to adjust to a school setting, one of the most important factors to consider is how to make the children *want* to be there. Learning situations planned to accomplish this goal will let the children know that the school atmosphere is designed for them. If the children's thinking is accepted, recorded, read back to them, and reread—if their words are saved for future use—the children will recognize the meaningfulness of this for them. Teachers often find this individualized approach a chore, but in the beginning of the adjustment period, the rewards far outweigh the trials involved in the effort.

In the language-experience approach, the youngsters commonly share experience. They have opportunities to discuss their common experience and clarify their thoughts on what happened. The teacher notes the common elements in the ways the children describe these experiences and writes up their ideas in the form of a story on the board. Follow-up activities can vary greatly. For example, the class as a whole might read a story once it has been recorded on the board. At times, the teacher might prefer the class to copy a story from the board so that each child will have a record of the story. This activity also reinforces handwriting skills for the children. In any case, the teacher keeps a copy of the story for later inclusion in a book for that particular class. The story itself becomes a treasury for future use in teaching important words which children must learn to recognize on sight. Practice with many experience stories is needed before a sufficient store of words will have been mastered by the children to allow them to read books on their own. One thing is certain when children enter school:

they are hungry for literature. We must provide a proper diet of adequate reading material, or we will lose them by the end of the school year.

Objectives

Teachers who use the language-experience approach usually have certain definite goals in mind. Showing children that there is a relationship between the written word and the spoken word is a very important goal. Ego-involvement helps make children feel comfortable enough to learn skills in a quiet, relaxed way. Also, helping children become able to share what they know with the teacher and with other children is a goal of this approach, as is teaching children to read from left to right. Teaching the concept of what a word is and the place which intonation and stress play in interpreting the printed word are additional objectives of the program.

Children who see their natural spoken language patterns in printed form where they can be read by others are thereby helped to feel better about themselves, their abilities, and their teacher. In a word, children feel better about being in school.

Advantages

The language-experience approach benefits children in a variety of ways.

1. Perhaps the greatest strength of this approach is that it is so personalized, which helps children's self-concept and holds their attention.
2. Children realize that the language arts are not four discrete school subjects to be mastered. They learn to use the natural flow of their own language to communicate with others.
3. The cost of materials is minimal. Later, trade books and supplementary materials are necessary, but most schools have such resources already available.
4. The real world of their preschool experiences can be readily used as a source of stories told individually. Common experiences of the whole class can be captured and preserved in stories dictated by the entire group.
5. The children work at levels commensurate with their abilities.
6. Under the gentle guidance of a teacher, children learn what the essential ingredients of a good written story are, and they proceed to follow these models when they themselves write stories.
7. The teacher is not burdened with highly structured lesson plans. The time for instruction is spent on individualizing the reading lessons for the many children who need such attention early in their school lives.

Disadvantages

The language-experience approach is not an educational panacea. Like other approaches to teaching reading, it has certain disadvantages.

1. It is impossible for the teacher to teach the many individual sight vocabularies in an entire class. The common-denominator approach is the usual alternative, except where teachers have the luxury of aides or volunteers available to assist with the many youngsters.
2. In any given class, the words used may often be those of the most vocal member of the class. It is necessary to control this situation so that not too many difficult words are introduced at one time.
3. The complaint most often heard has to do with the lack of a planned sequence of reading instruction. In this sense, the teacher finds it impossible to be aware of which individual skills each child has mastered.
4. Some teachers find it difficult to sustain interest in the children's stories because they are quite predictable. For example, in a particular community, there are just so many events that children talk about, and this can become a problem in sustaining students' interest for long periods of time.
5. Contrary to what some language-experience proponents would have us think, one of the difficulties with the approach is that teachers simply run out of material after a while and need to turn to a program such as a basal reading program. When we consider this endurance factor, it is apparent that the language-experience approach is not sufficient of itself.

BASAL READING PROGRAMS

In a recent issue of an educational journal, there appeared an advertisement for a set of the McGuffey readers. Now considered a collector's item, these books were the most popular set of beginning readers for children for many years in the mid-1800s. The basic format of reading series today has not substantially changed from that period. A reading book, a workbook, and a teacher's guide are still the core materials. Recent developments in such programs include the use of such supplementary materials as filmstrips, games, and dittoed exercises. It has been estimated that as many as 95 percent of our classrooms have such reading series in them (10), so it is proper that we now consider some important aspects of basal reading programs.

Rationale

Given the regularity with which basal reading programs are adopted and used in our elementary level classrooms, the justifications offered for their use are worth noting. The most common reason given is that children need structure. The basal reading program is highly structured. Major publishing companies commission authors whose expertise is well established in the field of reading. These individuals spend several years developing a single series. It is generally known that the production of a new series probably carries a price tag of over a million dollars. One of the reasons for this is the effort expended on putting together a structured and sequenced program so that all learners will be taught all the necessary skills in a logical progression from grade one through at least grade six or, possibly, grade eight. It is argued that the elaborate scope and sequence charts enable a teacher to know what children have been previously taught in a series, what they should be presently learning, and at what point of development they should be at the end of a school year. There is an effort to ensure that no skills will be overlooked or insufficiently learned. The entire basal reader program philosophy is based on the premise that sooner or later all learners can learn to read with this sort of detailed programming. The teacher's manual spells out in elaborate detail the myriad activities in which children should be engaged if they are to become proficient readers. Depending upon the specific series, activities designed to help the teacher evaluate a child's progress in reading may or may not be in evidence.

Characteristics

There are many features which differentiate the over twenty basal reading series now available. The origin of the words used in the stories is one such feature. One publisher may have materials based on a frequency listing of word occurrence. Such a listing often is itself taken from other basal series and readers commonly used in schools. Another publisher's books may emphasize words from recorded samples of children's natural language. Still another series might use words that reflect the author's preference. Such books are usually termed *linguistic*, and the words in the stories fit in definite word families—for instance, rhyming words such as "the fat cat sat on the hat." In any case, there is a rationale for the words used. Further, the rate at which words are introduced to children is controlled.

Once the question of word source is resolved, what remains for the authors of basal programs is to determine the format of the materials. For example, some series contain only reading books. Other series have workbooks for practicing and reinforcing skills. More elaborate programs contain recordings, filmstrips, games, and other supplementary materials. Teacher's manuals and tests are also commonplace in basal reading series.

Simply saying that a school has adopted a basal reading series does not sufficiently explain the nature of the reading program. It is important to know the overall emphasis of the particular program. For example, some programs concentrate greatly on phonics. Other series spend more attention on developing stories in tune with youngsters' interests. Some series might be known primarily for their linquistic emphasis. It is because of these differing emphases that skill sequences vary from series to series. Some programs spend a great deal of time on word recognition skills and vocabulary growth, while other reading books require that much time be spent on reading for meaning.

Publishers today have started to move away from assigning grade equivalents to their reading books and toward assigning levels. Typically there were books on the preprimer level, primer level, and each grade level through grade six or eight. Now it is not uncommon to see a series with fourteen to twenty levels. The basic content could be the same as in the older format, but the series is broken down into smaller units. One reason for this development is to ensure that youngsters have the greater satisfaction of completing more books in the course of learning to read through the elementary grades.

Recent Developments

Older teachers often stifle a laugh whenever reference is made to the basal reading programs by which they learned to read. The old Dick and Jane program served an important purpose in its day, but today fails to address the needs of our society. The Dick and Jane characters were white, middle-class people who lived in suburbia and, of course, had a dog. Jane never got her clothing dirty, and she was cast in the role of an onlooker whenever Dick was playing ball. Their mother's role was even more stereotyped. She was anchored to the house and regularly attended to chores in that one location and inquired as to the well-being of Spot, the family dog.

With the rising concern over social issues, there appeared a number of attempts to alter the content of these books. For example, instead of the character named Dick, there was the character Juan. The Jane substitute was allowed to run in a race. These efforts were feeble and did not satisfy the need for equality of representation of characters and locations in children's stories. Major overhauls and, in some instances, completely new series were the outcome. Today's materials reflect a greater sensitivity toward all classes of people in many different settings. In some states, a basal reading program will not be considered unless its content is free of sexist stereotypes and is multicultural in content.

Another change in the development of reading series has to do with author teams. Greater attention is paid to assembling experts in children's literature, linguistics, psycholinguistics, sociology, and related areas to work in the writing of basal programs. Many years ago, basal series were classified as phonics-oriented or linguistically programmed. Today, it would be more difficult to type some programs because they are so balanced by the input of the extensive author teams.

Objectives

A school's use of a basal reading program generally reflects confidence that all the necessary skills which children need for reading are logically and systematically taught by the particular series. At any point in any grade, it is possible to check what skills have been dealt with in a basal program. Ever since the public clamor resulting from Rudolph Flesch's *Why Johnny Can't Read*, school personnel have been conscious of the need to identify good reading programs. A basal program potentially allows this ready identification.

A few basal programs are known for their high literary quality in their efforts to develop in children an enjoyment of reading. A rather recent trend is to include reading materials with selections from different content areas so that students can have the opportunity to learn and practice reading skills in school subjects and not just in stories.

Advantages

The benefits that generally come from the use of a basal reading series are discussed in the following paragraphs:

1. There is a definite progression of skills development through the grades. This progression includes the most important vocabulary, comprehension, and study skills.
2. The materials in basal programs are usually attractively presented to capture children's interest.
3. Teacher's manuals are elaborately prepared and include many more ideas for teaching than could possibly be used by any one teacher. The manuals have extensive enhancement activities for children who need extra help or who need more challenging opportunities to exercise their skills.
4. Research has aided authors greatly in knowing what types of reading selections to incorporate in their programs. With the expansion of interest in children's literature and with more attention being paid to content-area reading, authors have a far greater range of choices of topics to include in their reading materials.

Disadvantages

Much can be said for reading series which can be used in virtually every school in the country. This does not, however, mean that there are not some drawbacks to basal programs.

1. The initiative of children is frequently stifled. Children are exposed to a preplanned sequence of skills and stories which are often not consistent with their own attitudes and abilities.

2. The controlled vocabulary may be quite different from the everyday speaking vocabulary which the children have mastered. This control limits children's ability to express themselves in a natural language pattern.

3. Reading is often seen as a separate subject along with spelling, handwriting, science, health, and so forth. Reading is presented in this manner as an isolated area of language arts rather than an integrated component.

4. The experiences in which children are to share vicariously are chosen by an author team, one hopes with the best interests of the child in mind. The selections do not necessarily provide for the varied interests of children across several years of their development.

Basal reading materials dominate most school programs. These materials have improved greatly over the past few years. How they are intended for instructional use is discussed in detail in Chapter 6.

INDIVIDUALIZED READING PROGRAMS

Background

One of the loftiest ideals espoused in educational circles is that of individualizing instruction for children. This ideal is commonly realized on a one-to-one basis in a reading clinic, but how well can individualization occur with an entire classroom of children? Is it possible to individualize with classes of twenty or thirty children? Veatch (13) and Jacobs (3) would certainly agree that this approach to reading is possible. In fact, they are undoubtedly two of the strongest proponents of individualized reading instruction.

The underlying idea of individualized reading seems to be that children seek the level of instruction they are ready for. In reading, children want to be taught when they feel the need for this type of communication. Once they are introduced to an individualized approach to reading, children will grow and learn reading skills while simultaneously enjoying materials of their own choosing, not those selected by the teacher.

Rationale

The reason for initiating an individualized approach lies in the belief that children will be far more interested in reading if they are allowed to select their own materials. Of course, a teacher still could exert a strong influence over the materials simply through the books and other printed matter made available for selection by the children. The amount of materials needed is great because there are as many different interests as there are children. It is the wise teacher who recognizes and tries to address the many interests of children. In all likelihood, that teacher will enhance the learning of those children. Instead of an imposed curriculum in reading, there are several tailored programs developing in a single classroom.

Philosophically, there is another major reason for considering this approach to reading. Children are the decision-makers. They are independent learners, and this is a lofty ideal in itself. Because of immaturity and other factors, perhaps some children will not be able to achieve this ideal, but at least the opportunity will have been provided by a conscientious teacher.

Characteristics

The individualized reading approach is characterized by three factors: seeking, self-selection, and self-pacing. Olson named these factors as essential to learning in children (6). Veatch is the reading authority most commonly acknowledged as applying these three factors to a reading program (13).

Children will seek out a teacher when they are ready to read. This suggests immediately that children in a first-grade classroom will start to learn to read at different points in the school year. When they have learned some essentials, they will be able to read materials which they choose themselves. The rate of teaching and learning will vary as the needs of the child dictate. It is very likely that a few children can be grouped for skills instruction to economize on time.

One of the major ingredients of an individualized reading program is the teacher-student conference. All children must participate in conferences regularly. It is a problem to arrange so many conferences, but without them the teacher cannot know how the children are doing. The children see the conference period as a time for sharing what they have read with the teacher. The teacher sees the conference period as a time for checking a student's skills and interests. In other words, this brief session is a time for diagnosis. Accordingly, using the individualized reading approach requires a great deal of background regarding the reading process and the skills needed to become a mature and proficient reader. It is not possible to teach thirty children to read individually under normal school circumstances. It is possible, however, to have that number of children reading on their own while the teacher is working with one child in a conference setting. At times, several children will be reading from their own books while the teacher is instructing a small group on a particular skill.

Objectives

Ultimately, the objectives of all reading approaches are the same, but one approach has emphases that other approaches do not have. More will be said later in this text on the role of children's literature in the reading program.

Obviously, the individualized approach is child-centered, and in a sense the structure of the program comes from within the child and not from a predetermined scope and sequence chart or a teacher's manual.

One of the main objectives in this approach is to expose children to many forms of good literature. More will be said later in this chapter and in Chapter 9 about children's literature in the reading program. Again, the choice of reading matter is made by the pupils. The number of books, magazines, pamphlets, newspaper articles, basal readers, and skill games which an individualized reading program requires is staggering. Some authorities suggest that there should be three times the number of books as there are children in a class. Others insist that as many as five hundred books are necessary in a fifth-or sixth-grade classroom.

The whole point of this kind of program is to make children independent readers and learners. This is a sensible philosophy, but the execution of an effective program is difficult because of the management skills necessary.

Advantages

There are a number of benefits that accrue from the use of the individualized reading approach.

1. The interests of children are emphasized. They read what they truly prefer to read.
2. Since the program is so personalized, there is an opportunity to focus attention on the individual child.
3. There is a greater likelihood that children will become more independent in their reading and learning.
4. Children are exposed to many different forms of printed materials. This variety is more consistent with what children have to read in their everyday world.

Disadvantages

A balanced judgment as to whether to use the individualized reading approach might be helped by considering some limitations.

1. The biggest problem with this program lies in the organization it requires and the time it takes. A new teacher would be advised not to initiate this type of program in the first year of teaching.
2. A vast knowledge about diagnosis, and skills development is necessary. The record keeping and the inclusion of reading-related independent activities also demand much time.

3. A regular flow of new materials places more demands on teachers to constantly become familiar with them.
4. An extensive background in children's books is also needed.

Motivational Activities

Aside from the experience necessary to initiate an individualized reading program, there is also a demand for a strong background in children's books. In addition, sustaining children's interest in books is of major importance. There are two activities which help teachers to build children's interest in new books: storytelling and sustained silent reading.

Storytelling

One of the saddest losses in most schools today is that of the artful storyteller. Storytelling used to be a very common way to teach and to entertain children. Unfortunately, in many schools, there is almost none of this old literary form in evidence. Today, the only locale where children can hear a practiced storyteller is the public library on Saturday mornings or in special summer programs. As a result, many children do not come into contact with excellent storytellers.

An obvious reason for the fading of this art is that teachers often do not know where to get the type of story suited for this activity. Two key resource items which contain excellent hints for storytelling are Ross (8) and Sawyer (9).

Some teachers feel that reading to children is neither educational nor important. This is an erroneous viewpoint, since encouraging children to read is of primary importance if we are ever to develop lifetime readers. At times, teachers feel inadequate for the task of reading to children. In these cases, other resources such as the following, are suggested (see Appendix H):

1. *Caedmon Records* has some invaluable selections on records and cassette tapes for all levels of learners. Usually the stories are rendered by professional actors and artists, and this provides a quality which any teacher might well share with children.
2. *Miller-Brody Productions* specializes in records and films of classics in children's literature. Many Newberry Award winners are included in this series.
3. Choral readings and group reading of plays are alternatives to reading aloud to children. *Plays for Reading*, published by Walker Educational Book Corporation, has thirteen titles in the series. The same publisher has series of American, African, Asian, Latin American, holiday, and mythology plays for classroom use.

The bumper sticker that says "Children Who Read Were Read To" is appropriate in the classroom and in the home.

Sustained Silent Reading

In order to provide scheduled time in class when all pupils are free to read what they choose, the teacher might initiate a sustained silent reading (SSR) program, described by Robert and Marlene McCracken (5). Sustained silent reading program develops the child's ability to "read silently and to sustain himself when reading silently for a relatively long period." There are six suggested rules to follow when initiating SSR.

1. Begin with the whole class.
2. Each child selects one book—no book changing is permitted.
3. Each child must read silently.
4. The teacher reads silently.
5. A timer is used so that students do not watch the clock.
6. There are absolutely no reports or records of any kind.

The teacher acts as a model in this program, and eventually the class and teacher should be reading for thirty minutes every day. Rules may be modified, though rules 2, 3, and 4 are generally followed exactly. Occasionally, an entire school participates in an SSR program. At a set time every day, everyone in the building reads, from principal to custodial staff. It is important that the school encourage pupils to read and provide time for them to do so. SSR is a good way of insuring that this time is made available.

CONTENT READING MATERIALS

There was a time when a subject such as biology was studied only in high schools. As with many other subjects, the inclusion of this discipline in the elementary-grades curriculum has focused attention on some problems specifically related to teaching reading as it applies to different subject areas. The first textbook for teachers with the words *content areas* in the title did not appear until 1970. The past decade has seen major developments in helping teachers at all levels of instruction to cope with problems originating with content-area reading materials.

The variations among classrooms require teachers to supplement the core reading program with many other materials. Some have been discussed earlier in this chapter. Others will be discussed later under the topic of "Supplementary Materials." There is a distinct problem in the typical class where there is a single book for each content subject. One is likely to find in a fifth-grade class a book for science, another for social sciences, perhaps one for health, and still another for mathematics. Since there is generally a dearth of other reading materials available to a teacher in this situation, there arises a situation where the emphasis becomes What can I do with *this* textbook? There are far fewer options for teachers in this case. Quite understandably then, the teacher is forced to focus on particular texts to determine ways to convey their content so that children can learn. It is the strategy which a teacher adopts and modifies that makes the difference in children's ability to read textbooks other than their reading books as such.

Readability Formulas

As children progress through the grades, the range of abilities in classrooms widens. For this reason, textbooks often do not fit individual students' instructional level. Two questions should be asked: Is the book suited to the child? Is the reading level of the textbook approximately that of the child? These questions are answered by applying a readability formula such as the one in Figure 5-1.

For primary-grade materials, the Spache readability formula is suggested (11). A popular device is the five-finger technique for assessing the difficulty of materials. Most measures of readability are designed to be applied by the teacher. Since the teacher is not always available to monitor students' recreational reading selections, it is helpful if the student can personally assess the difficulty level of the material. For years, teachers have directed intermediate-level children to use the five-finger method in order to avoid books that are too difficult.

The student is directed to read one page of a book, putting a finger up each time that he comes to a word which he does not recognize. If all five fingers go up before he finishes reading a page, the book is too difficult, and another book should be selected. For beginning readers, the same procedure may be followed; however, only two or three fingers per page would be sufficient to determine that a book is too difficult.

Another noncomputational procedure is the SEER technique, described in Appendix C.

Other commonly used formulas include

1. The Dale-Chall formula [Dale, E., & J. Chall, "A Formula for Predicting Readability," *Educational Research Bulletin*, 27:11–20 (1948)].
2. The Flesch reading ease formula (Flesch, R., *The Art of Readable Writing*, Harper & Row, New York, 1949, pp. 5–6, 43).
3. The Harris-Jacobson formulas (Harris, A. J., and E. Sipay, *How to Increase Reading Ability*, 6th ed., McKay, New York, 1975, pp. 658–665).
4. The Raygor reading formula (Raygor, A., *The Raygor Reading Estimator*, Twin Oaks, Rehoboth, MA, 1979).

FIGURE 5-1
Graph for Estimating Readability—Extended (Fry)*

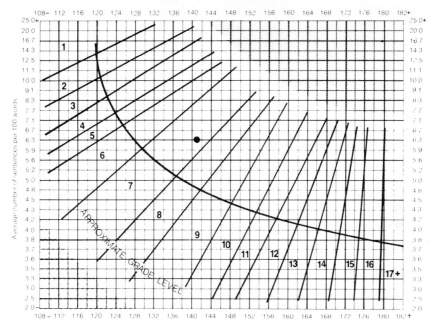

Average number of syllables per 100 words

Expanded Directions for Working Readability Graph

1. Randomly select three (3) sample passages and count out exactly 100 words each, beginning with the beginning of a sentence. Do count proper nouns, initializations, and numerals.
2. Count the number of sentences in the hundred words, estimating length of the fraction of the last sentence to the nearest one-tenth.
3. Count the total number of syllables in the 100-word passage. If you don't have a hand counter available, an easy way is to simply put a mark above every syllable over one in each word, then when you get to the end of the passage, count the number of marks and add 100. Small calculators can also be used as counters by pushing numeral 1, then push the + sign for each word or syllable when counting.
4. Enter graph with *average* sentence length and *average* number of syllables; plot dot where the two lines intersect. Area where dot is plotted will give you the approximate grade level.
5. If a great deal of variability is found in syllable count or sentence count, putting more samples into the average is desirable.
6. A word is defined as a group of symbols with a space on either side; thus, *Joe, IRA, 1945,* and & are each one word.
7. A syllable is defined as a phonetic syllable. Generally, there are as many syllables as vowel sounds. For example, *stopped* is one syllable and *wanted* is two syllables. When counting syllables for numerals and initializations, count one syllable for each symbol. For example, *1945* is four syllables, *IRA* is three syllables, and & is one syllable.

**Journal of Reading*, 21:249 (1977). Reprinted by permission.

5. The SMOG formula [McLaughlin, G. H., "SMOG Grading—A New Readability Formula," *Journal of Reading*, 12:639–646 (1969)].

Readability formulas should be perceived as aids in determining the difficulty of written works. The grade equivalents derived from their usage are approximations, not absolutes.

There are many times when a teacher might not know the reading ability of every child in the class. In such a case, the teacher should ask whether the children are suited to the book. To answer this question, another strategy, the cloze procedure, is used. The name is suggested by the psychological tendency to close (that is, focus attention) on something that is missing. The cloze procedure operates as follows:

1. Choose a passage from the textbook in question of approximately 275 words. This material should not be familiar to the students.
2. Type the passage on a ditto, leaving the entire first sentence of the passage intact and then deleting any one of the first five words in the second sentence and every fifth word thereafter until there is a total of fifty deletions. Use an underlined blank fifteen spaces long for each deletion. Type the last sentence intact.
3. Students may not refer to their textbooks while completing the exercise.
4. It might be wise, if students have never engaged in this activity previously, to show them some sample sentences the day before testing them with the cloze passage. Students should be told that the exercise is meant to measure the difficulty of the reading materials. You might illustrate the activity with such sentences as "The teams came out of the locker rooms and ran onto the ———— " or "The teacher took some ———— and started to write on the board."
5. Allow students an entire class period to finish the cloze passage.
6. When scoring, give two points for each word exactly supplied. Near-misses should not be counted as correct, because confusion can result from this practice.
7. Use the 40-60 rule for determining levels. For students below 40, the material spells trouble; it is at their frustration level. Students scoring between 40 and 60 should be able to function with this material; it is at their instructional level. The material is considered easy for students scoring beyond 60; it is at their independent level.

Some teachers feel that the time taken by children to complete the cloze procedure is too long. A recently developed similar procedure might be used, especially with younger children. This procedure is known as the maze technique (1). The difference between the cloze procedure and the maze technique is that the maze technique is a multiple-choice instrument. The following will serve to illustrate the maze technique:

This is the story of the first man to reach the North Pole.

Matt was the
$\begin{bmatrix} a. & \text{silly} \\ b. & \text{orphan} \\ c. & \text{certainly} \end{bmatrix}$
boy who ran away
$\begin{bmatrix} a. & \text{around} \\ b. & \text{fast} \\ c. & \text{to} \end{bmatrix}$
Washing-

ton, D.C. There he found
$\begin{bmatrix} a. & \text{work} \\ b. & \text{food} \\ c. & \text{young} \end{bmatrix}$
to earn some money.
$\begin{bmatrix} a. & \text{On} \\ b. & \text{Right} \\ c. & \text{At} \end{bmatrix}$

work he heard
$\begin{bmatrix} a. & \text{stories} \\ b. & \text{music} \\ c. & \text{funny} \end{bmatrix}$
that led him to
$\begin{bmatrix} a. & \text{want} \\ b. & \text{sour} \\ c. & \text{get} \end{bmatrix}$
to have some

real
$\begin{bmatrix} a. & \text{cross} \\ b. & \text{type} \\ c. & \text{adventure} \end{bmatrix}$
in the great wild
$\begin{bmatrix} a. & \text{lands} \\ b. & \text{rivers} \\ c. & \text{running} \end{bmatrix}$
north of

our country.
$\begin{bmatrix} a. & \text{The} \\ b. & \text{Soon} \\ c. & \text{A} \end{bmatrix}$
tales he heard as
$\begin{bmatrix} a. & \text{the} \\ b. & \text{a} \\ c. & \text{hand} \end{bmatrix}$
young man

he never
$\begin{bmatrix} a. & \text{told} \\ b. & \text{stomp} \\ c. & \text{forgot} \end{bmatrix}$

A passage of 100 to 120 words would be adequate. Approximately every fifth word should be presented as three alternatives. The rule to follow in selecting incorrect answers is to choose one word which is the same part of speech as the correct word and another which is another part of speech. For example, if the correct response is *airplane* (a noun), the two incorrect choices could be *man* (a noun) and *beautiful* (an adjective).

Scoring on the basis of the percentage of correct responses would then, in accordance with the table below, show whether a child read the selections at the independent, instructional, or frustration level.

SCORE ON GRADED MATERIALS	READING LEVEL	SCORE ON NONGRADED MATERIALS
85+	Independent	92+
60–70	Instructional	80–91
50 or less	Frustration	75 or less

Both the cloze procedure and the maze technique should be seen for what they are: methods for helping teachers to match students with textbooks. Neither device is perfect; both the cloze procedure and the maze technique must be interpreted with care by teachers.

Other Concerns

Other problems that arise in reading textbooks are discussed in the following paragraphs:

1.   What is the concept load of the book? At what rate are technical words (that is, words pertaining to the subject) introduced?
2.   At what rate must skills be acquired by a student reading the material? Is the pacing too demanding for your children?
3.   What kinds of graphics does the book contain? How many pictures, maps, graphs, charts, diagrams, sketches, and tables are there per chapter? What special skills does analyzing each require?
4.   Does the book have an introduction, a summary, and main-idea questions for every chapter?
5.   Does the book contain important supplementary information in the form of glossaries, appendixes, tables, and the like for quick reference.

Another question to consider is whether there are skills required in one area but not in another. Are there certain skills needed in most areas? Socher suggests that the following skills are exercised by readers in many different subjects (10):

1.   Reading for the main idea.
2.   Distinguishing significant from insignificant details.
3.   Following the sequence of events.
4.   Reading critically—that is, noting propaganda devices, distinguishing fact from opinion, judging the author's qualifications, judging the relevance of what is read.
5.   Interpreting graphic aids in books.
6.   Seeing relationships among ideas.
7.   Deriving generalizations from what is read.

Figure 5-2 details some of the important skills specially needed when reading science, literature, mathematics, and social studies. The teaching of a body of content implies the teaching of not only the facts of the subject but also the process involved in learning those facts. In other words, the teaching of a subject implies the teaching of how to learn in that subject, including how to read materials.

TEACHER-MADE READING MATERIALS

In any reading program, no matter what the approach, there will be ample opportunity to help children learn to read by using materials of the teacher's own making. Original materials developed by a teacher can take various forms.

Initially a teacher might consider using special objects, events, or lessons which require the identification of special words. Labeling such objects

FIGURE 5-2
Requirements for Reading in Different Content Areas

SCIENCE

1. Ability to use highly technical vocabulary; some knowledge of Greek roots.
2. Ability to use diagrams, formulas, and so on.
3. Ability to follow step-by-step directions.
4. Ability to work through problems.
5. Ability to note specific details.
6. Ability to recognize certain key patterns; ability to classify, and to understand experiments, technical process, and statements of facts.

LITERATURE

1. Possession of a wide general vocabulary; ability to understand figurative language.
2. Ability to appreciate different genres.
3. Ability to use general reference materials; such as a dictionary, an encyclopedia, and so on.
4. Ability to interpret clues to plot, character, motives, and so on.
5. Ability to see the organization of a story.
6. Ability to appreciate mood and feeling.
7. Ability to detect style and tone.

MATHEMATICS

1. Ability to understand technical vocabulary.
2. Ability to interpret signs and symbols.
3. Ability to analyze problems stated in words.
4. Ability to use a system to solve problems.
5. Ability to follow directions.

SOCIAL STUDIES

1. Ability to use abstract words and ideas.
2. Ability to use maps, graphs, and so on.
3. Ability to locate information in different sources.
4. Ability to organize and synthesize information.
5. Ability to refer to many sources.
6. Ability to recognize such patterns as cause and effect, comparison and contrast, and time order.

in the room as an aquarium or a faucet with repeated verbal references to the objects, helps children learn sight words in a way that differs from the way of other strategies. Survival words, such as *stop*, *exit*, and *walk*, make up another set of terms which can be focused upon by this incidental way of teaching vocabulary.

Posters dealing with important people and events, notices of changes in children's classroom assignments, and riddles and other enjoyable materials can be displayed and can emphasize single words, phrases, or whole sentences. In each case, the children would be exposed to increased numbers of words at all levels of instruction.

As children become more socially aware, the teacher can take advantage of opportunities to rewrite and show interesting columns from newspapers, as well as to share good, entertaining short accounts of people and events. At Christmas time, for example, the O. Henry story "The Gift of the Magi" could be presented in simplified language for children. Around the room the teacher can post such directions as "Place picture books here" or "Place storybooks on the shelf below."

Occasionally children's stories of experiences that have been shared with other children can be displayed. Teachers who have taken trips will have stories to tell about other children.

In any classroom, no matter what the nature of the reading program, many and diversified teacher-made materials may be used, according to the creativity of the teacher.

SUPPLEMENTARY READING MATERIALS

Supplementary materials include, but are not restricted to, kits and programmed materials; workbooks; high-interest, low-vocabulary books; games; and such audiovisual items as films, filmstrips, cassettes, and records.

Perhaps the best-known, and the most misused, type of materials is the reading kit. We know of times when entire classrooms of children have been diligently working on exercises from a kit. The manner in which the children were assigned to work on the various levels of materials was suspect, to say the least. Usually children were encouraged to work through the materials by color-coded levels of difficulty. When teachers were interrupted and asked why particular students were working at a given level, the explanations typically had to do with the students' success on prior levels. However, in virtually every kit series, there is a placement test and a skills locational index which are to be used to insure that children work only on those areas of reading in which they are deficient. Children are not meant to work through level after level. In one instance, a teacher explained that the manual needed for determining the specific cards with which children needed to work was securely hidden in the bottom of the file cabinet "to make sure it doesn't get lost." The kits are usually fairly well developed, but they are too often used in ways the authors never intended.

The most commonly known program of reinforcement materials is the Science Research Associates *Reading Laboratories*. Educational Development Laboratories has the *Study Skills Library* for grades three through nine. Macmillan's *Reading Spectrum* and Webster McGraw-Hill's *Classroom Reading Clinic* are other kits commonly found in our schools.

Another type of material whose purpose is largely misunderstood is the workbook. There is nothing wrong with workbooks *per se*; however, they are often misused. Teachers frequently assign workbook exercises as time fillers, and this is unwise since children soon learn that such work is a form of penance, not a beneficial exercise. The following are some of the most commonly used exercise books:

1. *Working with Sounds*, *Getting the Facts*, *Following Directions*, and others (Barnell-Loft, Ltd.).
2. *Phonics We Use*, primer to grade six materials (Lyons and Carnahan).
3. *New Phonics Skilltexts*, for grades one to six (Charles E. Merrill Company).

4. *Be a Better Reader*, Books A, B, C for grades four to six (Prentice-Hall, Inc.).
5. *McCall-Crabbs Standard Test Lessons in Reading*, for grades two to seven (Teachers College Press, Columbia University).

High-Interest, Low-Vocabulary Books

In the past several years, there have been some excellent reading materials published. Among these are books usually referred to as *high-interest, low-vocabulary*. They are intended for the reluctant reader, for the remedial reader, and for the reader who merely wants to enjoy some good stories. A list of the better-known materials and magazines of this type is included in Appendix B.

Games and Teaching Devices

Commonly used in remedial reading are games and similar types of materials. The *Dolch Basic Sight Cards*, *Consonant Lotto*, and *Vowel Lotto* are published by the Garrard Company. Milton Bradley produces the *See and Say Consonant Game*. The Remedial Education Center, in Washington, D.C., has developed the games *Go Fish* and *Vowel Dominoes*. *Word Wheels* is available from the Webster McGraw-Hill Company. One item youngsters enjoy is the Flash-X hand tachistoscope, which rapidly flashes words and parts of words.

Remember that most educational media centers carry a full complement of such materials which can be reviewed upon request.

SUMMARY

There are many materials for teaching reading: child-created materials, basal readers, trade books, teacher-developed materials, and supplementary materials. Which materials are used depends on the school's and the teacher's goals in teaching reading. Typically, a combination of approaches is found in elementary classrooms. In later grades, a greater emphasis is found on the use of content reading materials, which allow children to learn in various subject areas.

The level of difficulty of reading materials and the suitability of materials for different learners was discussed in this chapter. Some real concerns about textbook reading were also raised and will be treated further in the next chapter.

ACTIVITIES RELATED TO THE CHAPTER

1. Write a story like the ones found in basal readers. The story would be for use with grade three or lower. Share your story with some classmates. Discuss the insights which class members have into the writing and into the use of a basal program. What are some advantages of using this type of reading material?

2. Bring in a story dictated by a five-year old child. What are the implications raised by whatever prompted the stories? What does this activity suggest about teaching words to new readers? What does this activity suggest about the oral language development of children?

3. Prepare a book talk to sell the rest of the class on the merits of a Newberry or Caldecott award book. Discuss the criteria used to evaluate each type of book. What characteristics of award-winning books for children are most apparent?

4. How might children's literature and content-area reading be used to enhance instruction? For example, for a grade level of your preference, grade one might concentrate on picture books, grade two on tales from other lands, grade three on true adventure stories, grade four on science topics, grade five on information books, and grade six on biographies. Compile lists of books suitable for each level.

5. Ask a class of children to write on a sheet of paper two or three topics they would like to read about during the year. Collect the papers and tabulate the responses; then share the results with the entire group. Discuss the implications of this activity for a teacher initiating an individualized reading program.

6. Conduct a sustained silent reading activity. What are the merits of allowing children time to read what they prefer to read in school?

BIBLIOGRAPHY AND REFERENCES

1. Feely, Theodore M., Jr.: "The Cloze and the Maze," *The Social Studies*, 66:252–258. (1975).

2. Herber, Harold L.: *Teaching Reading in the Content Areas*, Prentice-Hall, Englewood Cliffs, NJ, 1970.

3. Jacobs, Leland B.: *One-to-One: A Practical Individualized Reading Program*, Prentice-Hall, Englewood Cliffs, NJ, 1970.

4. Lee, Dorris M., and Roach Van Allen: *Learning to Read through Experience*, 2nd ed., Appleton-Century-Crofts, New York, 1963.

5. McCracken, Robert A., and Marlene J. McCracken: *Reading Is Only the Tiger's Tale*, Leswing Press, San Rafael, CA, 1972.

6. Olson, Willard C.: "Seeking, Self-Selection, and Pacing in the Use of Books by Children," in Jeanette Veatch, *Individualizing Your Reading Program*, G. P. Putnam's, New York, 1959, pp. 89–98.

7. Russell, David H., and Caroline Shrodes: "Contributions of Research in Bibliotherapy to the Language Arts Program," *School Review*, 58:335–342 (1950).

8. Ross, Ramon R.: *Storyteller*, Columbus, OH, Merrill, Columbus, OH, 1972.

9. Sawyer, Rita *The Way of the Storyteller*, Viking Press, NY 1970.

10. Sochor, E. Elona: "Special Reading Skills Are Needed in Social Studies, Science, Arithmetic," *The Reading Teacher*, 6:4–11. (1953).

11. Spache, George D.: *Good Reading for Poor Readers*, rev. ed., Garrard, Champaign, IL, 1972, pp. 194–207.

12. Spache, George D., and Evelyn B. Spache: *Reading in the Elementary School*, 3rd ed., Allyn and Bacon, Boston, 1973, pp. 146–147.

13. Veatch, Jeanette: *Individualizing Your Reading Program*, G. P. Putnam's, New York, 1959.

Ned Haines/Photo Researchers, Inc.

Integrating Instructional Approaches

6

Overview

Instruction in vocabulary and comprehension skills, in study skills, and in handwriting and spelling are meant to be coordinated within and among classrooms in an elementary school.

Mostly, elementary teachers successfully integrate instruction in many of the above skills within a total language arts curriculum. Certain procedures and techniques allow for this integration of instruction that helps children deal realistically with the world of language they encounter daily.

This chapter looks at some of these procedures and techniques for developing and sustaining a total language arts curriculum in an organized and logical manner.

Definition of Terms

1. *Acuity*—the keenness of response of any of the senses.
2. *Co-basal*—basic reading books used in conjunction with another series to allow greater choices and levels of materials.
3. *Content areas*—school subjects or disciplines in which a body of knowledge is taught. Subjects such as English, health, history, and earth science are included in this category.
4. *Directed Reading Activity (DRA)*—a reading lesson which includes concept and vocabulary preparation, a strategy of motivation, purposeful silent reading, oral rereading, development of skills, and skill extension activities.
5. *Directed Reading-Thinking Activity (DR-TA)*—an alternative to the DRA in which the emphasis is placed on questioning and prediction strategies to which all students can respond simultaneously.
6. *Discrimination*—the way in which the senses determine similarities and differences in stimulus objects.

7. *Guided Reading Procedure (GRP)*—a study technique for assisting students in learning content-area textual materials.
8. *Word bank*—a special collection, usually on file cards, of words taken from a pupil's own stories dictated to the teacher or an aide.

The major approaches to the teaching of reading are not meant to be exclusive of other approaches. A good program always carries the feature of balance.

This chapter emphasizes the complementary nature of the approaches to reading along with key ways to teach a reading lesson in fiction and nonfiction materials.

A reasonable starting point is to consider what children bring to their initial reading lessons—their own experiences.

THE LANGUAGE-EXPERIENCE APPROACH

The language-experience approach is a model procedure for the teaching of reading. Smith and Strickland view this approach as part of a total communication process (4). Children tell their stories to the teacher, who writes them down. Later, the children read back what the teacher has written. The stories are repeated so that the children can enjoy what they have dictated. Children who can write should record their own stories. In this whole process, there are many opportunities for children to talk, listen, read, and write.

Organic Reading

Ashton-Warner has written a book which all elementary school teachers will enjoy (1). In this book, *Teacher*, you can readily appreciate the beautiful sensitivity and understanding that she had for her children. An outline of her method conveys the idea that her approach is child-centered.

The major premise on which Ashton-Warner based her teaching method is that reading begins with what is intrinsic to a child. Words must have *intense* meaning to the learner. A beginning reading vocabulary should not come from another person's list, especially not an adult's. Words must be "organically tied up, organically born from the dynamic life itself." The technique of organic reading can be described as follows:

1. Each morning, the teacher talks with students individually. At this time, key words are written on a card. The youngster studies the words until they are known. The word cards are then placed in a box provided by the teacher.

2. A brief test is given later in the period to see if the words have been retained.

3. The child is encouraged to use these key words in writing sentences and stories.

4. Writing and spelling are reinforced by having the child say the words as they are displayed or by having the child spell them.

5. The next day, the words are spilled on the floor for each child to find his own words. Words not recalled are then removed since they are not yet part of the living vocabulary.

6. Words recalled are rehearsed again by having each child share with a partner the words recognized during the search.

7. In time, two words are used per card, and the children repeat the steps above in reinforcing their learned words.

8. At this stage, children are ready to write their own storybooks or to read those made by the teacher, using their organic vocabulary.

9. Gradually, children can begin to share their stories with their peers. Then a transition is made to Maori books containing stories written by these other children from the same culture. Subsequently, other published materials are included in the reading repertoire.

Language-Experience Stories

In a manner similar to that in which Maori children learned from Sylvia Ashton-Warner, other children learn to read by sharing their own experiences. A sufficient supply of words is developed and stored in a word bank. At first the stories can be group-dictated and later, individually. In the latter case, teachers may find it worthwhile to suggest topics to children by having ideas posted for children to see. These ideas can be changed periodically so that children are not always prone to tell the same types of stories. One such set of ideas would be: "What is it like to live on the moon?" "What is it like to be famous?" "How does a snowflake live?" "Your best friend from summertime." "How does a pig ever get clean?" "Suppose you are a helmet." "Suppose you are a library book." The list should prompt children to think about many of the concepts which the teacher would like to develop in the course of the year.

With a class of youngsters, a teacher can suggest one of the above ideas for a story. Whatever the topic, ample time must be allowed for children to talk freely about it. The teacher attempts to broaden the scope of the story so that several children can contribute and not just a few. After the topic has been discussed, the teacher suggests that the class write a story. At times a picture can be used to stimulate children's thinking. When all are ready, the teacher asks for ways to start the story. For instance, a title might be requested first, in order to try to keep the children fairly close to the general idea of the story. The teacher writes as the children dictate. If it seems that the story will be fairly long, the teacher might pause and read aloud what has been composed to that point, passing a hand under each word as it is read.

When the story has been completed, and while it is still fresh in the minds of the class, have the children read it aloud together. This reinforces vocabulary words which often are already part of their word banks. In time, these words will be immediatley recognized sight words.

Next day, the teacher may want to read the story again as a way of reinforcing the vocabulary. This is an opportunity for good oral reading, where the teacher's overall fluency, intonation, and pacing can help develop these same skills in children.

There are in every story key words which a teacher can use when instructing in a skill area. For example, if three words in a story contain the long "a" sound, the teacher can review that sound. The teacher might concentrate on some inflectional endings, or all the compound words might be underlined and thereby marked for further study. Most of the word skills discussed in Chapter 3 can be worked on here, according to the teacher's purpose. Critics of the language-experience approach often bring up the lack of a systematic study of words as an objection to this approach. The approach requires that the teacher be alert and take note of which forms of word study are going on and which are not.

The following story may help you see how a first grader shared his thoughts with his teacher.

Our New Cat

My brother said Uncle Jim's cat had kittens. There were some for us. Mom said one was enough. Me and my brother wanted one. We got a brown and white one, and Scruffy was his name.

The story contains the following key words to be included in the child's word bank for further study:

my	*said*	*cat*	*had*
we	*were*	*Mom*	*one*
us	*was*	*and*	*for*
me	*got*	*his*	*there*

It can be very rewarding and, therefore, personally meaningful for children to have a collection of their own stories. Then, when a number of stories have been written, the children can make their own books. This is an excellent way of encouraging youngsters, by having them share their books with other children in the class. For detailed instructions on how to bind books, see Appendix A.

Should the language-experience approach be the only approach used in a reading program? We realize that the exclusive use of this approach might prove monotonous after some time; teachers will want to consider other methods. A teacher can introduce a basal program or use a co-basal series. It is also possible to introduce an individualized reading program, as described in Chapter 5. However, several hundred books will be needed for the class, and the teacher must be knowledgeable about the reading skills of children of many different abilities. It is probably true that most experienced teachers would not recommend such an approach to teachers who have not had several years of teaching. One of the obvious reasons for this is that it takes years for a teacher to build a list of good books for children.

For how long should the language-experience approach be used in the elementary grades? Is it a suitable approach for the middle grades? We feel some distinctions might be made here. In the primary grades, the language-experience approach takes proper advantage of children's natural language patterns and their enthusiasm. In addition, children are starving for reading. What better material than that which they have written themselves? In time, the teacher can introduce other materials (see chapters 5, 7, and 9). Many teachers prefer to begin with the language-experience approach and then gradually change to a basal reading program no later than grade two. Sometimes, however, children in the middle grades who are remedial readers might find the language-experience approach to be the self-concept booster that they need. Children who lack interest in reading might find that writing and reading their own stories is rewarding.

From time to time in the middle grades, a teacher may want to have a small group of students brainstorm a story on a given topic. Several groups can work independently on developing stories, and prizes could be awarded for the best story by a group. The activity verges on creative writing, and pupils should have the chance to listen to what others have done. This activity offers another way of integrating the language arts.

It is probably fair to say that in most cases our schools expect teachers to perform this sequence: First, build the children's sight vocabulary by reading extensively to them and eliciting stories from them. Then, continue to have children tell, write, and read their own stories, while introducing other books to them to sustain their interests. In this way, a teacher makes the class ready for the introduction of a basal reading program.

GUIDED READING TECHNIQUES

Today, the teaching of reading is done according to a fairly standardized, almost traditional practice. In cases where a teacher's manual for a basal reading program is used, this practice is known as the *directed-reading activity* (DRA). The DRA includes specific steps to be followed, and each will be described in turn.

Another method that has been widely used and has become quite popular in some circles is the *directed reading-thinking activity* (DRTA). This activity has been promoted especially by Stauffer (5), who suggests that perhaps the DRA is too stifling for children. The systematic steps of the DRA do not allow for much individual thinking; Stauffer's alternative will be discussed below. The activity has interesting implications with respect to content-area reading, an area where we are especially interested in looking at teaching possibilities.

There is also the guided reading procedure developed by Manzo for use in content areas (3). The more choices we have, the better the opportunities for varying our procedures in instructing children. One would do well to seriously consider using all these techniques, but at different times and for different reasons.

The Directed Reading Activity

Are reading lessons necessary? Why not just have the children read what they care to read and hope they will enjoy their books? The main reason given for having reading lessons as such is that required skills are taught in a logical sequence. Without lessons the reading program often appears to lack organization. Some children do very well in this kind of chaotic situation. Many children, however, need some type of order if they are to learn adequately. Lessons allow teachers to think through what they will do; they know why children are engaged in various activities; and they have opportunities to let learners practice skills under teacher direction. In large classes teachers can systematize lessons in a way that allows assessment of what is happening or not happening during the lessons. This information will then help teachers plan further instruction.

Teachers who plan lessons in this way must make decisions about the time and materials required and about how each lesson fits into an overall sequence.

Reading lessons implicitly raise certain considerations of which teachers should be aware. Among these is the notion that reading is a separate program of study in school. This idea is largely responsible for teachers' amazement that there is something called *reading in the content areas*. Most people remember reading as a school subject wherein they met such characters as Dick, Jane, Spot, and Puff. Also, overreliance on a teacher's manual is often cited as a problem in using the DRA approach.

While the newer series have made elaborate allowances for all kinds of additional activities, basal reading programs are still created with the idea that teachers will work along the lines of the DRA. Therefore, it behooves us to consider the DRA sequence of activities.

Preparation

When are children ready to begin to read? Readiness refers to more than chronological age. Readiness also is based on the initial parts of a lesson during which the teacher prepares the children to understand and enjoy what is to follow. Ordinarily, the first part of the preparation for reading the story is trying to relate children's experiences to the story. Often references to stories read previously can serve as connections. Curiosity is built by having children look at pictures. The teacher may ask questions to try to get the learners to predict what is to happen in the story.

The vocabulary words in the story are ordinarily written on the board in context. Words hard to pronounce should be singled out for this purpose.

The next part of the preparation for reading is to establish the purpose. Depending on the type of material to be read, it is at times beneficial to ask children to read the questions that follow the selection. This is especially true with content-area materials.

Silent Reading

Once preparation has been completed, children should be ready to read silently. Teachers should look for indications, usually nonverbal, of difficulties children manifest as they read. Moving the mouth or lips, squinting, and holding the book too close are some of the signs that children are having problems with the reading.

Developing Comprehension

In this part, discussion takes place, and some literal, interpretive, and critical and creative activities are suitable. Activities at these levels might not be considered for every story, but this part of the DRA is usually devoted to clearing up misunderstandings and to developing children's appreciation of language, character, and literary features.

Oral Reading

Oral reading continues to be a misused practice. Many teachers remember when they were children and were called upon to read aloud in groups. Commonly referred to as *round-robin reading*, this activity is discouraged today because it lends virtually nothing to developing children's reading interests.

It is appropriate to clarify the role of oral reading in a reading lesson. Children can be asked to support an answer by reading an excerpt from a story. In the first grade, the ratio of the times spent on oral and silent reading is usually about 1:1. By grade three, as children have developed their reading skills, the proportion of oral to silent reading time is usually about 1:3.

Oral reading can take the form of sight reading, in which children read aloud without any preparation. This activity, though denounced by most practitioners, has two valid uses: (1) If you are diagnosing children's reading abilities, sight reading is warranted. (2) If the teacher wants children to *practice* reading at sight, it is acceptable for children who feel secure enough to do this type of reading in small groups.

There are a number of reasons for our reluctance to recommend extensive oral reading, especially in the primary grades. Oral reading is decidedly more complex than is silent reading. In silent reading, the child must derive meaning. In oral reading, the child has the added burden of conveying meaning to others. Thus, another aspect of oral reading is that it requires accomplished listeners.

Another reason for being cautious about having children read aloud is the amount of preparation required. A public speaker, such as a politician, an announcer, or a preacher, prepares what is to be said; children also must be allowed to prepare by reading silently before reading aloud to their peers.

Developing Word Power

The words encountered in the preparation phase might be reviewed in context at this stage of the lesson. Additional words might be suggested by the manual. Usually, certain word analysis skills are discussed in the manual—for example, working with several words which contain roots and affixes in common. It is not uncommon to find workbook activities for the reinforcement of skills introduced in the lesson. This is fine, except that the use of workbooks may frequently become automatic. Keep in mind that nobody ever said children always have to do every exercise. A teacher with an eye for diagnosis can see quickly which children need extra work and which do not. Having the children complete exercises because there is nothing else to do is a form punishment.

Evaluation

The reactions of children often are the best clues to how well they appreciate what they read. Their performance in workbooks often reveals their comprehension and word study development. Teachers usually have to offer additional reading materials to children who express a preference for certain types of literature. The idea of the "teachable moment" suggests that many good and interesting books should be on hand for learners to browse through after reading their stories.

The following is a description of an excellent DRA. In reading it, please note that it contains the elements discussed on the preceding pages.

The format of the DRA rarely changes. Some feel that is its strength, while others adamantly feel that the procedure is too structured. It is our experience that most learners need both structure and some time to be on their own as far as reading is concerned. This is the reason why we support such fairly recent developments as the Read-a-Thon and Reading Is FUN-

The Happy Woman

The Happy Woman, pages 24-39
(Softcover: pages 24-39)
Part One: The School Bus
Part Two: A Sad Day
Part Three: The Old Woman at School
The Wheels of the Bus Go Round and Round, pages 40-41
(Softcover: pages 40-41)

SUMMARY

"The Happy Woman" is a realistic story in three parts about a friendship between a little girl and a happy woman who drives the bus that the girl rides to school.

In Part One, the children and the bus driver have fun singing on the bus and exchanging presents.

In Part Two, the happy woman is replaced by another woman who likes quiet on the bus. The little girl misses her friend. She goes looking for her and feels sad when she can't find her.

In Part Three, the little girl is delighted to see the happy woman at school one day. She has come to work in the lunchroom where she can be with her friends.

"The Wheels of the Bus Go Round and Round" is a poem describing the delightful experience of riding on a bus. (For teaching suggestions, see page 47.)

OUTCOMES

To demonstrate that friendship is possible between a child and an adult

To encourage the realization that different people have different ways of doing the same job

OBJECTIVES *(Part One:* The School Bus)

Comprehension/Literary Skills

- **Review/Test:** Understand and use vocabulary appropriate to grade level (page 23)
- **Introduce:** Recognize a paraphrase of a given sentence (page 28)

  Review: Demonstrate an understanding of a selection (page 24)

22

Decoding Skills

- **Review/Test:** Recognize the phoneme-grapheme correspondences for short vowels /i/i/ as in *pig* with the CVC and CVCC patterns and the graphemic bases *-ip, -ig, -id, -ick, -ill;* /a/o as in *top* with the CVC pattern and the graphemic bases *-ob, -op, -ot* (PHONICS; page 28)
- **Review/Test:** Recognize the phoneme-grapheme correspondences for initial consonant clusters: /pr/pr as in *pretty* (PHONICS; page 29)
- **Review/Test:** Recognize plural nouns that end in *-s* (page 29)
- **Introduce:** Recognize the phoneme-grapheme correspondences for initial consonant clusters: /dr/dr as in *dress;* /fr/fr as in *free;* /gr/gr as in *green* (PHONICS; page 29)

Language Skills

  Review: Recognize the characteristics of nouns (page 30)
  Review: Identify a given word as a noun (page 30)
  Review: Recognize the difference in meaning between a singular and a plural noun (page 30)

RESOURCES

Practice Materials

Workbook: pages 9-12
Skills Practice: pages 5-6

Supplementary Materials

Chart paper, oaktag cards, Story Card 21, Word Cards, Phonic Picture Cards

Classroom Materials

Chart paper, oaktag cards, picture of a pie, pictures that show one and more than one of something

---

Source of material reproduced on pages 113 through 118: Teacher's edition of *Opening Doors/ Amigos/Ups and Downs*, series r: *The New Macmillan Reading Program*, Carl B. Smith and Ronald Wardbaugh, Senior Authors. Copyright © 1980 Macmillan Publishing Co., Inc. Used by permission of the publisher.

1 INTRODUCING THE LESSON

Instructional Vocabulary: happy, woman, school, went, liked, drove, sang, gave

DEVELOPING VOCABULARY AND CONCEPTS

- **Understand and use vocabulary appropriate to grade level   (Tested Objective)**

Display Story Card 21 or write the following paragraph on the chalkboard or on chart paper. You may make your own word cards, or you may wish to use the prepared word cards for instructional vocabulary words and for the following known words: *walk, game, like, sad, woods, man, have.*

> Suzy and I go to school.
> One day, I went to a party at school.
> Suzy gave me a present.
> I liked my presents.
> We sang.
> A woman sang, too.
> Then we drove home.
> The happy woman drove Suzy and me.

school   Display the new word *school.* Elicit that school is a place you go to learn. Read the word *school* with the children. Have a child read the first sentence and frame the word *school.*

went   Display the new word *went* and the known word *walk.* Elicit that both words begin with the same consonant sound and letter, /w/w. Explain that *went* means "to have gone somewhere." Have a child read the second sentence and frame the word *went.*

gave   Display the new word *gave* and the known word *game.* Elicit that both words begin with the same sound and letter, /g/g. Elicit that *gave* means "handed over." Have a child read the third sentence and frame the word *gave.* Direct the children to use the new word in sentences of their own.

liked   Display the new word *liked* and the known word *like.* Call attention to the ending of *liked.* Have a child find the word *like* in the new word *liked* and frame it. Elicit that *liked* means "having enjoyed something." Have a child read the fourth sentence and frame the word *liked.*

sang   Display the new word *sang* and the known word *sad.* Elicit that both words begin with the same consonant sound and letter, /s/s. Help the children read *sang.* Point out that *sang* means "made music with the voice." Have a child read the fifth sentence and frame the word *sang.*

woman   Display the new word *woman* and the known word *woods.* Elicit that *woman* and *woods* begin with the same consonant sound and letter, /w/w. Tell the children that a woman is an adult female human being. Have a child read the sixth sentence and frame the word *woman.*

drove   Display the new word *drove.* Help the children read the word *drove.* Explain that *drove* means "having made a car go." Have a child read the seventh sentence and frame the word *drove.*

happy   Display the new word *happy* and the known word *have.* Elicit that both words begin with the same consonant sound and letter, /h/h. Elicit that *happy* means "glad or pleased." Have a child read the eighth sentence and frame the word *happy.*

After all the instructional-vocabulary words have been introduced and discussed, ask volunteers to read the paragraph aloud.

REINFORCING VOCABULARY AND CONCEPTS

Write the instructional-vocabulary and the following pattern of letters on the chalkboard:

happy	a	c	d	s	n	r	l
woman	w	o	m	a	n	g	i
school	e	c	i	n	r	o	k
went	n	w	x	g	a	v	e
liked	t	d	r	o	v	e	d
drove	s	c	h	o	o	l	b
sang	o	l	h	a	p	p	y
gave							

23

Tell the children that the eight words on the left are hidden in the word puzzle. Explain that the words are written either across the rows or up and down the columns. Then ask individual volunteers to read a word, find it in the puzzle, and circle it.

■ WORKBOOK: page 9

2 READING FOR COMPREHENSION

DEVELOPING INTEREST AND ORAL LANGUAGE

Tell the children that the story they are going to read is about a happy woman who drives a school bus. Ask the children if they have ever been on a bus, and, if so, to describe what the bus ride was like. *Was the ride short or long? Was the bus crowded?* Encourage different children to tell about their rides on a bus. For those children who may not have been on a bus, you might wish to ask them whether a bus passes their house, or what they think about when they see a bus. *Why are buses so large?* (They carry many people.) *How do buses help people?* (They take people from one place to another.)

SETTING PURPOSES FOR SILENT READING

Have the children turn to the Contents and locate the title, "The Happy Woman." Help them discover that the story has three parts. Ask a volunteer to read the title of the story aloud. Th:n have another volunteer read the title of Part One, "The School Bus." By using the Contents, the children should be able to locate the page on which Part One begins. Have them study the pictures on the first two pages. Then help the children to set their own purposes for silent reading by asking questions similar to these: *What are the children and the bus driver doing as they ride on the bus? How would you describe the bus driver? What do you think the children will do when they get off the bus?*

The children should read the entire first part of the story silently before proceeding to discuss and reread the story orally.

DISCUSSING AND REREADING ORALLY

Demonstrate an understanding of a selection

The comprehension questions that follow focus on a discussion of Part One as a whole. The questions under the reduced text pages should be used selectively after the general discussion. You may wish to have the children read orally in response to specific questions or for general enjoyment.

Literal Comprehension

1. *Who is telling this story?* (a girl; one of the children who rides the bus)
2. *Where did the bus take the children?* (to school)
3. *Who drove the bus?* (a woman)
4. *What did the woman do while she drove the bus?* (She sang to the birds, the dogs, and the children.)
5. *What did the children do on the bus?* (They sang, too.)
6. *What kinds of presents did the woman and the children exchange?* (funny presents)
7. *What presents did the little girl give the woman?* (a little mouse and a little car)

Interpretive Thinking

1. *Why do you think the children called the bus driver a happy woman?* (The woman loved to sing, and she let the children sing, too. When people sing, it's often a sign of happiness.)
2. *Why do you think the children liked to ride the bus?* (They liked to sing and they liked the woman. They felt happy on the bus.)
3. *Why did the woman and the children give presents to one another?* (Answers may vary but should suggest that they wanted to show their happy feelings.)

24

4. *What kinds of presents might be "funny" presents?* (Answers may vary but should suggest that the presents did not cost a lot of money. Rather, they were small things that the giver already had and thought would amuse the receiver.)

Critical Thinking

1. *Do you think it was a good idea to sing on the bus?* (Answers may vary but should include the idea that it is probably all right to sing as long as it does not bother other people or the bus driver.)
2. *Why do you think the woman and the children liked to sing?* (Answers may vary but should include the idea that singing is a fun activity that a group of people can enjoy together. The

woman and the children wanted to have a good time during the ride to school.)
3. *How old do you think the woman who drove the bus was?* (Answers will vary.) *Do you think she was too old to be driving a bus?* (Answers will vary.)

Creative Thinking

1. *If you were riding on a bus, what songs would you like to sing?* (Answers will vary.)
2. *If you had been one of the children on the bus, what kind of present would you have given the woman?* (Answers will vary but should include the idea that the present need not be purchased. The present might be something the child made or found.)

■ WORKBOOK: page 10

25

The Happy Woman

Dina Anastasio

Part One
The School Bus

I went to school on a bus.
My friends went on the bus, too.
We liked to ride
on the school bus.

A happy woman drove the bus.
We liked the happy woman
who drove the bus.
She drove and she sang.
She sang to the birds.
She sang to the dogs.
She sang to my friends.
And we sang, too.

Softcover: page 24

Softcover: page 25

Character's Behavior/Picture Clues   *Look at the picture. What are the children doing?* (They are looking out the windows. They are singing. They are all in their seats.) *Why are the children seated?* (It is probably a safety rule on the bus.)

Character's Feelings   *The children on the bus are smiling. What does that tell you about how they are feeling?* (They are happy.)

Vocabulary Development   *What words do you see in the picture that are also in the story?* (school bus; You might want the children to locate the words in the story again.)

First-Person Narration   *Who is telling the story?* (Direct the children to look at the word *I.*) *Who do you think the I is?* (Probably one of the children on the bus. Not until the last page in Part One do you know it is the little girl.)

Picture Clues   *Look at the picture of the bus. If this were real life, do you think musical notes would be coming out of the woman's mouth? Why or why not?* (No, just the sound of the music would be heard from the bus.) *Why do you think the notes are shown in so many different colors?* (To express the happiness of the children and the woman.)

Character Traits   *Why did the woman sing to the birds and the dogs?* (Answers will vary but should include the idea that she probably sang to them because she liked animals and wanted them to feel happy, too.) *Why do you think the woman liked to sing?* (It probably made her feel happy and joyful.)

26

The woman gave funny presents
to my friends and me.
And we gave funny presents
to the woman.

I gave little things,
like a little mouse
and a little car.

She liked the car.
She liked the mouse, too.

26

Softcover: page 26

Main Idea and Supporting Details   *What happened on this page?* (The woman and the children gave presents to one another.) *What are some of the presents they gave?* (They gave funny presents such as a little car and a little mouse.) *What other presents do you think the children gave?* (Answers will vary.)

Word Connotations   *According to the story the presents were funny. Why were the little mouse and the little car funny presents?* (Because they were not the type of presents one would ordinarily give to an adult.)

Relate to Personal Experience   *To whom would you like to give a present and why?* (Answers will vary.) *Is being a friend just as important as giving a present? Why or why not?* (Answers will vary but should include the idea that friendship is as important as giving presents. People give presents to show that they like their friends. They usually give presents their friends will like.)

27

damental (RIF) programs. The sensitive teacher will know when to change the format and pattern of teaching.

The Directed Reading-Thinking Activity

Like the DRA, this activity follows a general sequence of procedures, which might be as follows:

1. In the beginning the teacher selects the materials to be read. In time, children can be encouraged to bring stories they would like to use for their reading. The books children select will usually be at their instructional level.
2. Each child should have a "secret page," a piece of paper used to cover the story until they are directed to slide the page down to progressively unveil more and more of the story. At first, only the title should be seen by the children, who then tell what the title means to them. Be prepared for some wildly imaginative responses at this stage of the DR/TA as the children try to predict what the story will be about. The children then read to a point predetermined by the teacher, moving their secret pages down. Ask the children if their predictions are still true. There will now have to be some adjustments in their thinking from the initial guesses. There will be no doubt, however, still be many different views as to what will happen next. When the teacher is satisfied that the children have committed themselves as to what is to happen next, they move their secret pages down again and continue reading to a point designated by the teacher. It is helpful to number the story by sections to facilitate this step.

    In each case, the same types of questions are asked by the teacher: *What do you think will happen? How do you know that? What makes you say that?* Children who state their thinking aloud have a vested interest as readers in what is taking place. They can then read each section to check their guesses before they make new ones.
3. At the end of the story, it is not unusual to see children peeking ahead to read the ending. There are ways to avoid this situation. The teacher can make sure the children cover over the last part, or the teacher can simply keep the last page. Some teachers prepare the conclusion on a transparency for showing with an overhead projector. Other teachers like to run copies of the ending separately and distribute them for silent reading when the other paragraphs have been completed.

The DRTA is a valuable activity to use from time to time with students. As with so many other strategies, children would soon tire of the activity if it were used every day. One of the greatest advantages of using the DRTA is that the teacher can capitalize on the many different experiences which readers bring to a class. Children can learn much from others in a group. A sample, DRTA follows*:

1. On the third night of hunger, Noni thought of the dog. Nothing of flesh and blood lived upon the floating ice island except those two.

2. In the breakup, Noni had lost his sled, his food, his furs, even his knife. He had saved only Nimuk, his great devoted husky. And now the two, marooned on the ice, eyed each other warily—each keeping his distance.

    Noni's love for Nimuk was real, very real—as real as hunger and cold nights and the gnawing pain of his injured leg. But the men of his village killed their dogs when food was scarce, didn't they? And without thinking twice about it.

3. And Nimuk, he told himself, when hungry enough would seek food. "One of us will soon be eating the other, "Noni thought. "So . . . "

4. He could not kill the dog with his bare hands. Nimuk was powerful and much fresher than he. A weapon, then, was needed.

    Removing his mittens, he unstrapped the braces from his leg. When he had hurt his leg a few weeks before, he had made the brace from bits of harness and two thin strips of iron.

    Kneeling now, he wedged one of the iron strips into a crack in the ice and began to rub the other against it with firm, slow strokes.

    Nimuk watched him, and it seemed to Noni that the dog's eyes glowed more brightly.

    He worked on, trying not to remember why. The slab of iron had an edge now. It had begun to take shape. Daylight found his task completed.

    Noni pulled the finished knife from the ice and thumbed its edge. The sun's glare, reflected from it, stabbed at his eyes and momentarily blinded him.

5. Noni steeled himself.
    "Here, Nimuk!" he called softly.
    The dog suspiciously watched him.
    "Come here," Noni called.

    Nimuk came closer. Noni read fear in the animal's gaze. He read hunger and suffering in the dog's labored breathing and awkward crouch. His heart wept. He hated himself and fought against it.

    Closer Nimuk came, aware of his intentions. Now Noni felt a thickening in his throat. He saw the dog's eyes, and they were wells of suffering.

    Now! Now was the time to strike!

6. A great sob shook Noni's kneeling body. He cursed the knife. He swayed blindly, flung the weapon far from him. With empty arms outstretched, he stumbled toward the dog and fell.

    The dog growled as he circled the boy's body. And now Noni was sick with fear.

    In flinging away the knife, he had left himself defenseless. He was too weak to crawl after it now. He was at Nimuk's mercy, and Nimuk was hungry.

*Hugh B. Cave, *Two Were Left,* Crowell-Collier, New York, 1942. Copyright 1942 by the Crowell-Collier Publishing Co. Reprinted by permission of the author.

The dog had circled him and was creeping up from behind. Noni heard the rattle in the savage throat.

He shut his eyes, praying that the attack might be swift. He felt the dog's feet against his leg, the hot rush of Nimuk's breath against his neck. A scream gathered in the boy's throat.

7. Then he felt the dog's hot tongue licking his face.

Noni's eyes opened. Crying softly, he thrust out an arm and drew the dog's head down against his own. . . .

The plane came out of the south an hour later. Its pilot, a young man of the coast patrol, looked down and saw the large floating iceberg. And he saw something flashing.

It was the sun gleaming on something shiny, which moved. His curiosity aroused, the pilot banked his ship and descended. Now he saw, in the shadow of the peak of ice, a dark, still shape that appeared to be human. Or were there two shapes?

He set his ship down in a water lane and investigated. There were two shapes, boy and dog. The boy was unconscious but alive. The dog whined feebly but was too weak to move.

The gleaming object which had caught the pilot's attention was a crude knife, stuck point first into the ice a little distance away, and quivering in the wind.

It is necessary to help students realize what has transpired in the story. At times, the discussion will wander because of all the opinions expressed about what is to happen next.

A built-in advantage of using the DRTA is that students are reading to determine the accuracy of their own predictions. This means that students are reading for their own reasons, for their own purposes. That is far better than always reading for purposes established by another person, even if it is the teacher.

We would like to see an intelligent integration of the DRA and the DRTA, so that learners can have the advantages of both along with the variety each brings to a class setting.

CONTENT-AREA READING PROCEDURES

In the last chapter we noted that among the most common reading materials in a classroom are those related to particular subjects, or content areas. We have already discussed the level of reading difficulty of content-area materials and ways to determine the suitability of textbook materials for children.

The following discussion focuses on teaching reading in the content areas.

Content-Area Guidelines

We cannot stress enough how vital a part readiness plays in reading in any subject area. It is simply sound teaching to determine where children stand in their preparation for the important concepts we want to teach them. Anybody can teach the sophisticated learners. But what about the average and below-average pupils? Herein lies the excitement of being a professional teacher in the first place. Finding ways to move children to the point where they will want to learn, where they will want to read, is the very heart of teaching.

There is a true story of a professor who was told by a student that the reason she enrolled in a certain reading course was to learn about motivation. The professor said that the topic was usually discussed in psychology courses and therefore was not addressed as such in his class. The student decided to stay in the class anyway. On the last meeting of the class, the professor asked the class what they felt were the strengths and limitations of the course. The student said she was delighted to have so much with which to motivate her children. The professor reminded her of her remark on the first day. The point is that good materials and good methods, used by a concerned and enterprising teacher at any level of instruction, from kindergarten through graduate school, will motivate students again and again. There is no magic formula involved.

We related this story to underscore the idea that good teaching is not an accident. A good teacher knows the material well, and he knows techniques and strategies that work well because he has looked for them, tried them out, and adapted them as necessary. Teachers who fail to teach in the first place are wrong to blame the children.

Content-area classes yield many opportunities for integrating the language arts. The key is motivation, and half of motivation is readiness, so the preparation a teacher puts into this phase of teaching is always amply rewarded.

When assisting learners with their reading assignments, the cardinal principle is to guide them. For example, if a teacher says, "Read Chapter 4 and we will discuss it," then do discuss it, otherwise the children will feel that they do not have to read anything. Children who say, "The teacher never makes us," reveal the expectations they have of teachers. Discussion can help integrate reading with speaking, listening, and sometimes writing. Learners do not, however, discuss intelligently unless they themselves have been guided on how to carry on a discussion. It takes a little patience to help children formulate guidelines for a good discussion.

It goes without saying that the teacher should read the textbook before the children do. How many teachers do you know who cannot answer questions because they have not read the text themselves? It is essential for the teacher to be aware of the important concepts to be taught, the problems to be resolved, and the purposes of the reading assignment.

Another excellent way of integrating children's literature with content-area materials is to make available books related to units of study. School librarians will often pull some titles related to a unit topic and make these available to children. Biographies of historical figures or scientists, informational books, and how-to books are abundant at the elementary levels.

Strategies for Reading Content Materials

In Chapter 4 mention was made of the work of Herber in developing comprehension (2). We will not discuss here his principles for teaching reading in the content areas, since that would be an entire textbook in itself. We will, however, speak about three strategies which can be useful at the elementary level.

The DRA can be used in subject areas. Preparation, vocabulary development, silent and oral reading, skill teaching and reinforcement, and enhancement activities can be used with content-area reading. Variety is the key to sustaining interest in a subject.

Some teachers have found a good deal of positive response to the DRTA used with content-area reading materials. Again, the DRTA sequence discussed previously will be helpful in these cases.

More recently, another procedure, the guided reading procedure (GRP), has been suggested by Manzo (3). The GRP is intended to help students get accurate factual information from their textbooks as a preliminary to interpretive, critical, and creative comprehension. The GRP can be described as follows:

1. As preparation, the teacher should identify key concepts and vocabulary and set the purposes for reading.
2. For silent reading Manzo suggests assigning a selection of 500–900 words for students in the middle grades, which should occupy approximately five to seven minutes of reading time. The teacher should tell the students: "Read to remember all that you can."
3. When the students are finished, they turn their texts over. The teacher asks them to tell what they remember and writes their responses on the board in the order in which they are recalled.
4. The teacher should note how much information was missed or incorrectly provided.
5. Have students review the selection.
6. Put the recorded information in some type of outline. Ask some general questions, such as: What came to you as an important idea? What came first? How can you prove that it is important? Can you tell me more about that? Your questions can help pupils probe deeper into their reading and discuss it in relation to what they already know. Again the purpose of the preparation phase is obvious.
7. Schedule an evaluation time for testing students in a format that reinforces these learnings.

It can be seen that throughout this process the teacher is guiding the learners so that they can become students in the true sense of the word.

The DRA, the DRTA, and the GRP are not the only strategies available. Herber speaks about other strategies in his text (2), and you are directed to that and other sources which deal solely with reading in the content areas. It remains for us now to consider briefly some aspects of reading that are dealt with in all materials, including content-area texts.

Content-Area Vocabulary

Content-area vocabulary differs from general reading vocabulary only in that it is highly technical and specialized. For that reason, content-area words need to be regarded as the responsibility of the content teacher. No teacher knows science vocabulary better than a science teacher. It is logical, therefore, to suggest that science class is the appropriate forum for teaching this technical vocabulary. The reason this is usually not done is that, regretfully, content teachers have no background in the teaching of reading and therefore avoid this task. This is understandable, but it still does not resolve the problem which young readers have in dealing with their textbooks.

One of the most typical vocabulary problems in content subjects appears when words commonly used in one way are used in a different way in a subject area. There is a version of Lincoln's Gettysburg Address that begins

> Fourscore [that's something from a ball game] and seven years ago, our fathers [my blood father?] brought forth on this continent a new nation [did they launch it like a rocket?] . . .

The point is that so often what seems *obvious* to everybody is really not at all obvious. The words singled out in the extract above exemplify precisely what we mean when we say that children need to learn the meanings of words in the subject fields. Highly technical words also need to be taught. In history for example, we study many *-ism*'s. What does that affix mean? What does *-ocracy* stand for in a word? There are many roots whose use is common in the sciences, social sciences, and mathematics and which require direct instruction to young learners.

Content-Area Comprehension

The skills and levels of comprehension discussed in Chapter 4 apply to content subjects as much as they do to general or story reading. Oral reading as a regular activity is not encouraged here, for the same reasons we have stated above. There are times, however, when students can be asked to read a portion of a paragraph to prove a point or to clarify a concept (for instance, when using the GRP). In English and social studies classes particularly, there are times when reading aloud to classmates serves the purpose of entertaining and sharing.

The vast amount of information contained in content-area reading, forces consideration of the problem of how students retain the information. Teachers should endeavor to identify ways in which students can see relationships in what they read. Again, this is an area where the preparation phase of lessons becomes important. There are many ways to see relationships. Teachers should stress such major categories as the following:

1. *Cause and effect*—It might be helpful to refer to this relationship as *action and reaction* to vary the idea.
2. *Comparison and contrast*—Pupils can begin comparing and contrasting at the earliest level of elementary school. The real and the unreal, the factual and the fanciful, the animal world and the people world, the seasons of the year: all these are in the realm of experience of young learners. Children can be helped to see how things are the same and how they are different, as they move on to more difficult reading material.
3. *Simple listing*—With textbook materials, at times the only reasonable way to keep thoughts in order is to make lists. Categorizing often lends itself well to this way of organizing information.
4. *Sequence*—When reading literature or scientific experiments, there are many places where children can be helped to see ideas in a logical order. Information in the social sciences can also often be chronologically ordered.

Students who can see relationships, have a better chance of retaining information. As children progress through their years of school, the amount of information increases. Teachers need to be alert to ways of showing learners how to retain the information they are getting in their various classes. This is the whole point of outlining: to see relationships and to keep information organized in a realistic manner.

CONTENT-AREA STUDY SKILLS

All textbooks have titles, chapter headings, subheadings, and other aids to understanding what is important. All too often these aids are completely ignored. How many times have you encountered learners who cannot seem to determine what is really important in their reading? Perhaps you have the same difficulty. There are three ways to help students make this determination:

1. Point out the chapter subdivisions and headings. The headings can be rephrased as questions.
2. Read the summary at the end of any section and at the end of the chapter. This is another clue to what is really important.
3. Read the questions at the end of the chapter. They indicate the ideas and concepts that are most relevant.

These three brief activities can help students feel sure about what is really important in any chapter. This is necessary in order to prevent them from becoming inflexible readers who read everything at the same rate. Also, pupils can come to hate school if nobody ever lets them in on the secret of how to study and survive.

The content areas provide a logical place for working on unit projects with students. The variety and flexibility that can be built into this type of instruction allow the immediate application of the most needed study skills. Locating information for projects can afford the opportunities which children need to practice their skills. Teachers can readily diagnose the situation and teach accordingly. Unit work can include assignments which are suited to the different types of students; the gifted, the average, and the slow all profit with the proper planning.

The study skills we have suggested allow students the chance to transfer the skills learned in reading class to the content area. This is highly practical, since the content areas are where these skills are mainly used in the upper grades. In fact, the amount of general-purpose reading declines as learners move from the elementary to the secondary grades.

SUMMARY

Children in the earliest grades can find great satisfaction in the language-experience approach. In the majority of schools, basal reading programs or a systems approach is used to ensure the sequential learning of reading skills.

Basic procedures, including the directed reading activity, were described, along with the directed reading-thinking activity.

The application of basic procedures to content-area reading is emphasized in the guided reading procedure. It is important for teachers to deal with vocabulary, comprehension, and study skills when teaching fiction and nonfiction materials alike.

ACTIVITIES RELATED TO THE CHAPTER

1. Check the teacher's manual for a basal reading series in grades one, three, and five. Note the amount of time to be spent on oral reading during a directed reading activity. What conclusions do you draw?

2. Visit a classroom where more than one approach to reading is used. What practical problems arise? Discuss in small groups the pros and cons of the approaches you observe.

3. If you wanted to equip a classroom of your preferred level with trade books, where would you seek information on appropriate titles, other than from a librarian? List several resources, and compile a list of suitable titles.

4. Find a story suitable for the directed reading-thinking activity, and bring it to class. Discuss the criteria for choosing stories for this activity. By lot, choose three or four members of your class to demonstrate the activity.

5. From a chapter of a content-area textbook, develop a list of what you judge to be important vocabulary words. What criteria can you set for determining which words should be taught directly?

6. Determine the writing pattern used in another chapter of a content-area textbook. What does this imply about how you would teach from the chapter? What study skills would you focus on in the chapter?

BIBLIOGRAPHY AND REFERENCES

1. Ashton-Warner, Sylvia: *Teacher*, rev. ed., Simon & Schuster, New York, 1963.
2. Herber, Harold L.: *Teaching Reading in Content Areas*, 2nd ed., Prentice-Hall, Englewood Cliffs, NJ, 1978.
3. Manzo, Anthony V.: "Guided Reading Procedure," *Journal of Reading*, 18:287–291 (1975).
4. Smith, Nila Banton, and Ruth Strickland: *Some Approaches to Reading*, Association for Childhood Education International, Washington, D.C., 1969, p. 6.
5. Stauffer, Russell G.: *Directing the Reading-Thinking Process*, Harper & Row, New York, 1975.

Skills Related to Reading

7

Overview

When children begin school, they usually possess a high degree of proficiency in oral communication. We now turn to some special considerations in the teaching of oral and written language, designed to ensure that reading is seen as one of the language arts and to surround the child with sound language-development practices. This chapter also treats the topics of handwriting and spelling. Beyond the primary grades when children are reading to learn, other areas demand attention to ensure their continued development. Accordingly, we also deal in this chapter with an often-neglected topic: fluency and flexibility in reading. The chapter concludes with a discussion of techniques for teaching the study skills which children need in order to read to learn, particularly in content areas.

Definition of Terms

1. *Creative writing*—written expression in an original mode.
2. *Cursive writing*—handwriting with joined letters.
3. *Flexibility*—a skill by which readers adjust their rate of reading according to the purpose and the difficulty of the material.
4. *Fluency*—a skill which enables a reader to proceed with good modulation and rate when reading aloud or silently.
5. *Locational skills*—the abilities needed to find information readily.
6. *Manuscript writing*—handwriting with printed letters usually not joined. This form is common in grades one through three.
7. *Scanning*—reading very rapidly to locate specific information.
8. *Skimming*—reading to gain a quick overview.

eading does not stand alone as a school subject. It is more appropriate to consider reading with its expressive counterpart—writing. Handwriting and spelling are two skills needed to write well. Much of what a child can write about can be spoken initially. Our discussion begins, then, with the verbal expression of language.

ORAL EXPRESSION

One of the most beautiful gifts that a child brings to school is that of imagination. In the primary grades teachers work hard to show children how pervasive language is in our lives. Imaginative stories told to and by children form the nucleus of a strong oral language development program. Children who are heavily exposed to good language patterns soon come to appreciate the beauties of our language. We shall look at some of the many aspects of children's and teachers' oral language expression. Our first task, however, is to share some insights as to the objectives and overall dimensions of such a program.

Objectives

The most obvious objective is to help children be good speakers and listeners. Social context is important in both of these areas. In time, children come to understand their roles in a class group, and they come to see their roles in relation to the teacher. Youngsters who can express themselves to their peers grow rapidly in a social sense, as do youngsters who can express themselves with their teachers, who function as adult models for children to emulate. Another purpose of an oral-language program is to help children appreciate the fascination of their language. Who has not heard the laughter of children when they listen to silly rhyming tales told by an adult? They can listen to some stories repeatedly. What might seem repetitive to an adult can seem quite necessary to a child. At the same time, children are learning to appreciate the contributions of dialects other than their own. Moreover, all speakers need to cultivate a pleasant voice, to pronounce words clearly, to express organized thoughts, and to use verbal and nonverbal clues for interacting with others in oral-language situations.

Primary-Grade Activities

There are many enjoyable activities which lend themselves to the general objectives stated previously.

1. Children telling stories to the teacher, as in the language-experience approach, is more commonly seen today than several years ago. Chil-

dren can easily be encouraged to talk about pets, TV programs, or stories that have been read to them.

2. "Bring and Brag" is not a new activity, but it still gives children a chance to deliver a brief oral report on an event, a person, or an object. This type of activity allows for an increase of self-confidence in most children in speaking to their peers.

3. One of the best activities for instilling a love of reading is storytelling by the teacher. Another aspect of this art form is described in Chapter 9.

4. Children can develop their own vocabularies and at the same time gain an appreciation for what makes a good story if they are guided to make an oral presentation. The teacher's discussing with a class the ingredients of a good story and then being resourceful in seeking out those stories promotes critical analysis and locational skills simultaneously. Pupils should tell stories only if they feel comfortable doing so.

5. Timid children can be given an effective and rewarding activity, such as choral speaking and reading. The anonymity of the small group can overcome many of the teacher's and children's deficiencies. There are refrains and two-part selections for choral reading. There are also sequenced readings, in which children are assigned different parts while delivering certain lines in union. However, all these forms require practice led by the teacher. There are unlimited possibilities for presentations to parents, other students, and community groups.

6. The fantasy world of the young schoolchild can be depicted masterfully through the use of puppets. This activity, as well as storytelling, can be used by both the teacher and the pupils. Unusual opportunities to grow in oral language are offered to reluctant or shy youngsters who have available hand puppets made from old scraps. Senior-citizen groups or individual retired people could be encouraged to make puppets for children, and in this way a lot of goodwill for the educational community can be engendered.

7. Pictures cut from printed sources can be placed in boxes, and children can be encouraged to create their own original stories based on a selection of about ten pictures. This activity should be done by one group while the teacher is working with another group of students on a different activity. Similarly, teachers can use a flannel board to gradually unfold a story to children by adding pictures one at a time. Conducting these activities helps intern students and student aides.

Intermediate-Grade Activities

1. When children have developed a sense of the plot and the sequence of events in stories, they are ready to predict the endings. This does not always mean, however, that they will agree in their predictions. Good and suspenseful stories allow room for the imagination to roam and for students to suggest alternate endings to stories.

2. Another type of activity which middle-grade youngsters enjoy is role-playing. Portraying what it feels like to have scored the winning field goal in the Super Bowl is an example of this activity. A budding sports announcer could be prompted to interview this hero for a few minutes for the benefit of the listening audience. Introducing the governor of the state and sharing the first impressions of having survived a two-week trip to the Arctic are other role-playing possibilities. Taking a call from the White House would allow two pupils to role-play in an impromptu five-minute conversation.

3. One student could interview and then introduce to the class a new member who has moved from another state or part of the country. An interview by a class reporter could help the rest of the class understand the main concerns of running a bakery, a drugstore, a pet shop, or a sporting goods store.

4. If students are familiar with storytelling, there is a natural way of introducing dramatization activities. The material chosen must be familiar to the students who participate. Time must be allowed for the planning, the costuming, and the staging. Such productions can be performed for larger audiences than just their own classmates.

The purpose of these activities on the primary- and middle-grade levels is to develop children's vocabularies, both listening and speaking. Such development can continue indefinitely, and these extended vocabularies form a base for a richer reading and writing vocabulary. We now turn to a discussion of the development of written language in the elementary school.

WRITTEN EXPRESSION

Have you ever seen a story written by a three-year-old? Incomprehensible but appealing. Yet, to the child it is a complete story. If invited to do so, they will tell you what it says. This illustrates how children imitate the models that surround them. The following discussion is of activities related to helping children express themselves in the written mode.

Objectives

In a sense, a child who can tell a story while someone else writes it down, can be said to be composing; the child is writing. As with reading, children soon learn the value of this form of communication. Writing, an expressive form of encoding, can be difficult for many students. Unless they are provided the time and the opportunities to write, they will see this skill as unnecessary. Each writing activity must have a clearly stated purpose. Writing is labor that should not be needlessly allied with futility. As with the teaching of oral language communication, there are many novel and interesting ways of aiding children to become proficient writers.

Primary-Grade Activities

1. Have children find good illustrations from a collection of pictures for stories that they may have dictated in the language-experience mode. Ask them to write captions for their pictures.
2. Have children write to their grandparents or to other senior citizens. Encourage the use of sentences that tell and sentences that ask. With the home as a context, children in the early grades can write sentences about the five senses.
3. Story starters and stimulators can be shown to children, who then write the details of a sequence of events. These stories can then be read to the class by the authors. Follow-up stories might be suggested by the audience.
4. Children's writing can be improved by having them do some sentence combining. In this exercise, the reader must attend to the meaning and function of each word. For example, a teacher could ask children to combine the following three sentences into a single sentence: Susan B. Anthony was a leader for women's rights. She was laughed at by some people. She was a woman of courage.
5. A teacher can focus on the value of other forms of the arts by asking children to talk about and then write their impressions of a work of art. Playing a good musical piece and asking children to listen and discover the mood of the music can be a good way of encouraging them to express their ideas and feelings in writing. This free-flowing technique is similar to the sustained writing activity described by Greene in which students are given ample time during a few periods each week to write whatever they care to write (6). The teacher does not read the children's writing. Children simply are given the time to write—letters, stories, poems, notes—whatever they want to write.

Intermediate-Grade Activities

Cinquain and haiku are two of the most unusual and exciting written forms for children to experience at this level. Both are poetic, and both are easy to share with children via some useful models. For example, the following model of cinquain:

The title (one word or two syllables):	Helmet
Describe (two words or four syllables):	Hard Plastic
Action (three words or eight syllables):	Safe snug air
Synonym (one word or two syllables):	Lifesaver

Children should at first be encouraged to work in a group until they have acquired a feeling for this form of poetry. It emphasizes imagery and represents a variation of the Japanese tanka verse.

Another form of poetry from Japan which can be used to stimulate writing is haiku. An example of haiku follows:

Where? (five syllables):   In the open fields

What? (seven syllables:)   Golden stalks grow tall and proud

When? (five syllables):   As summer's sun shines.

At this level, still another good form for children is the limerick, We do not mean to suggest that only poetic forms are suited to the development of writing skills at the intermediate-grade level. Other activities are encouraged in the overall plan for writing at this level.

1. Factual writing can be practiced using the well-known "five W's" of newswriting. Given a choice among several events, class members could write a short news report that answers the questions Who? When? Where? What? and Why? Sometimes it is equally important to ask How? This type of activity shows children how to achieve brevity in certain forms of writing. It helps them to gain a greater appreciation for the people who gather and report the news to us.

2. An activity related to the DRTA described in the preceding chapter is to read stories to pupils and then stop at a point close to the ending but not close enough to give away the outcome. Students then write the ending they judge most plausible. When they are finished, their versions are compared to the actual ending of the original author.

3. Intermediate-grade pupils might also be encouraged to read to each other their attempts at writing dialogue. By comparing their efforts with actual transcripts of dialogue, students learn to appreciate the need to listen to others when trying to compose what would be judged good dialogue. These pieces of dialogue could be incorporated in dramatizations about famous people studied in social science or physical science.

4. Students who have completed a story or other written piece could be prompted the next day to look at what they have written. This fresh look might make students consider changing some words, particularly descriptive or action words, to tighten their writing somewhat. By eliminating such words as *said*, *make*, *nice*, and *interesting* sentences can be more succinctly worded.

HANDWRITING

In all writing activities, there is another area that needs attention. Especially in the lower grades, the students' ability to write *legibly* is important if others are to share in their products. Consequently, we now consider the teaching of handwriting in the elementary school.

Any teacher who analyzes the drawings of children in preschool through grade one can see the rudiments of handwriting. As the other skills we have discussed, this skill, too, develops over time. Children can illustrate stories which they previously dictated to the teacher. From these drawings, aware teachers can see when the basic strokes for beginning to write by hand are there. Before discussing some procedures for teaching handwriting, it would be well to delineate some objectives of such teaching.

Objectives

Those of you who have taken a typewriting course will find it easier to understand some of the objectives in teaching handwriting. Who ever enrolled in a typing course to become merely a fair typist? The goal of most people is to type well. That is to say, mastery is the purpose for beginning the lengthly exercises of the program.

With young children, some goals need to be stated so the children will know our expectations of them. Children should see handwriting as older students see typing, as a medium for expressing themselves in the most legible and efficient way possible. Handwriting should be taught with the ancillary goals in mind of neatness, durability, a sense of personal pride, and respect for the person who has to read what we have written. Using the little finger when beginning to type is awkward. So, too, children need to build the small muscles used in handwriting. Children's posture and the position of the writing instrument are not to be overlooked when teaching handwriting. Reaching these objectives involves keeping important considerations in mind before and during instruction.

Readiness

Readiness is to be considered in beginning handwriting as in beginning reading. The time established for handwriting should not be restricted to practice writing time. Handwriting should be incorporated into and integrated with other language-arts activities. Obviously, children need models; in handwriting, the teacher is usually the model children see more often than any other.

In time, more attention can be given to the ideas conveyed and less to the actual handwriting. There is no question that pupils can accumulate many stars on the tops of their papers. The question is why. Good handwriting should be its own reward; the student knows that the job has been done well. Ideas and thoughts can be presented more clearly by this means, and we owe that to the reader.

There are some signs that indicate when a child is ready to be instructed in handwriting. For example, it should be obvious when children can use crayons, scissors, and pencils for the purposes intended and with safety. There is the pride in writing one's own name which all writers enjoy.

A child using materials quickly reveals which hand is dominant. Finally, when children in their readiness-for-reading activities draw different shapes according to directions, they are not only building concepts, but also showing that they are ready to write by hand.

When children are ready to write and when they have the proper materials available, the next step to consider is the lesson itself. Ordinarily, pencils in the primary grades do not have erasers in order that children will be led to try the word again in its whole form. It is commonly held that ballpoint pens should not be used until grade three or later.

The Handwriting Lesson

Individualizing to the extent that children work at the level appropriate to their development is to be sought in handwriting, as well as in reading. The pencils and paper do not matter with second graders; what is important is their learning stage in handwriting. Some children will be forming their large loops and capitals correctly, and these children could be helped to write even more fluently. Other children might have some difficulty with writing smoothly, and these need to work as a group on forming letters. Other students have problems with the sizes of letters and need to concentrate on this aspect. And there are those who have enormous trouble with their coordination. In a class of children, there are bound to be distinct differences among handwriting abilities.

Teachers must be ingenious in introducing children to interesting ways of practicing their handwriting and not boring them. The commercial books we all came to dread need not be used without any purpose save skill development. Other possibilities include having children make their own name labels or picture captions, copy their own stories from the language-experience charts for inclusion in their books, and make signs. Children can write notes expressing thanks to the crossing guard, the principal, the teacher, aunts and uncles, or other supportive adults. Later, students can write announcements, make lists, write rosters, enter book titles in journals, copy stories and poems, and write to their parents and guardians at holiday and birthday time.

Manuscript and Cursive Writing

At some point, students must begin to make the transition from manuscript to cursive writing.

> This is an example of manuscript writing.
> This is an example of cursive writing.

Most of us tend to teach the way we were taught. There is the tradition of printing in the first two grades and then beginning to learn cursive writing at the end of grade two or the beginning of grade three. Often, the timing is dictated by the commercial materials we are using. It is interesting that adults often are overheard to say in admiration, "I wish I could print like that." It would be regrettable to lose this art form. Writers of fancy script are still in great demand. At times, it seems that manuscript should be used in all grades. People who have never changed to cursive achieve an obvious fluency and high speed in their own printing style. Nevertheless, there remains the traditional transition around grade three to cursive writing.

When to start children with cursive writing depends on their muscular coordination and overall handwriting maturity. Children who have a fair degree of rhythm in their writing, make no gross errors, and can read cursive writing are probably ready to learn cursive writing.

Left-Handedness

This question still plagues many teachers: Should a child be switched to the "right" way to write? Hand dominance can be determined by the teacher through some simple observations: Which hand does the child extend to accept a paper or book? Which hand is offered when pointing at distant objects? Which hand is used to comb the hair or hold a glass or a pair of scissors?

Once it is known that a child prefers the left hand, the most important thing is to avoid making an issue of it. Why call attention to this when you cannot and must not change it? There is nothing wrong with being left-handed. Some of the world's most successful people have been left-handed, including some of today's millionaire sports heroes!

There are some things which a teacher can do to help left-handed students develop legible writing. Allow these children more opportunities to use the board. Proceed more slowly on the transition from manuscript to a cursive script. By all means watch for correct posture. Often left-handed children contort in a way that could harm muscles. They distort their positions when writing. Left-handed writers should be encouraged to develop a slant that feels comfortable to them (4). Such a slant, if consistent, usually is quite legible in the long run. In time, left-handed writers should be encouraged to type, but that applies also to certain right-handed writers. Especially suited for third through sixth graders is Edward Fry's *Typing Course for Children* (Dreier Educational Systems). This program includes essential sight-vocabulary words, which often are needed by remedial students in the intermediate grades.

Whenever practical, students' efforts in handwriting should be related to their progress in all the language arts. What was said earlier about expressive writing activities can only be urged again; at the proper place and time, encourage students to write so that they can be read and understood.

SPELLING

Poor spelling, just as poor handwriting, can be a hindrance to progress in reading and in writing. Children should be encouraged to read widely to see how words are spelled.

There are several reasons for the existence of poor spellers. For instance, the teacher's handwriting can cause poor spelling in children. Also, an attitude that says good spelling is necessary should be conveyed by the teacher and other adults. Children may have to carry the burden of being poor spellers for a lifetime if it does not matter whether they spell words correctly.

There is a natural corollary to the ability to spell well. Good spellers use far more of the words in their speaking, reading, and listening vocabularies when it comes time for written expression. We all avoid writing words of which we are uncertain of the spelling, and mature writers use all kinds of strategies in this area. But what about children? Their usual strategy is to revert to stilted or flatly worded sentences.

Objectives

Good spelling is a sign that a student has a proper attitude toward work. Moreover, a planned program to teach spelling helps children become familiar with the alphabet. A good speller can partition words more readily when writing and knows how to use the diacritical marks in dictionary entries to figure out the pronunciation of a new word. Students can gradually come to understand some of the basic principles of correct spelling and can apply them to new words. Experience and practice lead to good spellers becoming good proofreaders. Such students also know strategies for mastering the spelling of unusual words.

Readiness

Readiness matters in spelling as much as in handwriting. Sensitive teachers look for signs that a child is ready to study spelling. A child who is not ready may develop a great aversion to spelling and much harm might result. The child may begin to hate school. There is little doubt that reading problems can be related to problems with spelling in the early grades.

To be ready for spelling instruction, children must be able to discriminate words visually and auditorially. Pupils also should have mastered the alphabet and should be able to write. The teacher can also judge whether a pupil is interested in learning how to spell.

The Content of Spelling

A common question from teachers is, "What spelling words should be taught?" If a commercial program is followed, the question is merely academic. If teachers wish to devise their own spelling program, the question is quite germane. Certainly, word lists are available and could be used for this purpose. An intriguing question arises with respect to lists of the most frequently used words: Is it necessary to include these words in spelling lessons? Perhaps just words with unusual spellings should be included, such as *enough*, *does*, and *about*, while omitting such words as *have*, *little*, and *make*. There is also the consideration of the later utility of spelling words. It seems senseless to learn words we probably will rarely encounter, or at least they should not be emphasized. A handy source both for spelling words and for words to be used in writing is a list contained in a book which resulted from a computer-aided study by Harris and Jacobson to determine word frequency (8). Some teachers prefer not to use a commercial speller and instead use words from the children's own writing. There is nothing wrong with using words from this source, as long as they are interesting words that will function for children later on.

The Spelling Lesson

Most teachers recall that Friday was spelling day when they were students. Either there was a test on the week's words or there was a spelling bee. Typically, twenty words were introduced during the week and reviewed in various ways before Friday's test. The problem with this procedure is the predictability. Children, as all learners, need a variety of activities.

It is a denial of what we know about individual differences to teach a whole class a prescribed number of words each week. By seeing how many words can be taught by sight, by grouping graphically similar words, and by teaching words in a variety of ways, a teacher should be able to judge how individual students learn best. Lessons need to be arranged accordingly.

It is important in teaching spelling that children be able to hear and see the word and to pronounce it several times correctly. Some learners concentrate better with their eyes closed; some learn faster by saying words aloud; others learn best by tracing words on paper or writing them several times. Writing words should not be a punishment, however.

Not all of us learn in the same way. Teaching in only one mode is, therefore, poor pedagogy. Some words are bound to be demons for many learners and should be stressed. For example, some irregular words need to be taught with the part usually misspelled in capital letters. In other cases, mnemonic devices can help: "Every *secret*ary should be able to keep a secret." "The princi*pal* is your *pal*."

Spelling lessons should be relatively short, perhaps no more than fifteen minutes, since often the attention span of youngsters will not be equal to much more time than this. Some teachers use a linguistic approach to spelling instruction, which develops spelling power by presenting words in patterns. Whenever feasible, the teacher should write the word on the board for all to see. Spelling is often a matter of incidental learning, and teachers should take advantage of the teachable moment.

Spelling Rules

The practicality of spelling rules, like that of phonic rules, is being questioned more and more. The reason is that there are so many exceptions to spelling rules. One thing is clear: if such rules are taught, they should be taught inductively. Children should be allowed time to figure out a rule after spelling several words that exemplify it. Rules should be introduced cautiously, and it is only fair to let students know that there are exceptions to every rule. Being able to apply a rule in doubtful cases is more important than being able to quote the rule at high speed. Some rules can be very helpful and are worth knowing, as many teachers will attest to from experience. Some of these are:

1. The letter *q* is always followed by *u*.
2. When you add a suffix beginning with a vowel to a word ending with an *e* drop the *e*.
3. Words ending in consonant +*y* change the *y* to *i* before adding suffixes (except suffixes that start with *i*).
4. *i* before *e* except after *c* unless *ei* is pronounced "aye."
5. When adding a suffix to a one-syllable word ending with a consonant, double the consonant. In the case of a two-syllable word ending with a vowel and a consonant and having the last syllable accented, also double the consonant.

Spelling Demons

Lists have been constructed of the most troublesome words to spell. What is rarely pointed out, as Greene and Petty indicate (7), is what to do about such words. Some of them are misspelled frequently because there is no regular phoneme-grapheme correspondence. This can be seen in the words *again* (try pronouncing it with *gain* emphasized), *because*, and *heard*. These words simply are not consistent with the expected sound-symbol correspondence, and they must be taught individually and repeatedly. Other groups of words, such as *there*, *their*, and *they're*, are spelled better if their meanings are taught, preferably with the help of pictures. Other words are troublesome because the rules do not apply. (for example, *sometimes* and *I'm*). Still other words are misspelled because they are misprounounced. (for example, *February* and *library*). We spoke earlier of some ways to highlight such words so that pupils can learn them more readily.

Spelling instruction can be tedious for children. For that reason, the use of commercial games often tends to lessen the burden on both teachers and students. However, the teacher must still teach spelling as a skill that facilitates writing.

Spelling and Reading

We can never know precisely how children learn to read or to spell. One thing we do know is that practice can promote skill both in reading and in spelling. Learners master material in many different ways. Some learn well when there is a lack of pressure to learn, and this is an advantage of incidental learning.

Vocabularies increase with exposure to new words. It is hoped that, in time, not only will students learn new words, but they will be able to spell those words as well as use them in writing and speaking.

FLUENCY AND FLEXIBILITY IN READING

It is common knowledge that expensive speed-reading courses are widely offered. Advertisements for such courses are directed at students in high schools and colleges, as well as at business executives. We feel that such courses would hardly be necessary if we could demonstrate the relative unimportance of speed reading. The problem, it seems, really takes root in the middle grades and beyond, where little if anything is done to develop fluent, flexible, and rapid readers.

There are reasons why children do not learn to read as they should. An overreliance on phonics instruction by the teacher can often make an individual a word-by-word reader, a habit that can persist for the person's entire life. A slow rate of reading can also result from children's being exposed to too much oral reading. In most classrooms, little time is devoted to instruction in how to vary the rate of reading. Children often fail to understand the real purpose for reading what they are asked to read, so they tend to read everything in the same manner. There can be no hope for flexibility in reading if the purpose of reading is not understood.

What are some reasonable goals for which teachers and children can strive when attempting to address the problem of inadequate rates of reading? It should be stressed that teacher expectations often play a crucial role, so teachers should be careful to set fair challenges for children. Harris and Sipay list median rates of reading for elementary grades as determined by several standardized reading tests (9). Teachers can aim for these rates when trying to assist slow readers.

GRADE	RATE OF SILENT READING (words per minute)
1	—
2	86
3	116
4	155
5	177
6	206

It must be stressed that nothing has yet been said about comprehension. However, it is probably true that in the middle grades, time should be spent on helping children improve their rate of oral and silent reading. Children should become proficient in both types of reading. Later, it will be necessary to look more carefully at what happens to students' comprehension of material as a result of increasing their rate of reading.

Improving Reading Rates

You will notice that *reading rates* is plural. The idea of a reading rate, even expressed in words per minute, can make no sense in isolation. Table 7-1 shows how reading rates vary according to the purposes of reading and the type of material.

At the elementary level, rate improvement does not just happen. It requires knowledge on the part of the teacher and training on the part of students. As you can see in Table 7-1 the rates vary greatly, depending on the goal set by the reader *before starting the assignment*. This is where it is critical for the teacher to state the goal clearly, so the children can adjust their rate accordingly.

It is also important that comprehension not be ignored for the sake of speed reading. However, there are times when children should be allowed to practice at extremely high rates of reading. This is part of training readers to read at times in one manner and at other times in a different way.

Probably the major task of any training in rate improvement with children is not to instill tension during the process. The teacher should give clear directions and clearly state the purpose of the task at hand. With wisely chosen materials, children will gradually perceive how and why reading rates differ.

The teacher selecting material with which to work must consider not only the difficulty of the material, but also the children's familiarity with the topic. Youngsters in Omaha may not be too well versed in subway systems, while children in Philadelphia are not very well acquainted with annual harvests or sheep shearing. A balance can be struck, using materials of different interests and reading levels, that will closely approximate the real world of children.

TABLE 7-1 Different Reading Rates

RATE	PURPOSES	TYPES OF MATERIALS
1. Scanning (1,500 wpm*)	To locate information	Directory, dictionary, or any other material which will give a specific answer.
2. Skimming (1,000 wpm)	To get overview and raise questions; to skim for main idea; to find out what happens next	Study material, difficult material, material that the reader must organize, textbooks
3. Speeded reading (400 to 600 wpm)	To read rapidly for details or main ideas	Any material from which main ideas and supporting facts are to be gleaned— newspapers, magazines, stories, easy texts, and so on
4. Study reading (250 wpm)	To read with maximum understanding; to apply SQ3R principles	Textbooks, technical articles, or any other material which is read in detail and is to be organized and presented to others
5. Careful and reflective reading (74 wpm)	To follow directions; to reflect on content; to evaluate; to enjoy; to read aloud and share an esthetic experience	Directions; profound or complicated materials; reports of current events; editorial pages; poetry, drama or anything else read orally

*Words per minute. These are rough estimates and will vary from reader to reader, depending upon the reader's familiarity with the material.

The Purposes of Reading

In the initial phases, the teacher should prepare children for increasing their rates by selecting materials which can be used to teach the skills of skimming and scanning. Later, study reading will be the focus. It is important to know the difference between skimming and scanning. Many teachers confuse these terms or use them interchangeably. It might help to think of skimming as a skill used when we are trying to get the gist of a selection, looking for the main idea (MI): skimMIng.

Another common purpose for reading is to find a particular point of information. For example, we might need a phone number or the date of the discovery of a country or the name of the representative from Connecticut who signed the Declaration of Independence. In seeking this type of information, we are scAnnING for a fact, A thING. The objective is usually singular. The way we scan a directory or an index is not the same as the way we survey an entire story to get a general impression.

Study reading has quite another purpose. It is most regrettable that commercial speed-reading courses give the impression that textbooks can be read with speed. That is not true, except for those already extremely proficient in the field of study. If you doubt this, try reading an advanced college physics book at several hundred words per minute. Students should realize that textbook reading is slow and often difficult. This is not to say, however, that there are not ways for them to read their text materials more efficiently. More will be said in the last section of this chapter about study skills.

Teachers cannot offer an entire speed-reading course in the elementary school; there are nevertheless many things a teacher can do to insure that children become efficient readers, where efficiency includes the ability to read at varying rates.

Flexibility

We have been talking in the preceding paragraphs about flexibility, or the ability to adjust one's reading rate to the difficulty of the materials and the purpose for reading. Braam (2) showed that although high school students are generally inflexible readers, they can be trained to become highly flexible readers with the right practice and good teaching. Flexibility must be acquired through practice. It does not come easily, and the concept in itself means nothing to a learner. It must be taught by a teacher who understands the reading and studying processes. At the elementary level, it probably is not prudent to emphasize speed reading. It does make sense, however, for the teacher gradually to begin using some sensible strategies for helping pupils to develop flexibility.

Activities for Improving Reading Rates

There are many kinds of activities that help students become more fluent, flexible, and rapid readers. In addition to the suggestions offered below, you may wish to consider those presented in *Mangieri and Baldwin* (10).

1. Use easy material at first, so that students are not unduly threatened by the difficulty. Use this material for timed practices.
2. Always keep charts for students to use, so they can see their progress in a concrete way.
3. Use dictionaries, encyclopedias, atlases, telephone directories, and the like to demonstrate and practice scanning.
4. Have one group of students skim a fairly long story for descriptions of characters. Another group skims the story for descriptions of settings. The last group skims for information about the plot. Give the children a reasonable time to complete this exercise, and then elicit the total group's response to the question of whether this story is one they would like to read or have read to them.
5. Prepare a set of warm-up exercises for increasing rates. A quick per-

ceptual exercise is to have children scan a list of words to find and circle the ones that are the same as the word at the head of the list.

6.   Time students while they find and circle the "glad" words or the "bad" words in a selection. (See the section "Critical Reading" in Chapter 4.) Ask yourself what impact these words have in the entire article or story?

7.   Read a statement to the class; then have them read a passage quickly (skim) to determine whether the statement is supported by the passage.

8.   Conduct weekly timed exercises on short selections, and have pupils maintain charts of their progress. Do this regularly over the course of the entire school year. This low-key approach is probably just as effective as any speed-reading course.

The main difficulty with most speed-reading courses for adolescents and adults is that of replacing old reading habits with new ones. It is reasonable to suggest that proper training in the earlier grades might make commercial courses unnecessary. The same is true of programs to assist learners in adopting new study habits. These habits should have been properly emphasized in the early years.

STUDY SKILLS

In the elementary school our purpose is to build new skills that will last a lifetime. Children learn the basics. They learn to expand their vocabularies; they learn to understand written materials better. One hopes that children will learn to read at acceptable rates, so they can read more. These basic skills can be used in subjects other than reading itself. It must be emphasized that children need to *use* study skills, especially if they are to be efficient learners in the years ahead of them. Our attention now turns to study skills which are used both at school and at home.

Readiness

To many, the word *readiness* suggests the results of some kind of instruction which children receive in kindergarten or first grade. We are using the term in a broader context: children and learners at all levels may or may not be ready for instruction in a particular skill or subject. For example, a fifth grader would have difficulty with schematic maps if the topic of maps in general had never been discussed in any previous class. In this case, the child is not ready. Some schemas for the development of study skills seem to suggest that the place to begin instruction is in grade three or beyond. We do not agree wholly with this view. Rather, we prefer to refer again to the idea of the teachable moment. It is true that teachers are already overburdened in the primary grades by the conglomeration of what should be taught and read to and written and spoken by children. It is certain, however, that there are many situations when it is simply good practice to teach children as the opportunity arises. Children's questions often can be starting points for impromptu lessons on study skills. This is another way of saying that it is not possible to state at what grade level certain study skills should be introduced and taught. We do know that once taught, study skills must be used, or they will have to be taught again.

What Are Study Skills?

The whole purpose of teaching study skills is to help the student become an independent learner. Teachers who do not help children achieve this goal probably prefer dependent learners. That desire is highly questionable. Ultimately, learners will be on their own and will not have the teacher as a resource.

In the primary grades, the following study skills are significant and should be taught:

Alphabetizing

Using a table of contents

Using the other parts of a text

Handling books correctly

Using the headings within chapters

In the intermediate grades, the following skills should be added:

Using side headings for outline development

Using guide words in key resource materials

Understanding the organization of encyclopedias

Using the card system to find books in a library

Reading and interpreting maps, charts, graphs, and so on

Cross-referencing what is read in one source

One way to help learners become independent is to assist them in setting their own purposes for reading. Though reading specialists have long used the SQ3R strategy for study reading (Survey, Question, Read, Recite, and Review), this technique is too difficult for most students. As an alternative, perhaps, the teacher could ask leading questions to guide the children's reading. Again, however, there is the problem of the learners being dependent on the teacher. Another possibility is to use selections which lend themselves to showing students how to read with a purpose. Children can be shown how to criticize, compare, discuss, solve, describe, explain, contrast, list, and evaluate. Gradually the children can begin to set their own purposes for reading.

Teaching Study Skills

It is important to consider content-area reading when instructing in reading rate, vocabulary, critical reading, and study skills. A logical focus is the content-area textbook. Any such text will contain a great amount of graphic materials, including maps, charts, diagrams, photographs, drawings, and tables. However, it is impossible simultaneously to teach children how to interpret all these items. In this case, a reasonable procedure is to analyze the entire series of content texts which your children have to read. Then, a given skill can be taught at a time when it is needed in another subject. For example, a teacher might decide to spend two weeks in October teaching how to use maps. Transferring skills from reading class to other subject classes is sorely neglected in most classrooms. The real test of student's ability to use their study skills comes in the subject areas, especially if the students are working on study units or assignments which require the use of the library.

It is far too common to hear students receiving the WHAT of an assignment but not the WHY or the HOW. Teaching can be so much more rewarding when we do not engage in guessing games with learners.

Activities for Teaching Study Skills

There are many opportunities to teach study skills in ways that help pupils become independent learners. Some useful activities for this purpose are described in the following paragraphs:

1. Give the class a list of sentences about subjects that can be looked up in encyclopedias or other reference works. Have them circle the key words in the sentences. Check the reference work immediately to see if there are any problems with this activity.
2. Write a humorous account in phonetic transcription. Give context clues so that learners are not too frustrated. Then refer students to the dictionary so they can see how the phonetic symbols are used in that source.
3. Take a long piece of wood and mark it off in thirds, i.e., A-H, I-P, and Q-Z. Use this to help students alphabetize key words by thirds of the alphabet. Use first-, second-, or third-letter alphabetizing, depending on the level of the learners.
4. Have students look up a few words in a glossary and compare their findings with the dictionary definitions for these words.
5. Have students combine skimming and scanning with study reading by converting chapter headings into questions and then reading to find the answers.
6. Have students make a partial outline of a content-area textbook chapter and complete it by using mainly the subheadings.
7. Assign pairs of students to consult different encyclopedias on the

same topics. Have these pairs of students report in class on their findings.

8. Provide the class with an essay test question and then a model answer. Have students make up questions of their own, based on text reading. Assist them in developing answers for their questions.

9. Have students bring to class a list of teams from the newspaper—such as hockey, basketball, or tennis teams. Then have students pin a flag on a map of the United States for each city or area represented. Discuss the implications this has for travel arrangements, scheduling of events, and players' time away from home.

10. Show students a completed outline of part of a chapter of a textbook. Present the same information first in the form of a series of bubbles around a core item and then as a hierarchy of three layers of ideas. What is the point of outlining? How do these ways of presenting information differ? How are they alike?

SUMMARY

In this chapter, the integration of reading and the other language arts was highlighted. The richness of children's oral language was seen as the basis for many activities employed in the classroom. Activities incorporating children's written expression were also featured.

Handwriting was discussed with respect to readiness, teaching a lesson, types of writing, and left-handedness. Spelling was also considered with respect to readiness, content, and teaching a lesson.

The role which fluency and flexibility play, especially beyond the primary grades, was stressed. A discussion of significant study skills and related activities completed this section dealing with specific instructional techniques.

ACTIVITIES RELATED TO THE CHAPTER

1. Taking the suggestions in this chapter and in Chapter 5, set up a creative-writing corner for an elementary classroom. Check some of the references for additional ideas for your center.

2. Develop a miniunit on puppetry which could actually be used with children. Select several scripts, and determine the puppet characters you will need. What are some possibilities for getting help in making the puppets?

3. Get some samples of children's writing, and group children with similar difficulties in handwriting. Do the same for spelling problems.

4. Read a few selections or tell a story to a group of children, and tape your reading. At a later time, analyze your performance.

5. Contact a local library and find out when and where a professional librarian will conduct a story hour for children. Try to attend a few of these sessions. What do you observe about the children? About the storyteller?

6. Take any two content-area textbooks for a grade level you are interested in

teaching. Consider these texts with respect to the study skills needed by readers. What conclusions do you draw as to how such needs might be filled?

7. Accumulate a file of good reading selections to augment classroom materials. Your purpose is to find suitable materials for helping students to develop fluency in oral reading. Other materials should be gathered for practice in skimming and scanning.

BIBLIOGRAPHY AND REFERENCES

1. Bamman, Henry A., Mildred Dawson and Robert Whitehead: *Oral Interpretation of Children's Literature*, Wm. C. Brown, Dubuque, Iowa, 1964.
2. Braam, Leonard S.: "Developing and Measuring Flexibility in Reading," *The Reading Teacher*, 16:247–251 (1963).
3. Burns, Paul C., and Betty L. Broman: *The Language Arts in Childhood Education*, 3rd ed., Rand McNally, Chicago, 1975.
4. Drummond, Harold: "Suggestions for the 'Lefties,'" *The National Elementary School Principal*, 38 (5):15 (1957).
5. Durkin, Dolores: *Teaching Them to Read*, 2nd ed., Allyn and Bacon, Boston, 1974.
6. Greene, Frank P.: "HIP: High Intensity Practice," Syracuse Univ. Reading Clinic, Mimeographed, Syracuse, NY, 1970.
7. Greene, Harry A. and Walter T. Petty: *Developing Language Skills in the Elementary Schools*, 4th ed., Allyn and Bacon, Boston, 1971, pp. 416–417.
8. Harris, Albert J., and Milton D. Jacobson: *Basic Elementary Reading Vocabularies*, Macmillan, New York, 1972.
9. Harris, Albert J., and Edward R. Sipay: *How to Increase Reading Ability*, 6th ed., McKay, New York, 1975.
10. Mangieri, John N., and R. Scott Baldwin: *Effective Reading Techniques*, Carfield Press, San Francisco, 1978, chap. 4.

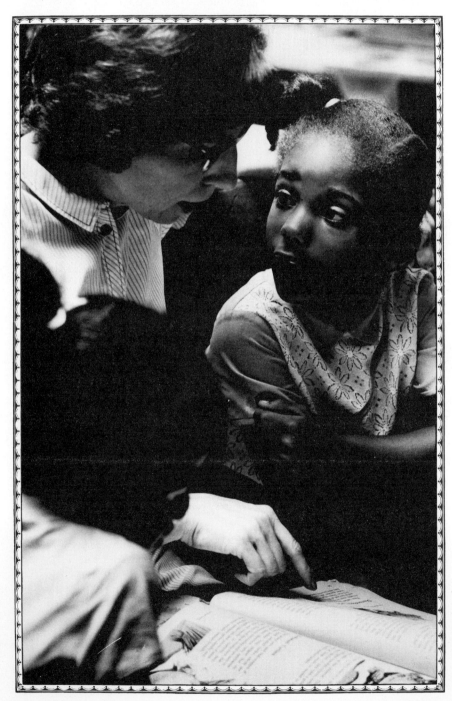

Assessment of Reading and Reading-Related Abilities

8

Overview

Assessment is important for several reasons. Teachers need information on each student's achievement levels, need for instruction in specific skills, interests, and attitudes so that they can plan appropriately. Parents need to know whether their children are progressing satisfactorily, and children need to know what they need to learn and how they are progressing. Administrators and school board members need information on achievement so that they can appropriately allocate resources.

This chapter describes procedures for collecting, organizing, and using data on reading and reading-related abilities.

Definition of Terms

1. *Conceptual background*—the concepts and ideas acquired by the learner prior to engaging in formal instruction.
2. *Criterion-referenced tests*—tests which use performance of specific tasks to reveal levels of mastery.
3. *Expressive vocabulary*—the words used in speaking and writing.
4. *Formal assessment*—using standardized tests to decide which children should use which basal readers and other multileveled materials.
5. *Frustration level*—the reading level at which the learner's reading skills are insufficient: fluency is lacking, there are frequent word-recognition errors, recall and comprehension are faulty, and discomfort and emotional tension are exhibited.
6. *Independent level*—the highest reading level at which a learner reads fluently and easily, with few recognition errors and good recall and comprehension.
7. *Informal assessment*—using teacher-made tests, interviews, and classroom observations for evaluation of student reading abilities.

8. *Informal reading inventory (IRI)*—an instrument for testing comprehension in which students read and respond to questions on a series of graded paragraphs.

9. *Instructional level*—the highest reading level at which a learner can read, given appropriate preparation and given direction by the teacher; word-recognition errors are not numerous, and recall and comprehension are satisfactory.

10. *Receptive vocabulary*—the words understood when heard or read.

tandardized testing is more and more being questioned in our classrooms. We need to understand the role of testing, the types of tests, and the part that classroom observation plays in this process. Our discussion begins with the distinctions between formal and informal assessment.

FORMAL AND INFORMAL ASSESSMENT

Standardized tests are used in formal assessment, and teacher-made tests and classroom observations are used in informal assessment. Both forms of evaluation have a place in school programs.

Formal Assessment

Group standardized tests are usually scaled on the basis of large numbers of children, so they are useful in making comparisons about reading achievement between a group of children in a particular school and the group on which the test was scaled. Group tests may also be used for screening purposes. Children who do poorly can be tested individually. Here are some important things to remember about using standardized tests:

1. The tests should measure skills related to achieving the objectives of the reading program.
2. The tests should be valid and reliable. (See Buros (5) and various indexes for *The Reading Teacher, Journal of Reading,* and *Reading World.*)
3. The tests should never be used as the sole means of establishing a child's ability in reading.
4. The test grade-equivalence score may not be appropriate for placing children in graded materials, because the test score may be somewhat inflated.

Criterion-referenced tests have become more widely known in the last ten years. These tests are not standardized by test makers seeking to determine how large numbers of children perform on the set of items in the instrument. Rather, tasks are devised to show whether children have mastered specified objectives. For example:

Objective—Given a list of eight one-syllable words containing the *ack* phonogram, the child should correctly pronounce at least six.

Criterion-referenced task—The child reads eight such words aloud—for instance, *back*, *lack*, *snack*, *pack*, *sack*, *tack*, *rack*, *track*.

As the example indicates, criterion-referenced tests specify which tasks indicate which levels of mastery. These tests are appealing to those who believe that reading can be analyzed into numerous tasks that can be developed and sequenced (and sold!) as a so-called system. Fry indicates a need for caution in using criterion-referenced tests (8). He believes that a specific order of learning makes sense in a curriculum area such as mathematics, where "mastery of lower units is necessary to master upper units." However, such a method works "rather poorly for other areas of the curriculum, such as appreciating literature, writing creative stories, or using . . . critical reading skills . . . ."

Testing every sound-letter association and large numbers of phonograms and keeping records for each child, uses a tremendous amount of time that could be devoted to instruction. Furthermore, this approach lends itself to testing and drill in isolation. Some children who can read fail isolated skill tests, and some who cannot read pass them. Because of the complex nature of the reading process, one cannot assume that performance on associative tasks in isolation is necessarily indicative of reading ability. Harris, in his research into the use of criterion-referenced tests (10), states: "Some sets of CR tests appear to measure so many separate skills that one wonders if all are really necessary for learning to read, and if all are of equal importance. . . . Some writers question whether CR tests can adequately measure such complex domains as reading comprehension."

In purchasing or constructing criterion-referenced tests, the following considerations are important:

1. Broader, more inclusive, objectives and test items are preferable to those that are constructed for each possible association.
2. It is better to keep careful records on a few important objectives rather than keeping records on a large number of objectives whose value is uncertain.
3. Tests of word recognition in isolation must be supplemented by tests that use context.
4. Tests should correspond to the reading program, not dictate it.

Standardized, or formal, tests can yield useful information to teachers who understand the proper uses and limitations of group tests. Although they are useful as screening devices, criterion-referenced tests are not designed to be diagnostic instruments or to specify placement or promotion.

These tests can be utilized to determine which children need further testing and can provide information on school or citywide performance. It is well for teachers to remember that a child's performance on standardized tests does not always correspond with the child's classroom performance. For example, a test which does not take account of the teacher's goals in reading will not be a true indicator of the child's performance in the classroom. The teacher's and child's attitudes toward group testing, as well as the child's sophistication in guessing the correct answer without real knowledge or skill, affect the child's performance on the test but do not necessarily relate to reading skills.

Informal Assessment

Informal assessment is a continuous process with an alert and knowledgeable teacher. Mike is observed skipping most multisyllabic words; Jim seems to enjoy figuring them out. Jim covers the affixes with his fingers to find the root word, pronounces the entire word softly, checks with the context of the sentence and says to himself, "yeah, that fits." Day to day observations, such as these with Mike and Jim are important and should not be discounted. Professionals in other fields—speech, audiology, psychology—are giving more attention to the behavior of individuals in their daily activities rather than depending on information obtained under formal test conditions.

In addition to making ongoing observations, teachers need to assess their students' abilities with regard to specified objectives. If the curriculum guide for a particular grade level or the manual for a basal the teacher is using as a guide, lists the development of dictionary skills as an objective, children should be tested to find out whether they already possess those skills. Each child might be given a dictionary and a list of words and asked to write down the page number where each word is found. The teacher can observe the group while this is done to note which children take an excessive amount of time. Other abilities related to dictionary skills can be tested in a similar fashion. Children who are successful will not require the dictionary lessons. This may seem obvious, but instructing children in areas where they are competent and requiring them to practice skills in which they are proficient are fairly common practices.

Another kind of assessment looks at enabling skills or concepts. A child who is unable to find words in a dictionary may be unaware that the words are listed alphabetically, or he may not know the alphabet. We have known adults who could not use dictionaries for these reasons. The moral? Do not take things for granted. Do not make unwarranted assumptions when teaching. Ask, "What does the learner have to know, or be able to do, to complete this task?" Then, test for these enabling abilities.

Informal assessment for the purpose of placing children in basals or other multileveled materials is as important as the testing of specific skills, if not more so. Children given materials on a level that is comfortable for them will be much more likely to develop necessary skills and to acquire fluency, which will increase their comprehension and enjoyment. The following suggestions are offered for your consideration:

1. Assessment for materials placement should include graded-paragraph testing of oral and silent reading and of listening comprehension.
2. Placement decisions should be open to adjustment after observation of children's responses to the difficulty of the material.
3. Children should be placed in two levels of material: an independent level with very easy material to build fluency and confidence and an instructional, or teacher-directed, level to increase word-recognition and comprehension abilities.

ASSESSMENT OF READING-RELATED ABILITIES

Language Development

Children speaking and listening give teachers their first clues concerning the children's abilities and feelings. Some of these abilities seem to be closely related to reading and some seem not to be, as you will recall from the discussion of language development in Chapter 2.

Receptive and Expressive Vocabulary

Generally, teachers can use their knowledge of language development to rule out certain explanations for some reading problems, but they cannot necessarily establish that a reading problem exists because of oral-language deficiencies. For example, Barbara, a fifth grade student, said, "When the mother country tried to increase tax revenues, she met with resistance in the colonies." To discover whether Barbara understood what she was saying and was not just repeating what she had heard, her teacher asked, "Can you say that in other words?" Barbara replied, "Well, England wanted people in the colonies to pay more taxes and they refused." Barbara had an excellent vocabulary, which is an important factor in reading comprehension. However, she often had difficulty in recalling information from her reading assignments. Her teacher quickly ruled out a vocabulary problem. Further investigation revealed that Barbara was inclined to read everything very fast and omit parts that were not interesting.

Richie and Mary were different from Barbara in that their speaking vocabularies seemed quite limited. They, too, had difficulty in recalling what they read. On a vocabulary-matching task that the teacher devised, Richie did very well, but Mary had a great deal of difficulty. On tasks requiring Richie to write definitions in his own words, he did poorly. Eventually, the teacher discovered that Richie's *expressive vocabulary* in speaking and writing was limited in comparison with his peers, but his *receptive vocabulary* was adequate and was therefore not the cause of his comprehension difficulty. Mary, however, was found to have a poor receptive vocabulary in listening and in reading. Richie needed help in using the words he knew when listening or reading; Mary needed help in learning the meaning of words she heard and saw. Ruling out vocabulary problems was fairly simple in Barbara's case, but more probing was required in assessing Richie and Mary's vocabulary.

	RECEPTIVE VOCABULARY	EXPRESSIVE VOCABULARY
Barbara	OK	OK
Richie	OK	Needs help
Mary	Needs help	Needs help

Guszak (9), in his article on measuring student understanding of written materials, analyzes several techniques which could be employed by the teacher. His discussion gives insight into the standard procedures for measuring such qualities as literal comprehension, ability to reorganize information, inferential comprehension, and ability to evaluate. He keeps a critical eye on how such measurements are conducted.

Oral Reading

Reading aloud is another aspect of oral-language expression troubling to some teachers, children, and parents. One second grader said he wasn't "good in reading" and, when asked why, said he didn't "read with expression." The child's lack of expression in reading might have been related to comprehension; however, some children who read aloud in a monotonous tone have excellent comprehension, while others do not. In the example, the child in fact did comprehend well; he read aloud in a toneless fashion because he was somewhat shy. On the student's report card "reads with expression" was listed. Why? It might have been taken from a checklist of reading behaviors on published oral-reading tests, or it might have been an objective of the language arts program. Inexpressive reading should not be mindlessly accepted as evidence that a child cannot read and comprehend well. As one youngster said, "When I read out loud, sometimes I spit and sputter, but I know what I'm reading." However, some children read in a halting, word-by-word, monotonous fashion because they don't comprehend or are struggling with word identification. In these cases, such reading indicates a need for further checking. The teacher might ask the child to read silently and then talk about, respond to questions about, or pick out true statements about what was read. The teacher should also keep in mind that those who do read with expression are not necessarily attending closely to what they are reading. Many adults have told of reading aloud for lengthy periods of time and using suitable inflection, pace, and stress, without a conscious awareness of meaning. One child said in response to questioning after oral reading, "I don't know; I wasn't listening to me."

Hearing Speech Sounds

Attempting to teach a child letter-sound associations when he cannot discriminate the individual sounds (phonemes) does not make sense; yet it happens, possibly because all children are assumed to have adequate auditory discrimination abilities. Generally, teachers test children for auditory disabilities by having them listen to pairs of words and tell if the words are the same or different. Examples of such pairs are *hat*, *bat*; *rake*, *lake*; *bid*, *bed*; *lap*, *lad*; *with*, *wish*; and *pin*, *pen*. Some pairs differ in the middle sound, others differ in the initial or final sound. If children are successful in this task, they should be tested on their ability to segment words phonemically. For example, they are shown pictures of a hat, a cat, and a bat and asked to point to or circle the picture whose name starts with the sound of the letter *k*. One should be careful to note whether the children know the names of the objects or actions pictured and whether they have the concepts denoted by such words as *same*, *different*, *beginning*, *middle*, and *end*, which are used in test directions. Next, dialect needs to be considered. Some children may pronounce and hear *pin* and *pen* in the same way because of their particular language background, but overall their sound-discrimination abilities may be quite good.

If vocabulary, test directions, and dialect are ruled out as causes of discrimination difficulties, other factors should be considered, such as a possible hearing loss, inexperience, or a perceptual problem. Sometimes children with hearing losses are undetected in a mass screening; therefore, a teacher should not hesitate to ask the speech therapist or school nurse to retest those children who have symptoms of an auditory acuity problem. If acuity is ruled out as a problem, the difficulty may be due to a lack of experience in attending to fine sound differences. In these cases an extended auditory readiness program may be helpful. Problems in auditory perception are difficult to diagnose. One hesitates to have a teacher or a psychologist assume the role of a neurologist. Generally, if all of the preceding factors have been tested and found not to be related to the child's inability to make fine sound discriminations, and if the child has not responded to instruction in auditory discrimination, the best course is to emphasize whole words and avoid a letter-sound approach to instruction.

Speech Difficulties

Children who stutter frequently, those with poor articulation, and those who use immature sentence patterns may need to be referred to a speech therapist. Exception should be made for children who are likely to overcome a temporary condition such as the absence of front teeth. There is no need to fill the speech therapist's office with happy lispers saying, "Thee the thurprithe I got from the tooth fairy!"

Oral Language Expression

Some children use language described as immature—that is, typical of oral expression at an earlier age. *I are ready* and *me want drink* are examples. This problem may result from an emotional factor such as competition with a younger sibling. Other atypical forms of language expression may result from learning English as a second language or from using a regional dialect. In all cases, children need acceptance and appropriate help, but the question faced by the teacher is whether a child with atypical oral expression requires special kinds of reading instruction. Generally, if children have an adequate comprehension of standard spoken English, they should be able to learn to comprehend standard printed English, even if they deviate in their speech from the standard English spoken by students of their own age. Therefore, teachers need to assess auditory comprehension of sentences and short passages. They may note how children respond to an oral direction such as, "Please put your pencil on your desk and take the lid off the paste." In addition, the teacher may read to the child and then ask the child to respond to questions. If the child understands what he hears, he can participate in the regular reading program. Children who cannot comprehend the language used in instruction need special programs or support. Care needs to be taken to distinguish between children with nonstandard oral expression who understand what they hear and those who do not. In other words, auditory comprehension is the key.

Written Language Expression

To some extent, the foregoing discussion of oral language expression also applies to written oral expression. A child may be able to read well but not write well. However, poor writing could indicate a problem in reading comprehension such as an inability to recognize a writer's organization, purpose, or main idea or an inability to comprehend complex sentence patterns.

The spelling of those in the beginning stages of reading reveals their knowledge of sound-letter associations and of phonics, as well as any problems of visual and auditory acuity and perception. Consider the following:

1. Certain words are spelled phonetically *(hit, fed, map, wish)*.
2. Some words are spelled with silent letters *(bite, wait, light, often)*.
3. Other words illustrate spelling rules *(stopped, coming, cookies, finally)*.

Children who spell correctly words in the first category demonstrate knowledge of sound-letter associations. Spelling correctly words in the second category indicates visual recall of word forms. Knowledge of common spelling conventions, or rules, is shown by correct spelling of words in the third group. Much can be learned by analyzing errors. A child who writes *cattle* as *katel* needs assistance but has demonstrated the ability to hear fine sound differences, a knowledge of letter sounds, and the ability to put letters in sequence. However, if *cattle* had been written as *gmi*, these abilities would not have been demonstrated. This is the kind of analysis teachers need to do as they examine the writings of children and plan instruction.

However, competence in spelling does perfectly correlate with reading ability. Readers use a combination of context and configuration to process print rapidly. They do not examine words in a letter-by-letter fashion and may have a poor visual memory for detail and may lack knowledge of common rules. A good reader may be a poor speller and vice versa.

Conceptual Background

Many of us take for granted the ideas about language and the ability to do school tasks that we have acquired. Young children and older students with reading difficulties may not have acquired some important concepts. However, children can make ingenious generalizations. One child reported problems with his *remembery*, another reported that her father had gone to *His*-ami (not *My*-ami).

Language Concepts Related to Reading

Language is abstract in that words are used to represent things and ideas. When we use an abstraction (language) to talk about an abstraction (language), we have moved to a very difficult level of understanding. This helps to explain why children can listen to the first-grade teacher talk about words for an entire school year and not have the concept of a word as a language unit with boundaries that represents an idea. In addition, some children may have the concept of word boundaries, but may not hear the boundaries. For example, one child thought *djeetjet? (did you eat yet?)* was a single word because she did not hear the phrase pronounced clearly. A teacher can informally assess children's knowledge of such language concepts by asking such questions as "Can you tell me some words?" or "Is _____ a word?" or "Is _____ _____ _____ a word?" It is not necessary to have a child recite a definition. In fact, some children can parrot definitions without understanding concepts.

Beginning readers need to acquire such language-related concepts as the following:

Experience precedes speaking and writing and determines what we can understand.

What is written becomes what is read.

A word is a meaning unit.

Words have boundaries (*cupacoffee* is not a word).

Any speech sound can be represented by letters of the alphabet.

Words that sound alike may have different spellings and meanings.

Word order provides cues to meaning.

Speech can be segmented into syllables and single letter sounds.

The letter sequence in written words is related to the phoneme sequence in spoken words.

The redundancy of language and of language patterns facilitate language production.

Punctuation provides cues to meaning.

Determiners *(the, an, a, this, my,* and so on*)* precede nouns in sentences.

Word, phrase, sentence, paragraph, and book meaning cannot be separated.

Concepts Related to School Tasks

Other concepts often erroneously assumed to have been acquired by children are those related to school tasks. These concepts underlie such directions as:

Underline or circle the correct answer.

Draw a line from the word in the first column to the matching word in the other column.

Cross out the incorrect word.

Mark the best answer.

Put an X over the word that does not belong.

Whether teachers use commercial materials and tests or those they themselves have constructed, they need to assess each child's ability to understand the tasks. When a child is asked to select the *best title* for a story from four or five possibilities, does he understand what he is to do? To one person, *best title* may mean *most interesting*; however, usually the child is required to choose the title that most completely summarizes the story. Children who are not aware that this is required, can hardly be evaluated fairly. Therefore, an assessment of their understanding of the task is essential. This is another area that can be assessed informally. Some tests have been published that may be useful, such as the *Boehm Test of Basic Concepts* (3).

Conceptual Background Related to Comprehension of Information

Our ability to comprehend what we see, hear, feel, or read depends to a great extent on our previous experiences. Read the following story:

> Linda got up early. Because she was very ganly, she are a big bowl of zibbie. It tasted so dorph she had another big bowl full. Then she had another! "Oh," said Linda, "I are too much. I feel ajib."

What do you think Linda might have eaten? Why do you think so? What else could it have been? How do you think Linda felt at the end of the story? What makes you think so?

You probably had no difficulty at all in making the inference that Linda felt ill from eating too much, since that is an experience most people in an area of the world with sufficient food have had. However, your guesses about what Linda ate are likely to have been closely tied to your particular cultural background.

Generally, young children can more easily understand stories that deal with familiar rather than unfamiliar events and relationships. When children differ in their experiences and cultures, their teacher should try to find materials that are within the grasp of all. If that is not possible, care should be taken to assess the children's conceptual backgrounds and explain ideas and relate experiences that will prepare the children for what they will read.

Two other effects of conceptual background need to be mentioned with regard to school experiences. First, tests are frequently culturally biased. A child who has never seen or heard about hoes, rakes, harrows, or furrows and who is required to take a test that uses such terms as these is at a tremendous disadvantage. Teachers need to read every item on every test given to their students in order to determine whether their children's experience is likely to have been extensive enough to enable them to take the test.

Second, as children mature, they are given materials to read, especially in content-area subjects, that contain concepts less universal in nature and more specific to the subject being studied. Many teachers fail to assess their students' conceptual background with regard to content-area reading. Textbooks are often seriously inadequate in this area: A widely used social studies textbook devoted an entire column to a discussion of what Washington wore to his inaugural and one brief paragraph to an explanation of the electoral college.

The use of synonyms is confusing to many children. One group of fifth-grade children thought that "the mother country," England, London, the British Isles, and Great Britain were five different countries from which the earlier settlers had come. It is difficult to imagine how any teacher can expect children to read and comprehend content-area material without the necessary conceptual background or how any teacher can plan a lesson in a content-area subject without first assessing the children's conceptual background. This can be done informally in discussion or by administering a test such as the following:

"We are going to study the planets. Here are some statements about the planets. Put a check (√) in front of the ones that are true."

_____ The planets closest to Earth probably have people living on them that are like us.
_____ Earth is a planet.
_____ The planets revolve about the moon.
_____ *Revolve* means *move in circles*.

Children who answer all or nearly all of the questions correctly can probably work more independently than those who know little about the subject. Assessment can help the teacher individualize instruction.

ASSESSMENT OF SPECIFIC READING ABILITIES

There are two major purposes for assessment of reading performance. The first purpose is placement in materials. Children should not be required to read materials day after day that are too difficult for them, nor should they be limited to very easy materials. The second purpose is identification of knowledge and abilities that have been acquired and knowledge and abilities that need to be acquired for improvement in word identification and comprehension.

Determining Levels of Reading Abilities

Although standardized group tests yield a grade-equivalent score, they are not very useful for placement in reading materials. As indicated earlier they are best used to compare groups and to screen for children who might need individual diagnosis. Scores on group tests may be misleading: children may not have understood the directions, or they may have simply guessed the answers without even reading the passages. Another reason group tests may be unsatisfactory is that the various published tests seem to measure different aspects of reading and may not reflect the goals of a particular program.

Probably the most satisfactory procedure for determining a child's placement in graded materials such as basal readers is to administer an informal reading inventory (IRI), which is described later in this chapter. However, the IRI can require at least twenty minutes of the teacher's time for each student; therefore, we suggest that the teacher make a quick group survey for the purpose of tentative placement in materials. Later, the teacher should see each child for a longer period of time in order to confirm or alter the initial placement decision.

Procedures for Tentative Placement

Three procedures are suggested for group placement: alternate oral reading, cloze testing, and word-list testing.

Alternate Oral Reading

Select a set of materials that most of the children in the class might be expected to be able to read. Also have available books on both easier and more difficult levels.

Call the children together in groups of eight or ten.

Explain that each child will read aloud for a short time so that you can find out whether the new book is right for them.

Ask each child to read a few sentences. Give assistance if needed while reading the selection.

Note each child's performance on a copy of the class list. (It is a good idea to make several copies of the class list for various record-keeping purposes.)

Retest on easier materials those children who had difficulty, and retest on more difficult materials those who seemed to be exceptionally capable. Note the estimated reading levels on the class list. Here is an example of an alternate oral reading record:

Name	pp	p	1	1.5	2.0	2.5
Allan, Sue			√			
Andrews, Jim			√			
Baker, Mike	√					

Cloze Testing

Cloze testing is described in detail in Chapter 5. It should be remembered that cloze testing can be used for group placement, as well as for the purposes described in Chapter 5.

Word-List Testing

Make a random selection of ten words from the list of new words introduced at each level of the graded material to be used for instruction. These words are usually listed in the back of each book or in the teacher's manual.

Type each set of words on a card. Use capital letters for preprimer and primer level words. Mark the level on the back of each card.

Make a scoring sheet such as the following:

Name _____ Date _____

pp	p	1.0	1.5	2.0
1. ____	1. ____	1. ____	1. ____	1. ____
2. ____	2. ____	2. ____	2. ____	2. ____
3. ____	3. ____	3. ____	3. ____	3. ____
4. ____	4. ____	4. ____	4. ____	4. ____
5. ____	5. ____	5. ____	5. ____	5. ____
6. ____	6. ____	6. ____	6. ____	6. ____
7. ____	7. ____	7. ____	7. ____	7. ____
8. ____	8. ____	8. ____	8. ____	8. ____
9. ____	9. ____	9. ____	9. ____	9. ____
10. ____	10. ____	10. ____	10. ____	10. ____

Ask each student to read to you alone. Have each begin with the highest level at which complete success is expected and read to a level where four or more words are not known.

Mark a check for words known instantly; a dash can be used to indicate that the child paused but recognized the word after analysis; an X can mark words not known. Write down the child's exact pronunciation of words read incorrectly. The highest level at which no words or one word was missed is termed the independent level; two words, the instructional level; and three or more words, the frustration level. A sample record is shown below (missed words are in parentheses).

p	1.0	1.5
1. ✓	1. ✓	1. ✓
2. ✓	2. ✓	2. —
3. was (saw)	3. —	3. —
4. ✓	4. —	4. ✓
5. ✓	5. —	5. X (everyone)
6. ✓	6. ✓	6. ✓
7. —	7. ✓	7. spot (stopping)
8. —	8. X (back)	8. —
9. ✓	9. ✓	9. —
10. ✓	10. frm (from)	10. nine (never)

The Informal Reading Inventory

Administering an IRI is a practical way of placing children in appropriate material and identifying their strengths and weaknesses in reading. A useful and well-written guide to IRIs, written by Johnson and Kress (11), contains a clearly stated rationale for such inventories and detailed suggestions for their development and use.

The IRI, which is widely used, generally requires students to read from a set of graded paragraphs and answer questions or talk about what was read. First, passages are read aloud. Then, other selections are read silently. Finally, the child listens to material read to him by the teacher, who then tests the child in order to determine the level at which the material was comprehended by the child.

After considering the child's performance in oral reading and in comprehension after oral and silent reading, the teacher makes a decision as to placement in graded materials, such as a basal reading series. The child's ability to comprehend what is read to him is revealed even if what is read is from a basal which is much too difficult for the child. Poor understanding may indicate a need for further language or conceptual development.

Betts has been widely quoted regarding placement of children in graded materials (2). He notes the following levels, with a guide to placement.

	ORAL READING	COMPREHENSION
Independent Level	95% accuracy	90% correct
Instructional Level	90% accuracy	75% correct
Frustration Level	85% accuracy	50% correct

The preceding numbers can be misleading: not all inaccuracies in oral reading and not all responses in comprehension testing are of equal importance. Bader (1), for example, points out that two students may have the same profile:

READER LEVEL	ACCURACY	COMPREHENSION
2.5	100%	100%
3.0	95%	100%
3.5	90%	80%
4.0	85%	80%

However, an examination of word-recognition errors may reveal that most of one student's errors were with multisyllabic words, whereas the other missed basic sight words and made inappropriate substitutions, confusing the meaning of the passage. The first student might be placed in the 3.5 reader and given help with affixes and syllabication, while the second student might be placed in the 3.0 reader and given more basic instruction before moving to material containing multisyllabic words and more complex sentence structures. Most authorities would agree that there is room for teacher judgment in the analysis of students' performance in the IRI.

We have found that teachers making such judgments occasionally place children in materials that are too difficult for them. It is better to err in the direction of placement in easier materials, because that can build fluency and confidence. Placement in materials that are too difficult is likely to retard growth and undermine the child's self-concept and interest in reading.

Directions for Preparing and Administering the Informal Reading Inventory

1. Near the beginning of each level of a basal reader, choose three selections that are representative of the book and self-contained as to content. The preprimer, primer, and first-grade selections should range in length from 50 to 100 words; the selections in grades two and three should range from 150 to 200 words; and the selections above third grade should range from 250 to 300 words. Students can read directly from the reader.

2. Make a mimeographed copy, double or triple spaced, of each selection. Label each copy with the book's level and the page number. The copy will be used to record student behaviors.

3. The open-response technique can be used. The teacher says, "Tell me everything you remember about what you read." The teacher then checks each item recalled, using an outline such as the following:

    ———— Tim's mother
    ———— took him to the circus.
    ———— They ate some peanuts
    ———— and a hot dog.
    ———— They saw a tiny monkey
    ———— and a big elephant.
    ———— Tim liked the tiger best.

    If questions are constructed about the selection, they should be on the same level of difficulty as the selection. Most should require factual answers, and should be based on information in the passage, not on previous knowledge. Five or six questions should be constructed for each passage.

4. Prepare a checklist of reading behaviors.
    Rate:

    ———— slow
    ———— appropriate
    ———— fast

    Phrasing:

    ———— appropriate
    ———— ignored punctuation
    ———— word-by-word

Approach to Unknown Words:

——— made meaningful substitutions
——— refused to guess
——— substituted graphically similar words
——— ignored context
——— made wild guesses
——— went back to correct miscues

Sound-Letter Associations:

——— made single-consonant errors
——— made consonant-combination errors
——— made single-vowel errors
——— made vowel-combination errors

Structural Analysis:

——— made errors on inflectional endings
——— made errors on prefixes
——— made errors on suffixes
——— made errors on compound words
——— made errors on multisyllabic words

Comprehension:

——— read with appropriate inflection
——— recalled events in sequence
——— recalled literal content
——— made appropriate inferences

Other Observations and Comments:

——————————————————————————
——————————————————————————
——————————————————————————
——————————————————————————

5. Administer the inventory in the following fashion:
    Out of the hearing of the rest of the class, try to help the child
    relax, and explain the purpose and procedure of the testing.
    Briefly introduce each selection. For example: "Here is a story
    about a dog who was lost. After you have read it, I will ask you to
    tell me about it. If you come to a hard word, do the best you can
    and go on."
    Begin with the selection for oral reading, and continue until the
    child has reached the frustration level. Say; "That was hard, wasn't
    it? Thank you for trying. Now we'll try something else." Then
    administer the selections for silent reading, from the highest inde-
    pendent silent-reading level to the silent-reading frustration level.
    Proceed similarly with the selections for listening comprehension.

6. Interpret the results. Using Betts' criteria, the checklist, and your own judgment, decide what level of reader would be most appropriate for the child. Next, note the child's instructional needs in word recognition, word analysis, vocabulary, use of context, and reading and listening comprehension.

7. Assess your judgments through instruction. Teachers need to remind themselves that test results or observations of behavior need to be checked; initial assessments may be in error. If further work with the child reveals that an adjustment in materials or methods is in order, the teacher should make the necessary changes.
   (A list of commercially prepared IRIs can be found in Appendix E.)

SUMMARY

Procedures for obtaining important information about children's abilities in reading and in related areas were described. We have suggested that tests can be useful but that they are not substitutes for continuous observation and evaluation within the instructional setting. The procedures described are helpful for initial placement, with adjustments to be made as more is learned about the children's capabilities.

ACTIVITIES RELATED TO THE CHAPTER

1. Interview a reading clinician or specialist. Find out what types of tests he or she customarily administers and why those particular instruments are used.

2. Observe two elementary school students in a variety of situations in which they employ expressive and receptive vocabulary. Based upon your observations, what judgments can you make about the expressive and receptive vocabulary of each student?

3. Develop your own inventory of prepared paragraphs and questions from a basal reading series used in a primary classroom.

4. Administer your own IRI or one developed by a teacher to a child in a primary classroom and to a child in an intermediate classroom. Discuss your placement decisions with the teachers in those classrooms. How do your placements compare with those made by the teachers?

5. Examine two or more published graded-paragraph tests, such as those developed by Durrell (6), Silvaroli (12), and Ekwall (7), and compare them with respect to how they interpret errors, the types of questions they ask, and their suggested conditions for testing. Which do you prefer? Why?

6. Which procedure for group testing—alternate oral reading, cloze testing, or word-list testing—do you feel would be most useful to a classroom teacher? Why?

BIBLIOGRAPHY AND REFERENCES

1. Bader, Lois A.: *Reading Diagnosis and Remediation in Classroom and Clinic*, Macmillan, New York, 1980.

2. Betts, Emmett A.: *Foundations of Reading Instruction*, American Book Company, New York, 1946.

3. Boehm, Ann E.,: *Boehm Test of Basic Concepts*, Psychological Corporation, New York, 1969-70.

4. Bormuth, John R.: "The Cloze Readability Procedure" in John R. Bormuth, ed., *Readability in 1968: A Research Bulletin*, published for the National Conference on Research in English by the National Council of Teachers of English, Champaign, IL, 40–47.

5. Buros, Oscar, ed.,: *The Mental Measurements Yearbook*, Gryphon, Highland Park, NJ, 1965.

6. Durrell, Donald D. and Jane H. Catterson: *Manual of Directions, Analysis of Reading Difficulty*, (3d ed.), The Psychological Corp., NY, 1980.

7. Ekwall, Eldon E.: *Graded Paragraph Tests*, Allyn and Bacon, Boston, 1979.

8. Fry, Edward: *Elementary Reading Instruction*, McGraw-Hill, New York, 1977, p. 252.

9. Guszak, Frank J.: "Strategies of Measuring Student Understanding of Written Materials," in Robert E. Leibert, ed., *Diagnostic Viewpoints in Reading*, International Reading Assoc., Newark, DE, 1971, p. 41.

10. Harris, Albert J., and Edward R. Sipay: *How to Teach Reading,* Longman, New York, 1979, p. 179.

11. Johnson, Marjorie S., and Roy A. Kress: *Informal Reading Inventories*, International Reading Assoc., Newark, DE, 1965.

12. Silvaroli, Nicholas: *Classroom Reading Inventory*, 3rd ed., Wm. C. Brown, Dubuque, IA, 1979.

Integrating Language, Literature, and Reading for Enjoyment

9

Overview

The purpose of this chapter is to explore the relationships among literature, reading, and language skills. Topics include the values of an elementary literature program; how the teacher can assess interests and attitudes toward reading; how to select appropriate reading materials and where to obtain them; and how to motivate children to read a variety of materials and to respond in different ways to them. A major curriculum objective should be the promotion of reading as a valued lifelong activity for all pupils.

Definition of Terms

1. *Active interests*—current interests.
2. *Annotation*—a brief description of the main points in a book or story.
3. *Bibliotherapy*—using books to aid children in their understanding of special problems of a personal nature.
4. *Independent reading level*—the level of material which pupils can read on their own without any assistance.
5. *Potential interests*—possible areas of interest that have not yet been explored or developed.
6. *Reading models*—adults or peers to whom reading is an important activity.
7. *Trade books*—paperback or hardcover books that are published as library books or supplementary materials.

R eading outside of the reading class is sometimes referred to as *free reading* or *recreational reading*; such reading generally involves material related to children's literature, such as trade books, magazines, and newspapers. All children—slower learners, average pupils and gifted or talented children—can enjoy such literature. It is the responsibility of the classroom teacher to expose pupils to appropriate literature and to encourage varied forms of pupil response to it.

The reading of literature outside the classroom should also be encouraged. Parents should become aware of the benefits of reading. It is sad but true that many children today do not enjoy reading in their spare time and seldom choose to read when other activities are available to them. Among the reasons why elementary pupils do not do much reading outside of school are

1. Television provides tough competition for books. Many children choose to watch television rather than read in their free time.
2. Many children are overscheduled by well-meaning parents. There are scout meetings, sports events, music or dance lessons, church activities, and so on, to the point where every night of the week is taken up. This often is not as much of a problem for pupils as the primary level (grades one to three) as at the intermediate level (grades four to six).
3. Children may not see their parents, siblings, or other relatives reading; lacking good models, they tend to undervalue reading.
4. The amount of oral reading or storytelling to children (usually by the teacher or a parent) tends to diminish as children grow up, and they are thus deprived of another source of motivation to read for themselves. Once a story has been told or read aloud, children almost always will want to read it again silently for themselves.

In order to encourage children to read, the school must include literature in the curriculum.

VALUES OF LITERATURE

The values of a literature program at the elementary level are many and varied. According to Helen Huus (7), the teaching of literature should have the following objectives:

1. to help pupils realize that literature is entertaining and can be enjoyed throughout their lives
2. to acquaint children with their literary heritage
3. to help pupils understand what literature is and, one hopes, to persuade them to prefer the best
4. to help children evaluate their own reading and extend their interests
5. to help pupils to grow up and to understand people

The reading of literature may also be of value to the child's overall creative development (14):

1. It can stimulate children to write for themselves.
2. It can function as therapy for troubled children.
3. It can help children build skills in expression, in defining, and in elaboration.
4. It can help children build a colorful vocabulary that will assist them in expressing themselves.
5. It can serve as a basis for constructive daydreaming and complete identification with a problem (necessary for creative problem-solving).
6. It can make children more discrete in passing judgment and making choices, especially in the use of words.
7. It can be a perpetual source of stimulation for every child's creativity.
8. It can help children develop sensitivity to places, sights, sounds, words, life problems, and people.
9. It helps children build a set of standards and values regarding creative writing.

Participation in a literature program will allow pupils to practice and extend their reading skills and related language skills involving oral and written expression. It is important for both teacher and pupils to value reading and to want to participate in a literature program.

CHILDREN'S INTERESTS

Children's interests are a key in motivating them to read. In a literature program, it is imperative that the teacher recognize what interests pupils and that this information be used to provide appropriate reading materials.

Children's interests are of two types: *active* (that is, current) and *potential*. The sharing of interests will usually reveal in what areas children are actively interested. It may also lead children to explore potential interests; for example, one child, seeing another's collection of sea shells, might decide that the assorted shells he or she has randomly picked up at the beach might also be displayed and labeled. Also, there is a good chance that in the process of classifying and labeling some reading will take place. The teacher must be prepared to capitalize on both types of interests for building motivation to read.

Assessing Children's Interests

There are several means, both formal and informal, by which a teacher can determine pupils' interests at any given time. Informal observation is one way to assess interests in the classroom. What do different pupils like to do best? What do they do when regular assignments are completed and they choose another activity? When there are options in activities, which do they choose? Informal conversations, or a more formal conference or interview, can also provide information for the teacher. An activity such as "Show and Tell," in which children can share the spotlight, can reveal what is currently important to them. This is a fine activity for any grade level, though the name must be changed for older pupils.

Teachers with older pupils may use a written questionnaire to assess pupils' interests. These are relatively easy to construct, and can consist of questions which do not invade the pupils' privacy. It is a good idea to give pupils the option of not answering questions they feel are inappropriate for them. Sample questions that might be used to assess interests are

1. What is your favorite television show? Why do you like it?
2. What is the best book (or story) you have read or had read to you lately? Why did you like it?
3. Do you have any pets? Tell what they are and give their names.
4. What chores or jobs do you like to do around your home?
5. What hobby (or hobbies) do you have? How long have you had it (them)?
6. Do you belong to any clubs or other organizations? Name them.
7. Where would you go for a perfect vacation? Why do you choose that place?
8. Who is a person you admire very much? The person may be famous or not, real or imaginary, living or dead.
9. What is the most enjoyable thing you do at home (or after school)?
10. What three wishes would you make right now?

(The reader is referred to Appendix D for further information on interest inventories.)

Since most children have hobbies, another possibility is to have a day or series of days when children share these hobbies by displays or demonstrations in the classroom. If the group is fairly large, it would probably be more beneficial to schedule a few children at a time so that equal time is given to all. The teacher should be sure to find out ahead of time what each pupil plans to do or bring. Some children may have pets as a hobby, and the classroom might end up with an incompatible menagerie of cats, dogs, gerbils, and canaries. If a child has a very large collection of some type, it would be prudent for only a few samples or favorite items from it to be brought to school. A vast collection of dolls or china figurines does not lend itself to class display very readily. However, a large insect collection that is mounted for display and easy to transport may be reasonable. The watchword is to plan ahead. If the teacher wants to make the sharing of hobbies an important class activity, the class could be organized as a hobby club and go more deeply into each hobby area.

Another way to assess pupil interests is to find out what the child is currently reading. A reading record or reading journal, which will be discussed in the next section, might be used for this purpose.

Children's Reading Interests and Their Attitudes Toward Reading

Considerable research has been devoted to finding out what elementary pupils like to read at different grade levels or ages (15). Some general findings are that children in grades one and two select books mainly because of their pictures; they enjoy stories about animals and mechanical objects, as well as folk and fairy tales. Children in grades three and four continue to enjoy fantasy and folklore but also like to read about their own world—in both the past and the present. Adventure, history, and biography are popular, as are animal stories. Boys like sports and science stories. In the upper grades five and six, boys' and girls' interests tend to diverge. Boys choose sports, adventure, and mystery, and they like a great deal of action. Girls begin to prefer light romance. Younger pupils like stories that involve pretending, and older ones prefer those picturing real life. But children at all levels enjoy stories with humor (12).

Some additional information that teachers might find helpful for dealing with the matter of reading preferences follows (15):

1. Children's interests vary according to age and grade level.
2. Girls usually read more books, but boys have a greater range of interests and read a wider variety of books.
3. Boys reading interests become different from girls' at about age 9.
4. Girls are more apt to read books that boys like than boys are to read books preferred by girls. There are some interest areas that boys and girls have in common regardless of age.
5. Socioeconomic background is not related to reading interests.
6. No single set of materials is likely to satisfy the reading interests of all pupils in any classroom.

What pupils like to read about varies greatly; therefore the teacher must be well informed about both the general reading interests of the class and active and potential interests of the individuals in the class.

In order to find out what reading interests individual pupils have, a reading design, reading record, or reading journal may be useful.

A reading design is a geometric design such as a circle, square, or triangle on which pupils use color coding to indicate the kinds of books they read.

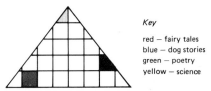

Key

red — fairy tales
blue — dog stories
green — poetry
yellow — science

Pupils fill in each section of the design with the color codes of the books they've read until the design is completed.

Designs can be made simple or complex, according to the amount of reading pupils do. Older pupils who are expert in the use of ruler, compass, and protractor may like to make their own reading designs. It is a good idea to have pupils list the books read and coded on the design at the bottom or on the back of the design or on a separate sheet. Each reading design is a record of the child's reading, which may be very useful for some pupils.

A reading record is a list of books that have been read by each pupil. Such a record can include not only the title, but also the author, the date of publication, a brief annotation, and so forth for each book.

A reading journal is a reading record that includes the child's reaction to each book or story read, plus a description of any project completed in response to the reading. A brief description of each book is also required in a reading journal. As the school year progresses, the child makes dated entries in a journal, which may take the form of a notebook or diary.

The reading design, record, or journal should be analyzed by the teacher from time to time during the year to assess the changing reading interests of each pupil.

How pupils feel about reading is another area that the teacher may wish to assess. A teacher-made inventory is useful for this purpose. Reading-attitude inventories generally consist of a series of statements expressing both positive and negative reactions to reading. The child responds with a yes or no to each statement. If the positive responses outweigh the negative, a positive attitude toward reading is indicated. Some sample reading-attitude items follow:

	YES	NO
1. I would rather play outdoors than read.		
2. I go to the school library on my own at least once every week.		
3. I often read before I go to sleep at night.		
4. I prefer watching TV to reading.		
5. I like to read magazines and comic books.		

When administering an attitude inventory to younger children, the teacher can read items aloud, and children show by their facial expression how they feel about each item.

Several reading-attitude inventories are available, such as the Reading Attitude Inventory by Paul Campbell (Livonia Public Schools, Livonia, Michigan), The Reading Interest/Attitude Scale (Right to Read Office, Washington, D.C.) and the Sartain Attitudes Toward Reading Inventory by Harry W. Sartain (University of Pittsburgh, Pittsburgh, Pennsylvania).

To encourage children at all levels in the elementary school to read widely, a literature program that is motivating and related to their interests is a vital part of the school curriculum. The classroom teacher should assume responsibility for assessing pupils' general interests, both active and potential, as well as their reading interests and their attitudes toward reading. Both formal and informal means of assessment may be utilized.

A teacher who is aware of pupil interests and attitudes naturally uses this information in the selection of appropriate, motivating, and challenging reading materials.

LOCATING AND SELECTING READING MATERIALS

It is not the purpose of this chapter to present a listing of so-called best or most appropriate books for elementary children. Rather, teachers should learn what to look for and where to look and then select those titles that seem best for the pupils in question. If a teacher reads widely and is enthusiastic about children's books, that zest for reading will make an impression on pupils.

In order to choose materials, the teacher needs some basic background in children's literature, background that is probably best acquired through a thorough course in the subject. The five types, or categories, of literature at the elementary level are folk literature, fiction, poetry, biography, and informational books. Some criteria are needed for selecting books within these major categories.

Criteria for Book Selection—Fiction

1. The *plot* should flow in an easy-to-follow sequence and should contain action and suspense.
2. The *characters* should be believable; they should act and talk like real people unless the story is a fantasy. The strengths and weaknesses of the characters should be portrayed. Pupils should be able to identify strongly with some of the characters.
3. If the book has a message, the *theme* should be clear and not overstated. Some books are purely for enjoyment and actually have no theme.
4. The *style of writing* can vary; some books are highly descriptive, some have a lot of dialogue, and some are straight exposition. More complex styles should be reserved for older pupils.
5. The *format*—that is, the illustrations (color, detail, accuracy), the size and clarity of the print, and the size of the book—and the books *durability* (quality of paper, binding) are considerations.

Criteria for Book Selection—Nonfiction

1. The book should be *accurate* and *authentic*.
2. The *content* should be appropriate for the age or grade level of the pupils.
3. Considerations with respect to the *style of writing* are the same as those given in the preceding section for fiction books.

4. The book should have a clear *organization*.
5. Considerations of *format* and *durability* are the same as for fiction books.

As children share what they enjoy reading, the teacher modifies or adds to the criteria used for book selection. Only through exposure to a wide variety of books can both teacher and pupils discover those literary qualities that have special appeal.

How does the teacher find out which books might be interesting to pupils in the class? There are many published sources that give information on books that are in print.

Books about children's literature used in college courses are useful for this purpose. They not only define categories of children's literature in more detail, but may also give historical background and include many sample selections and illustrations. All good texts of this type include information about many children's books. Two good books about children's literature are Sutherland and Arbuthnot (16) and Huck (6).

The teacher should also be acquainted with the Newberry Award and Caldecott Award books. The Caldecott Medal, first awarded in 1938, is given annually to the artist of the most distinguished American picture book for children. The Newberry Medal, first given in 1922, is presented each year to the author of the most distinguished contribution to American literature for children. Winners of these two prestigious awards are selected by a committee of the Children's Service Division of the American Library Association.

Generally the Caldecott Award books are picture books intended for primary-level readers; the Newberry Award books are appropriate for older children. Appendix B includes a complete list of the Caldecott and Newberry award-winning books.

Two widely available paperbacks that deal with books for children are Larrick (11) and Cianciolo (2). Belying its title, the Larrick book can also be very helpful to teachers who want to find out about books for children. It gives information on the development of language and reading and the role of parents in encouraging their children to read. The section of the book entitled "Books They Like" lists and categorizes children's books, with a brief annotation for each book and an indication of the age level for which it is appropriate. The Cianciolo book, an annotated and categorized listing of children's books, is most likely to be available in the school library or in the children's section of the public library. It is revised every few years.

Some other resources from the library that can help teachers find out about children's books, especially those that are newly published, are

1. *Best Books for Children* (an annotated bibliography for grades K-12, arranged by grades and subjects, and published annually by R. R. Bowker Company).

2. *The Horn Book Magazine* (published six times yearly and entirely devoted to children's and young adult's books; can be ordered by writing to *The Horn Book Magazine*, Park Sq. Bldg., 31 St. James Ave., Boston, MA 02116).
3. *The Calendar* (an official newsletter of the Children's Book Council published at eight-month intervals; it can be ordered from Children's Book Council, Inc., 67 Irving Place, New York, NY 10003).
4. *Bulletin of the Center for Children's Books* (published by the Center for Instructional Materials, University of Chicago Graduate Library School).

Although these sources are mainly intended for school librarians, teachers and other interested individuals are welcome to subscribe to them.

Additional sources which teachers may want to review are the book-review columns in such monthly educational publications as *Learning*, *Teacher*, *Instructor*, or *Early Years*. *The Reading Teacher*, published by the International Reading Association, and *Language Arts*, published by the National Council of Teachers of English, are journals which also review children's books and frequently contain articles about aspects of and issues in children's literature.

The children's section (or children's room) in the public library also may from time to time provide free book lists which are usually specific in nature, with such titles as An American Indian Booklist, Our Puerto Rican Heritage, or Nice and Easy to Look At. These lists usually have an eye-catching format and are offered free as a public service.

Some Other Materials for Children

Most of the sources in the preceding section serve to familiarize teachers with books, both hardback and paperback. In addition, teachers should be aware that magazines and newspapers are also valuable assets to the elementary literature program. Where funds are scarce, these materials may prove the least expensive.

Children's Magazines:

1. *Cricket: The Magazine for Children* (Box 2670, Boulder, CO 80322).
2. *Sesame Street* and *The Electric Company* (Television Workshop, 1 Lincoln Plaza, New York, NY 10023).
3. *Jack and Jill* (1100 Waterway Boulevard, Indianapolis, IN 46206).
4. *Highlights for Children* (Highlights for Children, Inc., P.O. Box 269, Columbus, OH 43216).
5. *Humpty Dumpty's Magazine* and *Children's Digest* (Parents' Magazine Enterprises, Inc., 685 Third Avenue, New York, NY 10017).
6. *Ranger Rick's Nature Magazine* (National Wildlife Federation, 1412 Sixteenth Street, NW, Washington, DC 20036).

7. *National Geographic World* (17th and M Streets, NW, Washington, DC 20036).
8. *Ebony Junior* (Johnson Publishing Company, 820 South Michigan Avenue, Chicago, IL 60605).
9. *Dynamite* (Scholastic Book Services, 50 West 44th Street, New York, NY 10036).

Children's Newspapers:

1. *My Weekly Reader* (Published in weekly editions during the school year for different grade levels. Also has summer issues available by subscription. Xerox Education Publications, 245 Long Hill Road, Middletown, CT 06457).
2. Scholastic Elementary Magazines—*News Pilot, News Ranger, News Explorer, News Trails, News Citizen, Newstime* (Published weekly during the school year. Scholastic Book Services, 50 West 44th Street, New York, NY 10036).

In addition to magazines and newspapers published especially for children, such general-interest magazines as *Sports Illustrated, Family Circle,* and *Travel and Leisure* might be made available in the classroom. The age of specialization is reflected in current magazines which deal with such specific topics of interest as scuba diving, home decorating, and CB radio. At the discretion of the teacher, such magazines could be included in the classroom. (See Appendix B for additional information on periodicals that are suitable for children.) Teachers should check their local newspaper to find out if it offers any special rate or programs for schools. Many newspapers have "Newspaper in the Classroom" or "Newspaper in Education" programs which are a valuable resource.

Underlying the preceding discussion on how to find out what is available for children to read is the idea that the librarian is a good resource person for both teacher and students. By showing genuine interest and enthusiasm for children's books, the teacher gains access to the librarian's knowledge and ideas for enhancing the classroom literature program. Probably the school or community librarian should head the list of teacher resources for literary reading.

GETTING MATERIALS INTO THE CLASSROOM

Once teachers start getting acquainted with good reading materials that should be in their school or classroom, they will want to do something about actually obtaining these materials. This can be very easy or extremely difficult, depending largely on the school's resources. If the elementary school has a fine library, the teacher can use its resources either by making arrangements with the librarian for pupils to visit the library often or by arranging to bring books from the library to the classroom on more-or-less permanent loan. If there is no school library but a children's section in the community library is available, the same arrangements might be made. In case no real library resources are available, the teacher might use any of the following means for acquiring elementary reading materials:

1. Conduct a book drive, in which good used books and other reading materials are solicited from parents or the community at large. Be sure to make it clear that you are collecting children's materials. It still may be necessary to exclude some titles that have been donated, but these might be sold as used books or as recycled paper.
2. Visit garage sales and used book stores to find bargains in children's books, as well as old magazines and newspapers.
3. If pupils can afford to purchase paperback books, join a book club. For a specific number of titles ordered, a free or bonus book is usually offered, and these books can go into the class collection. Pupils might also donate paperbacks bought through the book club when they have finished them. There are several school book clubs for children. Among these are

> 1. Scholastic Book Clubs
>
>   See Saw Book Club (for grades K and one)
>
>   Lucky Book Club (for grades two and three)
>
>   Arrow Book Club (for grades four, five, and six)
>
>   Teen Age Book Club (for upper intermediate and junior high or middle school)
>
>   (Information is available from Scholastic Book Services, 50 West 44th Street, New York, NY 10036).
> 2. Weekly Reader Children's Book Club (for ages 4 through 10; Subscription Office, 1250 Fairwood Avenue, Columbus, OH 43215).
> 3. Troll Book Clubs (320 Route 17, Mahwah, NJ 07430).
> 4. Firefly Book Clubs (P.O. Box 485, Pleasantville, NY 10570).

If the best idea seems to be to purchase new books, but the school budget does not fully support this, class fund-raising activities might be conducted. A bake sale, movies, a school carnival, and so on are all possible.

Another idea which might be investigated is the RIF (Reading Is FUNdamental) program. Sponsored by the federal government, this program supplies free reading materials to eligible schools. For additional information, teachers can write to RIF, 1833 South Burdick, Kalamazoo, MI 49001.

A CLASSROOM LIBRARY AND READING CENTER

The end result of acquiring resources for the class literature program may well be a small classroom library and reading center. If there is ample space available in the classroom, this library and reading center might include floor pillows, beanbag chairs, and other furniture to help create a relaxed reading atmosphere. Older pupils can learn valuable library and reference skills by setting up a library classification system, a check-out system, a system for the acquisition of materials, and a system for the repair of damaged materials. A floor plan for a classroom library and reading center might look like the following illustration:

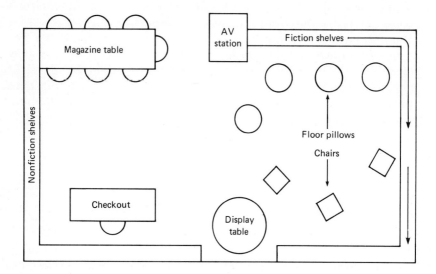

LITERATURE IN THE ELEMENTARY CURRICULUM

After introducing a variety of reading materials into the classroom, the teacher must motivate pupils to utilize them fully. The literature program is not just free reading time; it is integrated within the elementary curriculum. A good way for this integration to take place is through individualized reading, in which pupils choose what they want to read, pace their reading, and react to what is read in varied ways. It is possible to combine individualized reading with a basal or any other regular reading program by conducting one or more of the regular weekly reading classes according to an individualized plan.

In order to provide scheduled time in class when all pupils are free to read what they choose, the teacher might initiate sustained silent reading. A thorough discussion of this program is found in Chapter 5.

Oral Reading

Another way that the teacher can integrate the literature program with the overall language program is by making oral reading part of the school day. The teacher may be the reader, or willing and able pupils may read. A complete book, such as *Charlotte's Web* or *Johnny Tremain*, may be read in installments. Or a complete story can be read during a single session, which is preferable for younger pupils.

Storytelling

Storytelling can be used to enhance literary appreciation. Teachers who work to develop their storytelling skills are to be commended. Also, there are often persons available in the community who are trained in this art. Such media as tapes and recordings can be used, too. A good book for teachers interested in the art of storytelling is *Bauer* (1).

The Teaching of Poetry

The teaching of poetry should be carefully planned. Poetry should not be presented only as a yearly unit in an elementary language series. It should be taught through an ongoing series of activities that will involve pupils in both reading and writing poetry in its many forms. Too many people dislike poetry as adults because they were taught poorly in elementary school.

Pupils should be exposed to poetry gradually, in different forms and on topics that are related to their interests. The teacher could use a series of categories, introducing poems relating to each and encouraging pupils to write their own poetry in these categories. Such categories as the following are possibilities:

1. *Everyday things*—poems about pets, seasons, the family, and so on
2. *Fun and nonsense*—humorous poems that exaggerate or have funny rhymes; limericks
3. *Poetry with alliteration*
4. *Poetry with imagery*—poems that paint a picture in the mind as they are read or heard
5. *Poetry with unusual or uneven rhyme schemes*—poems that do not follow a regular pattern or do not rhyme at all; free verse.

The teacher should develop a collection of poems that fit such categories and then use poetry whenever it fits into the school program; teachers can also develop some specific poetry lessons. Eventually pupils should be exposed to such poetic forms as couplets, haiku (sometimes overdone in the elementary school), limericks, cinquain, and diamente. For further good ideas on the reading and writing of poetry, see Koch (8 and 9).

Pupils should be encouraged to select poetry books for their independent reading. The classroom collection should include a wide variety of poetry anthologies, as well as collections by children's poets, such as Dorothy Aldis, Rachel Field, John Ciardi, and David McCord.

Using Media

Another good way to enliven the literature program is through the use of such media as sound films, filmstrips, tapes and recordings, television, and radio. Weston Woods Media sells or rents many fine materials featuring children's stories and books, including a number of Caldecott and Newberry award winners. They also have sound films featuring interviews with famous children's authors. The Stanley Bowmar Company features children's literature in recorded form. There are also available many book-with-tape or filmstrip-tape combinations. Such materials may be teacher-made, as well as purchased. (See Appendix H for further information.)

Television and radio can also be incorporated in the classroom program. Educational television and radio offer several children's literature programs, including *Cover to Cover I* (for primary level) and *Cover to Cover II* (for intermediate level), by Bill Robbins, and *About Books* and *The Book Bird*. *Meet Barney Bookworm* is a radio show which enterprising teachers might tape for later use. Check with the local educational television or radio station for information on such programs.

Regular television networks occasionally feature specials adapted from books or stories for children. Teachers can write to the major networks for free information on such programming. For example, the American Broadcasting Company (ABC) publishes a guide to television for teachers, entitled *Watch The Program—Read The Book*. There is also a publication *Teacher's Guide to T.V.* (699 Madison Avenue, New York, NY 10021).

Other Techniques for Motivating Pupils

Teachers can use other means of maintaining a high level of interest in the reading materials available in the classroom.

Some visual motivators are wall charts, bulletin boards, and other displays relating to books and reading. Most of these should be made by pupils (see the section of this chapter "Activities That Promote the Sharing of Reading by Children"). Commercially available materials, such as posters, mobiles, book jackets, and reading progress charts, might be used. The Children's Book Council publishes many such items.

Teacher-made bulletin boards and displays of books and other materials relating to topics being studied or of special interest are also motivating. At the primary level, a class "bookworm" that "grows" is popular. The teacher makes the worm's head out of construction paper and many separate blank sections for the worm's body. Each title of a story or book read by the pupils is written on a section, and the section is added to make the worm grow. Eventually this bookworm could stretch across an entire classroom wall. Teachers must decide whether to include children's names on the bookworm sections. Including the names could add an element of competition to the activity.

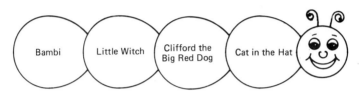

Another motivating activity is for the teacher to organize book discussion groups. Several children who have read a particular book gather together for a discussion of that book. The teacher or other leader must be prepared with questions that elicit children's reactions to the story on the literal, appreciative, and evaluative levels (see Chapter 4). This activity is popular with older pupils, and might lead to the creation of a book discussion club or literary club that would meet on a regular basis. It should be noted here that there are Junior Great Books Programs for children, along the same lines as the Great Books Programs of the University of Chicago. Leadership training is required in setting up a Junior Great Books Program.

Having the class order and purchase books from school book clubs, as mentioned previously, also stimulates reading. Group discussions could focus on popular books ordered by pupils from these clubs.

A commercial book fair is another interesting project, one that is probably best organized by a group of teachers. Contact is made with a publisher of children's books or a local bookstore to arrange a display and sale of books in the school. Pupils, teachers, and often parents are invited to attend the book fair. Sometimes a percentage of the total sales is given to the book fair's sponsors, possibly in the form of books rather than money. A book fair is a good pre-holiday or pre-summer vacation activity.

Finally, a motivator that should not be overlooked is the teacher. A teacher should show interest in and enthusiasm for children's books and what each child is reading. No teacher should ever be embarrassed about reading and enjoying materials for children; such materials are often more interesting and worthwhile reading than books on the best-seller list. Also, pupils will function as models for one another as they become involved in their reading. Open and constant communication is an important part of maintaining interest in literature. Interest in books is contagious; once the word is out that a particular book is "real good," its popularity with the children is assured—everyone will want to read it. There must be plenty of opportunity for such "advertisement" of good books in the school.

WHICH BOOKS FOR WHICH PUPILS?

Many teachers fear that when children have a choice of what to read, they choose books that are too hard or too easy for them. In the long run, however, children usually read both hard and easy books. For example, an intermediate-level pupil may enjoy rereading picture books or easy-to-read stories, yet may also tackle an occasional junior high or senior high book. However, most pupils find materials on their own independent reading level for the majority of their reading. A teacher who wants to help children select a book that is on their independent reading level, could use the five-finger technique (see Chapter 5). A more precise assessment of a child's reading level can be made with an informal reading inventory, such as the *Classroom Reading Inventory* or the *Botel Reading Inventory*.

BIBLIOTHERAPY

Bibliotherapy means *therapy through books*; it is a technique suited to the classroom teacher. Children can be helped to understand and, in some cases, come to terms with the variety of personal and social problems of everyday life by books in which these problems are presented. As pupils read such books and identify with the characters in them they learn to accept the problems dealt with therein. Such problems as divorce, cultural differences, sibling rivalry, family mobility, and handicapping conditions may be discussed. Bibliotherapy helps pupils identify and acquire information about such problems, but it cannot help pupils who are in need of clinical treatment for emotional or mental illnesses.

Bibliotherapy can be therapeutic (when a book presents a child's actual problem and suggests a solution) or preventive (when a situation presented in a book prepares a child to cope with similar situations in his or her own life). Many recent books for children deal with serious issues, and the number of books appropriate for bibliotherapy has grown rapidly in recent years. A valuable resource for the teacher wishing to pursue this technique is Dreyer (4), which lists books by subject or problem area, author, and title and includes a thorough description of each book. *The Book Finder* should be available in the school library or in the public library's children's section. (See Appendix B for a list of books which could be used for bibliotherapy.)

ACTIVITIES THAT HELP CHILDREN SHARE WHAT THEY READ

The activities described in this section have been highly successful in motivating children to respond to what they read, thus promoting the sharing of good literature. A traditional activity of this kind is the formal book report, but this often has a negative connotation for students and adults alike. The book report, though legitimate, is often overused or misused: it should not be the major way of holding children accountable for what they read.

There are many activities that can replace or supplement the formal book report. We have chosen to discuss four general categories of activities: (1) activities emphasizing written language, (2) activities emphasizing oral language, (3) activities emphasizing arts and crafts, and (4) miscellaneous activities. Within each category, we will present a number of carefully selected activities that can be used exactly as described or can be modified by the teacher. The activities are appropriate for a wide variety of grade and age levels, as well as for slow, average, and gifted learners. Other activities for gifted learners are discussed in Heimberger (5).

Activities Emphasizing Written Language

1. Write a letter nominating a book for the Caldecott Medal or Newberry Medal and giving the reasons for your nomination.
2. Write a different ending for a story or book.
3. Write an episode involving the characters in a book, or write a continuation of the story.
4. Write a scene from a book in script form, as for a play or television show.
5. Send a letter to a favorite author, asking how he or she happened to write a certain book or certain books, whether the writing is based on actual experiences, and other such questions. Most authors can be written to in care of their publishing company.
6. Be a literary critic. Write a book-review column, evaluating two or three books on the same topic. Compare them as to their accuracy, or realism, and as to how interesting and well written they are.
7. Write a diary as if you were one of the main characters in a book.
8. Write a conversation between characters in two different stories. Or write a letter from a character in one book to a character in another. A friend could write back as the other character.
9. Write a newspaper headline and news story about a major event in a book or story.
10. Write a brief annotation of a book on a file card to be placed in a class file which pupils can consult when they are looking for a good book. The annotation should include the following information:

    The title and author

    The reviewer (your name)

    A *short* description of the main events and characters

    The reason(s) why you would recommend this book to others

11. Make up a crossword puzzle or word search using characters and events from a book.
12. Write a poem about an entire book or about a main character, the setting, or an important happening in the book. Older pupils could write a ballad or ode.

Activities Emphasizing Oral Language

1. Dramatize a scene from a book with some classmates, or present a puppet show of a story or a scene from a book. Puppets may be especially made for this activity, or puppets available in the classroom or at home can be used.
2. Dress as one of the main characters from a book and tell the story, or part of it, from that character's point of view.
3. Tape-record informal book reports. The report should include the title and author of the book, your name, a brief description of the book's main events and characters, and the reason(s) why you would recommend this book to others.
4. Read part of a book or story into a tape recorder. The selection could be a dramatic incident, exciting conversation, or humor. Add sound effects or appropriate background music.
5. Auction a good book. This involves getting a group together and telling them about the book for two or three minutes in order to convince them to read it. Show the book as you try to sell it. Consider it auctioned off when someone agrees to read it.
6. Do a flannelboard presentation of your book. This activity is good for younger pupils in their own class or for older pupils to present to younger ones.
7. Present a program of oral readings on a particular topic. For example, excerpts from dog stories or from biographies of famous explorers could be read. Each pupil prepares a reading after the group has chosen the topic and appropriate selections.
8. Present a choral reading. The entire class, a group, or an individual can present a poem that has been prepared for choral reading.
9. Present a book quiz show. Use a twenty-questions format (to guess the title of a particular book) or a what's-my-line format (to identify characters from popular books).
10. Interview the author of a favorite book. This interview might be taped or done via telephone conference call so the whole group can participate. Or it might be a mock interview in which a second pupil acts as the author. It is important that the person acting as the author have a chance to look up or otherwise become familiar with the author's background, works, etc.
11. Read a "how to" book; then, give a demonstration showing what you learned from reading it (examples—plant care, macrame, making models).

12.   Play a Book Charades game in which each person draws the name of a book or a book character and, using pantomime or other means, gets other members of the team to guess the title or character being portrayed.

Activities Emphasizing Arts and Crafts

1.   Make a book mobile that represents the main events, characters, and setting of a book. Coat hangers are good for this purpose.
2.   Make a shoe-box diorama showing a scene from a book.
3.   Design and make a jacket for a book. Be sure to include information about the story and author on the flyleaf. Display such jackets on a bulletin board or put them on the actual books in the class library.
4.   Make a mural about a book. This is an activity for three to five pupils.
5.   Make puppets of the main characters in a book. Various materials can be used, from paper bags to wood.
6.   Make a five- or six-frame comic strip that tells a story or depicts an event in a book.
7.   Make a movie or a TV show based on a book. Draw a series of pictures showing the sequence of action in the story, then tape these together and roll them into a scroll. This "film" can be shown in a box with an opening for the screen by rotating the paper scroll around dowel sticks or empty paper-towel rollers.
8.   Make a filmstrip about a book. The pictures on an old filmstrip can be removed with a bleach and water solution; then draw new frames. Put lined paper under the blank filmstrip as a guide to keep the writing and drawing even. Put a paper towel on top of the filmstrip as a handrest while you are drawing or writing so you do not blur your marks.
9.   Make a map or series of maps to show where the story action takes place in a book.
10.   Make a picture dictionary about a book you have read.
11.   Make a poet-tree. This is a two-dimensional or three-dimensional tree made of paper or an actual tree branch on which favorite or original poems are hung.
12.   Make a collage or montage about a story or book. A collage is made of pictures and objects. A montage is made of pictures and photographs.

Miscellaneous Activities

1.   Advertise books. Advertisements may be designed as newspaper or magazine ads or written and taped or presented as live television or radio commercials.
2.   Make up book lists for different kinds of people—for example, sports fans, animal lovers, cooks, and outdoor types. Include the title, the

author, and a brief description of each book. This activity is good for a group or as an individual activity for older pupils.

3. Design and make a classroom bulletin board about some aspect of reading and books. This might be done during Children's Book Week or National Education Week, both of which fall in November.

4. Organize a book drive to get some new reading materials for your classroom.

5. Produce a class literary magazine. It might include original stories and poems, book reviews, cartoons about books, and so on. This might be a welcome alternative to the often overworked class newspaper activity.

Book Day: an Integrating Activity That Emphasizes Literature

A book day can be organized by a class, a combination of several classes, or an entire school. It is a fine end-of-school activity in which the literature program predominates. Classrooms are decorated with posters, book jackets, and other projects which pupils have done over a period of time. Arts and crafts and writing projects are displayed, and oral language projects are scheduled for presentation during the day. Books dealing with such content areas as math, science, and social studies are also featured.

If the book day becomes a large-scale endeavor involving several classes, parents and other interested adults might be invited to attend. School hallways and even outdoor areas can be used as display space. A parade of book characters might be held, for which each child dresses as a book or story character. Older pupils can collaborate and dress as the main characters in a single book or story—for example, Robin Hood, Little John, Maid Marian, and so on. The cafeteria can become involved in the activity by serving a "literary" lunch in which the menu includes items relating to books (for example, Since Soup, Journey Cake Ho, and King's Pudding). Teachers and all other members of the school staff should be encouraged to participate in and enjoy book day.

SUMMARY

There are multiple relationships among language, literature, and reading. The effective teacher provides a motivating environment and selects and makes available a wide variety of materials. Such a teacher also develops an ongoing literature program which permeates the elementary curriculum at various hours of the school day. Through such a program, pupils are helped to view reading as a lifelong activity.

ACTIVITIES RELATED TO THE CHAPTER

1. Prepare a short questionnaire of eight to ten items to assess pupil's interests at either the primary or the intermediate level. Try it out with a class, and analyze the results.

2. Examine an inventory designed to measure attitude and/or interest in reading. Complete it yourself and see what results you get. Could you have predicted the outcome?

3. Read approximately twenty-five books for children that are recommended in one or more of the sources listed in this chapter. On file cards, summarize the books with a brief annotation based on the criteria suggested for evaluating that type of book (fiction or nonfiction).

4. Make a list of and briefly annotate ten to fifteen books for children that are about topics of contemporary interest. Include, for example, multicultural stories or books about ecology.

5. Review four or five children's magazines after examining at least two consecutive issues of each. Compare them as to objectives, content, age level, appropriateness, and so on.

6. Draw a floor plan for your ideal classroom or library reading center. Describe how you would use it daily in class.

7. Choose, prepare, and tape a selection using oral reading or storytelling. Or present it live to pupils. Write an evaluation of the activity.

8. Begin a file of poetry you feel children would enjoy. Choose eight or ten categories, such as animals, family, seasons, fun and nonsense, and holidays. Find poems that fit well into each category. You might collect the poems in the form of an illustrated booklet. You could gear your file to the primary or the intermediate level or make it general enough for all elementary levels.

9. Set up a book display for the classroom that would motivate pupils to read. You might use a general theme, such as "holiday reading" or "fun with our pets" or a more specific one, such as "books about shells" or "America moves westward."

10. Prepare a book talk that would motivate your audience to read the book. Give your talk to a group of children or adults and report on your experience.

11. Visit an elementary school library or the children's section of a public library. Observe how it is arranged, what materials and displays are there, and what activities take place. Write a report on your visit.

12. Interview two or three elementary teachers and an elementary school librarian. Find out how they keep up with children's books and how they motivate pupils to read and respond to what they read. List all the ideas you collect.

13. Select and read several Caldecott Medal and Newbery Medal books. Write a brief annotation for each book and give your reaction to it.

14. Select and read several books by one children's author or poet; for example, books by Lois Lenski, Judy Blume, or John Ciardi would be appropriate. Write a brief analysis of how the books are similar to or different from each other; tell which books you prefer.

15. Examine some items related to children's literature, such as the Weston Woods materials or the Bowmar materials mentioned in this chapter. Write how you feel about them and how you might use them in a classroom.

BIBLIOGRAPHY AND REFERENCES

1. Bauer, Caroline Feller: *Handbook for Storytellers;* American Library Assoc., Chicago, 1977.

2. Cianciolo, Patricia, ed.: *Adventuring with Books*; National Council of Teachers of English, Urbana, IL, 1977.

3. Coody, Betty: *Using Literature with Young Children*, W. C. Brown, Dubuque, IA, 1973.
4. Dreyer, Sharon S.: *The Book Finder: A Guide to Children's Literature about the Needs and Problems of Youth Aged 2-15*, American Guidance Services, Circle Pines, MN, 1977.
5. Heimberger, Mary J.: *Teaching the Gifted and Talented in the Elementary Classroom*, National Education Assoc., Washington, DC, 1980.
6. Huck, Charlotte S.: *Children's Literature in the Elementary School*, 3rd ed., Holt, New York, 1976.
7. Huus, Helen: "Teaching Literature at the Elementary School Level," *The Reading Teacher*, 26:797-798 (1973).
8. Koch, Kenneth: *Rose, Where Did You Get That Red?: Teaching Great Poetry to Children*, Random House, New York, 1974.

9.   _____ : *Wishes, Lies and Dreams: Teaching Children to Write Poetry*, Chelsea House, New York, 1970.
10. Lapp, Diane, and James Flood: *Teaching Reading to Every Child*, Macmillan, New York, 1978.
11. Larrick, Nancy: *A Parent's Guide to Children's Reading*, 4th ed., Doubleday, New York, 1975.
12. Petty, Walter T., Dorothy C. Petty, and Marjorie F. Becking: *Experiences in Language*, 2nd ed., Allyn and Bacon, Boston, 1976, pp. 375-376.
13. Polette, Nancy: *E Is for Everybody*, Scarecrow, Metuchen, NJ, 1976.
14. Smith, James A.: *Adventures in Communication*, Allyn and Bacon, Boston, 1972.
15. Strain, Lucille B.: *Accountability in Reading Instruction*, Merrill, Columbus, OH, 1976, pp. 119-121.
16. Sutherland, Zena, and May Hill Arbuthnot: *Children and Books*, 5th ed., Scott, Foresman, Glenview, IL, 1977.

Will McIntyre/Photo Researchers, Inc.

Classroom Management 10

Overview

Probably few aspects of instruction are of as much concern to teachers as classroom management. Keeping track of students' needs and interests, selecting materials, scheduling time to meet with groups and individuals, and individualizing instruction are tasks that demand much time and expertise on the part of a teacher.

This chapter describes practical approaches to classroom organization. Topics include grouping, organizing materials, and techniques for individualizing instruction.

Definition of Terms

1. *Achievement-level grouping*—grouping children by reading level within a single classroom.
2. *Heterogeneous grouping*—grouping children in classes primarily on the basis of age. Children in these classes often vary greatly in ability.
3. *Homogeneous grouping*—grouping children in classes on the basis of ability (also called *tracking*); homogeneous grouping may simplify classroom organization by minimizing the variation of abilities within groups.
4. *Independent learning*—learning based on instructional procedures which focus on individualized planning and instruction, rather than on grouping.
5. *Interclass grouping*—grouping children from various classes according to general reading level.
6. *Skill-needs grouping*—grouping children according to areas of difficulty. These subgroups frequently cut across achievement-level groups.
7. *Special-interest grouping*—grouping children according to interests.

I n every grade from kindergarten through high school, teachers can expect that there will be a range of differences in their student's achievement and that the range will increase with age and experience. This means that some first-grade children will be able to read materials at a third-grade level, while there will be children in third grade who are barely able to read a primer. Harris and Sipay (8) presented an illustration of this. They programmed a hypothetical situation and studied the range of reading abilities in second-, fourth-, and sixth-grade classes in schools where there was one class for each grade (8). All children were promoted without regard for achievement, the reading program was typical, and the children were representative of the general population in intelligence. Harris and Sipay found that at the beginning of each grade, half of the children were reading below grade level, and half were at or above grade level. The reading ranges were as follows: second-grade reading scores ranged from readiness to at least third-grade level; fourth-grade reading scores ranged from low second grade to sixth-grade level; sixth-grade reading scores ranged from low third to ninth-grade level. Some teachers find this a difficult situation in which to manage instruction; unfortunately, advanced readers are sometimes not permitted to go beyond the highest basal-reader level within their designated grade placement, and very poor readers are placed in materials that are much too difficult for them. Clearly, this makes effective reading instruction very difficult.

There are several ways of dealing with a wide range of achievement. They include interclass grouping and independent learning.

INTERCLASS GROUPING

The best-known form of homogeneous grouping that cuts across classes and grade levels is the Joplin plan. The Joplin, Missouri, schools experimented with this form of organization several years ago. It has since been tried in various forms by other school systems. Schools using this approach group students according to general reading achievement for formal reading instruction. Children taught in interclass grouping receive all of their instruction from their homeroom teacher, with the exception of reading and, perhaps, a special subject such as music. The reading period is one to two hours long, depending on whether reading is integrated with language arts instruction.

Harris and Sipay (9), Durkin (4), and Smith, Otto, and Hansen (16) express some reservations about the effectiveness of the plan. Cushenberry (3), Newport (12), and Miller (11) give the plan mixed reviews. Only Cushenberry indicates that the advantages outweigh the disadvantages.

Although this method appears to meet the needs of children with different abilities—all third-grade readers meet with one teacher, and all second-grade readers meet with another—in practice the advantage of ease of teacher planning is offset by several limitations.

1. Children who receive the same score on a test may differ to a great extent in interests, learning rate, age, motivation, verbal abilities, learning styles, maturity, and reading subskills. Durkin believes that differences in reading interests will be especially noticeable among individuals who vary in age by two or three years. She questions whether an eight-year-old who is a high achiever is sufficiently like a ten-year-old reading on the same level for both to be provided with the same materials and type of instruction. It is probably fair to say that homogeneous grouping is an illusion, since similarity in one area does not necessarily mean similarity in others.

2. Large-group instruction in which all children read the same materials and complete the same assignments often fails to appeal to their individual interests, and work becomes routine. In their discussion of the disadvantages of the Joplin plan, Harris and Sipay express concern that teachers may be tempted to treat the class as homogeneous and rely on whole-class instruction. This is not to say the teachers cannot individualize instruction in interclass homogeneous groups, but many teachers believe that less individualization is needed in such settings.

3. Instruction that focuses on reading as a subject rather than as a process and a tool is less likely to be effective. One doesn't just read; one reads *something* for a *purpose*. Smith says (15): "Higher-level comprehension skills are more likely to be employed when students are reading material that interests them." Teachers who set aside a long period of time for formal reading instruction are less apt to provide the informal, immediate help in reading that is needed by children reading in content areas.

4. The teacher who is best acquainted with a child should teach that student. A story will illustrate this idea. One of us spent several days with a second-grade teacher who was doing a fine job of teaching. Children had made nature collections and labeled them; they had rewritten fairy tales into plays; in math learning centers, they had matched terms and operations or solved story problems written by the teacher to accord with their interests; and in the young author's corner were several creative writing projects. Although this teacher knew her children's interests and needs quite well, most of them left her and their room for reading for sixty minutes every day. Durkin asserts that interclass grouping prevents the homeroom teacher from knowing the reading abilities of all the children in the classroom, which can be a real problem when planning the teaching of other subjects, such as social studies and science.

Interclass grouping is effective when teachers inform each other about the children and plan instruction together. This approach can also help with a problem that few wish to discuss—the ineffective teacher who cannot be removed from the classroom. Some children are fortunate to be part of self-contained classrooms managed by excellent teachers; others are doomed to spend a year with a poor teacher. Interclass grouping does not solve the basic problem, but it provides occasional relief.

Spache and Spache argue that narrowing the range of reading levels in an interclass grouping system does not overcome the limitations of the method (18). They found that although grouping pupils of similar reading ability or mental capacity may make teaching easier, it does not solve the problem of attending to individual differences. Spache and Spache say: ". . . unless the number of pupils at a grade level is very large, and performances in a number of reading skills, plus intelligence, plus interests, plus learning modality, plus academic motivation are the criteria for the formation of the groups, . . . the group formed is not really homogeneous."

INDEPENDENT LEARNING

Another approach to the problem of organizing to meet individual differences is to provide for independent learning. This term is somewhat inadequate—in the final analysis, people always learn for themselves— *independent learning* refers to organizational procedures that focus on individualized rather than direct or group planning and instruction. In his discussion of teacher behavior and student learning (2), Brophy suggests that the success of individualized as opposed to direct instruction varies according to grade and ability level and subject matter.

Many forms of independent learning have been tried. Some are teacher-directed and highly prescriptive, involving the use of programmed workbooks, computer diagnosis And prescription, computer programmed instruction, and skills-management systems. Other approaches are student-directed, emphasizing self-selection, self-pacing, and exploration.

Teacher-Directed Approaches

How do some of these approaches look in practice? In one middle school, during the reading period students are assigned by reading-level range to tables in the cafeteria, where they work on boxed materials containing cards or small booklets with reading selections and questions. Answer keys and charts are provided so that the children can check their own work and graph their progress. Talking is discouraged in this area, since there are two hundred students. Teachers and aides move from table to table and hold brief conferences with students who have questions. While the reading selections are generally appealing and the exercises well constructed, children who use materials such as these day after day often start to find them boring and meaningless. Having to answer several questions after reading each passage is punishing; also, since the questions often fall into patterns, students learn to use a question-answering strategy rather than reflect on meaning. The major problem, however, is that time set aside in this way for reading is poorly used.

Another way of individualizing is to assign materials according to skill levels. Whether the setting is a classroom or a learning center, the procedure is the same: select a large number of objectives; sequence the objectives; select activities that will help students achieve the objectives; and test and prescribe for each child. The exercises in this kind of system are usually even more isolated from the natural reading process than are those in the kits. In fact, teaching on the basis of skill systems is usually quite dependent on isolating and sequencing such elements as sound-symbol associations. Drill on associations is emphasized, often through independent practice in programmed materials or workbooks. This plan, too, quickly becomes monotonous to the child who fails to see the relationship between skills and reading.

Some authorities question a dependence on a skill-system approach. Spache attacks conventional skill-deficit theory (17). He cautions that no one has been able to set forth a proper sequence for training within each skill area or even to suggest in which order identifiable abilities should be practiced. He also believes that it is a mistake to assume oral reading reflects what goes on in silent reading. In fact, says Spache, such an assumption "ignores the influences of the child's mediation and associative thinking while reading silently." In addressing the theory that reading is essentially decoding, Spache points out that readers "employ other word recognition clues such as familiarity with common sentence patterns, word function, graphic clues in letter clusters, context clues based upon probabilities, and so forth." Reading, therefore, involves more than decoding.

Harris and Sipay (9) deplore situations in which all users of a linear program must go through the same sequence of tasks. They are concerned about the disadvantages of repetitiousness and of the use of short, disconnected bits of material. Also, they find that not all aspects of the reading process can be programmed (for example, critical reading).

Veach (19), in discussing the difficulty of identifying skills deficiencies, compares learning to read with learning to walk: "If children are made conscious of what leg to move when, they will be confused in how to walk. We suggest that if children are made to be conscious of what they do to analyze reading material, they will be confused as to how to read."

We concur that instruction based on skill systems is limited and should be used sparingly.

Student-Directed Approaches

Student-directed approaches are also characterized by independent learning, but in contrast to teacher-directed approaches, children are helped to learn new skills or improve their abilities as they work on tasks they have chosen themselves and that are meaningful to them.

A classroom properly organized for activities that are largely student-directed will have reference materials readily available and an arrangement for free movement into and out of a library and media center. The person or persons working in the center need to work closely with classroom teachers and students so that appropriate materials can be easily checked out by children and teachers.

Within the classroom, tables, learning centers, conference areas, and writing and editing stations enhance both individual and small-group work.

The teacher plans with each student what is to be done, what materials will be used, what procedures will be followed, when the work is to be completed, and how the student will evaluate her or his own work. The teacher must take care to help the child plan realistically and to not needlessly control the child. This is a delicate matter. Some children are much more confident, independent, and well organized than others and seem to be better able to set reasonable goals for themselves. Teachers who wish to learn some practical techniques for helping children work independently will find Raths *et al.* a useful source (13).

Guidelines prepared by the Board of Education of the City of New York provide a carefully structured format for independent assignments and include such factors as basing assignments on previously learned materials, making them short enough to accomplish within the given time, having them written out, and being sure they are explained carefully so that children know exactly what to do (7). In addition, the guidelines suggest having necessary materials on hand or readily accessible and providing for free-time activities for children who finish their work early.

CLASSROOM ORGANIZATION FOR INSTRUCTION

Since it is obvious that children who are different in some ways share needs and interests, an approach to organization that combines grouping and individualizing seems a satisfactory one to many competent teachers.

Generally, research seems to show that a combination of large-group and small-group instruction is more efficient and produces better reading gains than instruction that occurs only in very small groups. However, it must be pointed out that the classroom setting includes a large number of interrelated variables that can confound research. As a result, teacher-effectiveness studies need to be interpreted with caution, especially when they are conducted by those with little or no classroom teaching experience. In fact, with regard to the size of the group, Brophy suggests that the most effective group size may vary with grade level (2). Basic skills must be mastered in the early grades, and the teacher needs to work with small groups in order to individualize response and feedback. In the later grades, learning involves a higher level of cognitive activity, and it is important to move the whole class along together.

Achievement-Level Grouping

Teachers organize groups for many purposes, but most teachers begin by focusing their attention on achievement-level groups. Since multileveled sets of materials, such as basals, lend themselves to group instruction, groups can be formed for placement in core materials. Both the characteristics of the materials and the abilities of the children should be considered as groups are formed. In addition, the teacher must decide how many groups can effectively be managed. A new teacher might start with two or three groups and add more later, as illustrated in the following table:

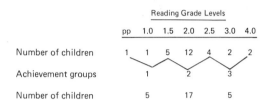

	pp	1.0	1.5	2.0	2.5	3.0	4.0
		Reading Grade Levels					
Number of children	1	1	5	12	4	2	2
Achievement groups		1		2		3	
Number of children		5		17		5	

In this second-grade classroom, the teacher felt able to manage only three groups, but achievement ranged across seven levels. Among the compromises was a decision to split the five children on the 1.5 level into different groups. Three had a very slow learning rate, lacked confidence, and required close attention; they were placed in the first group. The other two were placed in the second group, but would be watched carefully for signs of frustration and slow growth in reading. Similarly, one of the children on the 2.5 level was placed in group three and the other three were placed in group two. The number of children in the second group is quite large, but the teacher decided to work with them until classroom work routines were established and then divide them into two groups.

Achievement-level grouping is the core of the reading schedule, but consideration must also be given to grouping by skill needs and by special interests.

Skill-Needs Grouping

Using diagnostic tests and observations, the teacher forms subgroups of children with similar areas of difficulty. For example, a few children from groups 1 and 2 may stumble over words with silent letters, such as *night*, *right*, *through*, and *rough*. The teacher groups them together and meets with them for instruction. Another group may need practice in using context clues. Some children may need special help because they are learning English as a second language. Other children may benefit from such techniques as the Fernald technique (5) and the impress method developed by Heckleman (10).

The Fernald technique, an approach to remediation, emphasizes tracing and language-experience sequences. Visual, auditory, kinesthetic, and tactile (VAKT) senses are employed in the learning process. This is termed an *analytical* method, because whole words are studied from the beginning of instruction, in contrast to *synthetic* methods, which begin with letter sounds and word parts. Sound-letter associations are acquired inductively. Words are pronounced by syllables rather than letter by letter.

The impress method is neurologically based and is a system of unison reading, which differs from other remedial approaches in that the emphasis is on hearing and pronouncing words in context rather than on attending to sound-letter correspondences in words in isolation.

The block of time devoted to instruction on skill needs can include the use of such techniques. It is important to relate skill practice to other ongoing reading instruction so transfer can occur. Teachers should explain briefly why skills need to be practiced. A good method is to begin in context, then isolate to teach, and finally return to context (1).

Special-Interest Grouping

Reading instruction is aimed at enabling children to use reading to meet their needs. Reading is used to obtain information and aesthetic enjoyment. Children's and adults' enthusiasm for fiction and nonfiction writing waxes and wanes. Our experience suggests it is probably wise to work with a child's interest rather than against it. For example, a fifth-grade boy who had been reading on a third-grade level with some difficulty suddenly became interested in a particular box of adventure-story booklets. His teacher complained that he just wanted to read one after the other of these booklets and refused to do his skill-practice sheets. Should she put the booklets away? We think she would do better to put the skill sheets away, for he probably was inductively learning from the booklets the principles presented in the skill sheets. To capitalize on the boy's interest, the teacher could have asked him to look back through the stories and write down any words he did not know and mark lightly any parts he did not understand; he could also have been asked to write a sentence about a part he liked. The teacher should not require work after reading that would be negatively reinforcing. To do so would create unnecessary stress and would fail to take advantage of the boy's inner sense of timing. Veatch discusses the danger of strictly adhering to skills sequences when this may interfere with the child's own schedule for learning (19). As she puts it: "We insist that skills cannot be taught in sequence when that sequence lies in books rather than in the child. We insist that skills be learned in the PUPIL'S order, no matter what the child chooses to read."

Time set aside for special-interest assistance can also be spent helping children who want to obtain additional information related to a content area, a hobby, or any other topic. Children in each interest group may obtain information, organize it, and present it through displays, demonstrations, and reports to the class. According to Veatch, the children should organize such presentations themselves. " 'Interest Groups' should be set up and operate with relative independence of the teacher who can conduct his class in a roving fashion moving from one group of children to another . . . . The element of independence . . . is a key factor. The cohesiveness of the membership depends upon the responsibility undertaken."

Scheduling

The teacher must also decide how often to meet with the groups during the ninety minutes set aside for reading every day. After working with the children for a time it is appropriate to form additional groupings based on skill needs and special interests. The teacher might elect to divide the class into three types of groups for reading purposes: achievement-level groups, skill-needs groups, and special-interest groups. This system of multiple grouping can provide more flexibility in dealing with the myriad aspects of reading. It can also help alleviate the problem of children with a poor self-image in the lowest achievement-level group by combining them for specific purposes (either skill needs or special interests) with children in the higher achievement groups. By forming skill-needs groups, the teacher can work more efficiently with children having similar difficulties. Special-interest grouping can make it easier to lead children to read for a purpose and can increase the children's enjoyment of reading. The following table shows how a weekly schedule using such a system might look:

	MONDAY	TUESDAY	WEDNESDAY	THURSDAY	FRIDAY
Achievement-Level Groups (1—low; 2—average; 3—high)	1 (20)*	1 (20)	1 (20)	1 (20)	1 (20)
	2 (20)		2 (20)		2 (20)
	3 (20)		3 (20)		3 (20)
Skill-Needs Groups (a–d)	a (15)	b (15)	c (15)	d (15)	b (15)
		c (15)	d (15)	a (15)	
Special-Interest Groups (I–II)	I (15)	I (20)		I (20)	II (15)
		II (20)		II (20)	

* Numbers in parentheses represent minutes.

EFFECTIVE MANAGEMENT

Children need to learn to work well in groups, to work independently, and to move from one activity to another efficiently.

Studies of ineffective teaching reveal an inordinate amount of wasted time. As Zintz says (20): "Probably the most difficult task for new teachers to master is that of keeping two-thirds or more of the group actively working and personally motivated while he teaches or carries on a worthwhile discussion with a small group in the class."

Unfortunately, many teachers who improperly use their classroom time are unaware that they are doing so. Much of the time that could be spent on instruction in classrooms with low-achieving students is wasted by (1) inefficient transitional activities (putting away materials from the last activity and getting ready for the next), (2) vague assignments that must be repeated or explained individually to students, (3) interruptions by children who cannot work alone or in groups without a teacher, (4) lengthy admonishments, (5) work the children do not understand or need, and (6) excessive or inefficient correction of children's papers.

Rupley and Blair cite research on teacher effectiveness which correlates reading gains with "academic engaged time"—that is, the time that "students interact with pertinent academic materials at a moderate difficulty level, logically . . . under the direct supervision of the teacher" (14). They further state that "a structured reading program, the development of purposeful reading, systematic and meaningful development of reading skills, and the establishment of reading goals and objectives" are characteristics of effective reading instruction.

Research aside, common sense might tell us that more time spent on task would be likely to produce higher-achieving students. Children who do not have the opportunity to read very much are not likely to become good readers; those who do not have sufficient writing experience are not likely to become good writers. This does not mean that teachers should be so insensitive as to be unable to scrap plans once in a while—perhaps to help children care for a bird who has dashed itself against the window or perhaps just to have fun. A good way to evaluate one's efficiency is to invite a colleague or a sympathetic supervisor to observe, record, and discuss one's classroom routines. Also, a teacher might visit the classrooms of teachers who are known to be highly efficient and effective and learn some of their management techniques.

Establishing Work Routines

The teacher who has arranged the classroom furniture and materials carefully can then avoid some problems by visualizing the children's movements during planned activities and the transitions between them. It is easier to anticipate difficulties than to change routines later.

A generous amount of time should be devoted to establishing procedures for children to work independently and in groups. Children need to know

1. *How to obtain help.* The first group of children to understand and remember assignments, directions for using equipment, and so forth

should be assigned on a rotating basis to help their classmates. The names of the helpers should be posted weekly in a clearly visible place. Children can thus get the assistance necessary to do their work more quickly without frequently interrupting the teacher. Care should be taken to use different children as aides and to give all children an opportunity to be in charge of something within their capabilities.

2. *How to use equipment and materials.* Tape recorders, projectors, and other audiovisual materials can be operated by very young children, if sufficient time is spent instructing them. Also, children should be taught how to use, as well as to put away, such supplies as pencils, paste, paper, paint, and crayons.

3. *How to work in groups.* Children must learn to take turns, to give everyone a chance to participate, and to be polite to one another. A teacher might choose a child who is able to work well with others to be a group leader. The teacher should explain to the pupils why the leader was chosen: the student is able to take turns, stay on task, not tease or laugh at others, and so on. The teacher should also assure the children that all will be given an opportunity to be a group leader who demonstrates these traits.

4. *How to work in learning centers.* A learning center can be designed to help children learn isolated tasks with self-correcting materials or to explore a subject in depth. In either case, the procedures for working in the center must be clearly understood. Younger children and those new to centers might be taken through the steps of using the center in small groups. From time to time, teachers need to check on how the center is being used and alter procedures as necessary. The effectiveness of the center also needs to be evaluated in order to find out whether the children are learning the associations, skills, interests, or attitudes which the centers were designed to teach. Teachers can create short, informal tests or questionnaires to discover whether a center is effective.

Centers can be created within a classroom or in a library and media area to increase the availability of a particularly popular tape, a set of references, or whatever seems to be in demand by several children at once. For example, headsets can be used to decrease the waiting time for a desirable tape, or multiple copies can be made for in-school use of a map, a set of directions, or some other material that is in heavy demand.

Children can be helped to avoid dawdling and to take turns by a timer that can be set by each child according to the maximum number of minutes the teacher has decided upon for the center's use. Having children select numbers hanging on a hook, as in the systems set up by bakeries and meat markets, can help children estimate when their turns will come and avoid a scramble in a particular center. Children might also be assigned to a designated center at a prescribed time. Such a schedule should be posted. In each center, there should be a place for children to write their names and the dates and times they used the center. Very young children can be taught to use a simple system such as coloring squares on their name cards. Each center can be given a particular color or color combination, and color markers can be kept at each.

5. *How to work independently.* Children can be taught to work independently, but the teacher must create the right conditions for independent work by insuring that assignments are worthwhile, that directions are clear and available for review in writing or on a tape, and that a practice activity is done in the group as a preliminary. Children need to learn to start their work promptly, get help from designated sources if they need it, check or proofread their work, avoid distracting others, and move from an activity they have finished to another.

A PLAN FOR READING-MATERIALS MANAGEMENT FOR GROUP AND INDIVIDUAL LEARNING

The charts in this section have been designed to help teachers organize their reading materials for group and individual instruction.

Two major assumptions underlie the charts. The first is that teachers can best meet the needs of their students by planning both for group interaction and for individual learning. The second is that a sound program of reading development is one that integrates the use of multilevel trade books or basals with language-experience approaches.

Completing the Grade Level Charts

These charts may be completed as a cooperative project. Some teachers find it beneficial to share the task of charting materials available in their building. In this way, they complete the task quickly and can then simply make copies of the charts pertinent to the reading level of children within their classrooms.

A teacher working alone to chart materials need do so only for the range of reading levels within the classroom.

Step 1. Adjust the materials charts (Figures 10-1 to 10-7). Before beginning to chart materials, review the categories to be sure they agree with your teaching objectives. If necessary, some categories may be eliminated and others substituted.

Step 2. Chart materials. Only those commercial or teacher-made materials that have been found to be effective should be charted. Simply write the title of the material in the left-hand column, and place a check ($\sqrt{}$) under each category for which the material is appropri-

FIGURE 10-1
Materials Chart—Readiness

Materials	Discrimination (1) — Auditory				Discrimination (2) — Visual		Discrimination (3) — Visual-Motor		Letter (4) — Names			Letter (4) — Alphabetizing	Letter (5) — Sounds		Letter (6) — Format		Sight Words (7)				Language (8)		Development (9) — Language / Conceptual	Development (9) — Conceptual			
	Rhyming words	Beginning sounds	Middle sounds	Ending sounds	Letters	Words	Tracing	Copying	Capital	Small	Matching	Alphabetizing	Consonants	Vowels	Capital	Small	Colors	Numbers	Signs — Daily life	Other	Listening	Oral expression	Following directions	Categorizing	Sequencing	Predicting outcomes	General

FIGURE 10-2
Materials Chart—Grade 1

Materials	Sight Words 1				Sound-Symbol Association 2						Blending 3		Struct. Anal. 4			Comprehension 5				Language Experience 6				Concept Development 7			
	Daily life (TV, K-Mart)	Classroom (Color names)	Basic (the, and)	General	Consonants	Consonant-digraphs	Consonant blends	Vowels—short	Vowels—long	Vowel combinations	Left-to-right	Word-family substitution	Inflectional endings	Compound words	Preprimer	Primer	1.0	1.5	Word charts	Sentence expansion	Story starters	Listening	Following directions	Categorizing	General vocabulary	Sequencing

FIGURE 10-3
Materials Chart—Grade 2

Materials	1 Sight Words				2 Sound-Symbol Association						3 Blending		4 Struct. Anal.			5 Comprehension				6 Language Experience				7 Concept Development				8 Ref.
	Daily life	Classroom	Basic	General	Consonant digraphs	Consonant blends	Vowels — short	Vowels — long	Vowel combination	Spelling	Left-to-right in context	Word-family substitutions	Compound words	Multisyllable words	Common affixes	Literal	Interpretive	Critical	Creative	Word charts	Sentence expansion	Story starters	Listening	Following directions	Categorizing	Prepositions, conj., pronoun	General vocab.	Dictionary

209

FIGURE 10-4
Materials Chart—Grade 3

	Materials	Sight Words (1)			Sound-Symbol Association (2)				Structural Analysis (3)				Spelling (4)				Comprehension (5)				Content Area Reading (6)			Language Experience (7)					Concept Development (8)		
		Basic	Automaticity for words	Automaticity for phrases	Consonant comb.—review	Vowel comb.—review	Use of vowel generalization	Shifting accent	Multisyllable words	Prefixes	Suffixes	Word patterns	Useful generalization	Dictionary use	Literal	Interpretive	Critical	Creative	Vocabulary	Organizational patterns	Main ideas	Word charts	Sentence expansion	Written expression	Literary form experiments	Listening	Categorizing	Abstract ref: (who, which, etc.)	General

FIGURE 10-5
Materials Chart—Grade 4

	1 Word Identification			2 Spelling		3 Vocab.			4 Comprehension				5 Content Areas			6 Rate			7 Language Experience			8 Study Skills			
Materials	Sound-symbol assoc.—review	Structural analysis-review	Basic sight words—review	Word patterns	Useful generalization	Roots-affixes context clues	Connotation general	Sentence patterns	Literal	Interpretative	Critical	Creative	Concepts and vocabulary	Organization patterns	Main ideas	Skimming	Scanning	Flexibility	Oral expression	Written expression	Listening	Basic reference	Library use	Mapping	Outlining

FIGURE 10-6
Materials Chart—Grade 5

Materials	1 Spelling			2 Vocabulary				3 Comprehension							4 Content Areas				5 Rate		6 Language Experience			7 Study Skills				
	Word ident. review	Word patterns	Useful generalization	Word origins	Roots and affixes	Context clues	Connotation	Basic general	Sentence patterns	Organization patterns	Main ideas	Literal	Interpretive	Critical	Creative	Social Studies	Science	Math	Literature	Skimming	Flexibility	Oral expression	Written expression	Listening	Basic references	Library	Mapping	Notes, text, listening

FIGURE 10-7
Materials Chart—Grade 6

Materials	1 Spelling			2 Vocabulary				3 Comprehension							4 Content Areas				5 Rate		6 Language Experience			7 Study Skills			
	Word ident. review	Word patterns	Useful generalization	Word origins	Roots and affixes	Context clues	Connotation	General	Sentence patterns	Organization patterns	Main ideas	Literal	Interpretive	Critical	Creative	Social studies	Science	Math	Literature	Skimming	Flexibility	Oral expression	Written expression	Listening	Library references	SQ3R	Notes, text, listening	Report writing

213

ate. In the case of the comprehension category, however, indicate the reading level of the material—for example, 2.0, 2.5, 3.0, and so on.

An advantage of charting is that it becomes apparent for which categories few materials are available. Steps can be taken to make or obtain materials for these categories.

Completing the Group and Individual Plans

The teacher must decide how many groups to have. Factors such as the number of students, the range of abilities, and the time available to meet with each group should be considered. The group and individual plan (see Figure 10-8) provides for children being members of a primary group, but the teacher should also use multiple-grouping strategies in order to individualize. For example, a group may be formed for a short time to teach a

FIGURE 10-8
Group and Individual Plan

Group Reading Range: _____

Group Profile: _____

Materials/ Activities	Group (G) or individual (I)	Teacher assisted	Self-corrected	Time	Frequency	Students 1	2	3	4	5	6	7	8	9	10	11	12
1.																	
2.																	
3.																	
4.																	
5.																	
6.																	
7.																	
8.																	
9.																	
10.																	
11.																	
12.																	
13.																	
14.																	
15.																	
16.																	
17.																	
18.																	

skill, or children can be encouraged to form their own groups to gather information or for a creative project.

Next, the teacher must decide upon group membership. Factors such as social needs, personality, learning rate, overall level of functioning, abilities, and interests will be important. She may use formal and/or informal diagnostic procedures and a simple chart to record progress.

Step 1. On the group and individual plan form, record the group reading range and write a brief group profile. Next, write the names of the children in the group on the diagonal lines across the top of the form. Do this for each group you form.

Step 2. After reflecting on the needs of the students in a particular group, consult the materials chart or charts on the students' reading level and select the materials you wish to use in group and individual instruction. Keep a record of which materials are heavily used by the group and which materials are used for individual instruction.

Step 3. For each title listed, keep a record of

1. whether the materials will be used in groups or by individuals.
2. whether the material will be used in teacher-assisted activities.
3. whether the material is self-correcting.
4. how much time is required for the activity.
5. how often the material will be used each week.

Step 4. Indicate which materials and activities are for each child in the group by placing checks under a child's name opposite each title that child will be using. Materials and activities should be changed periodically.

SUMMARY

It is our conclusion that probably the best management system for today's classroom is one that includes small-group work, individualized work, and close attention to providing productive reading experiences within the classroom. Techniques stressing interclass grouping or focusing on independent learning by means of programmed materials are usually undesirable for purposes of attaining comprehensive reading instruction.

ACTIVITIES RELATED TO THE CHAPTER

1. Interview one or two classroom teachers in the primary and upper elementary grades. Find out through your interviews how they made decisions concerning the placement of children in appropriate groups, the number of groups to have, and so forth.

2. Take two levels of the reading materials charts in this chapter and visit a reading curriculum center. Classify at least ten pieces of material using the charts.
3. Visit three or four classrooms on the same grade level to compare methods of organizing with regard to the types of subgroups established, the use of learning centers, the use of materials for independent study, efficient transitional activities, and so forth.
4. Using what you learned from doing activity 3, design a room in which you would like to teach.

BIBLIOGRAPHY AND REFERENCES

1. Bader, Lois: *Reading Diagnosis and Remediation in Classroom and Clinic*, Macmillan, New York, 1980, p. 9.
2. Brophy, Jere E.: "Teacher Behavior and Student Learning," *Educational Leadership*, 37:33, 36 (1979).
3. Cushenberry, Donald C.: "The Joplin Plan and Cross Grade Grouping," in Wallace Z. Ramsey, ed., *Organizing the Individual Differences*, International Reading Assoc., Newark, DE, 1967.
4. Durkin, Dolores: *Teaching Them to Read*, 2nd ed., Allyn and Bacon, Boston, 1974, pp. 79-81.
5. Fernald, Grace M.: *Remedial Techniques in Basic School Subjects*, McGraw-Hill, New York, 1943.
6. Fry, Edward: *Elementary Reading Instruction*, McGraw-Hill, New York, 1977.
7. Division of Curriculum Development, Board of Education of the City of New York: *A Guide for Beginning Teachers of Reading*, New York, 1969, pp. 13-14.
8. Harris, Albert J., and Edward R. Sipay: *How to Improve Reading Ability*, (6th ed.) McKay, New York, 1975, p. 110.
9. ————: *How to Teach Reading*, Longman, New York, 1979, pp. 179.
10. Heckleman, R. G.: "Using the Neurological Impress Remedial Reading Technique," *Academic Therapy Quarterly*, 1:235-239 (1966).

8. Harris, Albert J., and Edward R. Sipay: *How to Improve Reading Ability*, (6th ed.) McKay, New York, 1975, p. 110.
9. ———: *How to Teach Reading,* Longmans, New York, 1979, pp. 179.
10. Heckleman, R. G.: "Using the Neurological Impress Remedial Reading Technique," *Academic Therapy Quarterly*, 1:235–239 (1966).
11. Miller, Wilma H.: "Some Less Commonly Used Forms of Grouping," *Elementary English*, 48:989–992 (1971).
12. Newport, John F.: "The Joplin Plan: The Score," *The Reading Teacher*, 21:158–162 (1967).
13. Raths, Louis, *et al.*: *Teaching for Thinking*, Merrill, Columbus, OH, 1967.
14. Rupley, William H., and Timothy R. Blair: "Characteristics of Effective Reading," *Educational Leadership*, 36:171–173 (1978).
15. Smith, Richard J.: "Developing Reading Maturity in the Elementary School," in Richard J. Smith and Dale D. Johnson, eds., *Teaching Children to Read*, Addison-Wesley, Reading, MA, 1976, p. 12.
16. Smith, Richard J., Wayne Otto, and Lee Hansen: *The School Reading Program*, Houghton Mifflin, Boston, 1978, pp. 128–129.
17. Spache, George D.: *Diagnosing and Correcting Reading Disabilities*, Allyn and Bacon, Boston, 1976, pp. 292–293.
18. Spache, George D., and Evelyn B. Spache: *Reading in the Elementary School*, 3rd ed., Allyn and Bacon, Boston, 1973, pp. 575–576.
19. Veatch, Jeannette: *Reading in the Elementary School*, 2nd ed., John Wiley & Sons, New York, 1978, pp. 216, 502–503.
20. Zintz, Miles V.: *The Reading Process*, 2nd ed., Wm. C. Brown, Dubuque, IA, 1975, p. 92.

Children With Special Needs

11

Overview

Teachers of reading are faced with the task of providing effective instruction to *all* children, not merely to those who conform to a particular image. This chapter describes some of the diversities found among elementary school children. Teachers are urged to be equally accepting of all children. Strategies for providing effective reading instruction to all children are described.

Definition of Terms

1. *Accommodation*—instructional, curricular, or logistical alterations made by a teacher so that a child with a physical problem can profit optimally from reading instruction.
2. *Auditory*—having to do with hearing.
3. *Dialect*—a way of speaking associated with a region of the country or a particular social class.
4. *Plan of action*—a precise account of the reading instruction a teacher intends to provide to a child or a group of children.
5. *Self-concept*—the perceptions that an individual has of himself or herself.

eet the individual needs. How often have you heard these words uttered by educators? The phrase is popular, but do teachers of elementary reading really meet the individual needs of children?

A colleague once remarked: "Schools meet the individual needs of students as long as the children are average in intelligence, average in reading ability, and neither introverted nor extroverted." On the same topic, Musgrave says (15):

> Everyone talks about individualized instruction. Undergraduate students preparing to teach talk about individualized instructional strategies in classes where theory and practice are poles apart. Graduate students attend education classes and become sophisticated talkers and writers concerning individualized instructional concepts and practices. Teachers attend local, state, and national meetings where the themes and entire programs are devoted to individualized instruction. Yet, few teachers actually practice individualized instructional strategies in their classrooms. Is it possible that teachers have been taught to teach and write about individualized instruction, while they have not been taught how to implement these practices in their classrooms?

To Musgrave's statement, the words of the International Reading Association's Commission on High-Quality Teacher Education can be added (24):

> Most beginning elementary teachers have been involved in only one or at best, two brief courses in teaching reading. They know a few of the reading skills that should be taught, and perhaps one method of teaching. But they have little or no knowledge of the limitless number of difficulties which children can encounter in learning to read, of how to diagnose those difficulties, and of the types of instructional adjustments that can be made for different individuals to produce better results.

In this chapter we want to focus on the uniqueness of children, on how the differences among children relate to their ability to acquire proficiency in reading, and on measures which teachers can take to meet the individual needs of children.

Naturally, it is impossible to discuss every way in which children may differ. Therefore we will confine ourselves to discussing the major differences found among American children. There are children with learning disabilities, children who exhibit slow learning rates, children who differ in their language or cultural background from some local or national norm, gifted children, and physically limited children.

LEARNING DISABILITIES

Court rulings and federal mandates have made it necessary for American elementary schools to educate children whose psychological or physical characteristics are such that they have great difficulty learning. Many school districts customarily served these children by placing them all into special-education classrooms and, despite their individual differences, usually giving all these children the same instruction.

In recent years, however, educators have come to the realization that not all children who fail to learn in regular classrooms do so for the same reasons. As a result, the instruction offered has become more suited to the individual children, and there has been development and growth of learning disabilities programs in elementary schools.

Definition

In the literature we found an almost unbelievable number of definitions of the term *learning disability*. Some were short and easy to comprehend, while others were long and extremely technical. There are disagreements among authorities as to what correlates with or constitutes a learning disability.

Kirk and Bateman contend (12):

A learning disability refers to a retardation, disorder, or delayed development in one or more of the processes of speech, language, reading, writing, arithmetic, or other school subjects resulting from a psychological handicap caused by a possible cerebral dysfunction and/or emotional or behavioral disturbances. It is not the result of mental retardation, sensory deprivation, or cultural or instructional factors.

Most elementary schools closely adhere to the definition of learning disability designed by the United States Congress (20):

The term "children with specific learning disabilities" means those children who have a disorder in one or more of the basic psychological processes involved in understanding or in using language, spoken or written, which disorder may manifest itself in imperfect ability to listen, think, speak, read, write or spell, or do mathematical calculations. Such disorders include such conditions as perceptual handicaps, brain injury, minimal brain dysfunction, dyslexia, and developmental aphasia. Such term does not include children who have learning problems which are primarily the result of visual, hearing, or motor handicaps, of mental retardation, of emotional disturbance, or of environmental, cultural, or economic disadvantage.

Kaluger and Kolson maintain that the following are characteristic of the learning-disabled child (10):

1. Intellectual capacity is average or better.
2. There is a discrepancy between expected and actual achievement.
3. There is a disorder in one or more of the basic psychological processes involved in using spoken or written language.
4. The deficiencies are not primarily due to visual, hearing, or motor hand-

icaps; to mental retardation; to emotional disturbance; or to environmental disadvantage.

Implications

We are presenting this information regarding learning disabilities for at least four major reasons. First, teachers of reading need to be fairly knowledgeable in the area of learning disabilities. This does not mean that teachers of reading should become learning disabilities specialists. Rather, teachers of reading should have a clear understanding of what a learning disability is. Teachers who know this are better able to identify students who might possess learning disabilities. Subsequent testing and observation by qualified personnel can then either confirm or refute the teacher's suspicions.

For the teacher who is unsure of which children to refer for assessment, the following description of the behaviors indicative of a learning disability may prove helpful. According to Smith (26), a child with a learning disability

usually

is an intelligent child who fails at school.

is a child who at school age reads *on* for *no*; writes 41 for 14; writes *p* for *d*, *q*, or *b*; or cannot remember the sequence of letters that make up a word.

is a child who loses homework, misplaces books, or doesn't know what day it is, what year, or what season.

is a child who calls breakfast *lunch*, who is confused by *yesterday* and *tomorrow*, or whose timing is always off.

frequently

is a child who cannot picture things in the mind—that is, who cannot visually remember what has been seen.

is a quiet child who bothers nobody in the classroom but does not learn.

is the older child whose language comes out jumbled, who stops and starts in the middle of a sentence or an idea . . . who talks about hospitals, animals, and enemies.

sometimes

is a child who can add and multiply but not subtract or divide, who can do math mentally but can't write it down.

is a child who skips, omits, or adds words when reading aloud.

Second, the role of reading in relation to learning disabilities should be understood. A child's disability may or may not be reading related. If the cause is, for example, medical, then the child's instruction generally should not be the responsibility of the teacher of reading. However, should the disability be reading-related, then in most cases the child should receive instruction from the reading teacher.

Third, when children are classified as having a learning disability, the teacher of reading should not think of them as slow or mentally retarded. As we previously pointed out, such children have average or better intelligence and possess the potential to perform better than they are. If a disability is in the area of reading, proper and effective instruction from the teacher of reading will be likely to improve the child's achievement considerably.

Fourth, the learning disabilities teacher is undoubtedly an experienced professional, with some definite ideas about children with learning disabilities. A child's disability may exist in reading and/or in another area. Obviously, the learning disabilities teacher cannot be an expert in every field. Therefore, teachers of reading should not necessarily assume that this individual has more knowledge about reading than they themselves possess.

It is our hope that you now have a philosophical understanding of learning disabilities. Let us now discuss some pedagogical issues.

Instruction

A child with a learning disability is a student who can learn. For some reason, the child is not achieving at a level commensurate with potential.

A child classified as learning disabled should be seen by teachers in positive, not negative, terms. This classification implies that the child can achieve more than he or she has previously achieved. Once the factors behind the low achievement have been recognized, the teacher must provide special instruction. Such personalized instruction will probably require an additional effort on the part of the teacher. However, providing maximally effective instruction for every child is one of the primary objectives of an elementary school.

For teachers of children with learning disabilities, we offer the following instructional suggestions:

1. A teacher should find out what a child's deficiencies in reading are and, once they are determined, correct those deficiencies through appropriate instruction. This is a two-step process. First, a diagnosis of the child's reading competence is conducted. This determines the specific strengths and weaknesses of the student's reading. Then, a program of instruction suited to the needs of the child can be initiated.
2. Once a child's deficiencies are determined, an instructional plan of action should be formulated, and this plan should be shared with the

child. In the plan, the teacher lists the skills to be acquired by the child and the activities to be employed in order to teach these skills. By sharing the plan with the child, the teacher helps the student understand the purpose of the subsequent instruction. It may also cause the child to cooperate with the teacher, as the plan is essentially shared between them.

3. The instruction should be child-oriented and should not be for the convenience of the teacher. Students with learning disabilities in general, and reading disabilities in particular, usually have not had successful school experiences. Although the past cannot be erased, we can make the future for these children brighter. This can be done by providing them with maximally effective instruction. Regrettably, some teachers do not do what can be most beneficial to children. Various factors—too many students, not enough time, insufficient instructional materials, and so on—are cited by teachers as reasons for not employing effective teaching practices. However, such rationalization arises from a single factor, the unwillingness of the teacher to be inconvenienced. Some teachers simply lack the motivation to do their utmost to create a situation of optimal learning for children.

4. The child should have successful experiences particularly in the early stages of an instructional program and throughout its duration. Educational psychologists have long affirmed the importance of positive reinforcement in the teaching-learning process. In discussing positive reinforcement, Fillbeck says (7): "Learning research has consistently shown that new responses are repeated as a function of the consequences of those responses. If the consequences are pleasurable, the learner tends to continue making the response to maintain the pleasurable consequences." For most of us, succeeding at a task leads to what Fillbeck terms *pleasurable consequences*, and we are likely to work at a high level in order to succeed. Therefore, a teacher who desires maximum effort from a child with a learning disability, must insure that the student attain some measure of success in the early stages of an endeavor. Then, if the student continues to have successful experiences and thus forms a positive perception of the activity, the student will be likely to be maximally cooperative and industrious in the instructional program.

5. Frequent feedback conferences should be held with parents to inform them of their children's successes in the program of instruction. Generally speaking, parents of children with learning disabilities tend to be active in education-related matters. They attend school functions, are especially interested in their child's well-being, and are willing to support the school's efforts for their child. Such parents should be informed of their child's achievement. They can become devoted allies of the teachers, and as a result, they can immeasurably enhance the school's accomplishments by their efforts at home with the child. Also, parental approval means a great deal to most children. Students usu-

ally work even harder when they are aware that their parents know of and care about their successes in school.

6. Instruction should be concerned not only with short-term gains, but also with long-range improvement on the part of the child. Otto *et al.* state (19): "Reading is a developmental, orderly, organized process and should be taught in just this manner. Many reading skills tend to progress from the easier to more complex ones. The easier skills combine to form more complex behaviors in the competent reader." Most teachers know that the process of learning to read takes place in a logical sequence; unfortunately, classroom instructional practices sometimes contradict this. Some teachers are so preoccupied with covering a book or a set of materials that they neglect to insure that individual children are truly mastering the materials' content. Thus, some children may show exemplary progress, but it will probably be short-lived. Clearly, this type of instruction must be avoided, not only because it is ineffective, but also because of its gross unfairness to students.

7. Instruction should not ignore the affective side of children. In recent years, research has reaffirmed the importance of the affective domain in the learning process. With regard to reading, the interests, attitudes, and self-concept of a child are particularly pertinent. As previously stated, a child possessing a positive attitude toward reading usually will work harder at learning to read than will one with a negative attitude. Quandt describes the relationship between reading and self-concept (21): "Studies that have correlated levels of reading achievement with levels of self-concept indicate that a positive association exists between the two." He adds: "Not only does poor self-concept interfere with learning to read but the resulting reading disability leads to an even poorer self-concept." Obviously, then, if teachers wish to be maximally successful, they will make sure their instruction complements, and does not conflict with, the affective side of children.

8. Children should be evaluated in terms of their past performance. Frequent evaluation lets both the teacher and the child know how successful their efforts have been. The achievements of learning-disabled children should not be compared with those of other children; rather, such children should compete with their prior performance. For example, did a child show more growth on the previous test or on the one just taken? How did the student's achievement after this assessment interval compare with the achievement after the preceding one? When learning-disabled children compete with their own performance, they do not become discouraged if their efforts consistently fall below those of their classmates. In this way, too, the teacher has a realistic standard against which to assess the children's performance.

The discussion in these eight paragraphs could apply as well to remedial readers who do not have learning disabilities. Since both remedial readers and learning-disabled children achieve at a level appreciably below their potential, for reasons which may or may not be the same, reading instruction for both groups may be quite similar. Both groups of children require special attention on the part of a teacher of reading.

SLOW LEARNING RATES

Educators employ many terms to characterize children who learn at rates slower than normal. Entire books have been devoted to discussing the differences in these categories. We will not attempt to do that in this book, but we will confine our remarks to children classified as *slow learners*. Dechant states (6): "The slow learner may or may not be retarded in terms of his ability level, but he is always retarded as to grade level. He generally has an IQ of between 70 and 90." Cruickshank and Johnson feel that slow learners "form 15 to 17 percent of the school population that cannot quite 'keep up' and are usually doing the poorest work in the regular classroom. Slow learners are essentially normal in their emotional, social, physical, and motor development" (4). If Cruickshank and Johnson are correct in their estimate that there is a rather high number of slow learners, then individuals charged with providing instruction to these students would do well to be informed about them. It is logical to assume that reading is an area in which it is especially difficult for slow learners to gain proficiency.

Reading

A student's success in acquiring the diverse skills needed in reading is frequently predicated upon earlier learning. As a result, since the reading curriculum is primarily designed for students of average intelligence or above, the slow learner usually falls behind the remainder of the class in achievement. Kephart describes the results (11): "Since later learning is based in large degree upon these earlier learnings, such a child finds himself in ever-increasing difficulty as his school experience continues."

Contrary to the opinions expressed by some, no single method has consistently proven to be most effective in providing reading instruction to children with slow learning rates. According to the Board of Directors of the International Reading Association (2): "No single method or approach nor any one set of instructional materials has proven to be most effective for all children."

The teacher must be able to present material in ways consistent with the abilities of slow learners. This seems to be the most crucial factor in instructing such students. The use of a particular method alone does not insure success with these children.

Students with slow learning rates may not achieve at or above their grade placement level in school. Teachers who employ ability grouping to facilitate reading instruction usually consign slow-learning students to the lowest achieving group. Some teachers come to feel a sense of futility regarding slow learners. These teachers contend that no matter how hard they work with these students the results are meager.

We can empathize with such teachers, but we do not agree with their opinion. Teachers of children with slow learning rates must remember that these students *can* learn. Clearly the expectations of a teacher of such children must be realistic. Generally, slow learners will not achieve as well as the average child, but they can learn to read according to their own potential.

We have also heard the opinion expressed that children with slow learning rates do not want to learn. We disagree with this viewpoint, too. Undoubtedly, some slow learners have a negative view of school and of reading. Such a reaction is natural, given the many failures and frustrations these children have experienced. Some slow-learning students have to be convinced that they can learn. But if they can be convinced, and if they begin to have successful experiences, their negative attitudes will greatly diminish or even disappear.

Instruction

On the basis of our own professional experiences, as well as those presented in the literature, we offer the following suggestions relative to teaching reading to slow learners:

1. Get to know the child as well as is professionally possible. By knowing the likes, dislikes, and interests of the children, you will probably be able to make them more responsive to your instructional efforts.
2. Make your instruction a low-risk venture for the child. A teacher should try to make the student have many more successes than failures at learning.
3. Remember that individual differences exist among slow learners. The differences among the reading proficiencies and deficiencies of these students will be as marked as the differences among those of their classmates.
4. Change your style of instruction if a child is not learning through your present manner of teaching. Many slow learners have a definite style of learning and will not achieve at a maximum level if instruction does not take account of that learning style.
5. Use concrete, practical learning examples as much as possible in your instruction. When slow learners can employ more than one sense (touch, sight, smell, and so on) in a learning situation, they tend to grasp the content better.
6. Have a high degree of repetition in your instructional program. Research suggests that slow learners need much reinforcement if they are to retain, on a long-term basis, concepts taught to them.

7. Remember that slow learners need to acquire the same basic reading skills as normal children. The rate at which the skills are presented should probably be somewhat slower, and the manner in which they are presented may be different, but the skills should be essentially the same as those of the regular reading program.

8. Emphasize oral language. Bond, Tinker, and Wasson state (3): "It is advisable to use more oral reading and oral prestudy in instructing slow learning children. Many of them need to vocalize what they are reading before they can comprehend it well. The fact that vocalization slows the reading is of little significance for these children."

9. When making up groups in order to teach reading, avoid having slow learners primarily associate with each other. It has been shown that slow learners achieve more when they interact with more able students.

10. Provide short-range goals. Slow learners should take frequent looks at their progress. Small successes can provide strong motivation.

Reger describes an elementary school's obligation to provide instruction to slow learners, as well as to all other children (22): "Schools are responsible for the instruction of children, and teachers are the agents who carry the burden of responsibility under the facilitating influence of the school administrator. The responsibility exists for all children, not just for those who are free of problems."

LINGUISTIC AND CULTURAL DIVERSITY

Our society is such that there will always be children from diverse cultural and linguistic backgrounds in our schools. Since providing education to all children is our continuing responsibility, it behooves us to ask the question: In the teaching of reading, how can we do a better job of taking children's culture and language into account?

When writing this section we interviewed a person who over the years has taught hundreds of children from diverse backgrounds and who has attained tremendous results. When we asked him to give us his formula for success, he replied: "Each night, I plan the next day's lesson as if it will be the last one I will ever teach. I remember that some of the children haven't learned how to learn, but it's my job to see to it they do learn. Each day, I teach a lesson with the same vigor, but hopefully with more ability, as I had on the first day I ever taught children. I try my utmost to insure *each* child learns to read better *each* day. And after teaching a lesson, I ask myself how can I do a better job of teaching reading to these youngsters? Teaching these children to read is the best gift I can ever give to them."

Thompson lists some of the terms educators have used in attempting to characterize the children of linguistic and cultural minorities (30). Philosophically, we find ourselves at odds with most of these characterizations. The majority of them have very negative connotations and can lead teachers to develop negative perceptions of children, consciously or subconsciously. This can result in teachers exerting less than their maximum efforts when providing instruction.

Instruction

We cannot give you a single, definitive answer relative to offering reading instruction that is responsive to linguistic and cultural variation among children. Nevertheless, the following seem to be appropriate ways of thinking about the problems involved:

1. Teachers should remember that all children are capable of learning, that all children do learn if afforded the proper opportunities, and that if motivated, all children will desire to learn.
2. The reading curriculum of most elementary schools does not take account of varying linguistic and cultural backgrounds among children. For this reason, particularly in the initial grades, many students fail to achieve the school's reading objectives. Schools should carefully analyze the reading curriculum with this consideration in mind.
3. In recent years, publishing companies have done an appreciably better job in developing instructional materials which reflect our pluralistic society. It is imperative that, whenever possible, such materials be employed. Students tend to be more interested in materials which have content and characters congruent with their own experiential background.
4. Children with a negative self-concept can come to believe they are incapable of learning in school and may develop a facade of indifference or hostility toward teachers and other educators. Teachers must learn to feel warmth and a genuine sense of concern for these children. Spache and Spache say that "the teacher must show the child that she trusts him, respects his judgments, expects him to succeed (in a task selected to be within his capacities), and believes he is making progress and that he wants to relate to her" (28).
5. The teacher should plan instructional activities so that children will experience success. Many students possess negative attitudes toward reading. These feelings can be countered if children begin to have successful experiences in reading.
6. The Task Force on Teaching English to the Disadvantaged reports (16): "Most of the elementary programs were doing work in oral language, but much of it was unstructured. Little work, for example, was done in analyzing the oral language difficulties and deficiencies of students and developing specific programs to correct these problems." Oral language is important in learning to read, and it must be given careful attention. Schools and teachers must thoroughly plan how they

will develop oral language skills with children who seem to be deficient in this area and how they will regularly assess children's proficiency.

7. Variations in language and culture imply variations in values and in behavioral standards. Teachers must realize this and not attempt to enforce a narrow value system or a rigid standard of proper behavior.

8. Language is probably the most controversial issue among educators. Children who are non–English speaking or who speak a nonstandard dialect may each present instructional difficulties for some teachers; however, it must be remembered that the two are indeed different.

Non-English-speaking children speak another language in their homes. Educators are beginning to understand the reading and educational needs of these children. Special educational programs exist in many schools to aid them in becoming competent readers of English. This task is rather specialized, and we refer you to sources which discuss the topic at greater length than can be afforded here (13, 23, 33).

Children who speak a nonstandard dialect present a different instructional challenge for teachers. *These children must not be ridiculed or assumed to be intellectually inferior.* Otto, McMenemy, and Smith put the question of nonstandard dialect in perspective (18): "The first function of the school is to accept each child's language as a basic personal characteristic and then to introduce the child slowly and without trauma to more socially acceptable language for expressing his experiences."

Sawyer dismisses the notion that these students speak unique languages (25): "No linguistic studies . . . have revealed enough variation to justify calling any of these dialects different languages." She adds: "If a new dialect is to be mastered by the students, the teacher must help them to form new language habits, just as the teacher of a foreign language does. For this reason, some of the techniques of pattern drill used to teach a new language are useful."

GIFTED CHILDREN

If you are wondering why a section of this textbook deals with gifted children, consider the words of Cutts and Moseley (5): "We in the United States have far surpassed the designs of the philosophers in establishing and maintaining universal schooling. But we have fallen short of the ideal of identifying our bright and talented children and providing them with an education adapted to their capacity."

It has been our experience that gifted children are largely neglected. These children are generally of high intelligence and read appreciably above grade level; neither administrators nor teachers devote much special attention to their needs. Gifted children do not usually pose severe problems in a school. They generally grasp lessons quite quickly. These children have not recently been the focal point of any massive federal educational program. Parents of gifted children usually are not organized or vocal. Is it any wonder then that schools by and large ignore gifted children?

Many teachers who attempt to provide meaningful reading instruction to gifted students consider their efforts to have been rather ineffective. There are many reasons given for this, including large class sizes, a lack of time for planning, a scarcity of suitable materials, and a lack of other teachers who understand how to effectively instruct such students.

Characteristics

For years, children who score very high on intelligence tests have been termed *gifted*. Many gifted children do score high, but educators presently recognize that intelligence tests do not infallibly identify these children. The cultural bias of some intelligence tests, as well as the fact that some children simply do not test well, have led educators to search for alternate ways in which to identify gifted children. Lee (14) contends research shows that gifted children usually

are in slightly better physical condition

have the same social and emotional needs as other children

have a wide range of interests and often follow up an interest in depth

are well adjusted emotionally and socially

have more positive self-concepts and make more realistic self-appraisals

are apt to achieve more than average as adults

show superior achievement in most school subjects

are selected as friends more than others

have fewer personality problems than the average child

seem to be more independent in judgment

come from homes with somewhat greater emotional stability

Witty (32) who has also studied the characteristics of gifted children, states: "In addition to their superiority in school work and related activities, they were found to be well-adjusted socially and to get along well with their peers."

Instruction

Teachers of gifted students play a crucial role in determining whether or not these children are going to attain *optimal* success in reading. Various research investigations have substantiated the teacher's importance in facilitating learning by such students. Nelson and Cleland say (17): "It is the teacher who sets the environment which inspires or destroys self-confidence, encourages or suppresses interests, develops or neglects abilities, fosters or banishes creativity, stimulates or discourages critical thinking, and facilitates or frustrates achievement." We would like to offer the following remarks to teachers of gifted children:

1. According to Nelson and Cleland (17), teachers should be cognizant "of certain traits and behaviors which characterize highly creative children:

    "Less concern with convention and authority;

    "More independence in judgment and thinking;

    "Keener sense of humor;

    "Less concern with order and organization;

    "A more temperamental nature."

2. These children are of superior intelligence, but they still must acquire certain reading skills. Teachers of gifted children sometimes assume that these students already possess, because of their intelligence, virtually every reading skill. One does occasionally encounter such a child, but in general care should be taken to insure that the child actually has learned essential reading skills. Herber contends (8): "If independent activity is expected and students have not been *shown how* to perform that activity, the teaching is assumptive. It neglects the critical factor in good instruction: that is, that students must be *shown how* to do whatever it is they are *expected* to do independently."

3. The rate at which gifted students learn will be markedly different from that of average learners. Gifted children will complete most tasks more quickly and will usually acquire concepts more rapidly than students of average ability. Unfortunately, some teachers consciously or subconsciously punish these children by giving them extra assignments of a tedious nature. They discourage these students by preventing them from enjoyably working up to their capacity.

4. Whenever feasible, assignments given to gifted children should be unusual rather than routine. Gifted children especially like to be challenged in learning situations. However, they should not be assigned impossible tasks or ones clearly beyond their intellectual level. Assignments should be interesting and challenging.

5. The teacher should provide gifted students with varied and ample opportunities to engage in recreational reading. This will broaden the children's range of reading interests and provide unusual opportunities for the children to employ acquired reading skills in materials that may then serve as the basis for enrichment-type activities for these learners.

6. Gifted children must be given the chance to engage in high-level reading tasks. In many elementary classrooms, teachers spend a great amount of time providing children with basic reading skills. Of course, care must be taken to insure that gifted children acquire essential reading skills; however, these learners should also attempt tasks requiring critical reading, creative reading, completion of story endings, the provision of alternatives to aspects of a story, and other comparable reading tasks.

7. Enrichment activities should be part of the instructional program offered to gifted children. Gifted learners often involve themselves in activities of an enrichment nature, but frequently in hastily conceived ways that are of dubious value. Often these activities are nothing more than glorified busywork. Clearly, such activities will do little to positively enhance the reading prowess of gifted children. We urge teachers to plan enrichment instruction carefully and with clear objectives in mind. The teacher should seek to design and implement novel and exciting activities that can further develop the reading abilities of gifted children.

Lee writes about both the current status and future prospects of the gifted children in our nation's schools (14): "The provisions for the gifted in our average systems lag markedly behind those of the better ones. So-called 'enrichment' procedures are too often an administrative alibi for inaction. Excellence can be achieved but only with united effort and commitment of community, school boards, administrators, and teachers."

CHILDREN WITH PHYSICAL LIMITATIONS

Children, like adults, may be affected by a large number of diverse physical maladies. We will confine our remarks to the visual and auditory conditions which directly affect a child's learning to read. Wilson states (31): "A physical limitation is considered a cause of a reading problem when it interferes with a student's potential and performance."

Vision

That vision plays a role in a child's learning to read is a contention about which few would argue. In Chapter 2, we described the role which vision and hearing play in reading readiness. Strang, McCullough, and Traxler (29) maintain that if a child is "to distinguish letter and word forms, . . . the child must receive a clear visual impression of them."

It is difficult, however, to determine the *extent* to which a vision deficit hinders a child's learning to read. The results of studies of the relationship between visual deficits and reading differ from each other. Spache contends (27): "Those who have reviewed the literature on the significance of visual deficits in learning disabilities, such as the present author, have experienced difficulty in reaching very definite conclusions." Both vision and reading authorities, however, are in general agreement as to the significance of visual discrimination and visual acuity in reading instruction.

Visual discrimination refers to the ability of a child to discuss likenesses and differences among graphic symbols. While visual discrimination is important at all levels of reading, it is particularly significant in the initial stages of reading. *Visual acuity* is the clarity with which one brings graphic symbols into focus. Students must possess the visual acuity necessary to see adequately both up close and at a distance (that is, must have *near-point* and *far-point* vision, respectively).

Visual discrimination and visual acuity are distinct, but they interact with each other, as in the following example. If a child looks at a book and sees all of the graphic objects clearly, this is visual acuity. If, at the same time, the student discerns the differences among the letters of the word *bad*, this is visual discrimination.

Assessment and Accommodation

Devices for the assessment of children's vision are available in abundance. The most popular device in American elementary schools is the Snellen Chart. The chart is placed 20 feet from a child, and the child is asked to identify specific letters. If a student receives a perfect score on this test, he is said to possess 20/20 vision.

It should be noted that the Snellen Chart, even if employed correctly, will not provide a comprehensive evaluation of children's vision. Strang, McCullough, and Traxler (29) point out that the Snellen Chart is of limited value since "unless special lenses are used, far-sighted children, who are the most likely to be poor readers, will not be detected." Additionally, they remind us of "the difference between *near* visual acuity and *far* acuity and of the fact that the Snellen and other tests made at 20 feet are likely not to be adequate for the appraisal of visual acuity in reading." The Snellen Chart is better than no vision screening test at all, but it is unfortunate that it is used in so many elementary schools.

Regrettably, some elementary schools screen children's vision only once every three years or every other year. We believe that vision, which has such pertinence to reading, must be evaluated every year. The physical changes which occur in elementary school children are enormous. Changes in height, weight, health, and vision can be rapid and dramatic.

Despite the inadequacies of the Snellen Chart and similar devices, we feel it should be used annually to assess children's far-point visual acuity. However, visual discrimination and near-point visual acuity should be assessed using other visual screening devices. A variety of measures, some formal and others informal, are being used by teachers to assess the visual discrimination of children. We especially recommend the *Harrison-Stroud Reading Readiness Profiles* and the *Murphy-Durrell Reading Readiness Analysis*.

There are also a number of devices that can be employed to assess comprehensively the visual acuity of students. We have found the *Keystone Visual Survey Tests, School Vision Tester, Spache Binocular Reading Tests*, and *Titmus School Vision Tester* to be particularly effective.

The school vision-screening program will be further enhanced if classroom teachers follow certain courses of action. Teachers must become more sensitive to the issue of vision. No elementary school vision-screening program, regardless of its scope, will detect every vision problem which emerges in children.

Teachers using apppropriate observational techniques may be able to identify vision problems and make referrals to specialists. Teachers must not only be willing to look for possible vision disabilities, but also knowing what to observe.

Most elementary teachers have a limited knowledge of the symptoms which a child possessing a vision problem will *tend* to exhibit in the classroom. This deficiency can be corrected by becoming familiar with the information conveyed in Figure 11-1, which was prepared by the American Optometric Association's Committee on Visual Problems in Schools (1). The committee's two recommendations are particularly worth noting: (1) all children in the lower third of the class, but particularly those with the ability to achieve more than their percentile ranking indicates, should be referred for a complete vision analysis and (2) children who, although achieving, are not performing reasonably close to their individual capacity should be referred for a complete vision analysis.

FIGURE 11-1
A Guide to Vision Problems

The following list can be used to indicate to parents, school nurses, or educators the need for a vision examination. One check ($\sqrt{}$) should be for signs or symptoms occurring occasionally and two checks ($\sqrt{}\sqrt{}$) for those occurring frequently.

Three areas of concern in determining possible vision difficulties are highlighted in this checklist.

Appearance of the Eyes:

Eyes crossed or turning in, out or moving independently of each other   _____

Reddened eyes, watering eyes, encrusted eyelids, frequent styes   _____

Behavioral Indications of Possible Vision Difficulty:

Avoiding close work   _____

FIGURE. 11-1. Continued

Unusually short attention span or frequent day-dreaming   _____

Turning head to use one eye only, or tilting head to one side   _____

Placing head close to book or desk when reading or writing   _____

Frowning or scowling while writing or doing chalkboard work   _____

Using unusual or fisted pencil grasp, frequently breaking pencil, and frequent rotation of paper when writing   _____

Spidery, excessively sloppy, or very hard to read handwriting; writing which becomes smaller and crowded or inconsistent in size   _____

Excessive blinking or excessive rubbing of eyes   _____

Closing or covering one eye   _____

Dislike for tasks requiring sustained visual concentration; nervousness, irritability, restlessness, or unusual fatigue after maintaining visual concentration   _____

Losing place while reading and using finger or marker to guide eyes to keep place while reading (tactile reinforcement)   _____

Saying words aloud or lip reading (auditory reinforcement)   _____

Difficulty in remembering what is read   _____

Omitting, repeating, and miscalling words   _____

Persistent reversals after the second grade   _____

Difficulty remembering, identifying and reproducing basic geometric forms   _____

Confusion of similar words   _____

Difficulty following verbal instruction   _____

Poor eye-hand coordination and unusual awkwardness including difficulty going up and down stairs, throwing or catching a ball, buttoning or unbuttoning clothing, tying shoes or being unaware of untied shoes   _____

Displaying evidence of developmental immaturity   _____

Low frustration level, withdrawn, and difficulty getting along with other children   _____

Complaints Associated with Using the Eyes:

Headaches, nausea, and dizziness ⎯⎯⎯

Burning or itching eyes ⎯⎯⎯

Blurring of vision at any time ⎯⎯⎯

Double vision ⎯⎯⎯

Please include the following information so that the educator can forward a vision report upon completion of the examination:

_____

Student's Name

_____

Teacher's Name

_____

School

_____

Address

_____

School Nurse's Name

_____

Remarks

_____

_____

_____

We are not suggesting that classroom teachers become vision specialists. Clearly, the assumption of such a role falls outside of a teacher's training and professional experience. We are, however, recommending that the teacher identify children with possible visual problems and refer these children to appropriate specialists for more definitive assessment.

The referral of a child for vision testing should not be perceived as the end of a teacher's responsibility. The teacher should also seek to make the classroom as accommodating as is realistically feasible to that child. The teacher might make instructional, curricular, or even, logistical alterations so that the child can profit optimally from reading instruction, and these alterations should continue until the vision problem is corrected or some other cause is established for the symptoms observed by the teacher. Wilson states that the creation of a comfortable and efficient visual environment "may be accomplished by placing the student in a position of maximum lighting, by eliminating glare, by adjusting seating to ease board work, or by reducing the reading load" (31).

Hearing

Children who have an auditory deficiency usually experience some degree of difficulty in learning to read. As in the case of vision, the *degree* to which such a deficiency limits a child in learning to read is a point of disagreement among reading authorities. There is little debate, however, as to the *ways* in which auditory deficiencies hinder one in reading. When children can hear sounds but cannot differentiate among them, the student is said to have an *auditory discrimination* problem. If a student is unable to hear a word or hears the sound in a distorted manner, the child has an *auditory acuity* problem. In instances of the former, educational practices can be of use with the difficulty. However, auditory acuity problems are physically caused and require medical attention.

Regardless of the method used to teach reading to elementary school children, their ability to hear sounds and words correctly and replicate them accurately in subsequent activities is highly important. The child who does not hear sounds correctly will not be able to perform in the same manner as the rest of the class and will probably not profit from phonic instruction in reading. This is particularly true with respect to instruction concerned with consonants. Many consonants are high-frequency sounds, and the majority of hearing problems affect an individual's ability to deal with high-frequency sounds.

Students with hearing problems also often experience difficulty with lecture-type presentations made by teachers. While this form of instruction may seem to be an expeditious way of teaching, it is a hardship to the hearing-impaired child, and such a child will probably miss a significant portion of the material presented.

Wilson mentions other reading problems encountered by students with auditory deficiencies (31). He states: "Students with hearing difficulties are hindered as well by their inability to follow directions since they may not hear them clearly. They are, therefore, likely to lose their places in oral reading activities when listening to others, fail to complete homework assignments, and appear inattentive and careless."

Assessment and Accommodation

As with vision, assessment of hearing is frequently inadequate in elementary schools.

The overwhelming majority of elementary schools do not assess the auditory competence of their students every year. Some schools test once every two years or once during the primary grades (1–3) and once during the intermediate grades (4–6). As a result of this infrequent testing, a child who develops an auditory problem will often remain undetected for long periods, and the child may not be able to profit from reading instruction.

Most schools' lack of an adequate auditory-screening program is not the result of a lack of high-quality measures. Auditory acuity is probably most accurately assessed by means of an audiometer. Some schools do not use audiometers because their cost is deemed to be relatively high or because the person using the device must possess special skill. Despite these considerations, children should be tested annually with an audiometer.

We also feel that a school's auditory-screening program can be enhanced through the use of two supplementary measures. Elementary teachers of reading should know how to administer, score, and interpret Wepman's *Auditory Discrimination Test*. This test is inexpensive, can be used quite readily in an elementary classroom, and can provide a teacher with significant information as to the auditory discrimination abilities of children.

As in the case of vision difficulties, teachers should seek to observe children with auditory difficulties in their classes. Kaluger and Kolson describe children having auditory difficulties in the following ways:

1. The child looks strained and frowns when trying to hear.
2. The child retains directions poorly; directions must be repeated.
3. The child confuses words which sound alike (for example, *big* and *pig*, *bad* and *bed*).
4. The child finds phonetics difficult and confusing.
5. The child enunciates poorly and may have speech defects.

If a teacher perceives a child with one or more of these characteristics, the student should be referred to the proper authorities for auditory testing.

The teacher's responsibility to a child is not fulfilled by referring the child for auditory assessment. Until it is established that the child has no problem or until a problem is corrected, the teacher must make some adjustments for the child.

The exact nature of this accommodation depends upon the suspected nature and severity of the auditory problem. Obviously, the teacher should make instructional and logistical modifications that would help the child in learning to read. Some such actions are (1) whenever possible, teaching reading through modes other than auditory (for example, visual or kinesthetic), (2) moving the child's seat to a central place, (3) repeating directions and portions of lessons, and (4) providing appropriate corrective instruction.

SUMMARY

"No one ever said that teaching was going to be easy" is commonly heard among educators. Indeed, anyone who has ever taught children to read knows what a simultaneously frustrating and rewarding experience it can be for both teacher and student.

The children described in this chapter are not easy to teach. In order for them to learn to read, teachers must be patient and perservering and carefully plan their instruction. The benefits to the children make the expenditure of effort more than worthwhile.

ACTIVITIES RELATED TO THE CHAPTER

1. Visit a classroom in which children with learning disabilities are taught. Observe the teacher providing reading instruction to these students. In what ways are the instruction, materials, and curriculum different from those offered to children in regular elementary classrooms? How are they similar?
2. Select an elementary school and arrange a meeting with the school's principal. Seek answers to the following questions: (a) Are children with slow learning rates given instruction within the confines of the regular classroom or in special-education classes? Why? (b) How does the reading instruction these children receive compare to the suggestions in this chapter?
3. Compile a list of commercial materials designed for the children of cultural or linguistic minorities. State what you consider to be the strengths and weaknesses of each set of materials.
4. Interview several teachers who have had gifted children in their classrooms. What special forms of reading instruction were given to these students? What problems did the children cause the teachers?
5. Ask ten teachers to individually list the symptoms which a child with a vision problem *tends* to exhibit within a classroom. How do the teachers' responses compare with the list in Figure 11-1?
6. Select several elementary children who are experiencing difficulty in reading. Administer Wepman's *Auditory Discrimination Test* to those children. What do the test results indicate to you about each child?

BIBLIOGRAPHY AND REFERENCES

1. American Optometric Associaton: "Teacher's Guide to Vision Problems with Check List," 243 N. Lindbergh Boulevard, St. Louis, MO 63141.
2. A Position Statement Adopted by the Board of Directors, International Reading Assoc., November 3, 1979.
3. Bond, Guy L., Miles A. Tinker, and Barbara B. Wasson: *Reading Difficulties: Their Diagnosis and Correction*, 4th ed., Prentice-Hall, Englewood Cliffs, NJ, 1979, p. 314.
4. Cruickshank, William M., and G. Orville Johnson, eds., *Education of Exceptional Children And Youth*, 2nd ed., Prentice-Hall, Englewood Cliffs, NJ, 1967, p. 195.
5. Cutts, Norma E., and Nicholas Moseley: *Teaching the Bright and Gifted*, Prentice-Hall, Englewood Cliffs, NJ, 1957, pp. 18–26, 237.

6. Dechant, Emerald: *Diagnosis and Remediation of Reading Disability*, Parker, West Nyack, NY, 1968, pp. 162–163, 167.

7. Filbeck, Robert: *Systems in Teaching and Learning*, Professional Educators Publications, Lincoln, NE, 1974, p. 9.

8. Herber, Harold L.: *Teaching Reading in Content Areas*, 2nd ed., Prentice-Hall, Englewood Cliffs, NJ, 1978, pp. 215–216.

9. Houston, Susan H.: "A Re-examination of Some Assumptions about the Language of the Disadvantaged Child," in John F. Savage, ed., *Linguistics for Teachers; Selected Readings*, Science Research Assoc., Chicago, 1973, p. 81.

10. Kaluger, George, and Clifford J. Kolson: *Reading and Learning Disabilities*, 2nd ed., Merrill, Columbus, OH, 1978, pp. 2–3, 329.

11. Kephart, Newell C.: *The Slow Learner in the Classroom*, Merrill, Columbus, OH, 1960, p. 20.

12. Kirk, Samuel A., and Barbara Bateman: "Diagnosis and Remediation of Learning Disabilities," *Exceptional Children*, 29(2):73 (1962).

13. Lapp, Diane, and James Flood: *Teaching Reading to Every Child*, Macmillan, New York, 1978, Chap. 13.

14. Lee, J. Murray: *Elementary Education Today and Tomorrow*, Allyn and Bacon, Boston, 1966, pp. 198, 207.

15. Musgrave, G. Ray: *Individualized Instruction*, Allyn and Bacon, Boston, 1975, p. ix.

16. Task Force on Teaching English to the Disadvantaged: *Language Programs for The Disadvantaged*, National Council of Teachers of English, Urbana, IL, 1965, p. 87.

17. Nelson, Joan B., and Donald L. Cleland: "The Role of the Teacher of Gifted and Creative Children," in Paul A. Witty, ed., *Reading for the Gifted and the Creative Student*, International Reading Assoc., Newark, DE, 1971, pp. 47, 48.

18. Otto, Wayne, Richard A. McMenemy, and Richard J. Smith: *Corrective and Remedial Teaching*, Houghton Mifflin, Boston, 1973, p. 370.

19. Otto, Wayne, *et al.*: *Focused Reading Instruction*, Addison-Wesley, Reading, MA, 1974, p. 304.

20. Public Law 94-142, *Education of All Handicapped Children Act*, 94th Congress, November 29, 1975.

21. Quandt, Ivan: *Self-Concept and Reading*, International Reading Assoc., Newark, DE, pp. 7, 9.

22. Reger, Roger: "Diagnosing and Prescribing for Individual Needs," in James F. Collins and Joseph A. Mercurio, eds., *Meeting The Special Needs of Students in Regular Classrooms*, National Dissemination Center, Syracuse Univ. Press, Syracuse, NY, p. 79.

23. Rupley, William H., and Timothy R. Blair: *Reading Diagnosis and Remediation: A Primer for Classroom and Clinic*, Rand McNally, Chicago, 1979, pp. 73–80.

24. Sartain, Harry W., and Paul E. Stanton, eds.: *Modular Preparation for Teaching Reading*, International Reading Assoc., Newark, DE, 1974, p. 3.

25. Sawyer, Janet: "Dialects, Education, and the Contributions for Linguistics," in *Language Programs for the Disadvantaged*, National Council of Teachers of English, Urbana, IL, 1965, pp. 216–217.

26. Smith, Sally L.: *No Easy Answers: Teaching the Learning Disabled Child*, Washington, D.C.: National Institute of Mental Health, Stock No. 017-024-00687-4.

27. Spache, George D.: *Investigatng the Issues of Reading Disabilities*, Allyn and Bacon, Boston, 1976 p. 213.
28. Spache, George D., and Evelyn B. Spache: *Reading in the Elementary School*, 3rd ed., Allyn and Bacon, Boston, 1973, p. 335.
29. Strang, Ruth, Constance M. McCullough, and Arthur E. Traxler: *The Improvement of Reading*, 4th ed., McGraw-Hill, New York, 1967, pp. 16, 156–157.
30. Thompson, Ruby, "The Culturally Different Child as a Learner," in Arthur W. Heilman, *Principles and Practices of Teaching Reading*, 3rd ed., Merrill, Columbus, OH, 1972, p. 57.
31. Wilson, Robert M.: *Diagnostic and Remedial Reading for Classroom and Clinic*, 3rd ed., Merrill, Columbus, OH, 1977, pp. 43, 48.
32. Witty, Paul A.: *Reading for the Gifted and the Creative Student*, International Reading Assoc., Newark, DE, 1971, p. 12.
33. Zintz, Miles V.: *Corrective Reading*, Wm. C. Brown, Dubuque, IA, 1966, Chap. 5.

Program Development and Improvement 12

Overview

Maintaining and improving an elementary school reading program is just as important as establishing one. Classroom teachers and reading specialists play a key role in reading program evaluation and improvement.

In this chapter, techniques for determining the effective and the ineffective features of a program are presented. In addition, ways of improving an elementary school reading program are described.

Definition of Terms

1. *Evaluation*—determination of the merits of something.
2. *Grade placement*—the grade in which a child is enrolled in a school.
3. *Objective*—an aim of a program or endeavor.
4. *Reading expectancy*—the level at which a child can potentially read.
5. *Special services*—functions performed in schools by professionals (for example, guidance counselors and librarians) who do not teach children directly.

reading program might be compared to a car. Just as an automobile needs certain repairs during its life, so too does a reading program. Instead of automotive parts, a reading program requires curricular adjustments.

Changes in a program should not be made merely for the sake of change. To proceed in this way would serve little or no purpose. A reading program requires regular, professional evaluation, and where deficiencies are found to exist, program improvements should be made. The process of programmatic evaluation and improvement is a necessary but not easy job.

PROGRAM EVALUATION

After an elementary school's reading program has been operating for a period of time, one question should be foremost in the minds of those affiliated with the program: Does the program provide maximally effective instruction to all students, thereby insuring their optimal growth in reading?

It will not be possible to discuss the many measures which can be employed to answer this question, but three of the most popular will be presented: (1) testing, (2) programmatic objectives, (3) checklist questionnaires. The three are not mutually exclusive; an elementary school's evaluation may include a combination of them.

Testing

Many educators hold testing in the same regard as the bubonic plague: something to be avoided at any cost. When one considers some of the educational travesties which have been committed under the rubric of testing, is it any wonder that many educators view testing in a negative manner?

We agree that tests have been used for many of the wrong reasons—to place blame on teachers, to label children, and so on—in our elementary schools. Nevertheless, with proper administration and interpretation, testing can be an integral part of the evaluation of a school's reading program.

In this discussion, the term *testing* refers to standardized, informal, and teacher-made tests of reading. The diagnostic nature of tests have been discussed in another section of this textbook, so this aspect of testing is not treated here.

The function of testing in an elementary school is to determine the degree to which students are acquiring proficiency in reading. There are at least two standards against which student competence can be measured: (1) grade placement and (2) potential.

246

Grade Placement

The most popular method for ascertaining the effectiveness of an elementary school's reading program is comparison with students' grade placement in school. Usually, in this form of assessment students are administered equivalent forms of a test at the beginning and end of a school year. The number of correct responses made by a child on the test yields a reading score (for example, 4.5) that indicates the grade level in school (in this case, fourth grade, fifth month) corresponding with the child's performance.

By conducting such testing with every child in every grade, the percentage of students who are reading above or below their grade placement level in school can be ascertained. For example, as indicated in Table 12-1, 70 percent of the second graders at the Roosevelt School read above their grade level in school at year's end. However, only 39 percent of the school's third graders read above their grade placement level at this time.

Officials of the Roosevelt School probably would be displeased with the scores obtained by their third, fourth, and fifth graders, would attempt to determine the causes of these relatively poor scores, and would then seek to improve the reading program appropriately.

Potential

Studies of reading and intelligence have frequently shown correlations of .50 to .80 between scores on intelligence tests and scores on reading tests. Some feel that the actual correlation between the two may be even higher. Therefore, a child's general intelligence is used by educators as a standard against which the child's reading performance is measured.

Various attempts have been made in recent years to ascertain the level at which children should be reading. These estimates of children's reading

TABLE 12-1   Report of Testing—Roosevelt School (June)

GRADE	NUMBER OF CHILDREN IN GRADE	NUMBER OF CHILDREN READING AT OR ABOVE GRADE LEVEL	PERCENTAGE OF CHILDREN READING AT OR ABOVE GRADE LEVEL
1	26	14	54
2	23	16	70
3	31	12	39
4	32	15	47
5	29	14	49
6	27	18	67

ability are frequently referred to as *reading potential* or *reading expectancy*. Of all of the methods offered for determining potential, the formula developed by Bond and Tinker is the probably best known (1):

$$\left[\frac{IQ}{100} \times \text{(years of reading instruction)}\right] + 1 = \text{reading expectancy}$$

Using this formula, one could calculate that a child with an IQ of 87 would be expected to read at 2.74 after two years of reading instruction,

$$\left(\frac{87}{100} \times 2.0\right) + 1 = 2.74$$

Similarly, a child with an IQ of 170 after two years of reading instruction would have a reading expectancy of 4.4. These two figures contrast with the figure of 2.9 which would be obtained using a grade placement standard.

Bond and Tinker offer the following three considerations to users of their formula:

1. The time of reading instruction is the years and months in school from the time systematic instruction was started. This typically begins with first grade.
2. Readiness training in kindergarten is not counted even though such programs do much to diminish the chances of disabilities from occurring once reading instruction is started.
3. If an IQ obtained from a Binet or Wechsler Intelligence Test is not available, it is suggested that a Slosson Intelligence Test given by the teacher or a group performance intelligence test score be substituted temporarily.*

This form of evaluation could be implemented by computing the reading potential of each student in a school. After these reading scores have been procured, the reading test scores could be compared to the reading potential scores.

It should be noted that the kind of data resulting from this type of assessment is different from that resulting from assessment based on grade placement. Children in the fifth grade may read below the fifth-grade level but commensurate with their reading expectancy level. Conversely, second-grade children may attain a third-grade level on a reading achievement test but may achieve below their reading expectancy level.

Also, it is not realistic to expect all children to read up to their potential, just as all children cannot be expected to read at or above their grade-

*Reprinted by permission of Prentice-Hall, Inc., Englewood Cliffs, NJ.

placement level. A reading expectancy level should mainly be perceived as a goal.

Finally, in some elementary schools, it may be difficult or impossible to determine the reading potential of children through use of a reading expectancy formula. Teachers may not be able to use such a formula because interpretation of these measures depends upon having an assessment of students' intelligence, and for various reasons the administration of intelligence tests to the entire population of an elementary school is rare.

As a result, in some schools, scores derived from a listening comprehension test or an arithmetic computation test substitute for determinations of the reading potential of children. A child's grade equivalent on one of these measures is compared to the student's reading achievement score. If the two are similar, the student is achieving at a level in accordance with potential. However, should a significant difference exist between the two, the student is said to be reading at a level above or below potential. For a student in grades one to three, a difference of 0.5 or more between a reading achievement test score and an arithmetic computation or a listening comprehension test score may be considered significant. For a child in grades four to six, a significant difference exists when there is a difference between the two of 1.0 or more.

Programmatic Objectives

Every well-conceived reading program includes a list of programmatic objectives. These objectives indicate what the program seeks to have students attain in reading achievement. It is only logical to assume, therefore, that an evaluation of a reading program should include an assessment of its programmatic objectives.

Most, if not all, educators would agree that a reading program must have objectives, but evaluating these objectives presents some very real problems for those affiliated with the program. As Tyler says (17): "To say that evaluation should begin with the educational objectives is simple enough, but to obtain a list of objectives clearly enough defined to guide the construction of means of appraisal is not easy."

We agree wholeheartedly with Tyler's statement. It is an easy task to determine the percentage of fifth graders who read above fifth-grade level at the end of a year's schooling. It is an equally simple matter to ascertain how many students achieve a specified degree of proficiency on a certain reading test. Some objectives readily lend themselves to assessment and are easily measurable.

However, not every aspect of reading can be defined in explicit terms or evaluated precisely. For example, how does one determine whether or not a child appreciates reading materials? Can we measure precisely the attitudes of children toward reading? How is a child's interest in reading objectively assessed? It is difficult to evaluate these kinds of elements. Program evaluators should assess children's progress with respect to such objectives by agreeing among themselves on how to define such terms as *appreciation*, *attitude*, and *interest*.

Checklist and Questionnaires

Checklists and questionnaires are popular means of evaluating an elementary school reading program. Typically, these devices have served to rate the key elements of a program. Figure 12-1 is an example of a high-quality questionnaire.

FIGURE 12-1
Questionnaire on Elementary Reading Instruction*

Your school system has requested a survey of instructional practices in order to discover what new steps can be taken to help you accomplish more fully educational outcomes that you desire for your pupils. Since we cannot talk to each teacher separately, your frank, thoughtful, responses to the questions on the following pages will be extremely valuable.

Although the questionnaire looks quite long, very little writing is required because most responses can be made by making check marks. Please complete the form at the designated time so that it will not be overlooked, and return it folded with the response inside. Your *individual* answers will be kept *completely confidential*; therefore, you are asked *not* to sign your name. Thank you for your cooperation. The Survey Committee.

Please check each statement that describes the teaching of reading as it usually occurs in your classroom.

Availability and Use of Instructional Materials

1. One set or series of basal or other developmental materials is used almost exclusively for reading instruction.   1. _____
2. Two sets of basal/developmental materials are used.   2. _____
3. Three or more sets or series of materials are used.   3. _____
4. An adequate school library is provided.   4. _____
5. The whole class goes to the library on schedule.   5. _____
6. Individual children go to the school library when they wish to locate materials or read.   6. _____
7. A classroom library of supplementary and literary readers, as well as trade (library) books is being developed.   7. _____
8. The classroom library contains 150 titles or more.   8. _____
9. The books in the classroom library have a difficulty range of four grade levels or more.   9. _____
10. Teacher's manuals that accompany basal/developmental materials are used to guide the teaching of reading skills.   10. _____

*From Sartain (12).

11. Occasional duplicated seatwork exercises are provided as needed by individual or small groups.   11. _____
12. Large amounts of duplicated seatwork or extra workbooks are provided to keep children working at their seats.   12. _____
13. Films, filmstrips, or tapes are used to develop background or teach skills in reading at least every ten days.   13. _____
14. Transparencies, language masters, or audio-flashcard devices are used in reading at least every ten days.   14. _____
15. Illustrations and stories in developmental materials regularly present minority groups honestly and favorably.   15. _____

Evaluation and Diagnosis in the Classroom

1. Most diagnosis is done through listening to oral teaching.   1. _____
2. Workbook exercises are used to evaluate reading skills growth.   2. _____
3. An individual reading inventory (informal or standardized) is used to determine instructional level and locate major reading difficulties.   3. _____
4. Published tests that accompany the reading program are administered.   4. _____
5. Standardized tests that are independent from the basal materials are administered at least once a year.   5. _____
6. Pupil progress is judged individually by comparing achievement scores with mental age or some other mental capability index.   6. _____
7. Published diagnostic tests are used to isolate difficulties of individuals having general vocabulary weaknesses.   7. _____
8. Published diagnostic tests are used to isolate difficulties of individuals having general comprehension weaknesses.   8. _____
9. Published diagnostic tests are used to isolate difficulties of individuals having general study skills weaknesses.   9. _____
10. Teacher-made diagnostic tests are used to plan what skills teaching is needed by individuals and groups.   10. _____
11. An informal procedure is used to determine which perceptual modality is most conducive to learning for each child.   11. _____
12. A checklist or other screening device is used to determine which children have subtle learning disabilities.   12. _____
13. Intelligence tests which are not heavily dependent upon reading are used to obtain an estimate of mental ability.   13. _____
14. A psychologist or counselor studies children who have special reading difficulties to determine whether there are social or emotional problems which contribute to the difficulty.   14. _____

Differentiation of Instruction

1. All children in the room are taught reading as one group.   1. _____
2. Children are divided into 2 or 3 groups for reading.   2. _____
3. Children are divided into 4 or more groups for reading.   3. _____
4. In addition to above developmental power grouping, children from several groups are drawn into a flexible, changing group

FIGURE 12-1 *(continued)*

for additional skills instruction at least twice weekly.   4. _____

5. Children are regrouped frequently for reading projects such as preparing programs for puppet shows.   5. _____

6. One basal (developmental) reader series is used for teaching all power groups.   6. _____

7. A different reader series is used for each of two or more groups.   7. _____

8. Fully individualized reading is practiced all of the time (each child taught separately in a different book).   8. _____

9. Individualized reading is practiced with some children part of the time.   9. _____

10. Children regularly work independently in pairs or small groups with skills development games or exercises.   10. _____

11. Word wheels or other skills game devices are used every week with each group.   11. _____

12. Small instructional groups usually are racially integrated (if the school has multiracial population).   12. _____

13. Approximately once a week or more frequently groups read stories or poems that present minority groups favorably either as authors or characters in the material.   13. _____

Developing Readiness for Reading Instructional Selections

1. Selections for reading are chosen because they relate to children's everyday lives and have immediate application for practical or pleasurable reasons.   1. _____

2. Pictures, charts, maps, films, tapes, field trips, and other realistic experiences are used at least twice a week to develop understanding of new vocabulary.   2. _____

3. New vocabulary for each story is introduced in phrase or sentence context (or through a word analysis technique).   3. _____

4. Vocabulary phrases and other preparatory work are placed on the chalkboard or charts *before* classes begin.   4. _____

5. The new vocabulary for a story is introduced in 10 minutes or less.   5. _____

Direct Learning

1. Each developmental group is met by the teacher once daily.   1. _____

2. Each group is met by the teacher both in the morning and in the afternoon.   2. _____

3. Children are given or are encouraged to suggest something to look for as they begin silent reading.   3. _____

4. Children set oral reading purposes that are somewhat different from the purposes for reading material silently.   4. _____

5. Most of the developmental assignment is reread orally.   5. _____

6. Other children usually close their books and listen while one child is reading part of selection orally.   6. _____

7. Children are encouraged to find other stories on the topic of the developmental reader unit to read independently.   7. _____

8. Children set up exhibits or plan projects to make reading each set of stories interesting and purposeful.   8. _____

9. A choral reading activity is undertaken once a month or more frequently.   9. _____

10. Reading frequently is correlated with or integrated in units with English, spelling, and handwriting.   10. _____

11. Children discuss specific literary qualities that make certain stories interesting.   11. _____

12. The able readers frequently are asked to think beyond the bare facts to consider implications or judge the value of a reading selection.   12. _____

13. The follow-up discussion takes no more than half of the time that was required for reading the selection.   13. _____

Teaching Content Reading and Study Skills

1. The difficult words in an assignment in science or social studies are introduced before the children study.   1. _____

2. Pictures, charts, films, tapes, objects, field trips, and other direct experiences are used to develop meanings of content vocabulary at least twice a week.   2. _____

3. Children are taught to select main points in a paragraph and to outline at certain stages of development.   3. _____

4. Children are taught to summarize in oral or written form what they have read from sections or chapters of material.   4. _____

5. Children are given frequent practice in locating material in library references.   5. _____

Public Relations

1. Parents are invited to visit the classroom to observe reading instruction once or twice a year.   1. _____

2. Short bulletins are sent home periodically (three or more times a year) explaining some phase of the reading program.   2. _____

3. One or more group conferences with parents are held each year to explain some phase of the program and to invite them to help their children by such means as setting an example of reading, reading aloud to them, and providing books.   3. _____

4. Individual conferences are held with each child's parents at least once during the year to discuss individual progress and problems.   4. _____

5. Parents are involved every couple of years in listing some desired goals of reading instruction or in tentatively judging some of the library reading materials.   5. _____

Personal Growth and Professional Satisfaction

1. I especially enjoy teaching reading.   1. _____

FIGURE 12-1 (*continued*)

2. I feel that most of the pupils in our school become successful readers.   2. _____

3. I know how to correct in the classroom most of the reading difficulties that my pupils have.   3. _____

4. I know a consultant or specialist in the district on whom I can call for advice and assistance in dealing with special difficulties of pupils.   4. _____

5. During the last two years I have learned effective teaching techniques or received especially valuable assistance in teaching reading from:

    a. A building principal   5a. _____
    b. A reading consultant   5b. _____
    c. A remedial reading teacher   5c. _____
    d. An administrator from the central office   5d. _____
    e. Another teacher in our school   5e. _____

6. During the past two years I have become acquainted with or learned to use:

    a. New basal/developmental books   6a. _____
    b. A packaged "laboratory" set of individualized lessons   6b. _____
    c. Fifteen or more new books in the classroom library   6c. _____
    d. A set of practice games in word analysis   6d. _____
    e. New materials for enhancing teaching of minority groups   6e. _____
    f. New procedures for individualizing instruction   6f. _____
    g. Diagnostic tools or techniques   6g. _____
    h. Other: _____   6h. _____

General Options

1. In my opinion, the greatest *strengths* of the reading program are:

    a. _____
    b. _____
    c. _____

2. In my opinion, the greatest *weaknesses* of the reading program are:

    a. _____
    b. _____
    c. _____

Instruments such as the preceding can be distributed to every elementary teacher, completed anonymously by these individuals, and the data provided tallied. The strengths and weaknesses of a program can then be delineated, and recommendations for programmatic improvements offered.

In other instances, a reading committee can be formed. Such a group generally is composed of teachers, administrators, and community members. They work in a collaborative manner. On the basis of test results, discussions with teachers, and any other pertinent sources of data, they attempt to respond collectively to each item contained in the checklist or questionnaire. The committee determines the strengths and weaknesses of the reading program, and the group presents ideas for improving the program.

The use of checklists and questionnaires can be very effective or a great waste of effort. It is relatively simple to determine what's wrong with an elementary school's reading program. Rectifying these deficiencies while maintaining a program's strengths is a much more difficult task.

PROGRAM IMPROVEMENT

The improvement of a reading program follows naturally from its evaluation. The step from assessment to improvement is a logical one, but, unfortunately, it is not easily accomplished. Anyone who has ever sought to alter any curriculum or educational program knows how difficult it is to achieve a desired change.

As recently as ten years ago, reading program development or revision was an area generally untouched by teachers' hands. Reading programs were developed by administrators, aided by outside experts, and dutifully implemented by teachers. Most teachers had little or no input into the content of a reading program.

It is to be hoped that those days are gone. If revisions are to be made in a reading program, then "individuals who are to be involved in a reorganization directly affecting them, and upon whom the ultimate success of that reorganization depends, should actively participate in the process of change" (2). To do otherwise, would be to ignore both contemporary educational conditions and the recommendations of the literature. It will, in all likelihood, result in the failure of the program.

Teachers and others—that is, community members—whose support for a reading program is essential should be actively involved. Several guidelines should be followed when trying to change a reading program. Among them are the following:

1. A reading program should not be revised merely for the sake of change or for punitive purposes. The program should not be implemented in order to punish teachers or to focus publicly on their deficiencies. Rather, improvement should be the reason for programmatic change. Remember that individuals are more likely to support a change when they understand why it is being proposed.
2. The committee responsible for planning revisions in a reading program should have adequate teacher representation. The teachers selected or elected for the committee should be chosen on the basis of their professional competence in reading and the contributions which they can make to the committee.
3. Since teachers are responsible for the implementation of the changes

being planned, the differences among teachers should be kept in mind. Teachers differ in their experience, expertise, intelligence, and motivation and in the types of positions they occupy. Programmatic changes that are being considered should be realistically evaluated in terms of whether the teachers have the skill and the desire necessary to implement them.

4. Reading is one of the most important subjects taught in elementary school, if not the most important. But it is not the only subject being acquired by children. As programmatic changes are being considered, care must be taken to insure that the modifications will not conflict with the other goals and programs within the school. Such potential conflicts should be resolved *prior* to the implementation of the revised program.

   In addition, the reading program should not become so extensive that a teacher has little time for other aspects of the curriculum. The developers of such a reading program may indeed have improved the program, but only at the expense of other important objectives.

5. A committee to revise a reading program must be afforded enough time to accomplish the job. Revising a reading program is an arduous task that can consume as much time as is needed to plan a program. Given normal conditions, a reading program cannot be significantly revised by a committee after one hour's work or after a single meeting. Usually, several meetings, held over numerous weeks' time, will be needed to accomplish this task.

   Some of the committee's activities may be conducted after school, but released time from regular teaching or administrative duties must be given to the committee's members. Incentives such as release from certain duties or remuneration for service can be effective in getting maximum effort from the committee.

6. As many persons as possible should be involved in the process of revising an elementary school reading program. This is not meant to imply that all should have an equal amount of responsibility. Some teachers will have a greater role in the change process than others. Every teacher who will be affected by the revised program should be part of the process of revision. There will then be a greater likelihood that a sense of ownership of the new program will develop and that the teachers will support the revised program.

7. Remember that evaluation is an integral part of programmatic change. Evaluation makes the need for specific changes apparent. The question of how revised parts of the program will later be evaluated should be considered. The committee responsible for revising the program should answer the question: How will we be able to show whether or not the changes improved our school's reading program?

These seven guidelines do not, of course, cover everything. They do, however, deal with important issues, and adherence to them will help bring about effective programmatic change.

ADDITIONAL RESOURCES

Revisions in an elementary school reading program usually focus upon the content taught in the classroom and on the materials and techniques used by teachers. With regard to content, new skills may be inserted into the curriculum and others deleted from it, or the sequence in which skills are taught may be altered. As for materials and techniques, teachers may change the basal reading series employed, use several basals concurrently, or use no series at all. Teachers may change their instructional technique and begin using an individualized approach to reading, a language-experience approach, or some other pedagogical procedure.

We agree that content, materials, and technique should receive emphasis when revising a reading program. They should not, however, be the only items being considered. Schools desiring to improve their reading program should also examine the role which special services, administrators, and parents could each potentially play.

Special Services

Educators have long recognized the necessity for teaching reading in elementary school. However, there has been little or no agreement among educators concerning whose responsibility it is to teach the necessary skills.

Some maintain that teachers of reading are solely responsible for teaching reading, but it is our belief that *all* educators must be involved in their school's reading program. Reading specialists, guidance counselors, and librarians—among many others in the area of special services—must become aware of the role they should play in the process of teaching reading.

Special services includes those professionals whose major responsibility is not primarily one of providing direct instruction to children. While many different roles fall within the category of special services, our discussion focuses on reading specialists, guidance counselors, and librarians. These are the ones with the greatest potential for enhancing an elementary school reading program.

Reading Specialist

Depending on the size of a school district, the title and the responsibilities of a reading specialist may vary. The position is sometimes titled Director of Reading or Reading Coordinator. Individuals in this position may or may not have other professionals working with them and may or may not be responsible for providing direct instruction to children.

Generally speaking, a reading specialist possesses at least a master's degree in the area of reading and has had several years of successful experience as a teacher of reading. The Heath City Schools in the state of Ohio have arrived at the following excellent description of what a reading specialist can reasonably be expected to do (13):

1. Develop knowledge and understanding as to what constitutes a good reading program as well as knowing the methods and materials that are necessary to carry out the programs.
2. Work directly with the Director of Instruction and the Principals in developing a coordinated, articulated reading program in grades K–12.
3. Be actively involved in the reading inservice program in grades K–12. Specifically, the specialist should: provide leadership and direction in curriculum-guide revision, provide assistance in basal-textbook selection, demonstrate effective teaching methods and materials, and help arrange and organize local inservice education programs.
4. Meet with teachers and administrators to provide for the harmonious articulation of language arts experience in grades K–12.
5. Develop implementation strategies to assist teachers in the teaching of reading in the content areas.
6. Provide leadership and direction in developing a diagnostic, prescriptive type of individualized reading instruction in the school district.
7. Cooperate with the guidance department in helping to select assessment tools that will enable the school district to evaluate reading instruction.
8. Help classroom teachers and librarians in the selection of supplementary materials to assure readability of materials.
9. Help classroom teachers diagnose individual and class weaknesses and strengths.
10. Assist counselors and primary teachers in the prescreening of grades K–1.

It is obvious that reading specialists are key to the development and maintainence of a high-quality reading program. One should also expect that a reading specialist will play a significant leadership role in redesigning an elementary school's reading program.

Guidance Counselor

In 1972, Mangieri conducted a study involving sixty-three school guidance counselors. The study sought to determine (1) how much counselors knew about their school's reading program and (2) the degree to which the expertise of the counselor was being used in the program. The findings of the study were, unfortunately, quite predictable. Guidance counselors knew their school had a reading program, knew that there were large numbers of children who were unsuccessful in learning to read, but were virtually ignorant of the objectives and ingredients of the program itself. Not surprisingly, sixty-one of the sixty-three counselors had little or no involvement in their school's reading program.

We believe, however, that counselors can immeasurably enhance the reading effort within a school if they are given the opportunity. Stanton suggests that a counselor can become involved in the reading program as a diagnostician, a counselor, and a consultant (14).

From their knowledge of tests and measurements, counselors can provide teachers with diagnostic information concerning the vision, intelligence, personality, and reading ability of individual students. This information can help teachers set realistic instructional goals for each student.

The counselor as described by Stanton helps students to understand their relationship to themselves and society. In this capacity, the counselor can give an individual the opportunity to think creatively and, as an outgrowth of this, to read with flexibility. Stanton states: "One of the interesting phenomena of the academic environment is the student who has all the tools to be successful, but a negative self-concept prevents his success. Regardless of how many skills a person has, if he does not feel that he can do the job, his chances of success are very limited. The alterations of an individual's reading self-concept is one of the most interesting and challenging duties that the counselor can perform."

As a consultant, the counselor helps to maximize the teacher's effectiveness and aids teachers in developing a framework for understanding human behavior. Children differ in terms of intellectual and physical ability and in emotional makeup, and the counselor as a consultant can foster an awareness in teachers of these differences.

Librarian

A librarian, who daily comes into contact with students, parents, and teachers, can be a potent force in an elementary school reading program. Unfortunately, as with guidance counselors, librarians are generally ill-informed about their school's reading program and uninvolved in it.

New books suitable for children and adolescents are being produced at what seems an ever-increasing rate. As a result, the majority of elementary teachers find it impossible to become familiar with most newly published books. The school librarian can be the bridge between recently published materials and the elementary classroom.

The school librarian can also represent continuity in an elementary school child's life. Huck and Kuhn point out (8): "Each year the child meets a new teacher, but the librarian remains as a familiar friend who is ready to help with his reading. The librarians see each child's developing interests, abilities, and needs. When new books come across the desk, individuals who would enjoy them are remembered."

One of the goals of most elementary school reading programs is to help children enjoy reading books. Schools typically engage in many such activities as book fairs, young authors' contests, and other special projects to achieve this goal. The school librarian could be a consultant to such activities. Chisholm addresses the role of libraries in a reading program (4): " . . . reading students must have access to a great diversity of materials in order to foster their love of reading, to stimulate their interest, to broaden reading ability, and to fulfill their informational and recreational needs. This program of support can be provided most effectively through organized library or media center service. A school library or media program is indispensable to an exemplary reading program." It is up to reading personnel and school administrators to recognize the value of the school librarian.

Administrators

In most instances, administrators are key members of a school district's professional staff. It is these individuals who designate teachers' assignments, establish a school's instructional priorities, allocate fiscal resources within a building, and make decisions about the creation, continuance, or termination of a program within a school.

Recent studies have confirmed that the role which an administrator plays in a school's reading program is especially significant. A school's reading program generally is successful if it has active administrative support. Conversely, when administrators are indifferent toward a reading program or insist upon adhering to policies or practices inimical to the program, then reading achievement is undoubtedly hampered. In the opinion of many educators, administrators more often hinder than help a school's efforts in reading. Dechant probably best expresses this view when he says: "The weakest link in many reading programs is often an untrained or a disinterested administrator" (6).

Dechant's viewpoint is no longer wholly accurate. It is true that, generally speaking, administrators are ill-prepared when it comes to reading instruction. In fact, a survey conducted by Mangieri in 1972 showed that of fifty-one institutions of higher education, only three reported offering a graduate level course dealing specifically with the theme of administrators and reading (10).

It is our opinion that administrators are indeed interested in improving the quality of reading instruction within their schools. Perhaps this interest is due to public outcries about the failure of schools to produce students proficient in reading. Other reasons may be the movement in many states toward minimum competency tests, the implementation of accountability measures in some schools, or an emphasis on going back to the "basics."

Regardless of the reason, there is interest among administrators in reading. This is illustrated by a program conducted during the 1977-78 school year by the Ohio Department of Education (7). The program had two major purposes: (1) to provide administrators with a rationale for becoming involved in the reading programs of their schools and (2) to supply administrators with the expertise necessary to enhance the reading programs of their schools. There were 301 administrators, representing 201 Ohio school districts, who participated in the program. Of these 301 administrators, 175 were superintendents. This degree of participation makes it clear that administrators are interested in reading.

When administrators do want to be involved in their schools' reading efforts, the question arises of what this involvement should be. At present, there is little consensus among reading authorities on this question. Almost all authorities advocate that administrators be involved in their schools' reading efforts, but differences of opinion exist as to the proper scope of this involvement.

Peterson provides one of the most comprehensive assessments of this issue (11), including the following "list of competencies related to reading instruction which should be expected of principals" (the word *administrators* could easily be substituted for *principals*):

1. Knowledge of the elements which make up a balanced reading program.
2. Ability to create a climate in the school which enhances reading instruction.
3. Ability to help teachers to identify and define immediate and long-range goals and objectives.
4. Ability to assist individual and/or groups of teachers to identify specific reading needs and to develop prescriptions to meet those needs.
5. Ability to plan and guide a total buildingwide reading program on the basis of standards which have been established by the staff.
6. Ability to organize and schedule a buildingwide or classroom testing program to assess reading needs and strengths.
7. Ability to encourage the effective use of resources by staff personnel.
8. Ability to assess the total reading program (criterion tests, ranking tests, diagnostic tests), the problems of early identification, and methods for keeping records.
9. Ability to organize a comprehensive reading program which includes developmental reading, reading improvement, and remedial reading.
10. Ability to provide information to the community regarding the school's reading program.
11. Ability to interpret test data to staff, students, and community.

12. Ability to help teachers coordinate and integrate reading into the total school curriculum.
13. Ability to assist teachers to design programs, experiences, and activities which will help students to maintain reading skills they have learned.
14. Ability to provide for the optimum effective and efficient utilization of space.
15. Skill in planning for the expenditure of funds to satisfy reading requirements identified by teachers.
16. Ability to integrate and coordinate the use of material and personnel resources (library, media, pupil personnel services).
17. Ability to design and implement staff development programs utilizing a variety of procedures such as meetings after school, released-time, etc.
18. Ability to make the most effective use of the teaching staff in terms of the overall reading program and the needs of the pupil population.
19. Ability to maximize the use of available materials and technology.
20. Knowledge of available research in reading which is shared with staff in terms of its implication for improving instruction.
21. Ability to organize staff and pupils for reading instruction.
22. Ability to provide meaningful on-site assistance to teachers relating to reading approaches, methods, and techniques.
23. Ability to organize a program which provides for continuous evaluation of reading instruction.
24. Ability to make materials and personnel resources available and readily accessible to teachers and pupils.
25. Ability to provide leadership in developing criteria to guide in the selection and purchasing of reading materials.
26. Ability to help teachers utilize paraprofessional personnel such as aides and volunteers and to establish a tutorial program.
27. Ability to organize tutoring programs, including the use of peer tutors.
28. Ability to help teachers to write specific behavioral objectives and to implement them in their program.
29. Ability to interpret and use data from educational research.

In conclusion, we feel that administrators can and should be involved in their school's reading efforts. We would urge any individuals seeking to improve reading within their schools to examine whether or not they have been utilizing their expertise to the fullest.

Parents

The literature about effective reading programs invariably brings one to the realization that parents are an integral aspect of such programs. For a reading program to achieve success, the support and involvement of parents is essential. Strang, McCullough, and Traxler say (15): "Parents and teachers are partners. A school reading program can stand or fall on parental understanding and cooperation. In fact, reading is not an in-school program; a lot depends on what happens outside the school."

Many elementary schools fail to involve parents in their reading programs. In fact, instead of parents being perceived as potential assets, they frequently are seen as adversaries. This is unfortunate, because parents are so important in the life of a child. According to Tinker and McCullough (16), "the parent sets an example for the child, not only because the child is basically imitative but because, as the child develops, he is apt to view his father and mother as people whose example is worthy of emulation."

Parental involvement in reading can be two-fold. First, parents need to be informed by educators as to how they can assist a school's reading efforts. Second, parents can use this information and be of real help to the program through direct contact with their children.

Many parents adopt a hands-off policy about reading simply because they lack knowledge. These individuals may be intelligent and avid readers themselves, but their relative ignorance about the reading process makes them choose to remain uninvolved in their child's learning to read. Some may have made attempts to become involved, but were consciously or unconsciously rebuffed by educators.

Parents can immeasurably enhance an elementary school's reading program, provided they are given proper guidance. The Dallas Independent Schools designed publications to show parents how to help their children in reading. The Muskingum County Public Schools in Zanesville, Ohio, offers the following suggestions to parents of preschool children in their publication "Parents As Partners:"

1. Talk to your child. From the time he/she is a baby, sing songs, say nursery rhymes, and talk to your child to develop family closeness and language ability.
2. Read to your children every day. When you look at a picture book with your children, take time to look at and discuss the pictures. Hold your children on your lap or have them sit close to you.
3. As you read to your children, have them join in chants and rhymes that are repeated in a story.
4. Read aloud simple, step-by-step directions and help your children follow them. Following simple recipes and then baking is a good beginning.
5. Expect your child to follow directions and pay attention.
6. Listen to your children. Give them time to tell about their interests.
7. Monitor TV viewing so your children watch valuable programs but still have time for plenty of exercise.
8. Provide crayons, paper, and scissors for your children to use.

This same publication provides the following guidelines for parents of school-age children:

1. Read to your child even after he/she has learned to read.
2. Encourage your child to read to you.
3. Buy books for your children and introduce them to the library.
4. Provide your children a place for their books.
5. Talk together about the day's experience and your child's interests.
6. Watch for opportunities to praise your child.
7. Watch TV with your children and discuss programs with them. Limit television time.
8. Set a regular time for doing homework, and make sure your child does it.
9. Get to know your child's teacher. Find out how your child is doing at school and any suggestions of how you can help.
10. See that your child gets enough rest.
11. Provide your children with nutritious meals. A good breakfast is particularly important.
12. Get your child to school. When your child is absent, important lessons may be missed.
13. See that your child gets plenty of exercise.

The degree to which parents can be involved in an elementary school's reading efforts is limited only by the school's wishes. We have seen schools which have shown parents how to teach or reinforce some rather specific skills in reading. Other schools have asked parents to convey their strong support for reading to their children and to set an example by reading for themselves at regular times within the home.

There is no right degree of parents' involvment in the reading program of an elementary school. A sense of realism, however, should prevail. Parents are not formally trained to be educators; therefore, care should be taken not to ask parents to perform tasks for which they are unprepared. When such care is taken, parents can make a very significant contribution to a school's reading program. (See Appendix G for information about materials and suggestions on how to involve parents in school reading efforts.)

SUMMARY

In this chapter, we have discussed the importance of evaluating and improving an elementary school's reading program on a regular basis. This is not an easy task, but it is a vital one. Good reading programs do not just happen; rather, they grow out of hard and well-directed work.

ACTIVITIES RELATED TO THE CHAPTER

1. Formulate a strategy for evaluating a school's reading program. You may use one or more of the devices described in the chapter or devise a plan of your own. In addition to selecting an evaluation plan, state what strategy you would

use for convincing the school's administration and teaching staff of the necessity for engaging in programmatic evaluation.

2. Select students from a particular grade in a designated elementary school. How many of these students are reading on or above their grade placement? What percentage are reading at their reading expectancy level? What conclusions can you draw from these scores?

3. Visit an elementary school, and find out when the school's reading program was last revised. What process was used to make the change? Was the procedure employed at the school comparable to any of those recommended in this chapter?

4. Select one of the professionals (for example, librarian or counselor) included in special services. Read professional literature to find ways in addition to the ideas presented here that the particular professionals can play a role in an elementary school's reading efforts.

5. Is active administrative involvement in a reading program a myth or a reality? Ask ten teachers and ten administrators this question. How do their responses compare?

6. Select an elementary school. What is that school's philosophy about parents and reading? What, *specifically*, is the school doing to encourage parents to become involved in their children's reading?

BIBLIOGRAPHY AND REFERENCES

1. Bond, Guy L., Miles A. Tinker, and Barbara B. Wasson: *Reading Difficulties: Their Diagnosis and Correction,* Prentice-Hall, Englewood Cliffs, 1979, pp. 62–63.

2. Burg, Leslie A., *et al.: The Complete Reading Supervisor: Tasks and Roles,* Merrill, Columbus, OH, 1978, p. 27.

3. Burns, Paul C., and Betty D. Roe: *Teaching Reading in Today's Elementary Schools,* Rand McNally, Chicago, 1976, pp. 501–514.

4. Chisholm, Margaret: "The Role of Libraries, Media Centers, and Technology in the Reading Program," in T. R. Carlson, ed., *Administrators and Reading,* Harcourt Brace Jovanovich, New York, 1972, p. 135.

5. Dallmann, Martha, *et al.: The Teaching of Reading,* 4th ed., Holt, New York, 1974, pp. 511–537.

6. Dechant, Emerald: *Reading Improvement in the Secondary School,* Prentice-Hall, Englewood Cliffs, NJ, 1973, p. 16.

7. Eberhart, Nancy A., and John N. Mangieri: *Administrative Involvement in Reading,* Ohio Department of Education, Columbus, OH, 1977.

8. Huck, Charlotte S., and Doris Young Kuhn: *Children's Literature in the Elementary School,* 2nd ed., Holt, New York, 1968, p. 562.

9. Lapp, Diane, and James Flood: *Teaching Reading to Every Child,* Macmillan, New York, 1978, pp. 130–133.

10. Mangieri, John N.: "An All-School Attack on Secondary Reading," *American Secondary Education,* 3:24–25 (1972).

11. Peterson, Ruth I.: "One Model of Inservice for Instructional Leadership," in *Leadership: Principals and Reading Programs.* Project LEAD/The Right to Read, Washington, DC, 1974, pp. 11–12.

12. Sartain, Harry W.: "Questionnaire on Elementary Reading Instruction," School of Education, Univ. of Pittsburgh Press, Pittsburgh, PA, 1971.

13. Smith, Henry A.: "Role of the Reading Specialist," Heath City Schools, Heath, OH 43055.

14. Stanton, Paul E.: "The Counselor and the Reading Program," in Donald L. Cleland, ed., *Reading in Its Sociological Setting*, School of Education, University of Pittsburgh Press, Pittsburgh, PA, 1967, pp. 93–99.

15. Strang, Ruth, Constance M. McCullough, and Arthur E. Traxler: *The Improvement of Reading*, 4th ed., McGraw-Hill, New York, 1967, p. 101.

16. Tinker, Miles A., and Constance M. McCullough: *Teaching Elementary Reading*, Appleton-Century-Crofts, New York, 1962, p. 361.

17. Tyler, Ralph W.: "What Is Evaluation?" in S. L. Sebesta and C. J. Wallen, eds., *The First R: Readings on Teaching Reading*, Science Research Associates, Chicago, 1972, p. 434.

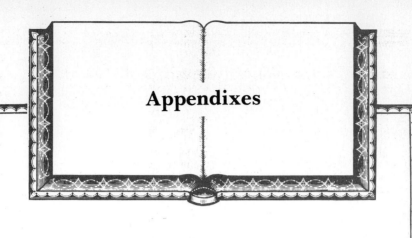

Appendixes

APPENDIX A: Materials and Procedures for
               Classroom Reading Instruction   269

APPENDIX B: Recreational and Supplemental
               Reading   301

APPENDIX C: Informal Techniques for Assessing
               Readability   395

APPENDIX D: Assessing Reading Interests   399

APPENDIX E: Published Tests   405

APPENDIX F: Organizations and References
               for Reading Professionals   413

APPENDIX G: Materials and Suggestions
               for Working with Parents   417

APPENDIX H: Names and Addresses
               of Publishers   423

Materials and Procedures for Classroom Reading Instruction

A APPENDIX

Observation Checklist: Reading   270
Titles, Levels, and Grade Equivalents of the Basal
Reading Series   271
High-Interest, Low-Vocabulary Materials   278
Elementary School Dictionaries   282
Picture Dictionaries   283
Checklist for Evaluating Games   284
How to Bind Books   284
Sixty-five Ways to Say "Good for You"   286
Checklist of Instructional Needs   288
Objectives for the Developmental Reading Program:
Grades K-6   290

OBSERVATION CHECKLIST: READING

This checklist was developed as a tool for principals to use in evaluating teacher instruction. Teachers of reading may find it beneficial to use this set of criteria in reviewing their own instructional procedures for teaching reading.*

Teacher_____ Grade _____ Date _____

		YES	NO
1.	Is the teacher using the manual accompanying the reading series being used?	—	—
2.	Is the teacher following the five steps in the directed reading lesson (DRL) as she conducts the reading group?	—	—
3.	Is the teacher successful in stimulating good discussion of a selection?	—	—
4.	Is the teacher enthusiastic and responsive as she conducts the reading group?	—	—
5.	Is the teacher following the skills-development section as outlined in the manual?		
6.	Are the children in their seats being provided with differentiated meaningful seatwork?		
7.	Is the teacher making judicious use of mimeographed material to reinforce skills, or does this material comprise the sole diet for seatwork?	—	—
8.	Are completed workbook pages corrected by the teacher with the pupils in a group situation?	—	—
9.	Is the teacher using workbooks in the proper manner as outlined in the manual, or are pages being assigned indiscriminately?	—	—
10.	Are children in their seats being given a variety of options to fruitfully occupy their time?	—	—
11.	Are supplementary materials being used along with the basic text?	—	—
12.	After one group is conducted, does the teacher circulate about the room answering questions before calling up the next group?	—	—
13.	Are children being administered the diagnostic tests accompanying the texts so as to pinpoint deficiencies and note strength?	—	—
14.	Do the children appear to be operating at their suitable instructional reading levels?	—	—
15.	Is there an attractive Reading or Interest Corner in the room?	—	—
16.	Is a rich and varied sampling of trade books available for the children as part of the reading program?	—	—

Comments: _____

_____

*Nicholas Criscuolo, Reading Center, New Haven Public Schools, New Haven, CT 06513. Reprinted by permission from the author.

TITLES, LEVELS, AND GRADE EQUIVALENTS
OF THE BASAL READING SERIES

In recent years publishers of basal reading series have designated individual student reading placement by levels rather than by traditional grade equivalents. Since the levels are not uniform across the publishers, this creates some confusion when children are transferred from one basal series to another or when more than one set of basal readers is used within a classroom.

The titles of the readers in the most commonly used basal series are listed here, together with the level assigned by the publisher and the corresponding grade equivalent. In examining the grade equivalents, note: R = readiness, PP = preprimer, and P = primer.

TABLE A-1   Basal Reading Series

TITLE	LEVEL	GRADE EQUIVALENT
Allyn and Bacon		
Pathfinder (1978)		
Families	1	R
Big and Little	1	R
How Do You Look? How Do You Feel?	1	R
Good Morning, Mouse!	1	R
What Is That?	1	R
Mysteries	1	R
Hello, Caterpillar	2	R
Winter Coats and Springtime Flowers	2	R
City Walk	2	R
Birthday Pizza	2	R
The Hiding Place	2	R
I Am a Wrecking Ball	3	R
Baker, Baker, Bake Me a Pie	3	R
Circus Work	3	R
Small One	3	R
Sounds of a Rainbow	3	R
Moving Days	4	PP
Summer Fun	5	P
Rides and Races	6	1
High Wires and Wigs	7	1
Surprises and Prizes	8	1
Upside and Down	9	1-2

TABLE A-1 Basal Reading Series (*Continued*)

TITLE	LEVEL	GRADE EQUIVALENT
Inside and Out	10	2
Moon Magic	11	2
Riding Rainbows	12	2–3
Sunshine Days	13	3
Handstands	14	3
Person to Person	15	4
Free Rein	16	4–5
Majesty and Mystery	17	5
Standing Strong	18	5–6
The Widening Path	19	6
Time and Beyond	20	6
American Book Company Reading Program (1980)		
Starting Off		R
Looking Out		PP
Climbing Up		PP
Going Far		PP
Finding Places		P
Moving On		1
Marching Along		2
Turning Corners		2
Building Dreams		3
Catching Glimpses		3
Clearing Paths		4
Crossing Boundaries		5
Making Choices		6
Changing Views		7
Meeting Challenges		8
Economy Keytext Program (1978)		
Sundrops	1	R
Crossovers	2	PP
Timespring	3	PP
Sky Lights	4	P
Puddlejumpers	5	1
Castlebuilders	6	1
Summerdaze	7	2
Street Songs	8	2
Thundercover	9	3
Turnstyles	10	3
Daystreaming	11	4
Bootstraps	12	4
Worldwind	13	5
Forerunners	14	5

TABLE A-1   Basal Reading Series (*Continued*)

TITLE	LEVEL	GRADE EQUIVALENT
Ginn		
Reading 720 Rainbow Edition (1979)		
Ready for Rainbows	1	R
Hello Morning!	1–2	R
A Pocketful of Sunshine	2	R
A Duck Is a Duck	3	PP
Helicopters and Gingerbread	4	P
May I Come In?	5	1
One to Grow On	6	2
The Dog Next Door and Other Stories	7	2
How It Is Nowadays	8	3
Inside Out	9	3
A Lizard to Start With	10	4
Tell Me How the Sun Rose	11	4–5
Measure Me, Sky	12	5–6
Mountains Are for Climbing	13	6
To Make a Difference	14	7
Gifts of Promise	15	8
Harcourt Brace Jovanovich		
The Bookmark Reading Program (1974)		
Look, Listen, and Learn		PP
Sun Up	1	P
A Happy Morning, A Magic Afternoon	2	P
Sun Up	3	P
Sun and Shadow	4	1
Together We Go	5	1
A World of Surprises	6	2
Going Places, Seeing People	7	2
Widening Circles	8	3
Ring Around the World	9	3
Goals in Reading	10	4
Much Majesty	10	4
Reading to Learn	11	5
Wider Than the Sky	11	5
Reading Power	12	6
First Splendor	12	6
Harper & Row		
Reading Basics Plus (1980)		
Get Ready!		R
Get Set!		R
Go Read!		R
Places and Puzzles		PP
Fish and Fables		PP
Rain and Riddles		PP
Webs and Wheels		P

TABLE A-1 Basal Reading Series (*Continued*)

TITLE	LEVEL	GRADE EQUIVALENT
Socks and Secrets		1
Wings and Wishes		2
Pets and Promises		2
Clues and Clocks		3
Trouble and Turnips		3
Dreams and Dragons		4
Moccasins and Marvels		5
Time and Tigers		6
Phantoms and Fantasies		7
Gnomes and Knots		8

Holt, Rinehart & Winston
  Basic Reading Systems (1980)

TITLE	LEVEL	GRADE EQUIVALENT
About Me	1	R
Hear, Say, See, Write	2	R
Rhymes and Tales	3	PP
Books and Games	4	PP
Pets and People	5	PP
Can You Imagine?	6	PP
A Place for Me	7	P
A Time for Friends	8	1
People Need People	9	2
The Way of the World	10	2
Never Give Up	11	3
Special Happenings	12	3
Time to Wonder	13	4
Freedom's Ground	14	5
Rides on the Earth	15	6
To See Ourselves	16	7
Great Waves Breaking	17	8

Houghton Mifflin
  Reading Series (1976, 1978)

TITLE	LEVEL	GRADE EQUIVALENT
Ready Steps		R
Getting Ready to Read	A	R
Rockets	B	PP
Surprises	C	PP
Footprints	D	PP
Honeycomb	E	P
Cloverleaf	F	1
Sunburst	G	2
Tapestry	H	2
Windchimes	I	3
Passports	J	3
Medley	K	4
Keystone	L	5
Impressions	M	6
Encore	N	7
Accents	O	8

TABLE A-1   Basal Reading Series (*Continued*)

TITLE	LEVEL	GRADE EQUIVALENT
Laidlaw Brothers		
Reading Program (1977)		
Purple Popcorn	2	R
Dancing Ducks	2	R
Blue Bananas	3	PP
Runaway Monkeys	3	PP
Red Reindeer	4	P
Green Geese	4	P
Ferocious Fish	4	P
Blue-Tailed Horses	5	P
Pots and Polka Dots	5	P
Pink Pumpkins	6	1
Checks and Double Checks	6	1
Toothless Dragons	6	1
Orange Owls	7	2
Tricky Troll	7	2
Pockets and Patches	8	2
Wide-Eyed Detectives	8	2
Lavender Lizards	9	3
Whispering Ghosts	9	3
Circles and Squares	10	3
Thundering Giants	10	3
Wheels	11	4
Reflections	11	4
Baskets and Balloons	11	4
Mobiles	12	5
Patterns	12	5
Wizards and Witches	12	5
Spotlights	13	6
Voyages	13	6
Oceans and Orbits	13	6
Macmillan		
Macmillan Reading (*Softbound*, 1980)		
Starting Out	1	R
Make Your Mark	2	R
Off We Go	3	PP
Who Can?	4–6	PP
Lost and Found	4–6	PP
Hats and Bears	4–6	PP
Amigos	7–8	P
Ups and Downs	7–8	P
Colors	9–10	1
Being Me	9–10	1
Believe It	11–12	2
Feelings	11–12	2
Stand Tall	13–14	2
A Second Look	13–14	2
Secret Spaces	15–16	3
Good News	15–16	3

TABLE A-1 **Basal Reading Series** (*Continued*)

TITLE	LEVEL	GRADE EQUIVALENT
Beginnings	17–18	3
Endings	17–18	3
Growing	19–21	4
Pastimes	19–21	4
Messages	19–21	4
Cycles	22–24	4
Impressions	22–24	4
Happenings	22–24	4
Moments	25–27	5
Birds and Beasts	25–27	5
Signals	25–27	5
Wonders	28–30	5
Outlets	28–30	5
Explorations	28–30	5
Awakening	31–33	6
Journeys	31–33	6
Dialogues	31–33	6
Inroads	34–36	6
Expressions	34–36	6
A Horse Came Running	34–36	6

Macmillan Reading (*Hardbound*, 1980)

Opening Doors		P
Rainbow World		1
Magic Times		2
Mirrors and Images		2
Secrets and Surprises		3
Full Cycle		3
Rhymes and Reasons		4
Echoes of Time		5
Catch the Wind		6
Roots and Wings		7
Dreams and Decisions		8

Merrill
Linguistic Reading Program (1975)

I Can	A	1
Dig In	B	1
Catch On	C	1
Get Set	D	2
Set Up	E	2
Lift Off	F	2
Take Flight	G	3
Break Through	H	3
Making Choices	I	4
Looking Around	J	5
Easy Going	K	6

TABLE A-1   Basal Reading Series (*Continued*)

TITLE	LEVEL	GRADE EQUIVALENT
Open Court		
The Headway Program (1979)		
Blue Book	A	1
Gold Book	B	1
On a Blue Hill	C	1
A Flint Holds Fire	D	2
From Sea to Sea	E	2
The Place Called Morning	F	3
Cities All About	G	3
Burning Bright	H	4
The Spirit of the Wind	I	5
Close to the Sun	J	6
Rand McNally		
Young America Basic Readers (1978)		
ABC and Me	1	R
Little Pig	2	PP
C. A. Zoo and Kangaroo	3	PP
Lost and Found	4	P
Magic Rings and Funny Things	5	P
Red Rock Ranch	6	1
Boxcars and Bottlecaps	7	2
Cartwheels and Caterpillars	8	2
Moonbeams and Microscopes	9	3
Telephones and Tangerines	10	3
Twirling Parallels	11	4
Soaring Plateaus	12	5
Shifting Anchors	13	6
Science Research Associates		
Basic Reading Series (1976)		
Readiness Book		R
Alphabet Book		R
A Pig Can Jig	A	1-2
A Hen in a Fox's Den	B	1-2
Six Ducks in a Pond	C	1-2
A King on a Swing	D	1-2
Kittens and Children	E	1-2
Purple Turtles	F	1-2
Tony's Adventure	G	1-2
The Story of Roger	H	1-2
Captain Bunker's Ghost	I	3
The Old-Fashioned Ice-Cream Freeze	J	4
The Big Abzul-Raider Game	K	5
Station Four	L	6

TABLE A-1   Basic Reading Series (*Continued*)

TITLE	LEVEL	GRADE EQUIVALENT
Scott, Foresman		
Basics in Reading (1978)		
Hello, Sunshine		R
First Feathers		R
Puppy Paws		PP
Jumping Jamboree		PP
No Cages, Please		PP
Dragon Wings		P
Calico Caper		1
Daisy Days		2
Hootenanny		2
Ride a Rainbow		3
Step Right Up!		3
Flying Hoofs		4
Fins and Tales		5
Racing Stripes		6
With the Works		7
Batter Up!		8
The New Open Highways		
Program (1973–1975)		
Starter Concept Cards		1
Get Set		1
Ready to Roll		1
Rolling Along		1
More Power		2
Moving Ahead		2
Splendid Journey		3
Speeding Away		3
Seeking Adventure		4
Discovering Treasure		5
Exploring Afar		6
Blasting Off		7
Orbiting Earth		8

TABLE A-2   High-Interest, Low-Vocabulary Materials (These materials are designed for the student with more mature interests who requires easy-reading material.)

PUBLISHER AND TITLE	*Reading Level* (GRADE)	*Interest Level* (GRADE)	*Components*
Addison-Wesley			
Checkered Flag Series	2.0–4.0	6.0–12.0	book series; filmstrips with records; read-along cassettes

TABLE A-2   High-Interest, Low-Vocabulary Materials (*Continued*)

PUBLISHER AND TITLE	Reading Level (GRADE)	Interest Level (GRADE)	Components
Deep Sea Adventure Series	1.8–5.0	3.0–9.0	book series
Morgan Bay Mysteries	2.3–4.1	3.0–8.0	book series
Top Flight Readers	2.3–3.5	5.0–10.0	book series; filmstrips and cassettes; read-along cassettes
Benefic			
Animal Adventure Series	PP–1.0	1.0–4.0	book series
Butternut Bill Series	PP–1.0	1.0–6.0	book series
Button Family Adventures	PP–3.0	1.0–3.0	book series
Cowboys of Many Races	PP–5.0	1.0–6.0	book series
Dan Frontier Series	PP–4.0	1.0–7.0	book series
Exploring and Understanding Series	4.0	4.0–9.0	book series
Horses and Heroines	2.0–4.0	5.0–7.0	book series
Moonbeam Series	PP–3.0	1.0–6.0	book series
Mystery Adventure	2.0–6.0	4.0–9.0	book series
Racing Wheels Series	2.0–4.0	4.0–9.0	book series
Sailor Jack Series	PP–3.0	1.0–6.0	book series
Space Age Books	1.0–3.0	3.0–6.0	book series
Space Science Fiction Series	2.0–6.0	4.0–7.0	book series; activity book
Sports Mysteries Series	2.0–4.0	4.0–9.0	book series
What It Is Series	1.0–4.0	1.0–8.0	book series
World of Adventure Series	2.0–6.0	4.0–9.0	book series
Bobbs-Merrill			
Childhood of Famous Americans Series	4.0–5.0	4.0–9.0	book series
Bowmar/Noble			
Play the Game	2.5–4.0	3.0–8.0	book series with cassettes
Reading Incentive	3.0–4.0	3.0–7.0	book series; filmstrips with cassettes
Search	2.0–2.5	3.0–7.0	book series
Young Adventure Series	4.0–6.0	3.0–12.0	book series; posters
Childrens Press			
About Books	1.0–4.0	2.0–8.0	book series
Fun to Read Classics	5.0–8.0	5.0–12.0	book series
The Frontiers of America Series	3.0	3.0–8.0	book series
I Want to Be Series	2.0–4.0	4.0–6.0	book series
True Book Series	2.0–3.0	1.0–6.0	book series

TABLE A-2 High-Interest, Low-Vocabulary Materials (*Continued*)

PUBLISHER AND TITLE	Reading Level (GRADE)	Interest Level (GRADE)	Components
Crestwood House			
Monster Series	4.0	4.0–12.0	book series with cassettes: posters; bookmarks
Doubleday			
Signal Books	4.0	5.0–9.0	book series
Economy			
Guidebook to Better Reading	2.1–5.6	4.0–9.0	book series
Educational Activities			
Sea Hawk Books	1.5–4.3	4.0–9.0	book series
Fearon • Pitman			
Adventures in Urban Reading	2.9–3.4	4.0–7.0	comic book series
American West Series	5.0	4.0–12.0	book series
Pacemaker Classics	2.1–2.8	5.0–12.0	book series
Pacemaker Story Books	1.9–2.6	4.0–8.0	book series
Pacemaker True Adventures	2.1–2.5	5.0–10.0	book series
Garrard			
American Folktales	3.0	2.0–5.0	book series
Americans All	4.0	3.0–6.0	book series
Around the World Holidays	5.0	4.0–7.0	book series
Discovery	3.0	2.0–5.0	book series
Famous Animal Stories	3.0	2.0–5.0	book series
Good Earth Books	3.0	2.0–6.0	book series
Holidays	3.0	2.0–5.0	book series
Indians	3.0	2.0–5.0	book series
Jimmy and Joe	1.0	K–3.0	book series
Old Witch Books	1.0–2.0	K–4.0	book series
Sports	4.0	3.0–6.0	book series
Target Books	3.0–4.0	5.0–12.0	book series
Globe			
Adapted Classics	4.0–8.0	5.0–12.0	book series
E. M. Hale			
Getting to Know Books	4.0–5.0	4.0–9.0	book series
How and Why Series	4.0–5.0	4.0–9.0	book series
We Were There Books	4.0–6.0	5.0–9.0	book series
Harper & Row			
American Adventure Series	2.0–6.0	4.0–9.0	book series

TABLE A-2 High-Interest, Low-Vocabulary Materials *(Continued)*

PUBLISHER AND TITLE	Reading Level (GRADE)	Interest Level (GRADE)	Components
D. C. Heath			
Reading Caravan Series	3.0–6.0	5.0–10.0	book series
Teen-Age Tales	3.0–6.0	6.0–11.0	book series
Jamestown			
Attention Span Books	2.0–4.0	5.0–8.0	book series
Jamestown Classics	5.0–6.0	6.0–adult	book series; cassettes
Mafex Associates			
Citizens All	1.0–3.0	4.0–8.0	book series
Magpie Series	1.0–3.0	4.0–8.0	book series
Target Series	2.0–4.0	4.0–9.0	book series
McCormick-Mathers			
Turning Point	1.8–3.1	5.0–10.0	book series; duplicating masters
Morrow			
Morrow's High Interest Easy Reading Books	1.0–8.0	4.0–10.0	book series
Oxford Univ. Press			
Wildrush Books	3.0–4.0	5.0–9.0	book series
Random House			
All about Books	4.0–6.0	5.0–11.0	book series
Beginner Books	1.0–2.0	1.0–4.0	book series
Gateway Books	2.0–3.0	3.0–8.0	book series
Landmark Books	5.0–7.0	5.0–11.0	book series
Step-Up Books	2.0–3.0	3.0–9.0	book series
World Landmark Books	5.0–6.0	5.0–11.0	book series
Reader's Digest Services			
Reading Skill Builders	1.0–4.0	2.0–5.0	book series
Scholastic Book Services			
Firebird Books	5.0–6.0	5.0–12.0	book series
Sprint	1.0–5.0	4.0–8.0	book series; duplicating masters; skills books
Steck-Vaughn			
Reading Essential Series	1.0–8.0	4.0–10.0	book series
Read Better with Jim King Series	2.0–8.0	4.0–10.0	book series
Watts			
First Books	2.0–9.0	3.0–12.0	book series
Let's Find Out	2.0–4.0	5.0–6.0	book series

TABLE A-2   High-Interest, Low-Vocabulary Materials (*Continued*)

PUBLISHER AND TITLE	Reading Level (GRADE)	Interest Level (GRADE)	Components
Xerox Education Publications			
Flash Gordon	2.5–3.5	5.0–8.0	reading cards with filmstrips, duplicating masters; posters
Reading Mastery	2.0–6.0	4.0–6.0	book series
Scrambler Reading Series	2.5–4.0	5.0–9.0	comic book series

TABLE A-3   Elementary School Dictionaries

TITLE	GRADE LEVEL	COPYRIGHT	PUBLISHER
The Charlie Brown Dictionary	K–3	1973	Random House (hardcover); Scholastic Paperbacks (paper)
The Children's Dictionary	3–6	1970	A. Wheaton, distributed by British Book Centre
The Ginn Beginning Dictionary	2–4	1973	Ginn
The Ginn Intermediate Dictionary	3–8	1974	Ginn
The HBJ School Dictionary	2–8	1977	Harcourt Brace Jovanovich
Macmillan Beginning Dictionary	2–4	1971	Macmillan
Macmillan School Dictionary	3–8	1978	Macmillan
The New Horizon Ladder Dictionary of the English Language	2–6	1970	New American Library
The Oxford Children's Dictionary in Colour	1–3	1976	Oxford Univ. Press
The Picture Dictionary for Children	K–3	1977	Grosset & Dunlap
Scott, Foresman Beginning Dictionary	3–8	1976	Scott, Foresman
Thorndike-Barnhart Beginning Dictionary	3–8	1974	Scott, Foresman
Troll Talking Picture Dictionary	K–3	1974	Troll Associates
Webster's New Elementary Dictionary	3–8	1975	G. & C. Merriam (trade edition); American Book Company (text edition)

TABLE A-3 Elementary School Dictionaries *(Continued)*

TITLE	GRADE LEVEL	COPYRIGHT	PUBLISHER
Webster's New World Dictionary for Young Readers	3–8	1976	Collins + World
The Weekly Reader Beginning Dictionary	2–4	1973	Grosset & Dunlap
Word Wonder Dictionary	2–4	1966	Holt, Rinehart & Winston
The Xerox Intermediate Dictionary	3–6	1974	Xerox Education Publications, distributed by Grosset & Dunlap

TABLE A-4 Picture Dictionaries

TITLE	GRADE LEVEL	COPYRIGHT	PUBLISHER
The Cat in the Hat Beginner Book Dictionary	K–1	1964	Beginner Books
The Golden Picture Dictionary	K–1	1976	Western
Grosset Starter Picture Dictionary	K–1	1976	Grosset & Dunlap
International Visual Dictionary	K–1	1973	Clute International Institute
My First Golden Dictionary	K–1	1957	Western
My First Picture Dictionary	K–1	1977	Lothrop, Lee & Shepard (library edition); Scott, Foresman (text edition)
My Dictionary	K–1	1970	Lothrop, Lee & Shepard (library edition); Scott, Foresman (text edition)
My Second Picture Dictionary	K–3	1971	Lothrop, Lee & Shepard (library edition); Scott, Foresman (text edition)
The New Golden Dictionary	K–1	1972	Western
Storybook Dictionary	K–3	1966	Western
The Strawberry Picture Dictionary	K–1	1974	Strawberry Books
Two Thousand Plus Index and Glossary	K–3	1977	Macdonald-Raintree

For further information on children's dictionaries the reader is referred to K. F. Kister, *Dictionary Buying Guide*, R. R. Bowker, New York, 1977.

CHECKLIST FOR EVALUATING GAMES*

In selecting and constructing games, the teacher should keep the following criteria in mind:

1. Can the game be played without specific previous knowledge (does it teach)?
2. Do all players have the required prerequisite knowledge?
3. Does the game require a task which seems useful in developing reading ability?
4. Does the game require integration of component reading skills?
5. Are frequent decisions and responses required of each player?
6. Does the game provide intrinsic motivation (related to the joy of learning, rather than merely winning over others)?
7. Does the game seem more useful than reading some interesting material?

The greater the number of positive answers, the more valuable the game is as a classroom activity.

HOW TO BIND BOOKS†

So many teachers have shown an interest in bookbinding. The suggestions below are included to assist in their classroom publishing.

First, the pages that are to be bound should be stacked in order, with a blank page before the title page and after the final page. Next, fasten the pages together along the left edge by stapling, or preferably, by sewing with a long stitch.

For hardcover bindings, enlist the help of the students in collecting shirt cardboards, gift boxes, and tablet backs. Cover materials may include colorful contact paper, fabric scraps, adhesive shelf paper, and wallpaper.

Cut two pieces of cardboard approximately ¼ inch larger in each direction than the page size. Next, tape the two pieces of cardboard together with about a ¼-inch separation when the two covers are lying flat so that the cover is hinged. Now, choose contact paper, fabric scraps, or whatever covering is desired and cut a piece large enough to extend 1 inch around the outer edge of the cardboard. Fold the edges of the cover material around the hinged cardboard, pulling the edges of the cover tightly to

*R. L. Allington and M. Strange, "The Problem with Reading Games," *The Reading Teacher*, **31**:274 (1977). Reprinted by permission from the authors and the International Reading Association.

†Prepared by Thomas Cloer, Director of Reading and Study Skills Laboratory, Furman University, Greenville, SC 29613. Reprinted by permission from the author.

remove puckers. Using contact paper, construction paper, or wallpaper, cut a piece large enough to cover the entire inside of the book cover. Finally, fasten the bound pages into the book with short strips of tape, and cover the tape with the same colored paper used for the inside cover.

The results are hardcover books in beautiful bindings by classroom authors. A publishing committee can accomplish the above procedures with a little guidance in the beginning.

The Cover

Cut two identical pieces of cardboard and place on cover paper, which has been precut.

Step 1.   The distance between the back and front covers should be between ⅛ and ½ inch, depending on the thickness of the pages.

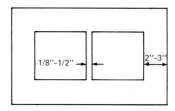

Step 2.   Turn in corners.

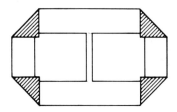

Step 3.   Turn in edges.

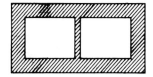

Three Ways to Insert Pages

1. Cut a piece of paper ½ inch smaller than book cover and glue on inside for inside cover. Use two strips of contact paper to put in pages, one on the front and one on the back.

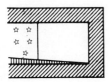

2. Staple your pages together and attach with two pieces of contact paper cut exactly double the size of one page.

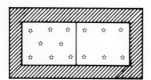

3. Sew pages together down the middle with a piece of contact paper for the inside cover underneath, face up. Glue the inside section to cover, being sure to match stitching up with the space between the two covers.

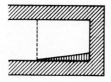

SIXTY-FIVE WAYS TO SAY "GOOD FOR YOU"*

Everyone knows that a little praise goes a long way in any classroom. But a "little praise" really needs to be something more than the same few phrases repeated over and over ad nauseum. Your students need more than the traditional "Good," "Very good," and "Fine" if encouragement is in the cards. Here are some additional possibilities.

---

*Reprinted by permission from the Exemplary Center for Reading Instruction, South Highland Drive, Salt Lake City, UT 84106.

That's really nice.

Wow!

I like the way you're working.

Everyone's working so hard.

Much better.

It's a pleasure to teach when you work like this.

What neat work.

This kind of work pleases me very much.

That's right! Good for you.

I bet your Mom and Dad would be proud to see the job you did on this.

Thank you for (sitting down, being quiet, getting right to work, etc.).

Right on.

Sharp!

I like the way Tom is working.

My goodness, how impressive!

That's "A" work.

Mary is waiting quietly.

Ann is paying attention.

That's clever.

Very interesting.

That's an interesting way of looking at it.

That's the right answer.

Exactly right.

Superior work.

That's a very good observation.

That's an interesting point of view.

You've got it now.

Nice going.

You make it look easy.

I like the way Bill (the class) has settled down.

Sherrie is really going to town.

That's coming along nicely.

Thank you very much.

That's great.

Keep up the good work.

That's quite an improvement.

Keep it up.

Good job.

Excellent work.

You really outdid yourself today.

Congratulations. You had _____ right.

Beautiful.

Terrific.

I'm very proud of the way you worked today.

I appreciate your help.

Very good. Why don't you show the class?

Marvelous.

Groovy.

For sure.

That looks like it's going to be a great report.

You're on the right track now.

John is in line.

Dickie got right down to work.

It looks like you put a lot of work into this.

Very creative.

Good thinking.

Now you've figured it out.

Clifford has it.

Now you've got the hang of it.

Super.

That's a good point.

That certainly is one way of looking at it.

Thank you for raising your hand, Charles. What is it?

Out of sight.

Far out.

TABLE A-5 Checklist of Instructional Needs*

NON READER OR PREPRIMER LEVEL	PRIMARY GRADE READING LEVEL	INTERMEDIATE GRADE READING LEVEL
Needs help in:	*Needs help in:*	*Needs help in:*
1. Listening comprehension and speech	1. Listening comprehension and speech	1. Listening comprehension and speech
—Understanding of material heard	—Understanding of material heard	—Understanding of material heard
—Speech and spoken vocabulary	—Speech and spoken vocabulary	—Speech and oral expression
2. Visual perception of word elements	2. Word analysis abilities	2. Word analysis abilities and spelling
—Visual memory of words	—Visual memory of words	—Visual analysis of words
—Giving names of letters	—Auditory analysis of words	—Auditory analysis of words
—Identifying letters named	—Solving words by sounding	—Solving words by sounding syllables
—Matching letters	—Sounds of blends, phonograms	—Sounding syllables, word parts
—Copying letters	—Use of context clues	—Meaning from context
3. Auditory perception of word elements	—Remembering new words taught	—Attack on unfamiliar words
—Initial or final blends	3. Oral reading abilities	—Spelling ability
—Initial or final single sounds	—Oral reading practice	—Accuracy of copy; speed of writing
—Learning sounds taught	—Comprehension in oral reading	—Dictionary skills: location, pronunciation, meaning
4. Phonic abilities	—Phrasing (eye-voice span)	
—Solving words	—Errors on easy words	
—Sounding words	—Addition or omission of words	3. Oral reading abilities
—Sounds of blends—phonograms	—Repetition of words or phrases	—Oral reading practice
—Sounds of individual letters	—Ignoring punctuation	—Comprehension in oral reading
5. Learning rate	—Ignoring word errors	—Phrasing (eye-voice span)
—Remembering words taught	—Attack on unfamiliar words	—Expression in reading; speech skills
—Use of context clues	—Expression in reading	—Speed of oral reading
6. Reading interest and effort	—Speech, voice, enunciation	—Security in oral reading
—Attention and persistence	—Security in oral reading	—Word and phrase meaning
—Self-directed work		

288

7. Other
___
___
___
___

4. Silent reading and recall
___ Level of silent reading
___ Comprehension in silent reading
___ Attention and persistence
___ Unaided oral recall
___ Recall on questions
___ Speed of silent reading
___ Phrasing (eye movements)
___ Lip movements and whispering
___ Head movements; frowning
___ Imagery in silent reading
___ Position of book; posture

5. ___ Reading interest and effort
___ Attention and persistence
___ Voluntary reading
___ Self-directed work; workbooks

4. Silent reading and recall
___ Level of silent reading
___ Comprehension in silent reading
___ Unaided oral recall
___ Unaided written recall
___ Recall on questions
___ Attention and persistence
___ Word and phrase-meaning difficulties
___ Sentence-complexity difficulties
___ Imagery in silent reading

5. ___ Speeded reading abilities
___ Speed of reading (eye movements)
___ Speed of work in content subjects
___ Skimming and locating information

6. ___ Study abilities
___ Reading details, directions, arithmetic
___ Organization and subordination of ideas
___ Elaborative thinking in reading
___ Critical reading
___ Use of table of contents; references

7. ___ Reading interest and effort
___ Voluntary reading
___ Variety of reading
___ Self-directed work

OBJECTIVES FOR THE DEVELOPMENTAL READING PROGRAM: GRADES K–6*

The following is a list of objectives for developmental reading instruction for kindergarten through grade six. These materials were developed as a part of the Basic Skills Assessment Program by the South Carolina State Department of Education.

The objectives are included in this appendix to serve as a scope and sequence reference to reading skills. School administrators and classroom teachers may use this list as a model in developing their own set of objectives for reading instruction.

*Reprinted by permission from the South Carolina State Department of Education.

TABLE A-6   Developmental Reading Instruction

KINDERGARTEN

Objective: The student performs tasks involving gross motor skills.

Explanation: The student uses large muscles to coordinate eye-hand movements, eye-foot movements, and body positions in maintaining balance while performing physical activities. Demonstrations of large muscle control include activities such as marching; hopping on either foot; skipping; jumping and landing on both feet; galloping; climbing stairs while alternating feet; and bouncing, throwing, catching, and kicking a ball.

Objective: The student performs tasks involving fine motor skills.

Explanation: The student uses small muscles to coordinate eye-hand movements and body positions while manipulating objects, tracing, copying, drawing, and painting. Demonstrations of eye-hand coordination include activities such as buttoning, zipping, lacing, and tying articles of clothing; folding paper; assembling puzzles; opening a book and turning the pages one at a time from front to back; building with blocks and construction toys; cutting straight and curved lines while holding scissors properly; tracing objects and symbols (for example, finger-tracing in sand or tracing wooden letters and numerals); and copying shapes, letters, own name, words, and numerals.

Objective: The student remembers visual stimuli.

Explanation: The student recalls, after a brief lapse of time, stimuli presented visually. (The "brief lapse of time" will vary depending upon the activity.) Demonstration of visual memory involves the student's recalling by pointing to or naming one to six visual stimuli after the stimuli have been presented and removed or covered. Visual stimuli might include colors, shapes, numerals, letters, or patterns.

Objective: The student determines likenesses and differences in visual stimuli.

Explanation: The student distinguishes likenesses and differences by comparing visual stimuli. Demonstrations of visual discrimination include activities such as matching identical colors; sorting objects on the basis of color; matching identical pictures; selecting the picture that is different; matching identical shapes; sorting objects on the basis of shape; assembling simple

TABLE A-6 Developmental Reading Instruction (*Continued*)

puzzles; matching objects of identical sizes; sorting objects on the basis of size; and matching identical symbols (numerals, letters, and words).

Objective: The student remembers auditory stimuli.

Explanation: The student recalls, after a brief lapse of time, stimuli presented auditorily. (The "brief lapse of time" will vary depending upon the activity.) Stimuli might include sounds made by animals, people, or objects and sound patterns. Demonstrations of auditory memory include activities such as repeating sounds made by animals, objects and people; repeating rhythmic sequences; counting from one to ten by rote; and repeating nursery rhymes, fingerplays, poems, and songs.

Objective: The student determines likenessess and differences in auditory stimuli.

Explanation: The student distinguishes likenesses and differences by comparing sounds. Demonstrations of auditory discrimination include activities such as matching sounds made by objects, animals, or people; matching sounds according to rhythmic pattern, pitch (high-low), or volume (loud-soft); recognizing words that sound the same (for example, "dog" and "dog") and words that sound different (for example, "dog" and "doll"); matching words that rhyme (for example, "cat," "bat," and "mat"); and matching sounds at the beginning of words (for example, "boy," "ball," and "book").

Objective: The student communicates with others by using expressive language.

Explanation: The student communicates with others by using a simple oral vocabulary and by expressing ideas with an expanding oral vocabulary. Vocabulary development may include naming such things as colors, parts of the body, people, animals, foods, objects, sounds, days of the week, seasons, occupations, letters, numerals, coins and textures. Demonstrations of expression of ideas include activities such as initiating verbal communication with others, relating personal experiences to classroom activities, and dictating personal experiences for teacher's recording in a written form.

Objective: The student is receptive of language in communicating with others.

Explanation: The student communicates with others by listening attentively and by utilizing the information presented. Demonstrations of receptive language include activities such as listening and responding to the conversations of others; listening to and making comments about a selection read; and listening to and following directions.

Objective: The student expresses an interest in language.

Explanation: The student seeks out information or initiates actions related to words or books. Demonstrations of an interest in language include behaviors such as asking the meaning of words; asking to have a story read; looking at pictures in books; and sharing books with the class.

Objective: The student classifies stimuli on the basis of one or more attributes.

Explanation: In order to be able to classify, the student must first recognize similarities in stimuli (such as objects) with respect to some attribute or characteristic (such as size). The student must then group the stimuli according to one or more attribute(s). Demonstrations of classification include activities such as classifying objects according to color, size, or shape and classifying by functions and/or relationships such things as objects, foods, animals, or people.

TABLE A-6   Developmental Reading Instruction (*Continued*)

Objective: The student compares stimuli on the basis of one or more attributes.

Explanation: In order to be able to compare, the student must first recognize similarities and differences in stimuli (such as objects) with respect to some attribute or characteristic (such as size). The student must then compare the stimuli according to one or more attribute(s). Demonstrations of comparison include activities such as comparing two groups of objects using the terms more than, less than, or same as; comparing two objects according to length, height, weight, size, shape, or distance; comparing opposites or positions (for example, behind/in front of, between/beside, above/below).

Objective: The student sequences stimuli on the basis of one or more attributes.

Explanation: In order to be able to sequence, the student must first recognize differences in stimuli (such as objects) with respect to some attribute or characteristic (such as size). The student must then order the stimuli according to one or more attribute(s). Demonstrations of sequencing include activities such as counting up to ten objects; ordering objects according to length, height, weight, or size, identifying the correct object to complete the pattern; completing an incomplete pattern or picture; retelling a short story in sequential order; arranging in correct order three pictures; and stating the sequential steps involved after completing a three-step activity.

Objective: The student begins to understand the concept of conservation of number.

Explanation: The student recognizes that a group has the same number of objects regardless of the arrangement of the objects. Demonstrations of conservation of number involves the teacher presenting the student with five to ten objects and asking the student to count the objects. After the student counts the number of objects correctly, the teacher rearranges the objects and asks, "How many objects are there?" A student who responds, without recounting, that the number of objects is the same understands conservation of number.

Objective: The student interprets and infers on the basis of oral or illustrative selections.

Explanation: The student demonstrates understanding of selections, for example, stories presented orally or in picture form, by interpreting or making inferences on the basis of the selection. The student interprets selections by summarizing what has been seen or heard. The student makes inferences by going beyond the content of the selection. Demonstrations of interpretation and inference include activities such as listening to a selection, expressing the main idea, and making inferences; supplying a logical ending to a story after being presented with only two-thirds of the story; supplying appropriate answer(s) to questions on the basis of context clues; and making up a story about a picture.

Objective: The student controls emotions and expresses them in a socially acceptable manner.

Explanation: The student exhibits the ability to control and express emotions by appropriate use of words or actions. Demonstrations of self-control include behaviors such as expressing feelings or needs in a controlled and constructive manner; accepting socially imposed limits; and adjusting to changes in routine.

Objective: The student displays a positive attitude toward self.

Explanation: The student exhibits a positive self-concept through favorable actions and words concerning self. Demonstrations of positive self-concept include behaviors such as taking finished work home; asking to have work displayed; showing work to others; working inde-

TABLE A-6   Developmental Reading Instruction (*Continued*)

pendently and asking for help from others when needed; completing tasks, tidying up after self; taking responsibility for personal belongings; and developing independent personal hygiene habits.

Objective: The student displays a positive attitude toward school.

Explanation: The student exhibits a positive feeling about school through favorable actions and words concerning school. Demonstrations of a positive attitude toward school include behaviors such as using materials correctly and participating voluntarily in a wide variety of classroom activities.

Objective: The student interacts with others in a socially acceptable manner.

Explanation: The student cooperates with others by being considerate of and sensitive to their needs. Demonstrations of appropriate school interaction include behaviors such as sharing materials; listening to ideas and opinions; respecting the property of others; and reacting positively toward the achievements of others.

READING: GRADE ONE

Decoding and Word Meaning

Objective: The student can use word recognition skills and can determine the meanings of words.

Suggested Measurement Strategy: Identifying the meanings and/or pronunciations of given words. These may be words selected from a basic sight vocabulary list; words selected to exemplify phonetic rules; root words with prefixes or suffixes added; words used in context; inflected nouns or verbs; compound words; or contractions.

Details

Objective: The student can accurately comprehend the details in a reading selection.

Suggested Measurement Strategy: Answering questions that ask "who," "what," "where," "when," "why," "how," "how many," or "in what sequence" about information that has been directly stated in oral, pictorial, or written communications. These communications may be pictures, sentences, sets of directions, paragraphs, stories, or poems.

Main Idea

Objective: The student can determine the main idea of a reading selection.

Suggested Measurement Strategy: Identifying or generating statements that most accurately and comprehensively summarize the contents of oral, pictorial, or written communications. These communications may be pictures, paragraphs, or stories.

Reference Usage

Objective: The student can locate and utilize desired information in reference sources.

Suggested Measurement Strategy: Locating and utilizing requested information in reference sources such as books' tables of contents, picture dictionaries, and calendars.

TABLE A-6 Developmental Reading Instruction (*Continued*)

Inference

Objective: The student can make valid inferences about a reading selection.

Suggested Measurement Strategy: Identifying or generating reasonable answers to questions about information not directly stated in oral, pictorial, or written communications. The questions asked may require determining themes or authors' purposes, making comparisons, deducing causes or effects, drawing conclusions, predicting outcomes, or applying information presented in communications to different situations. The communications may be pictures, paragraphs, stories, or poems.

Analysis of Literature

Objective: The student can critically analyze a reading selection.

Suggested Measurement Strategy: Answering questions that ask for analyses of the structure or content of oral or written communications. The questions may require identifying a communication's genre (e.g., fairy tale, nursery rhyme, etc.); identifying structural elements (e.g., plot, setting, etc.); identifying rhetorical devices (e.g., rhyme, exaggeration, etc.); or identifying the nature of the information presented (e.g., realism, fantasy, etc.). The communications to be analyzed may be pictures, sentences, paragraphs, stories, or poems.

READING: GRADE TWO

Decoding and Word Meaning

Objective: The student can use word recognition skills and can determine the meanings of words.

Suggested Measurement Strategy: Identifying the meanings and/or pronunciations of given words. These words may be words selected from a basic sight vocabulary list; words selected to exemplify phonetic rules; root words with prefixes or suffixes added; words used in context; inflected nouns or verbs; compound words; contractions; or words with a synonym, antonym, or homonym.

Details

Objective: The student can accurately comprehend the details in a reading selection.

Suggested Measurement Strategy: Answering questions that ask "who," "what," "where," "when," "why," "how," "how many," or "in what sequence" about information that has been directly stated in oral, pictorial, or written communications, These communications may be pictures, sentences, sets of directions, paragraphs, stories, or poems.

Main Idea

Objective: The student can determine the main idea of a reading selection.

Suggested Measurement Strategy: Identifying or generating statements that most accurately and comprehensively summarize the contents of oral or written communications. These communications may be paragraphs or stories.

TABLE A-6   Developmental Reading Instruction (*Continued*)

Reference Usage

Objective: The student can locate and utilize desired information in reference sources.

Suggested Measurement Strategy: Locating and utilizing requested information in reference sources such as books' tables of contents, glossaries, picture dictionaries, calendars, and maps.

Inference

Objective: The student can make valid inferences about a reading selection.

Suggested Measurement Strategy: Identifying or generating reasonable answers to questions about information not directly stated in oral or written communications. The questions asked may require determining themes or authors' purposes, making comparisons, deducing causes or effects, drawing conclusions, predicting outcomes, or applying information presented in communications to different situations. The communications may be pictures, paragraphs, stories, or poems.

Analysis of Literature

Objective: The student can critically analyze a reading selection.

Suggested Measurement Strategy: Answering questions that ask for analyses of the structure or content of oral or written communications. The questions may require identifying a communication's genre (e.g., fairy tale, nursery rhyme, etc.); identifying structural elements (e.g., plot, setting, etc.); identifying rhetorical devices (e.g., rhyme, exaggeration, etc.); or identifying the nature of the information presented (e.g., realism, fantasy, etc.). The communications to be analyzed may be pictures, sentences, paragraphs, stories, or poems.

READING: GRADE THREE

Decoding and Word Meaning

Objective: The student can use word recognition skills and can determine the meanings of words.

Suggested Measurement Strategy: Identifying the meanings and/or pronunciations of given words. These may be words selected from a basic sight vocabulary list; words selected to exemplify one or more phonetic rules; root words with one or more affixes added; words used in context; inflected nouns or verbs; compound words; contractions; or words with a synonym, antonym, or homonym.

Details

Objective: The student can accurately comprehend the details in a reading selection.

Suggested Measurement Strategy: Answering questions that ask "who," "what," "where," "when," "why," "how," "how many, " or "in what sequence" about information that has been directly stated in reading selections. These selections may be sentences, sets of directions, paragraphs, stories, or poems.

TABLE A-6 Developmental Reading Instruction (*Continued*)

Main Idea

Objective: The student can determine the main idea of a reading selection.

Suggested Measurement Strategy: Identifying or generating statements that most accurately and comprehensively summarize the contents of reading selections. These selections may be paragraphs or stories.

Reference Usage

Objective: The student can locate and utilize desired information in reference sources.

Suggested Measurement Strategy: Locating and utilizing requested information in reference sources such as books' tables of contents, glossaries, dictionaries, encyclopedias, the library card catalog, maps, graphs, tables, and charts.

Inference

Objective: The student can make valid inferences about a reading selection.

Suggested Measurement Strategy: Identifying or generating reasonable answers to questions about information not directly stated in reading selections. The questions asked may require determining themes or authors' purposes, making comparisons, deducing causes or effects, drawing conclusions, predicting outcomes, or applying information presented in selections to different situations. The selections may be paragraphs, stories, or poems.

Analysis of Literature

Objective: The student can critically analyze a reading selection.

Suggested Measurement Strategy: Answering questions that ask for analyses of the structure or content of reading selections. The questions may require identifying a selection's genre (e.g., fairy tale); identifying structural elements (e.g., plot, setting, etc.); or identifying the nature of the information presented (e.g., realism, fantasy, etc.). The selections to be analyzed may be sentences, paragraphs, stories, or poems.

READING: GRADE FOUR

Decoding and Word Meaning

Objective: The student can use word recognition skills and can determine the meanings of words.

Suggested Measurement Strategy: Identifying the meanings of given words. These words may be words selected from a content field such as social studies or the sciences; words with one or more affixes; compound words; words with a synonym, antonym, homonym, or multiple meaning; words used connotatively; words used figuratively; or words defined by their context.

Details

Objective: The student can accurately comprehend the details in a reading selection.

Suggested Measurement Strategy: Answering questions that ask "who," "what," "where," "when," "why," "how," "how many," or "in what sequence" about information that has been directly

TABLE A-6   Developmental Reading Instruction (*Continued*)

stated in reading selections. These selections may be sentences, sets of directions, articles from newspapers or magazines, stories, poems, or excerpts from books or plays.

Main Idea

Objective: The student can determine the main idea of a reading selection.

Suggested Measurement Strategy: Identifying or generating statements that most accurately and comprehensively summarize the contents of reading selections. These selections may be paragraphs, articles from newspapers or magazines, stories, or excerpts from books.

Reference Usage

Objective: The student can locate and utilize desired information in reference sources.

Suggested Measurement Strategy: Locating requested information in reference sources such as books' tables of contents, indexes, and glossaries; dictionaries; encyclopedias; the library card catalog; graphs; tables; charts; maps; and telephone directories.

Inference

Objective: The student can make valid inferences about a reading selection.

Suggested Measurement Strategy: Identifying or generating reasonable answers to questions about information not directly stated in reading selections. The questions asked may require determining themes or authors' purposes, making comparisons, deducing causes and effects, drawing conclusions, predicting outcomes, or applying information presented in selections to different situations. The selections may be paragraphs, stories, poems, or excerpts from books or plays.

Analysis of Literature

Objective: The student can critically analyze a reading selection.

Suggested Measurement Strategy: Answering questions that ask for analyses of the structure or content of reading selections. The questions may require identifying a selection's genre (e.g., myth, fable, etc.); identifying structural elements (e.g., narrator, climax, etc.); identifying rhetorical devices (e.g., simile, personification, etc.); or identifying the nature of the information presented (e.g., fact, opinion, etc.). The selections to be analyzed may be sentences, paragraphs, articles, stories, poems, or excerpts from books or plays.

READING: GRADE FIVE

Decoding and Word Meaning

Objective: The student can use word recognition skills and can determine the meanings of words.

Suggested Measurement Strategy: Identifying the meanings of given words. These words may be words selected from a content field such as social studies or the sciences; words with one or more affixes; compound words; words with a synonym, antonym, homonym, or multiple meaning; words used connotatively; words used figuratively; or words defined by their context.

TABLE A-6 **Developmental Reading Instruction** (*Continued*)

Details

Objective: The student can accurately comprehend the details in a reading selection.

Suggested Measurement Strategy: Answering questions that ask "who," "what," "where," "when," "why," "how," "how many", or "in what sequence" about information that has been directly stated in reading selections. These selections may be sentences, sets of directions, articles from newspapers or magazines, stories, poems, or excerpts from books or plays.

Main Idea

Objective: The student can determine the main idea of a reading selection.

Suggested Measurement Strategy: Identifying or generating statements that most accurately and comprehensively summarize the contents of reading selections. These selections may be paragraphs, articles from newspapers or magazines, stories, or excerpts from books.

Reference Usage

Objective: The student can locate and utilize desired information in reference sources.

Suggested Measurement Strategy: Locating requested information in reference sources such as books' tables of contents, indexes, and glossaries; dictionaries; encyclopedias; the library card catalog; graphs; tables; charts; maps; and telephone directories.

Inference

Objective: The student can make valid inferences about a reading selection.

Suggested Measurement Strategy: Identifying or generating reasonable answers to questions about information not directly stated in reading selections. The questions asked may require determining themes or authors' purposes, making comparisons, deducing causes and effects, drawing conclusions, predicting outcomes, or applying information presented in selections to different situations. The selections may be paragraphs, stories, poems, or excerpts from books or plays.

Analysis of Literature

Objective: The student can critically analyze a reading selection.

Suggested Measurement Strategy: Answering questions that ask for analyses of the structure or content of reading selections. The questions may require identifying a selection's genre (e.g., myth, fable, etc.); identifying structural elements (e.g., narrator, climax, etc.); identifying rhetorical devices (e.g., simile, personification, etc.); or identifying the nature of the information presented (e.g., fact, opinion, etc.). The selections to be analyzed may be sentences, paragraphs, articles, stories, poems, or excerpts from books or plays.

READING: GRADE SIX

Decoding and Word Meaning

Objective: The student can use word recognition skills and can determine the meanings of words.

TABLE A-6   Developmental Reading Instruction (*Continued*)

Suggested Measurement Strategy: Identifying the meanings of given words. These words may be words selected from a content field such as social studies or the sciences; words with one or more affixes; compound words; words with a synonym, antonym, homonym, or multiple meaning; words used connotatively; words used figuratively; or words defined by their context.

Details

Objective: The student can accurately comprehend the details in a reading selection.

Suggested Measurement Strategy: Answering questions that ask "who," "what," "where," "when," "why," "how," "how many," or "in what sequence" about information that has been directly stated in reading selections. These selections may be sentences, sets of directions, articles from newspapers or magazines, stories, poems, or excerpts from books or plays.

Main Idea

Objective: The student can determine the main idea of a reading selection.

Suggested Measurement Strategy: Identifying or generating statements that most accurately and comprehensively summarize the contents of reading selections. These selections may be paragraphs, articles from newspapers or magazines, stories, or excerpts from books.

Reference Usage

Objective: The student can locate and utilize desired information in reference sources.

Suggested Measurement Strategy: Locating requested information in reference sources such as books' tables of contents, indexes, and glossaries; dictionaries; encyclopedias; the library card catalog; graphs; tables; charts; maps; and telephone directories.

Inference

Objective: The student can make valid inferences about a reading selection.

Suggested Measurement Strategy: Identifying or generating reasonable answers to questions about information not directly stated in reading selections. The questions asked may require determining themes or authors' purposes, making comparisons, deducing causes and effects, drawing conclusions, predicting outcomes, or applying information presented in selections to different situations. The selections may be paragraphs, stories, poems, or excerpts from books or plays.

Analysis of Literature

Objective: The student can critically analyze a reading selection.

Suggested Measurement Strategy: Answering questions that ask for analyses of the structure or content of reading selections. The questions may require identifying a selection's genre (e.g., myth, fable, etc.); identifying structural elements (e.g., narrator, climax, etc.); identifying rhetorical devices (e.g., simile, personification, etc.); or identifying the nature of the information presented (e.g., fact, opinion, etc.). The selections to be analyzed may be sentences, paragraphs, articles, stories, poems, or excerpts from books or plays.

Recreational and Supplemental Reading

B

APPENDIX

The Newberry Award-Winning Books and Their
  Grade Equivalents   302
The Caldecott Award-Winning Books   303
Children's Choices   305
Bibliotherapy: Helping Children Cope   382
High-Interest, Low-Vocabulary Magazines   391
Children's Magazines   392

THE NEWBERRY AWARD-WINNING BOOKS AND THEIR GRADE EQUIVALENTS

The Newberry Award is presented to the author of the most outstanding contribution to American children's literature published during the previous year. This award is sponsored by the Children's Services Division of the American Library Association. Listed below are the year in which the award was received, book title, author, publisher, and reading grade level.*

1922 *The Story of Mankind* by Hendrik Willem van Loon. Liveright. Grade ten.
1923 *The Voyages of Doctor Doolittle* by Hugh Lofting. J. B. Lippincott. Grade six.
1924 *The Dark Frigate* by Charles Hawes. Little, Brown. Grade seven.
1925 *Tales From Silver Lands* by Charles Finger. Doubleday. Grade seven.
1926 *Shen of the Sea* by Arthur Bowie Chrisman. E. P. Dutton. Grade five.
1927 *Smoky, the Cowhorse* by Will James. Scribner's. Grade seven.
1928 *Gayneck, the Story of a Pigeon* by Dhan Gopal Mukerji. E. P. Dutton. Grade seven.
1929 *The Trumpeter of Krakow* by Eric P. Kelly. Macmillan. Grade eight.
1930 *Hitty, Her First Hundred Years* by Rachel Field. Macmillan. Grade seven.
1931 *The Cat Who Went to Heaven* by Elizabeth Coatsworth. Macmillan. Grade four.
1932 *Waterless Mountain* by Laura Adams Armer. Longmans. Grade four.
1933 *Young Fu of the Upper Yangtze* by Elizabeth Lewis. Winston. Grade five.
1934 *Invincible Louisa* by Cornelia Meigs. Little, Brown. Grade eight.
1935 *Dobry* by Monica Shannon. Viking. Grade six.
1936 *Caddie Woodlawn* by Carol Brink. Macmillan. Grade three.
1937 *Roller Skates* by Ruth Sawyer. Viking. Grade seven.
1938 *The White Stag* by Kate Seredy. Viking. Grade six.
1939 *Thimble Summer* by Elizabeth Enright. Rinehart. Grade three.
1940 *Daniel Boone* by James Daugherty. Viking. Grade nine.
1941 *Call It Courage* by Armstrong Sperry. Macmillan. Grade seven.
1942 *The Matchlock Gun* by Walter D. Edmonds. Dodd, Mead. Grade four.
1943 *Adam of the Road* by Elizabeth Janet Gray. Viking. Grade six.
1944 *Johnny Tremain* by Esther Forbes. Houghton Mifflin. Grade seven.
1945 *Rabbit Hill* by Robert Lawson. Viking. Grade six.
1946 *Strawberry Girl* by Lois Lenski. J. B. Lippincott. Grade two.
1947 *Miss Hickory* by Carolyn Sherwin Bailey. Viking. Grade three.
1948 *The Twenty-One Balloons* by William Pène du Bois. Viking. Grade eight.
1949 *King of the Wind* by Marguerite Henry. Rand McNally. Grade six.
1950 *The Door in the Wall* by Marguerite de Angeli. Doubleday. Grade three.
1951 *Amos Fortune, Free Man* by Elizabeth Yates. Aladdin. Grade six.
1952 *Ginger Pye* by Eleanor Estes. Harcourt, Brace. Grade four.
1953 *Secret of the Andes* by Ann Nolan Clark. Viking. Grade three.
1954 *. . . and now Miguel* by Joseph Krumgold. Crowell. Grade three.
1955 *The Wheel on the School* by Meindert DeJong. Harper. Grade six.
1956 *Carry On, Mr. Bowditch* by Jean Lee Latham. Houghton Mifflin. Grade six.

*The Fry Graph for Estimating Readability was used in assessing the reading grade levels of the books listed here. The calculations were performed by Richard Ingram, Reading Department, Winthrop College, Rock Hill, SC 29730.

1957 *Miracles on Maple Hill* by Virginia Sorensen. Harcourt, Brace. Grade three.
1958 *Rifles for Watie* by Harold Keith. Crowell. Grade six.
1959 *The Witch of Blackbird Pond* by Elizabeth George Speare. Houghton Mifflin. Grade four.
1960 *Onion John* by Joseph Krumgold. Crowell. Grade four.
1961 *Island of the Blue Dolphins* by Scott O'Dell. Houghton Mifflin. Grade six.
1962 *The Bronze Bow* by Elizabeth George Speare. Houghton Mifflin. Grade two.
1963 *A Wrinkle in Time* by Madeleine L'Engle. Farrar, Straus. Grade four.
1964 *It's Like This, Cat* by Emily Neville. Harper & Row. Grade five.
1965 *Shadow of a Bull* by Maia Wojciechowska. Atheneum. Grade three.
1966 *I, Juan de Pareja* by Elizabeth Borton de Trevino. Farrar, Straus & Giroux. Grade five.
1967 *Up a Road Slowly* by Irene Hunt. Follett. Grade seven.
1968 *From the Mixed-Up Files of Mrs. Basil E. Frankweiler* by E. L. Konigsburg. Atheneum. Grade four.
1969 *The High King* by Lloyd Alexander. Holt, Rinehart & Winston. Grade three.
1970 *Sounder* by William Armstrong. Harper & Row. Grade three.
1971 *The Summer of the Swans* by Betsy Byars. Viking. Grade four.
1972 *Mrs. Frisby and the Rats of NIMH* by Robert C. O'Brien. Atheneum. Grade six.
1973 *Julie of the Wolves* by Jean Craighead George. Harper & Row. Grade five.
1974 *The Slave Dancer* by Paula Fox. Bradbury. Grade two.
1975 *M. C. Higgins, the Great* by Virginia Hamilton. Macmillan. Grade six.
1976 *The Grey King* by Susan Cooper Atheneum. Grade ten.
1977 *Roll of Thunder, Hear My Cry* by Mildred D. Taylor. Dial. Grade ten.
1978 *Bridge to Terabithia* by Katherine Paterson. Crowell. Grade seven.
1979 *The Westing Game* by Ellen Raskin. E. P. Dutton. Grade eight.
1980 *A Gathering of Days: A New England Girl's Journal, 1830-32* by Joan M. Blos. Scribner's. Grade six.
1981 *Jacob Have I Loved* by Katherine Paterson. Crowell. Grade seven.

THE CALDECOTT AWARD–WINNING BOOKS

The Caldecott Award is presented annually to the illustrator of the most outstanding picture book published during the previous year. This award is sponsored by the Children's Services Division of the American Library Association. Listed below are the year in which the award was received, book title, illustrator, author, and publisher.

1938 *Animals of the Bible*. Illustrated by Dorothy P. Lathrop. Text Selected by Helen Dean Fish. J. B. Lippincott.
1939 *Mei Li* Illustrated and written by Thomas Handforth. Doubleday.
1940 *Abraham Lincoln*. Illustrated and written by Ingri and Edgar d'Aulaire. Doubleday.
1941 *They Were Strong and Good*. Illustrated and written by Robert Lawson. Viking.
1942 *Make Way for Ducklings*. Illustrated and written by Robert McCloskey. Viking.
1943 *The Little House*. Illustrated and written by Virginia Lee Burton. Houghton Mifflin.
1944 *Many Moons*. Illustrated by Louis Slobodkin. Written by James Thurber. Harcourt, Brace.

1945 *Prayer for a Child*. Illustrated by Elizabeth Orton Jones. Written by Rachel Field. Macmillan.

1946 *The Rooster Crows*. Illustrated by Maud and Miska Petersham. Macmillan.

1947 *The Little Island*. Illustrated by Leonard Weisgard. Written by Golden Mac-Donald (pseudonym of Margaret Wise Brown) Doubleday.

1948 *White Snow, Bright Snow*. Illustrated by Roger Duvoisin. Written by Alvin Tresselt. Lothrop, Lee & Shepard.

1949 *The Big Snow*. Illustrated and written by Berta and Elmer Hader. Macmillan.

1950 *Song of the Swallows*. Illustrated and written by Leo Politi. Scribner's.

1951 *The Egg Tree*. Illustrated and written by Katherine Milhous. Scribner's.

1952 *Finders Keepers*. Illustrated by Nicolas (pseudonym of Nicolas Mordvinoff) Written by Will (pseudonym of William Lipkind) Harcourt, Brace.

1953 *The Biggest Bear*. Illustrated and written by Lynd Ward. Houghton Mifflin.

1954 *Madeleine's Rescue*. Illustrated and written by Ludwig Bemelmans. Viking.

1955 *Cinderella, or the Little Glass Slipper*. Illustrated and translated from Charles Perrault by Marcia Brown. Scribner's.

1956 *Frog Went A-Courtin'*. Illustrated by Feodor Rojankovsky. Text retold by John Langstaff. Harcourt, Brace.

1957 *A Tree is Nice*. Illustrated by Marc Simont. Written by Janice May Udry. Harper.

1958 *Time of Wonder*. Illustrated and written by Robert McCloskey. Viking.

1959 *Chanticleer and the Fox*. Illustrated by Barbara Cooney. Adapted from *The Canterbury Tales*. Crowell.

1960 *Nine Days to Christmas*. Illustrated by Marie Hall Ets. Written by Marie Hall Ets and Aurora Labastida. Viking.

1961 *Baboushka and the Three Kings*. Illustrated by Nicolas Sidjakov. Written by Ruth Robbins. Parnassus.

1962 *Once a Mouse*. Illustrated and retold by Marcia Brown. Scribner's.

1963 *The Snowy Day*. Illustrated and written by Ezra Jack Keats. Viking.

1964 *Where the Wild Things Are*. Illustrated and written by Maurice Sendak. Harper & Row.

1965 *May I Bring a Friend?* Illustrated by Beni Montresor. Written by Beatrice Schenk de Regniers. Atheneum.

1966 *Always Room for One More*. Illustrated by Nonny Hogrogian. Retold by Sorche Nic Leodhas. Holt, Rinehart & Winston.

1967 *Sam, Bangs & Moonshine*. Illustrated by Evaline Ness. Holt, Rinehart & Winston.

1968 *Drummer Hoff*. Illustrated by Ed Emberley. Adapted by Barbara Emberley. Prentice-Hall.

1969 *The Fool of the World and the Flying Ship*. Illustrated by Uri Shulevitz. Retold by Arthur Ransome. Farrar, Straus & Giroux.

1970 *Sylvester and the Magic Pebble*. Illustrated and written by William Steig. Windmill.

1971 *A Story, A Story*. Illustrated by Gail E. Haley. Retold by Gail E. Haley from an African folk tale. Atheneum.

1972 *One Fine Day*. Illustrated by Nonny Hogrogian. Adapted by Nonny Hogrogian from an Armenian folk tale. Macmillan.

1973 *The Funny Little Woman*. Illustrated by Blair Lent. Retold by Arlene Mosel. E. P. Dutton.

1974   *Duffy and the Devil*. Illustrated by Margot Zemach. Retold by Harve Zemach from a Cornish tale. Farrar, Straus & Giroux.

1975   *Arrow to the Sun*. Illustrated by Gerald McDermott. Adapted by Gerald McDermott from a Pueblo Indian tale. Viking.

1976   *Why Mosquitoes Buzz in People's Ears*. Illustrated by Leo and Diane Dillon. Retold by Vera Aardema. Dial.

1977   *Ashanti to Zulu: African Traditions*. Illustrated by Leo and Diane Dillon. Written by Margaret Musgrove. Dial.

1978   *Noah's Ark*. Illustrated and written by Peter Spier. Doubleday.

1979   *The Girl Who Loved Wild Horses*. Illustrated and written by Paul Goble. Bradbury.

1980   *Ox-Cart Man*. Illustrated by Barbara Cooney. Written by Donald Hall. Viking.

1981   *Fables*. Illustrated and written by Arnold Lober. Harper.

CHILDREN'S CHOICES*

Since 1975, the International Reading Association/Children's Book Council Joint Committee has compiled a list of recommended children's books published during the previous year. The unique feature of this list is that books are selected by children throughout the United States.

The lists are published annually in *The Reading Teacher* and have been consolidated here under the following headings: beginning Independent Readers (7 years and under); younger Readers (7 to 10 years); middle Grades (over 10 years); older Readers; All Ages. The year preceding each section indicates the year in which those books appeared in *The Reading Teacher*, not the year of publication.

Reprints of this annotated bibliography may be obtained by sending a stamped, self-addressed envelope to The Children's Book Council, Inc, 67 Irving Place, New York, NY 10003.

Beginning Independent Readers (7 Years and Under)
1975

Albert's Toothache.   Barbara Williams. Illustrations by Kay Chorao. E. P. Dutton. Unpaged (32 pp.).
  Young children related sympathetically to a turtle with a problem. They chuckled over the humor in the story. Pictures carry some of the humor which can be seen by groups of listeners who will be eager to predict the ending.

Amy's Dinosaur.   Story and illustrations by Sid Hoff. Windmill/E. P. Dutton. 48 pp.
  Ecology theme mingled with the return of a dinosaur into modern times makes this popular with children and useful to teachers. An easy-reading book that deals with a comtemporary problem.

*Reprinted from *The Reading Teacher*, 1975–1980, by permission from the International Reading Association.

And I Mean It, Stanley. Story and illustrations by Crosby Bonsall. Harper & Row. 32 pp.
Young children will wonder whether there really is a Stanley hiding behind the fence. There is humor in the pictures and surprise when Stanley turns out to be a dog. An easy-to-read book.

Circus. Jack Prelutsky. Illustrations by Arnold Lobel. Macmillan. 32 pp.
Circus appeals to K–2 because of its beautiful full-color illustrations. The poems are sophisticated reading and are most effective when presented by the teacher. This book lends itself to creative writing and language expression.

The Compost Heap. Story and illustrations by Harlow Rockwell. Doubleday. 24 pp.
Simply written description in picture-book format of how to build a compost heap. Sound advice in easy-to-read prose for ecology-minded children.

Dinosaur's Housewarming Party. Norma Klein. Illustrations by James Marshall. Crown. Unpaged (39 pp.).
Children enjoyed hearing this one read aloud mainly for the humor in the many incidents showing a dinosaur moving into a house. One to read for fun and to prove reading is worth doing.

Dreams. Story and illustrations by Ezra Jack Keats. Macmillan. Unpaged (33 pp.).
Excellent book for primary language arts. Kids love it. The words paint pictures. Beautifully illustrated. Promotes oral discussion and writing as kids relate their own dreams.

An Elephant in My Bed. Suzanne Klein. Illustrations by Sharleen Pederson. Follett. 31 pp.
A light-hearted story of a boy who tries every possible hiding place for an elephant but finds none large enough. The ending, with the elephant returning to the circus with its father, satisfies children. An easy-to-read book.

Everett Anderson's Year. Lucille Clifton. Illustrations by Ann Grifalconi. Holt, Rinehart & Winston. 31 pp.
This book is appealing both for the woodcuts and the poetry. Children are involved because their year is much like Everett Anderson's year. Most effective if read aloud so that the poetic quality comes through to the listener.

Giants, Indeed! Story and illustrations by Virginia Kahl. Scribner's. Unpaged (32 pp.).
Story recounts small boy's trials when he travels from home in the days of giants and monsters. Contains delicious synonyms: "sneered," "scoffed," and so on. Should be read aloud to enjoy inflection changes and multiple meanings of words.

Herman the Helper. Robert Kraus. Illustrations by Jose Aruego and Ariane Dewey. Windmill/E. P. Dutton. 32 pp.
One child's comment, "He helped others and finally helped himself," states the essence of the book. The humorous comments interwoven with Aruego's and Dewey's illustrations amplify the ideas in the text. The repetitive story structure will be an aid to beginning readers.

Hooray for Pig. Carla Stevens. Illustrations by Rainey Bennett. Seabury. 48 pp.
This book about a pig who is afraid to swim was seldom on the shelf. Once children heard it, they were eager to read it themselves. Children in primary grades could handle the vocabulary easily. Could serve as basis for discussions about overcoming fears and trying new things.

Humbug Rabbit. Story and illustrations by Lorna Balian. Abingdon. Unpaged (32 pp.).

Children solve the mystery of the missing Easter eggs as they see the rabbits, below ground, and Granny, above ground, prepare for Easter. Detailed pictures, humorous touches, and a satisfying ending add to reader enjoyment.

If I Had My Way. Norma Klein. Illustrations by Ray Cruz. Pantheon. Unpaged (33 pp.).

Children can identify with this fantasy of role-playing in which a little girl becomes parent to her mother, father, and baby brother. Excellent for children with new siblings. Gratifying fantasy with implicit lesson in human relationships.

Lyle Finds His Mother. Story and illustrations by Bernard Waber. Houghton Mifflin. 48 pp.

Another adventure with Lyle the crocodile. This story will give children a chance to sympathize as well as to laugh. Good for reading aloud.

Mary Louise and Christopher. Natalie Savage Carlson. Illustrations by Jose Aruego and Ariane Dewey. Scribner's. Unpaged (40 pp.).

Used first for reading aloud, but children soon took book individually to see small and more detailed illustrations. Leads into discussions about being friends and the consequences of playing unkind tricks.

Morris and Boris. Story and illustrations by Bernard Wiseman. Dodd, Mead. 64 pp.

The stories produce laughter at a rather stupid moose getting the better of a conceited bear. They provide good material for beginning readers to enjoy.

Mushroom in the Rain. Mirra Ginsburg. Illustrations by Jose Aruego and Ariane Dewey. Macmillan. Unpaged (32 pp.).

Young readers enjoyed this story, about how one mushroom was able to protect many animals from the rain, for the colors and because they thought they could "learn something from this story." Many were able to read it themselves by the end of first grade.

The Mystery of the Missing Red Mitten. Story and illustrations by Steven Kellogg. Dial. 32 pp.

This is one that children in primary grades discovered for themselves and responded to with joy and increased self-confidence. They followed the plot even before they could read the words. For many, it was an excellent transition from basal reader to trade book.

Otter in the Cove. Miska Miles. Illustrations by John Schoenherr. Atlantic/Little, Brown. 48 pp.

Animal lovers and ecology students will worry, with Maggie, about her father's threat to shoot the otters so they will not destroy his abolone harvest. Beautiful illustrations add to the effect of the story.

Owliver. Robert Kraus. Illustrations by Jose Aruego and Ariane Dewey. Windmill/E. P. Dutton. 32 pp.

Owliver, the owl, has the problem many people have of choosing a career. Although both parents have plans for him he makes his own decision. The illustrations by Aruego and Dewey add an amusing dimension to the book.

Paper Party. Story and illustrations by Don Freeman. Viking. Unpaged (40 pp.).

Led to some imaginative thinking from young children about what it would be like to step into a television set. Could lead to creative writing or drawing experience. Excellent for reading aloud.

Rebecca Hatpin. Robert Kraus. Illustrations by Robert Byrd. Windmill/E. P. Dutton. 32 pp.
About a self-centered little girl who learns that it is satisfying to help other people. Good for approaching social responsibility and consideration for others.

The Seal and the Slick. Story and illustrations by Don Freeman. Viking. 32 pp.
Without being moralistic this picture book recounts what happens to marine life, in this case a seal, when a spill occurs in the ocean. Excellent both in text and in illustrations. High appeal to children in primary grades.

Send Wendell. Genevieve Gray. Illustrations by Symeon Shimin. McGraw-Hill. Unpaged (32 pp.).
Six-year-old Wendell's family sends him to do errands others are too busy to do. After an uncle's visit, Wendell's availability decreases but his sense of self increases. Shimin's art enriches characterization.

She Come Bringing Me That Little Baby Girl. Eloise Greenfield. Illustrations by John Steptoe. J. B. Lippincott. Unpaged (32 pp.).
Great to start discussion about a new baby in a family and the feelings older children might have about the baby. Children enjoyed listening to the story and took the book for closer study of illustrations.

The Summer Night. Charlotte Zolotow. Illustrations by Ben Shecter. Harper & Row. 32 pp.
A tender story of a father and his daughter preparing for bedtime on a summer night when sleep comes slowly. Companionship, understanding and love are communicated through the story and Ben Shecter's delicate illustrations.

Two Good Friends. Judy Delton. Illustrations by Giulio Maestro. Crown. Unpaged (32 pp.).
Children related to the friendship between Bear and Duck and their willingness to help each other in everyday household tasks. The vocabulary and the sentence structure are especially good for reading aloud. By spring first-grade children could read it aloud, and it was judged a favorite.

Watch Out for Chicken Feet in Your Soup. Story and illustrations by Tomie de Paola. Prentice-Hall. Unpaged (32 pp.).
Unique beginning to story prepares the reader for a peek into the "old ways" of an Italian grandma. Text encourages tolerance for different life styles and concludes with a recipe for making grandma's special bread dolls.

You're the Scaredy-Cat. Story and illustrations by Mercer Mayer. Parents' Magazine. 40 pp.
Read it aloud once and from then on children will take it and read it themselves. Idea, text, and illustrations are all hilarious for young children. One child, when introduced to a basal text word, answered, "We already know it; it's in *Scaredy-Cat.*"

1976

The Bear's Bicycle. Emilie Warren McLeod. Illustrations by David McPhail. Atlantic/Little, Brown. 32 pp.
Bicycle safety is demonstrated through colorful pictures leavened by a parallel set of humorous pictures of a teddy-bear-turned-real who takes the hazardous

consequences of ignoring the safety rules. With teacher guidance, this book can be not only amusing but an effective teaching tool.

The Chicken's Child.   Story and illustrations by Margaret A. Hartelius. Doubleday. Unpaged (40 pp.).

The humorous plot of this wordless picture book makes it useful for storytelling with primary children and as an aid in teaching about plot structure. The pictures at the point in the story when the hen is in danger, turning the rapid growth of her child into an asset, offer an opportunity for introducing children to the skill of predicting outcomes.

Cunningham's Rooster.   Barbara Brenner. Illustrations by Anne Rockwell. Parents' Magazine. Unpaged (28 pp.).

Nice, bright illustrations, and a good basic story idea of why and how composers, compose music. Excellent for use in music class and to further reading about music and musicians.

Dig, Drill, Dump, Fill.   Tana Hoban. Illustrated with photographs by Tana Hoban. Greenwillow. Unpaged (32 pp.).

Black-and-white photographs of heavy earth moving equipment will engage the youngest reader of this wordless book. Useful for categorizing, labeling, language experience stories and just liking, this book will fit in many areas of the curriculum.

Dinner at Alberta's.   Russell Hoban. Illustrations by James Marshall. Crowell. 40 pp.

Teaching about manners is fun with this book about Arthur Crocodile and his family. This humorous tale offers an opportunity to work with interpretive reading skills and will stimulate discussions dealing with social behavior and the need to change.

The Field of Buttercups.   Story and illustrations by Alice Boden. Walck. Unpaged (32 pp.).

Michael O'Grady catches a leprechaun, and in turn, the crafty little fellow tricks Michael in this amusing and beautifully illustrated Irish tale. Children love the leprechaun's cleverness and Michael's good-natured attitude. Good for creative writing and storytelling.

Georgie's Christmas Carol.   Story and illustrations by Robert Bright. Doubleday. 48 pp.

Georgie, the friendly ghost, charms children again as he organizes an unusual Christmas surprise for two children and their uncle, gloomy Mr. Gloams. Children chuckle at the sight of a cow with evergreen antlers pulling a sleigh and at Georgie coming down the chimney. A good reading-aloud book that shows children what the spirit of giving to others accomplishes.

I'm Not Oscar's Friend Anymore.   Marjorie Weinman Sharmat. Illustrations by Tony DeLuna. E. P. Dutton. Unpaged (32 pp.).

For any child who has ever had a fight with his or her best friend and doesn't even remember how the whole thing got started. Younger children are especially pleased that there is a happy ending.

The Lady Who Saw the Good Side of Everything.   Pat Decker Tapio. Illustrations by Paul Galdone. Seabury. Unpaged (32 pp.).

An improbable story of a supreme optimist (and her silent cat) who smilingly survives a series of calamities with confidence. A natural springboard to creative writing and illustrating of equally preposterous happenings, this book is also good for reading aloud and is excellent for drawing discussions from older children.

Little Rabbit's Loose Tooth.   Lucy Bate. Illustrations by Diane DeGroat. Crown. Unpaged (28 pp.).

Reading this book aloud to children promotes lively discussions about what tooth fairies do with teeth and if, indeed, there is such a being at all. Text lends itself to creative writing. Bold illustrations add to the appeal of the book.

Louie.   Story and illustrations by Ezra Jack Keats. Greenwillow. Unpaged (32 pp.). As children are putting on a puppet show, shy Louie interrupts the show to talk with Gussie, one of the puppets. At first there is disappointment for Louie but a thoughtful surprise appears in the satisfying ending. Consideration for others is shown in the action while encouragement of puppetry in the classroom may be a side effect.

The Maggie B.   Story and illustrations by Irene Haas. Atheneum/McElderry. Unpaged (28 pp.).

Stunning pictures are an integral part of the story. Molly is the ship's captain, her brother is her passenger. Children in grade one listened in quiet enchantment; one boy said, "the words moved like the ship." Creates moods children can recognize.

Mary Alice Operator Number 9.   Jeffrey Allen. Illustrations by James Marshall. Little, Brown. Unpaged (26 pp.).

Mary Alice is sick and can no longer quack the correct time. Other animals try and fail to bark or oink the time correctly or pleasantly, as the callers are accustomed to Operator Number 9. At last, Mary Alice is well and all are happy, to hear her familiar quack return. Humorously written with equally colorful and funny illustrations. Good for acting out the roles.

Michael.   Liesel Moak Skorpen. Illustrations by Joan Sardin. Harper & Row. 41 pp. A stormy mood is conveyed and developed with words and pictures. Michael and his dog Mud share attention with a baby rabbit. Solution is subtle, in a way children appreciate. Children naturally *start* the discussion after oral reading.

No Dogs Allowed, Jonathan!   Mary Blount Christian. Illustrations by Don Madden. Addison-Wesley. Unpaged (32 pp.).

The mixed blessings of owning a dog are experienced by Jonathan, whose dog is much too big for the city apartment. The trail of disaster that the dog leaves convinces Jonathan that he must find a more appropriate home for him. The slapstick humor comes through the illustrations as well as the text. This book stimulates lots of stories about escapades with dogs.

Rabbit Finds a Way.   Judy Delton. Illustrations by Joe Lasker. Crown. Unpaged (32 pp.).

Children sympathize with Rabbit when he fails to get his usual treat of Bear's carrot cake. They enjoy his resourceful solution (calling up for the recipe). A good book to call attention to kind deeds that friends do for one another. Some children chuckled over the picture of Goldilocks and the three bears hung on Bear's wall!

The Tutti-Frutti Case.   Harry Allard. Illustrations by James Marshall. Prentice-Hall. Unpaged (32 pp.).

Delightful story and pictures of a national disaster that would be very realistic to children. Imagine, no more ice cream because it always melts. Very logical

solution, and kids love the President's menu at the White House. Good story to
read aloud because children are fascinated by "big" words.

When the Wind Stops.   Charlotte Zolotow. Illustrations by Howard Knotts. Harper &
Row. 32 pp.

At the end of a happy day, a little boy asks his mother, "Why does the day have
to end?" Each answer brings another question about the continuity of life and
seasons and nature. This quiet mood book can be used to develop understand-
ings about the cyclical nature of events and reassurance about the future. A
good book to compare with Zolotow's *The Sky Was Blue*.

1977

Amy for Short.   Laura Joffe Numeroff. Macmillan. 48 pp.

Amy, the tallest girl in her class, was often called "stringbean" or "beanpole." At
least her friend Mark was as tall as she—until one summer when she grew
faster than he. Would she lose her friend? The solution of this story told in
three chapters involves a coded message and Captain Crunchy's Secret De-
coder Ring.

Arthur's Pen Pal.   Written and illustrated by Lillian Hoban. Harper & Row. 64 pp.
Paper ed., Xerox Education Publications.

Having a new pen pal named Sandy starts Arthur wishing he had a brother
rather than his bothersome baby sister Violet. When he discovers Sandy is a girl
who uses karate on her big brother, Arthur decides Violet is "pretty neat" after
all. Illustrations in soft red, yellow and green throughout.

Bullfrog Grows Up.   Rosamond Dauer. Illustrated by Byron Barton. Greenwillow.
56 pp.

Chris and Matt, young mice, find a tadpole, take him home in a bucket, and
raise him. Eventually he becomes such a huge bullfrog that he can no longer
live in the little mouse house. Tearfully, he is sent out into the world to raise his
own family. Colorful pictures illustrate this cheerful fantasy of animals acting
like humans.

Detective Mole.   Written and illustrated by Robert Quackenbush. Lothrop, Lee &
Shepard. 63 pp.

Each of the five short mysteries has enough action and suspense to keep children interested throughout. Humorous touches in the writing and illustrations
add to the enjoyment. This book is especially appealing to children who are
reluctant readers, since the stories are short enough to hold their attention.

Eliza's Daddy.   Ianthe Thomas. Illustrated by Moneta Barnett. Harcourt Brace
Jovanovich. 64 pp. Paper, Harcourt Brace Jovanovich.

Eliza's daddy has a new wife and children, but spends Saturday with her. Sure
that his new daughter is more talented than she, Eliza finds, on meeting her
stepsister, that Mandy is just like herself. This book was liked for its warm
father-daughter relationship.

The First Morning.   An African myth retold by Margery Bernstein and Janet Kob-
rin. Illustrated by Enid Warner Romanek. Scribner's. Unpaged (44 pp.).

Before there was any light in the world, Mouse volunteered to bring light to
earth. His friends Spider and Fly helped to outwit the selfish king in the
kingdom above the sky; and they returned to earth with a surprising way to

provide light. Attractive stylized drawings add dignity to the carefully simplified version of a charming African myth.

First Pink Light.　Eloise Greenfield. Illustrations by Moneta Barnett. Crowell. Unpaged (36 pp.).

Tyree wants to stay up and wait for his daddy' who has been away a whole month, but his mother objects. Finally they agree on a comfortable place he can curl up in and wait for that "first pink light" that appears before the sun rises. A warm look at a child's private world in a loving family.

Frog and Toad All Year.　Written and illustrated by Arnold Lobel. Harper & Row. 64 pp.

Six more tales about the friendship of wise and bumbling Frog and Toad. Illustrations in green and brown complement the good-natured humor in the stories.

The Littlest Leaguer.　Written and illustrated by Syd Hoff. Windmill. 48 pp. Paper ed., Scholastic Book Services.

Harold's legs are so short he can't move fast enough to catch a fly; he's so small no bat is light enough for him. He sits on the bench until the last game of the season when in a pinch he learns how to use his size to advantage. Humorous drawings and no more than seven lines on a page encourage the immature reader.

May I Visit?　Charlotte Zolotow. Illustrated by Erik Blegvad. Harper & Row. 32 pp. Paper ed., Xerox Education Publications.

A married woman visiting her childhood home evokes many questions from her younger sister. An especially popular book with children who have older siblings. Readers enjoy the delicate illustrations that match the theme of the story.

Mooch the Messy.　Marjorie Weinman Sharmat. Illustrated by Ben Shecter. Harper & Row. 64 pp.

Mooch, a rat who lives in a hole under a hill, hangs his clothes on doorknobs, lamps, pictures, and chairs. When his father comes to visit and calls the place messy, Mooch cleans it up, but when Father leaves, Mooch brings the socks, belts, sheets, and sweaters back out where he "can see them all at once." Such a messy room! It's obvious why the children giggled all through the book. Illustrations in brown and gold.

Some Swell Pup or Are You Sure You Want a Dog?　Story by Maurice Sendak and Matthew Margolis. Illustrated by Maurice Sendak. Farrar, Straus & Giroux. Unpaged (26 pp.).

This cautionary tale of two children and a rambunctious new pup presents the problems and frustrations associated with owning a puppy. A combination of humor, patience, and some sage advice produces a satisfactory solution. The cartoon format catches and holds young readers' attention.

The Trip and Other Sophie and Gussie Stories.　Marjorie Weinman Sharmat. Illustrated by Lillian Hoban. Macmillan. 64 pp.

Four short stories about two lady squirrels tell of the delights and problems of friendship. The noodle-head humor makes readers feel complacently superior.

Two Is Company.　Judy Delton. Illustrations by Giulio Maestro. Crown. 47 pp. Paper ed., Xerox Education Publications.

Bear learns to share even when he's the third member of the party and "the seats on the Ferris wheel only have room for two." The story is well sustained. "A good story," commented one second-grader. "I could read it."

What's Inside the Box?   Ethel and Leonard Kessler. Illustrated by Leonard Kessler. Dodd, Mead. 48 pp. Paper ed., Firefly.

This easy-to-read book, while remaining humorous and suspenseful, helps children to develop their conceptual thinking. Treatment of such concepts as near, behind, over, and inside are part of a sequence of events that lead to a surprise ending.

Witch, Goblin, and Sometimes Ghost: Six Read-Alone Stories.   Sue Alexander. Illustrated by Jeanette Winter. Pantheon. 61 pp. Paper ed., Xerox Education Publications. Short tales of childhood problems—a lonely walk, a windless day for kite-flying—faced by friends Witch, Goblin, and Ghost, popular characters no matter what guise they take. Children enjoyed seeing these usually magical creatures deal with real situations and liked the idea of friendship among them.

1978

Birth of a Foal.   Jane Miller. Photographs by the author. Lippincott. Unpaged (44 pp.). Paper ed., Scholastic Book Services.

Black-and-white photographs and straightforward text describe the birth and first days of a Welsh mountain pony. The easy-reading format includes large print and short sentences, but does not simplify vocabulary. Children were fascinated with the photographs and subject matter.

Bony.   Frances Zweifel. Illustrated by Whitney Darrow, Jr. Harper & Row. 64 pp.

Kim finds a motherless baby squirrel and raises it until it becomes a nuisance, even to him. Then he has to teach it to become an outdoors squirrel. A nice version of a story about a child's love for an animal that is an inappropriate house pet.

Fish Story.   Robert Tallon. Illustrated by the author. Holt, Rinehart & Winston. Unpaged (27 pp.) Paper ed., Scholastic Book Services.

Bored within the confines of his small pond, Little Fish accepts the invitation of Big Cat to be carried to the ocean and view the bright and beautiful world along the way. But Big Cat takes Little Fish to his kitchen instead. To save himself, Little Fish appeals to the appetite and greed of Big Cat with a fish story of his own. The brilliance of the watercolor illustrations helps make the book a delight.

The Great Thumbprint Drawing Book.   Ed Emberly. Illustrated by the author. Little, Brown. 37 pp.

Simple thumbprint drawings and instructions on how to make them are presented in a readable and understandable format. The cheery illustrations may encourage children to design their own original thumb creatures, which can then serve as story starters.

Harry and Shelburt.   Dorothy O. Van Woerkom. Illustrated by Erick Ingraham. Macmillan. 48 pp.

Shelburt the Tortoise, while sharing his dinner with his good friend Harry the Hare, tells him that once, because of a certain race, hares didn't like tortoises at all. The ensuing challenge provides an enjoyable new twist to this old fable. The detailed illustrations offer additional amusement and charm.

Little Otter Remembers.   Ann Tombert. Illustrated by John Wallner. Crown. 64 pp.
In the first story Little Otter tries to find a birthday present for his mother, in the second he finally remembers where he hid his prized pinecone, and in the third he plans a party for friends who cannot come. The three charming, quite different stories, and the colorful illustrations, provide good reading for children with skills at high second-grade level and above.

Mother Rabbit's Son Tom.   Dick Gackenbach. Illustrated by the author. Harper & Row. 32 pp. Paper ed., Scholastic Book Services.
Two stories: in "Hamburgers, Hamburgers" Tom eats so many hamburgers his mother and father worry that he will turn into one; in "Tom's Pet" Tom finally finds a pet his mother will let him keep. The stories are short and use repetition to advantage.

Mouse Soup.   Arnold Lobel. Illustrated by the author. Harper & Row. 64 pp. Paper ed., Scholastic Book Services.
A captive mouse tells four tales to keep himself out of the soup. The tales are funny and so is the book's tricky ending, which might serve as a commercial for reading (and remembering) stories. First-grade readers prefer "the story about the noisy crickets and the lady mouse who couldn't get to sleep."

Nate the Great and the Phony Clue.   Marjorie Weinman Sharmat. Illustrated by Marc Simont. Coward, McCann & Geoghegan. 48 pp.
Detectives in fiction are seldom modest, and Nate is no exception. His belief in his own "greatness" encourages readers to outguess him. They like Nate despite his bragging, and they like the author's easy style with its put-down of detective ego. They also like the way the exaggerated drawings tease the story.

Oops.   Mercer Mayer. Dial. Unpaged (30 pp.). Paper ed., Pied Piper.
Ms. Hippo goes on a trip to the city and ends up causing disaster for everyone she meets. As she innocently makes her way from china shop to museum, she leaves a trail of destruction behind her. The anticipation of the impending catastrophe is half the fun of this wordless book.

Penny-Wise, Fun-Foolish.   Judy Delton. Illustrated by Giulio Maestro. Crown. Unpaged (48 pp.).
Ostrich and Elephant are saving for a trip to America. Though Elephant is determined to enjoy the good things in life as well as save, Ostrich spends all her time saving. A trip to the carnival convinces Ostrich that maybe life should be lived every day. A pleasant book with a moral that children seem to enjoy.

The Surprise Party.   Annabelle Prager. Illustrated by Tomie de Paola. Pantheon. 44 pp.
Nicky doesn't have enough money to give himself a birthday party, so he talks Albert into planning a surprise party for him. But Nicky's continual suggestions for the "surprise party" almost ruin the plan. In the end the party is a real surprise for him. A funny, suspenseful book in easy reading format.

1979

Arthur's Prize Reader.   Lillian Hoban. Illustrated by the author. Harper. 64 pp. Paper ed., Harper & Row.
Arthur's little sister is the best reader in the first grade; to hear him tell it, he taught her all she knows (even the "hard words"). But we find out differently as

the story unfolds. A sensitive, comic story of sibling rivalry and its resolution, this book will parallel most children's experiences at home.

The Farmer in the Dell.   Diane Zuromskis. Illustrated by the author. Little, Brown. Unpaged (32 pp.).

Delft-blue stenciled endpapers of the dog, the cat, the mouse, and the cheese begin this charming book about how the farmer in the dell and his family might have looked. The title page shows seven children moving in a circle to the traditional rhyme, which sets the scene for the detailed illustrations found in circular frames.

Freight Train.   Donald Crews. Illustrated by the author. Greenwillow. Unpaged (24 pp.).

The simple words of this picture book suggest the action of the boldly colored illustrations. Each section of the train is identified and pictured before the whole freight train moves across the landscape. Words and pictures work together to create a scene representative of most children's experience with trains: the quick loud commotion of the locomotive; then . . . gone.

Grasshopper on the Road.   Arnold Lobel. Illustrated by the author. Harper. 64 pp. Paper ed., Harper & Row.

Grasshopper follows a road wherever it will lead. He meets a host of compulsive characters unable to change, unwilling to see value in a varied existence. Among them are a housefly attempting to sweep the world clean and a hilarious mosquito so stuck on rules that he can't see when Grasshopper is humoring him. Soft pinks and greens whisper aspects of Lobel's philosophy and blend beautifully with his gentle wit.

If the Dinosaurs Came Back.   Bernard Most. Illustrated by the author. Harcourt Brace Jovanovich. Unpaged (32 pp.).

"If the dinosaurs came back, they would scare away robbers" and . . . "dentists would have plenty of teeth to work on." Bold lines accentuate imaginative, humorous ideas. The dentist lies in the dinosaur's mouth to work, for example. A natural for student response: students formulated their own outcomes about what would happen if the dinosaurs returned. An overwhelming favorite in the early grades.

Is It Red? Is It Yellow? Is It Blue?   Tana Hoban. Illustrated with photographs by the author. Greenwillow. Unpaged (32 pp.) Paper ed., Random House.

In her first book of color photographs, Tana Hoban has created a unique offering for young children. Bold, simple pictures of childlike interests fairly compel little ones to squeal with delight. "Sunglasses!" "Jelly-bean shoes!" "Jack-o'-lantern!" Relationships (an opened umbrella opposite a collapsed one) and hidden information such as size, shape, and design were also noticed.

Jenny and the Tennis Nut.   Janet Schulman. Illustrated by Marylin Hafner. Greenwillow. 56 pp.

Jenny's Dad is a tennis nut. So is her Mom. But Jenny isn't. And this is a story of how she convinces her folks that tennis just isn't her racquet. Kids are sure to identify with Jenny's exasperation and pride at "teaching" her parents something for a change.

Lambs for Dinner.   Betsy Maestro. Illustrated by Giulio Maestro. Crown. 32 pp.

Mama Sheep warns her four little lambs that Mr. Wolf wants to "have them all for dinner!" Children are delighted with the surprise switch in this modern spoof of *The Wolf and the Seven Little Kids*—comparison is inevitable. The illustrations in soft blue, orange, and grey are as intriguing as the story. An overwhelming favorite with younger children.

Morris Has a Cold. Bernard Wiseman. Illustrated by the author. Dodd, Mead. Unpaged (48 pp.). Paper ed., Scholastic Book Services.

Morris the Moose has a *walking* (not *running*) nose. He refuses to have his *forehead* felt because he insists that he has just *one* head. He is fortunate to have Boris the Bear for a friend, for Boris forebears Morris' *faux pas* (to say nothing of hoofs). The jokes in the story, both verbal and visual, are right on target for beginning readers.

Oh, Were They Ever Happy! Peter Spier. Illustrated by the author. Doubleday. Unpaged (40 pp.).

The sitter doesn't show up, so the Noonan children help out by painting their home's exterior. The contrast of a pastoral suburban street with the splashy mess they make is uproarious. While giving nearly every indication of what's happening, Spier keeps the audience waiting until the last page for a good look, causing youngsters to squeal with delight and anticipation. The pacing works beautifully, and readers overlook the inconsistency—that children old enough to stay alone wouldn't paint windows yellow and throw every conceivable color onto their house.

Snake In, Snake Out. Linda Banchek. Illustrated by Elaine Arnold. Crowell. Unpaged (29 pp.).

It could happen to anyone's grandmother!? Unexpectedly finding herself the owner of a snake, this is the up-down-in-out-over-under-on-off (the only eight words used in the book) story of how a lovable little old lady and her pet finally become friends. Wonderful pictures and few words make this a good choice for a child's retelling.

Tony Dorsett. S. H. Buchard. Illustrated with photographs. Harcourt. 64 pp. Paper ed., Harcourt Brace Jovanovich.

Tony Dorsett's career is outlined from his early days as a high school defensive football player to his first season with the Dallas Cowboys. Emphasis is given to motivating factors in his background, and to his drive to be a star. The vocabulary is suitable for beginning independent readers.

UFO Kidnap! Nancy Robinson. Illustrated by Edward Franklin. Lothrop, Lee & Shepard. 63 pp.

Barney and Roy discover a mysterious object on their street that looks like a giant Frisbee. Their investigation of the UFO leads to their being whisked off to the Pink Planet. Children love reading about Roy's and Barney's adventures with alien beings and of their cleverness in planning their escape back to Earth.

1980

The Animals Who Changed Their Colors. Pascale Allamand. Illustrations by the author. Lothrop, Lee & Shepard. Unpaged (32 pp.).

A cute tale about some animals who decide they want to be as beautiful and colorful as parrots. The delightful pictures show the results: a red whale, blue crocodile, green polar bear, and orange tortoise.

Arthur's Eyes. Marc Brown. Illustrations by the author. Atlantic/Little, Brown. 32 pp.

The hero of this story, Arthur the Aardvark, has a problem shared by many children. He must wear glasses and is teased by his second-grade friends. Arthur discards his glasses only to discover that his troubles increase. An understanding principal helps Arthur to wear his glasses with pride.

The Bean Boy.   Joan Chase Bowden. Illustrations by Sal Murdocca. Macmillan. 62 pp.

In this cumulative folktale, an old man responds to the repeated requests of his wife and carves a little boy from a bean. The old woman thereupon carries the bean boy into the world in the hope of making them rich.

But No Elephants.   Jerry Smath. Illustrations by the author. Parents' Magazine. Unpaged (42 pp.).

Grandma Tildy takes in all sorts of pets who help her, but no elephants. One cold winter day she allows an elephant in and her troubles begin. The easy-to-read text allows children to join in with the title phrase, "But no elephants."

Cat at Bat.   John Stadler. Illustrations by the author. E. P. Dutton. 32 pp.

A delightful collection of animal doings, each accompanied by a humorous illustration. Short, easy sentences relate the improbable adventures of such unlikely creatures as nice mice on ice, a crocodile who runs a mile, and a sheep deep in sleep.

Chameleon Was a Spy.   Diane Redfield Massie. Illustrations by the author. Crowell. Unpaged (40 pp.). Paper ed., Scholastic Book Services.

Chameleon, a mischievous little lizard, decides to apply his unique disappearing ability to detective work. The successful completion of his first assignment earns him the undying gratitude of pickle lovers throughout the world.

Everyone Ready?   Franz Brandenberg. Illustrations by Aliki. Greenwillow. 55 pp.

Despite the traditional clothing and some stereotypic behavior, this story of a field mouse family's difficulties staying together on a trip has some contemporary touches. The pictures of family life are realistic and humorous.

Ig Lives in a Cave.   Carol Chapman. Illustrations by Bruce Degen. E. P. Dutton. 56 pp.

Five very short stories about a cave boy deal with concepts that are universal: sharing, jealousy of a new baby, making a birthday present for Mom, reacting to danger with fear, and tearful relief in finding safety. The earth-colored drawings enhance the story.

Lost in the Museum.   Miriam Cohen. Illustrations by Lillian Hoban. Greenwillow. Unpaged (32 pp.). Paper ed., Dell.

The problems of a group of first graders temporarily lost in a large museum are resolved when Jim courageously volunteers to go and find the teacher. Attractive illustrations depict some famous exhibits at what is obviously New York's Museum of Natural History.

Nini at Carnival.   Errol Lloyd. Illustrations by the author. Crowell. Unpaged (26 pp.).

This Jamaican variation of the Cinderella theme is boldly and brilliantly illustrated. Nini is distressed when she realizes that she does not have a costume for Carnival. An older girl disguised as a fairy godmother creates a costume and sends Nini off to the Carnival where she is crowned queen.

One Little Kitten.   Tana Hoban. Photographs by the author. Greenwillow. Unpaged (24 pp.).

Adorable photographs of an exploring kitten, plus an easy, rhyming word pattern equal an irresistible book for the primary set. Hoban captures the delight of a mischievous kitten as it travels from one discovery to the next.

Ottie and the Star. Laura Jean Allen. Illustrations by the author. Harper & Row. 32 pp.

Headstrong Ottie the otter dives into the sea to find a star, only to capture a starfish. Simple vocabulary offset by watercolor picture cues facilitates mastering the words of this story.

Samuel's Tree House. Bethany Tudor. Illustrations by the author. Philomel. Unpaged (28 pp.).

It's even more fun to do things together than by oneself, says Samuel. Charming, pastel-colored drawings of animals illustrate this easy-to-hold, 6-inch-square book.

Scarlet Monster Lives Here. Majorie Weinman Sharmat. Illustrations by Dennis Kendrick. Harper & Row. 64 pp. Paper ed., Random House.

The new monster in the neighborhood fears rejection by the other monsters. The story conveys two important messages: things are not always what they seem and never give up hope.

Ugbu. Ora Ayal. Illustrations by the author. Trans. from Hebrew by Naomi Löw Nakao. Harper & Row. Unpaged (32 pp.).

Ugbu, a dog whom we never see, is an imaginary playmate created by little Maya. Readers are encouraged to consider that Ugbu may one day be transformed into whatever their own imaginations desire.

Where Does the Teacher Live? Paula Kurzband Feder. Illustrations by Lillian Hoban. E. P. Dutton. 48 pp.

Children have always wondered where their teachers go after school. In this simple story three children try to solve the mystery. They discover the answer and are even rewarded for their curiosity.

Younger Readers (7 to 10 Years)
1975

All Upon a Sidewalk. Jean Craighead George. Illustrations by Don Bolognese. E. P. Dutton. Unpaged (48 pp.).

A fascinating account of a yellow ant's search for an ant-loving beetle, a journey that brought her into danger from birds, spiders and enemy rats. The fine illustrations add much information about the ecology of a small, but busy, area of city sidewalk.

Animals and Their Ears. Olive L. Earle with Michael Kantor. Illustrations by the author. Morrow. 64 pp.

An informational book about the forms and functions of animal ears. Explanations of some unique hearing devices will appeal to children's curiosity. Good for use with a science unit.

Bus Station Mystery. Gertrude Chandler Warner. Illustrations by David Cunningham. Whitman. 125 pp.

The Alden children, while waiting out a storm in a bus station, discover many mysterious happenings involving a paint factory and a polluted river. Very easy reading, but will hold reader's interest.

The Case of the Silver Skull.   Scott Corbett. Illustrations by Paul Frame. Atlantic/Little, Brown. 123 pp.
Snooping proves to be dangerous work, and Roger vows to devote himself to his egg business until some hot leads convince him that his heart is in being a detective.

Cross Your Fingers, Spit in Your Hat: Superstitions and Other Beliefs.   Collected by Alvin Schwartz. Illustrations by Glen Rounds. J. B. Lippincott. 159 pp. Notes, sources, and bibliography.
Older children enjoy reading parts of this book aloud to each other. It is full of short superstitions and need not be read cover to cover. Reading some aloud gets children interested. This book could supplement a study of American subcultures or early American history.

Danny Dunn, Invisible Boy.   Jay Williams and Ray Abrashkin. Illustrations by Paul Sagsoorian. McGraw-Hill. 159 pp.
Science and adventure are combined in the Danny Dunn series, and the books are always popular with children. The book lends itself to studying science through science fiction.

The Ears of Louis.   Constance Greene. Illustrations by Nola Langner. Viking. 89 pp.
Until the big boys called him "Ears" when they invited him to play football, Louis's ears had meant only teasing and trouble. Readers appreciate and identify with the change that brought Louis's new status in the eyes of classmates.

Encyclopedia Brown Lends a Hand.   Donald J. Sobol. Illustrations by Leonard Shortall. Elsevier-Nelson. 95 pp.
One of a series of eleven books. It is readable and appealing to reluctant or below-grade readers. Children read ten short mysteries, devise their own solutions, then find Encyclopedia Brown's.

Free to Be . . . You and Me.   Marlo Thomas. McGraw-Hill. 138 pp.
Suited for pupil or teacher use from grade two up. It is factual and honest—teaches self-pride and beauty of individuality. Used for creative writing, oral discussion and music. Fun for just browsing.

Front Court Hex.   Matt Christopher. Illustrations by Byron Goto. Little, Brown. 136 pp.
Can a warlock be hexing Jerry's arm so he cannot throw the basketball successfully? Another easy-to-read Christopher sports story.

The Ghost on Saturday Night.   Sid Fleischman. Illustrations by Eric Von Schmidt. Atlantic/Little, Brown. 63 pp.
All easy-to-read tall tales to tickle the funny bone and chill the spine as the younger protagonist helps to solve a crime. The humor and suspense are enhanced by Eric Von Schmidt's pictures.

The Great Custard Pie Panic.   Scott Corbett. Illustrations by Joe Mathieu. Atlantic/Little, Brown. 48 pp.
An easy-to-read funny book in which Nick and his dog, Bert, outwit the wicked magician, Dr. Merlin, in a fake bakery. The slapstick humor is well illustrated by Mathieu and adds to the humor of the story.

Henry Aaron: Sports Hero.   Marshall and Sue Burchard. Illustrated with black-and-white photographs. G. P. Putnam's. 96 pp.
This biography of a modern sports hero covers Aaron's life through the record-breaking home run. The drama of the life of a great man shines through every phrase.

Hut School and the Wartime Homefront Heroes.   Robert Burch. Illustrations by Ronald Himler. Viking. 138 pp.
This World War II story interestingly portrays the difficulties of life during a war. The cooperative attitude of the children in helping pick cotton, accepting a makeshift school and being supportive when a child's brother is killed are strong points of the book.

James Weldon Johnson.   Ophelia Settle Egypt. Illustrations by Moneta Barnett. Crowell. 48 pp.
This moving book instills a strong feeling of the pride and dignity of black people as personified in this remarkable, gentle man. High interest and easy readability for primary-grade children. Promotes further discussion and stimulates creative writing. Appealing illustrations.

Jinx Glove.   Matt Christopher. Illustrations by Norm Chartier. Little, Brown. 48 pp.
Chip willingly exchanges his dad's old baseball glove for a new one until he discovers it's "jinxed." Text relates Chip's maturing and encourages thoughtfulness for the feelings of others.

Langston Hughes, American Poet.   Alice Walker, Illustrations by Don Miller. Crowell. 40 pp.
Third and fourth graders find it easy to read and comprehend. Factual and honest. Good reference for social studies. Permits black children to relate and other children to understand minority problems.

Maria's House.   Jean Merrill. Illustrations by Frances Gruse Scott. Atheneum. 59 pp.
Fourth graders found this book excellent and identified with Maria. It enhances the value of truthfulness. Used for literature and as impetus to creative art and writing.

Me and the Terrible Two.   Ellen Conford. Illustrations by Charles Carroll. Little, Brown, 121 pp.
A funny, fast-reading story about Dorrie, sad because her best friend, Marlene, has just moved away to Australia. Into Marlene's old house moves a family with two boys, identical twins who delight in finding ways of annoying Dorrie.

Mirror of Danger.   Pamela Sykes. Nelson. 175 pp.
Lucy, left alone after the death of her aunt, moves into the old house of distant relatives. They have children her age, but the girl who intrigues and frightens Lucy is the old-fashioned one who appears mysteriously in the mirror in the attic and who tries to get Lucy to leave the real world forever.

Moose, Goose and Little Nobody.   Story and illustrations by Ellen Raskin. Parents' Magazine. 32 pp.
A nonsense adventure of a mouse looking for his mother and his house. Children in first grade chose to read this one for themselves. It has a format and vocabulary different from easy readers. Bold, clear colors. Children enjoyed it for the fun in the characters and their actions and they liked hearing it read aloud.

More Fables of Aesop.   Retold and illustrated by Jack Kent. Parents' Magazine. 56 pp.
The pupils love to listen to these stories or read independently. Promotes open discussion and gives impetus to creative writing. Can be used in social studies classes and for browsing.

Muhammad Ali.   Beth Wilson, Illustrations by Floyd Sowell. G. P. Putnam's. 64 pp.
Good for upper primary. Format simple and easy on the eyes. Promotes un-

derstanding among the races. Useful for social studies and language arts or as a supplemental reader.

My Animals.   William Armstrong. Illustrations by Mirko Hanak. Doubleday. 32 pp.
Sensitive prose about the small animals that live in Green Meadow, paired with beautiful watercolor illustrations. Text encourages reverence for wildlife. Could be used in study of ecosystems. Needs to be read aloud to appreciate beauty of the language.

No Arm in Left Field.   Matt Christopher. Illustrations by Byron Goto. Little, Brown. 135 pp.
Terry, a new member of a baseball team, hits and catches well but has difficulty making long throws. Terry's main concern, however, is about Tony, a team member who resents him because he is black.

The Pack Rat's Day and Other Poems.   Jack Prelutsky. Illustrations by Margaret Bloy Graham. Macmillan. 31 pp.
Humorous poetry that shows life from the animal's point of view. The lilting language draws the reader through the pages and into the fun. A stimulus for creative writing and study of different points of view.

The Return of the Great Brain.   John D. Fitzgerald. Illustrations by Mercer Mayer. Dial. 157 pp.
The Great Brain's adventures in this story involve him in a train robbery, a murder, an impressive magic show and, above all, a charge that he must stop swindling his friends. Great Brain's fans will enjoy it.

Roberto Clemente.   Kenneth Rudeen. Illustrations by Frank Mullins. Crowell. 40 pp.
A biography of the selfless Clemente whose baseball fame was surpassed only by his service to humankind. The easy-reading level expands the age range that can enjoy the story.

Save the Earth: An Ecology Handbook for Kids.   Betty Miles. Illustrations by Clarie A. Nivola. Knopf. 95 pp.
This book would be welcome material for a study of ecology, developing the idea of the importance of caring for our land. The suggested projects reinforce concepts developed in the text about land, air, and water.

Seeing Things: A Book of Poems.   Robert Froman. Lettering by Ray Barber. Crowell. 59 pp.
Concrete poetry written so that graphic form becomes a part of the message. It will motivate children to experiment with writing and to visualize words in new ways.

They Put on Masks.   Byrd Baylor. Illustrations by Jerry Ingram. Scribner's 48 pp.
A fine blend of words and illustrations describing Indians' uses of masks in ceremonial messages to their gods. Children are challenged to plan messages and masks they would like to produce. An excellent resource for anthropology and general social studies.

Thor Heyerdahl and the Reed Boat Ra.   Barbara Beasley Murphy and Norman Baker. Illustrated with photographs. J. B. Lippincott. 64 pp. Foreword by Thor Heyerdahl.
An account of the voyage of Ra II, enhanced by clear and interesting photographs. Resource for social studies and anthropology.

What Can She Be? An Architect.   Gloria and Esther Goldreich. Photographs by Robert Ipcar. Lothrop, Lee & Shepard. 46 pp.
An excellent introduction to the job experience of an architect. A straightfor-

ward book. Shows a female as a functioning, creative individual in a traditionally male role.

Why Noah Chose the Dove.   Isaac Bashevis Singer. Illustrations by Eric Carle. Farrar, Straus & Giroux. 28 pp.

Vivid illustrations and sparse text reveal a powerful theme about a gentle voice being heard above the clamor. Good for reading aloud and helping children read beyond the literal level.

The Wish at the Top.   Clyde Robert Bulla. Illustrations by Chris Conover. Crowell. 32 pp.

Jan risked his life on a high church steeple to make a wish that would make his mother happy. His rescue by the outlaw, Laszlo, and the outcome of that brave act are beautifully told in folktale style.

1976

Abracadabra!   Written and illustrated by Barbara Seuling. Messner. 96 pp.

These magic tricks may not all be new and original, but children comment that they find the directions complete and easy to follow. A book that makes reading for information fun and useful.

Becky and the Bear.   Dorothy van Woerkom. Illustrations by Margot Tomes. G. P. Putnam's. 48 pp.

In this true story of Colonial Maine, Becky ingeniously captures a bear which is much needed for meat, oil and a new rug. With many colorful illustrations and few words on each page, this book helps children understand colonial life.

The Blue Lobster.   Carol Carrick. Illustrations by Donald Carrick. Dial. Unpaged (26 pp.).

The drawing on the cover looks like a giant moon monster but don't let that stop you from reading this life-cycle story. Children like it for listening and for close-up study of the natural-looking watercolor drawings. Fine example of a book to prove nonfiction is worth studying as literature.

A Calf is Born.   Joanna Cole. Photographs by Jerome Wexler. Morrow. Unpaged (48 pp.).

A book kids pick up again and again because of the photographs of real live animals and the birth of a calf. This could be used as supplemental material for a unit in career education and life on a farm. It is also good to read before visiting a dairy farm.

Danny, the Champion of the World.   Roald Dahl. Illustrations by Jill Bennett. Knopf. 196 pp.

A hilarious "Robin Hood" tale of an English father and son outwitting a rich man by poaching his pheasants before the annual hunt. Action, good pacing and characterization make this story of filial devotion a winning read-aloud. Possible follow-up discussion on legalities of and public provision for hunting.

Do You Love Me?   Story and illustrations by Dick Gackenbach. Seabury. Unpaged (48 pp.).

A well-written and thoughtful story of a small boy, who, in accidentally killing a hummingbird, realizes finally that all wild things cannot be pets. Good characterization, especially of an understanding older sister, nice illustrations, and a generally low-keyed tone make this an excellent book about family relationships, and for discussions and written compositions about death, pets, and families.

Escape King. John Ernst. Illustrations by Ray Abel. Prentice-Hall. Unpaged (28 pp.).

The great Houdini inspires immediate interest. This is a factual account of his life and spectacular tricks, illustrated with black-and-white drawings and photos. Particularly stimulating for below-grade-level readers.

Football Players Do Amazing Things. Mel Cebulash. Illustrated with photographs. Random House. 72 pp.

This book proves excellent for sparking interest in further reading among below-average middle-grade readers. Each of eleven short selections highlights a special triumph, a mistake, or a humorous happening. Readers want to collect, retell, and write about other sports episodes for their own "amazing" class book.

The Great Brain Does It Again. John D. Fitzgerald. Illustrations by Mercer Mayer. Dial. 127 pp.

The Great Brain shows an occasional bit of goodwill in this latest book but, as usual, most of his schemes are based on greed for money. Some readers show scorn for his selfish behavior as he hardheartedly refuses to consider the feelings of others. Most, however, are captivated by the humorous incidents such as wearing a devil suit to scare a fat boy into losing weight.

Grizzly Bear. Berniece Freschet. Illustrations by Donald Carrick. Scribner's. Unpaged (40 pp.).

The story line of this informational book takes a mother grizzly and her twin cubs through a season of training for survival that leads to independence. Action-filled watercolor illustrations enhance the already engrossing text which reads aloud effectively as well as giving accurate facts. No indexing.

Hamburgers—and Ice Cream for Dessert. Eleanor Clymer. Illustrations by Roy Doty. E. P. Dutton. 48 pp.

The perfect book to share with kids who won't try new foods, this story shows the folly of rigidity. Text encourages discussion and can be used in connection with study of food groups and lunchroom eating habits.

Handmade Secret Hiding Places. Written and illustrated by Nonny Hogrogian. Overlook Press. Unpaged (40 pp.).

Demonstrates in easy-to-follow directions many different types of secret hiding places for both the city and country child that are made from materials easily available in homes or in nature. This book charmed young readers who read or heard it read, and then pored over the illustrations. Some classes read one or more similar books (for example, *A Very Special House, A Little House of Your Own, The Secret Garden*). Some classes composed booklets about their own "secret hiding places."

The House on Pendleton Block. Ann Waldron. Illustrations by Sonia O. Lisker. Hastings House. 151 pp.

Both boys and girls chose this mystery as a favorite for pleasure reading. They identified with Chrissie, lonely and friendless when her family moved. A realistic account of a young girl's growing acceptance of life's common problems.

Let's Make a Deal. Story and illustrations by Linda Glovach. Prentice-Hall. 48 pp.

Tom and Dewey share a secret tree house and a puppy named Lucy until Tom has to move and Lucy's home must be decided upon. Love and friendship do win in this story of two boys and their dog.

The Lion in the Box. Story and illustrations by Marguerite de Angeli. Doubleday. 64 pp.

A story of a widowed mother and her five children for whom a bleak Christmas is transformed into a glorious one. The treasures are overshadowed by the love that the members of the family display toward one another. A story in the de Angeli tradition that brought forth quiet meditative reactions from sensitive children.

Maggie Marmelstein for President. Marjorie Weinman Sharmat. Illustrated by Ben Shecter. Harper & Row. 128 pp.

Maggie's adventures and misadventures in her bid for class presidency make humorous and exciting reading, and promote class discussions of the relationships between friendship and competition. Following reading of the story, social studies classes have enjoyed staging mock elections, making speeches or writing short articles about a current political issue or candidates.

The Magic Cooking Pot. Story and illustrations by Faith M. Towle. Houghton Mifflin. 40 pp.

Ancient folktale from India in which a good man is granted an endless supply of rice but must rescue a magic pot from a treacherous innkeeper. Good for reading aloud, comparison with other versions, discussion of hunger and food production in study of India. Traditional Indian batik illustrations lead to related art lesson.

Make a Circle Keep Us In: Poems for a Good Day. Arnold Adoff. Illustrations by Ronald Himler. Delacorte. 26 pp.

A classroom favorite. A group of poems about getting up, growing up, living, rain and thunder. The arrangement of the words on the printed page, as well as the excellent choice of words by the author, present a new and interesting adventure in reading. Children prefer handling this book themselves. Older children like the rhythm of the words. Leads to individual creative writing experiences.

Mr. Mysterious's Secrets of Magic. Sid Fleischman. Illustrations by Eric von Schmidt. Atlantic/Little, Brown. 81 pp.

What a great positive self-image a child gets by reading this book and putting on his own magic show. Secrets of magic are revealed in such simple language and drawings that even the most reluctant reader wants the book.

Movie Monsters. Thomas Aylesworth. Illustrated with photographs. J. B. Lippincott. 80 pp.

The movie book for children who love monsters is now available. All a child needs to know about King Kong, Godzila, Frankenstein and Bride, the Wolf Man, the Mummy, the Fly, Dracula, Mr. Hyde, the Invisible Man, and Dr. Moreau's creatures. The photographs and unusual historical and human interest touches excite and educate the movie monster buff.

My Daddy Is a Cool Dude. Karama Fufuka. Illustrations by Mahiri Fufuka. Dial. Unpaged (40 pp.).

A book of poetry that depicts black people in non–stereotypical roles, the text is recorded through the eyes of a black child. The topics of the twenty-seven poems show the reader that children have universal feelings and needs. Delicate charcoal drawings pair perfectly with the spirit of the text.

Near the Window Tree: Poems and Notes.   Written and illustrated by Karla Kuskin.
Harper & Row. 64 pp.
Children are interested in the format of this book as well as in the poems. The
ideas that grow into a poem are presented on one page with the poem itself on
the facing page. A fine book to introduce ideas or situations that inspire a poet
to create a poem and to call attention to interesting use of words.

New Life: New Room.   June Jordan. Illustrations by Ray Cruz. Crowell. 53 pp.
With a new baby coming, 6-year-old Linda must move in with her two brothers,
but they don't want her and she doesn't want to share a room with them. The
planning finally becomes a game with the children painting old furniture,
discarding old toys and creating a room that they all enjoy. This warm family
story encourages creativity and provides new ideas about how to cope.

Nonna.   Jennifer Bartoli. Illustrations by Joan E. Drescher. Harvey House. 48 pp.
Because children relate to the death of Grandma, the text provides opportunities for students to express their emotions. Sensitive treatment of a difficult
topic brings introspective thinking and lively discussions when this book is read
aloud. One first-grader observed, "It tells how you feel when somebody dies."

Old Mother Witch.   Carol Carrick. Illustrations by Donald Carrick. Seabury. 32 pp.
Unusual Halloween story of children saving an old woman's life instead of
playing a trick on her. In return they are rewarded by Old Mother Witch who
really is not a witch at all. Good story for any time of year.

The Old Woman and the Red Pumpkin.   Besty Bang. Illustrations by Molly Garrett
Bang. Macmillan. 32 pp.
Rhythmic folktale in which skinny old woman gets fat at granddaughter's, then
outwits hungry animals on the way home by rolling inside a pumpkin. Comical
Indian folk art illustrations and Bengali inscriptions for animal names (with
glossary) add spice to this satisfying read-aloud about cleverness. Useful with
unit on India.

Owl at Home.   Story and illustrations by Arnold Lobel. Harper & Row. 64 pp.
Five easy-to-read stories are enlivened by gently humorous prose and warm
illustrations. Young readers use the book as a model for creating their own
stories of cozy homes and peaceful fantasies.

The Princess and Froggie.   Harve and Kaethe Zemach. Illustrations by Margot
Zemach. Farrar, Straus & Giroux. 46 pp.
Three child-like tales about a princess and her very obliging froggie. The
natural child language and the simple plots are enriched by the gentle humor
in the illustrations. This book encourages the beginning reader, for the story is
worth the effort of reading.

Ramona the Brave.   Beverly Cleary. Illustrations by Alan Tiegreen. Morrow.
192 pp.
Lively Ramona continues to captivate her fans as she enters first grade. Her
antics infuriate her teachers, annoy her big sister, and perplex her parents.
Ramona does not understand why others won't see her the way she really is.
The new Ramona book is welcomed and loved by children and teachers.

Sea Star.   Written and illustrated by Robert M. McClung. Morrow. 48 pp.
An informational book about seashells that starts with the starfish. Accurate
information for identification of the shells is presented with clear, soft illustrations. Useful for science, trips to the shore, and for labeling and categorizing
treasures brought back from the sea.

Small in the Saddle.   Story and illustrations by Mark Allan Stamaty. Windmill/E. P. Dutton. Unpaged (32 pp.).

A highly appealing plot with a child hero and humorous, detailed black-and-white illustrations cause children to pore over this book repeatedly. One child summarized, "Everything is funny about this book!" Most effectively used individually or in small groups because of details in the pictures.

Sports Hero: O. J. Simpson.   Marshall Burchard. Illustrated with photographs. G. P. Putnam's. 96 pp.

This biography is written for first through third graders. Well written and well documented. Excellent for use in social studies class. Easy introduction to discussions on ethnic groups, attitudes, interdependence. A clean-cut story in good taste for children to enjoy and use as a model for hero stories of their own.

Strega Nona.   Story and illustrations by Tomie de Paola. Prentice-Hall. 32 pp.

Children laugh at Big Anthony's predicament because he is proud of turning on Strega Nona's pasta-making pot but can't remember how to stop it. As pasta engulfs the town, they think of ways to make use of it. In the end, most children enjoy Big Anthony's punishment, but they also sympathize with his ordeal of having to eat more than he can comfortably hold.

The Terrible Thing That Happened at Our House.   Marge Blaine. Illustrations by John C. Wallner. Parents' Magazine. 40 pp.

When Mother took an outside job, everything seemed to change at home! A good read-aloud story that leads to discussion of the real meaning of family love and cooperation. Some classes made picture caption books about "Mothers at Work."

Top Secret: Alligators!   Story and illustrations by Harold Goodwin. Bradbury. 95 pp.

Kids who have mysteriously lost a flushable pet will delight in this story where alligators live in a big city sewer and talk. Relates to scientific study of hatching and normal habitat of alligators with some ecology and humanism thrown in.

1977

Annie's Rainbow.   Written and illustrated by Ron Brooks. Collins + World. Unpaged (28 pp.).

Soft, delicate pictures enhance a simple story of a young girl's desire for a rainbow. This quiet mood story may inspire creative art or poetry writing.

Arthur's Nose.   Written and illustrated by Marc Brown. Atlantic/Little, Brown. 31 pp.

Arthur the Aardvark has the common problem of being dissatisfied with his looks. Marc Brown's text and amusing illustrations tell of Arthur's attempts to change his features and the way his friends help him learn to be happy with himself.

The Bear and the Fly.   Paula Winter. Crown. Unpaged (32 pp.).

An outrageously funny variation on Goldilocks. A fly is the intruder at the three bears' dinner and Father's pursuit of it leaves everyone, including the dog, unconscious and the house a wreck. The fly sails away untouched. A textless book for which children loved to create their own words. Returned too often.

Bear by Himself.   Written and illustrated by Geoffrey Hayes. Harper & Row. 32 pp.
   Bear, dressed in striped pants and turtleneck, likes to be alone at times, wander
   off by himself, and enjoy his home. Children responded to the sensitive, quiet
   mood, and agreed that they liked some time to themselves, just as Bear did.

Bearymore.   Written and illustrated by Don Freeman. Viking. Unpaged (36 pp.).
   Paper ed., Puffin.
   Bearymore, the amazing circus bear, must create a new act as well as hibernate
   before the next circus season. This is a great problem-solving exercise for
   young listeners. Get children to help Bearymore solve his problem so he can get
   to sleep before his alarm clock awakes him on April 1.

Cranberry Christmas.   Wende and Harry Devlin. Illustrated by Harry Devlin. Parents' Magazine. Unpaged (29 pp.).
   Mr. Whiskers was in deep gloom when, with Christmas approaching, there
   were no skaters on his pond. His new neighbor, Cyrus Grape, claimed ownership of the pond and chased the skaters away. This is an unusual Christmas
   story that can be enjoyed as a read-aloud book. Children liked the colorful
   illustrations and the contrast in personalities of the two main characters.

Crystal Is the New Girl.   Shirley Gordon. Illustrations by Edward Frascino. Harper &
   Row. 32 pp.
   Susan is determined not to like the new girl, Crystal, but she can't help it.
   Crystal *is* funny, and she soon wins the friendship of Susan and her readers.
   The author has the gift of being specific about the activities of childhood
   friendship.

Deep in the Forest.   Brinton Turkle. E. P. Dutton. Unpaged (32 pp.).
   A wordless picture book, *Deep in the Forest* tells the familiar Goldilocks story in
   an unusual way. Children readily accept the role reversals and identify with the
   characters. Turkle's illustrations fit the mood of the story.

The Dog Who Insisted He Wasn't.   Marilyn Singer. Illustrated by Kelly Oechsli. E. P.
   Dutton. 32 pp.
   Konrad runs away from a good "dog's life" and finds a family who accepts him
   as a person; he sits at the table to eat, sleeps in a bed, and goes to school. When
   the situation gets out of hand, Konrad "pretends to be a dog" and enjoys his
   new "dog's life" immensely. Black-and-white-illustrations round out the text,
   which children found hilarious.

Don't Forget the Bacon!   Written and illustrated by Pat Hutchins. Greenwillow. Unpaged (32 pp.).
   Surely anyone could remember four items on a grocery list! A play on words,
   however, leads the shopper into interesting predicaments. Children gleefully
   follow the strange replacements that result. A great book for developing visual
   literacy and wordplay.

The Easter Egg Artists.   Written and illustrated by Adrienne Adams. Scribner's.
   32 pp.
   The Abbotts, rabbits who design Easter eggs, are worried that son Orson will
   not follow the family trade. On a winter vacation Orson and the family paint a
   car, a house, an airplane, a bridge, and Orson becomes a committed Easter Egg
   Artist. Children rated this charming story with its lovely illustrations one of the
   most beautiful picture books of the year.

Eric Carle's Storybook: Seven Tales by the Brothers Grimm.   Retold by Eric Carle. Illustrated by the author. Watts. 94 pp.

Eric Carle chose seven of the tales by the Grimm brothers to retell in versions based on research from the original and from childhood memories. His brilliant illustrations give an added dimension to the characterizations and humorous tone of the text.

The Girl on the Yellow Giraffe.   Written and illustrated by Ronald Himler. Harper & Row. 32 pp.

The giraffe is a toy; the stone castle is a slum building; the monsters and dragons are the machines digging foundations in the crowded city. Few books combine text and pictures so movingly to reveal a child's point of view.

Hamilton.   Robert Newton Peck. Illustrated by Laura Lydecker. Little, Brown. 32 pp.

Hamilton, a greedy piglet, becomes a greedy pig, the butt of farmyard jokes. The night the wolf appears Hamilton is dreaming of food. The wolf's tail finds its way into Hamilton's mouth and dream. The scared wolf flees for his life. Hamilton is a hero! Lighthearted verses and color illustrations tickled young funnybones.

Hiccup.   Written and illustrated by Mercer Mayer. Dial. Unpaged (29 pp.).

An *almost* wordless book in which a male and female hippopotamus set off on an outing in a rowboat. Their tranquil trip is interrupted by the female's unexpected case of hiccups. Unfortunately, the cures attempted by her companion are worse than the problem. Only two words appear in the text—hiccup and boo. This book was enjoyed by both readers and nonreaders and was useful as a starter for creative writing and storytelling.

I Sure Am Glad to See You Blackboard Bear.   Written and illustrated by Martha Alexander. Dial. 32 pp.

Children who have been teased by others will wish they had a friend like Blackboard Bear. Anthony gains the confidence to face Gloria and Stewart when his fantasy friend joins him. The simple text is complemented by Martha Alexander's charming illustrations.

It's Not Fair! Robyn Supraner. Illustrated by Randall Enos. Warne. 32 pp.

Children identify with the problems of being an older sister. Sibling rivalry is an almost universal experience, and many children appreciated the difficulties enumerated here.

The King's Cat Is Coming.   Written and illustrated by Stan Mack. Pantheon. 28 pp.

Appealing illustrations delight younger readers as they try to predict what the king's cat is like. A further source of enjoyment for the more mature student lies in discovering the pattern of alphabetical characteristics attributed to the cat by the townspeople.

Kittens for Nothing.   Robert Kraus. Illustrations by Diane Paterson. Windmill. Unpaged (27 pp.).

A pet cat gives birth to nine kittens in a family with a father allergic to cats. The problem in trying to find homes for nine kittens is gently but humorously presented both in the text and the excellent black-and-white illustrations. The story focuses on the problem from the child's point of view. Indeed, the children produce the solution which is extremely satisfying to all concerned (including young readers or listeners).

Little Love Story.   Fernando Krahn. J. B. Lippincott. 24 pp.

A wordless tale of a Valentine's Day gift—a heart-shaped balloon—a little boy gives a little girl. The expressive illustrations, with only a touch of red, captured

children's attention; children were also much amused at the blowing up of
the balloon. Useful for encouraging conversation and storytelling among
younger students.

The Magic Porridge Pot. Written and illustrated by Paul Galdone. Seabury. Unpaged (30 pp.).

A magic pot provides porridge for a hungry girl and her mother until one day
the mother attempts to make the pot boil without knowing the magic words to
make the pot stop. The pot bubbles over and covers the entire village. This
traditional tale is great for a storytelling session as well as an incentive for
discovering variations from other countries (for example, Japan—*The Magic
Mortar*).

Max. Written and illustrated by Rachel Isadora. Macmillan. Unpaged (32 pp.).

Max discovers that ballet class is a great warm-up for his Saturday baseball
games. Bouyant illustrations captivate children and make this a favorite book to
be read and reread alone. Simple text makes it possible to be read by young
children.

Monster Mary Mischief Maker. Written and illustrated by Kazuko Taniguchi.
McGraw-Hill. Unpaged (37 pp.).

This book about monsters and mischief is bound to be popular with younger
readers. The simple story carries an important message about kindness and
friendship, demonstrating that one can change from a mischief maker to a
"lovingheart."

Mr. and Mrs. Pig's Evening Out. Written and illustrated by Mary Rayner.
Atheneum. Unpaged (32 pp.).

When Mr. and Mrs. Pig decide on an evening out, the agency sends them a
babysitter for their ten piglets. The babysitter is a wolf, and the ensuing evening is adventurous and humorous. This was an overwhelming favorite; the
children enjoyed both text and illustrations.

Mr. Gumpy's Motor Car. Written and illustrated by John Burningham. Crowell.
Unpaged (30 pp.). Paper ed., Puffin.

Mr. Gumpy is off on another unpredictable outing. Children and animals pile
in his old red touring car, but trouble lies ahead. The car gets stuck in the mud
and Mr. Gumpy needs help. The old "not me" response comes from his passen-
gers. However, in the end all help and the trip is a success. Children enjoy and
appreciate the outstanding full-color illustrations that accompany the story as
they learn that they can glean satisfaction from doing something that has to be
done.

Old Mother Hubbard and Her Dog. Sarah C. Martin. Illustrated by Ib Sprang Olsen.
Coward, McCann & Geoghegan. 32 pp.

A new English translation of the Swedish version of the old English rhyme adds
droll humor and zest to the familiar chant. The illustrations, bold literal interpretations of each line, give double pleasure to the humor.

One Dragon to Another. Written and illustrated by Ned Delaney. Houghton Mifflin.
Unpaged (48 pp.).

A dragon and a caterpillar/butterfly find much in common and, learning to
reconcile their differences, inspire a beautiful friendship. The illustrations are
delightful and children pore over the book with pleasure.

Paddy Pork's Holiday. John S. Goodall. Atheneum/McElderry. 59 pp.

Paddy Pork's wordless walking tour turns into a riotous romp as he wrestles with a storm, a railroad train, and a piano when he's mistaken for the real performer, Herr Grunt. Giggles galore greeted every page of this textless story, which was popular with both readers and nonreaders.

Poor Goose: A French Folktale.   Retold and illustrated by Anne Rockwell. Crowell. Unpaged (34 pp.).

A warm, charming and handsomely illustrated retelling of an old Gallic cumulative tale. Poor Goose has a headache and decides to cure it by seeking a cup of peppermint tea at the castle. She is joined along the way by three curious animals. Frightened by the cry of a wolf, they seek shelter in a humble hut and find a surprise inside. Full-color drawings displayed against old provincial textile patterns. An excellent choice for reading aloud and initiating discussion.

Rotten Ralph.   Jack Gantos. Illustrated by Nicole Rubel. Houghton Mifflin. 48 pp.

Though Ralph and his mischievous behavior will amuse young readers, they will think he deserved the treatment he gets from the circus people. All is well in the end when Ralph vows never to be rotten again.

Six Little Ducks.   Chris Conover. Crowell. 27 pp.

Children examined the illustrations, full of sly, inventive detail, with great attention, and responded to the rhythm and humor of the old song. Fun for classroom and music room.

Spots Are Special.   Kathryn Osebald Galbraith. Illustrated by Diane Dawson. Atheneum/McElderry. Unpaged (27 pp.).

After reading *Spots Are Special*, children with chicken pox will want to try Galbraith's game. Eric realized adversity can be an occasion for fun as he tries to join in Sandy's games, but can't because "You don't have any spots. Only people with real spots can play."

The Sweet Touch.   Written and illustrated by Lorna Balian. Abingdon. Unpaged (37 pp.).

Every candy-loving child will be enchanted with the pleasures and problems Peggy faces when, rubbing her shiny, genuine plastic gold ring, she becomes the mistress of an inept genie and requests that everything she touches turn into something sweet. It takes the genie's mother to save Peggy from the sticky problems she creates.

The Terrible Troll-Bird.   Written and illustrated by Ingri and Edgar Parin d'Aulaire. Doubleday. 45 pp.

Can a bird fly away with a horse? Yes, if it's the terrible troll-bird. With fine lithographic art, the author-artists show what to do about the situation. The scary story will delight young readers and listeners.

Three Wishes.   Lucille Clifton. Illustrated by Stephanie Douglas. Viking. 32 pp.

Everybody knows that if on New Year's Day you find a penny from the year of your birth you can make three wishes . . . and they will come true. After wasting two wishes Zenobia ("everybody call me Nobie") makes a wise wish and gets her good friend back. Told in dialect. Bright colorful pictures.

Two Greedy Bears.   Mirra Ginsburg. Illustrated by Jose Aruego and Ariane Dewey. Macmillan. 32 pp.

Children watched with delighted foreknowledge the way in which two greedy bear cubs were outwitted by a wily fox, who stole almost all their cheese. The cubs vowed never to be fooled in like manner. The large bright pictures and minimal text were very attractive to children.

The Tyrannosaurus Game.   Steve Kroll. Illustrations by Tomie de Paola. Holiday House. Unpaged (40 pp.).

A boring day at school sparks the tyrannosaurus game in which each person helps create the story. Children respond to the simplicity of the tale and make up their own stories about the tyrannosaurus.

Wild Robin.   Written and illustrated by Susan Jeffers. E. P. Dutton. Unpaged (40 pp.).

Glorious illustrations accompany this retelling of a Scottish ballad. Wild Robin runs away from home and is captured by the fairies. His sister Janet rescues him by means of her love. The outstanding illustrations capture the attention of readers immediately. One child's eyes actually "lit up" when he saw the picture of the jewel-encrusted castle. Also appropriate for older grades.

Zoo City.   Stephen Lewis. Photographs by the author. Greenwillow. 32 pp.

A game of matching city images (for example, a crane) with animals (for example, a giraffe), played by pairing black-and-white photographs on split halves of the page. When the match is correct on the right, the name of the animal appears on the left. The photographs are ingeniously chosen, clear and well matched in images and size. A unique exercise in visual discrimination for children.

1978

Amifika.   Lucille Clifton. Illustrated by Thomas Di Grazia. E. P. Dutton. Unpaged (28 pp.).

When Amifika's daddy is coming home from the Army, Mama and Aunt Katy discuss getting rid of some things he won't remember in order to make room for him. Amifika is convinced *he* is what they will get rid of. A warm, happy ending makes it easy to see why this was a favorite with young readers.

Apple Pigs.   Ruth Orbach. Illustrated by the author. Collins + World. Unpaged (32 pp.).

When an apple tree rewards its owners by overproducing, the whole community, including the zoo, comes to help consume the apples. Rhymed verse and bright-colored drawings enliven this clear, fast-paced story. One group of primary pupils gave their shared reaction in a word: "Superb!"

Bah! Humbug?   Lorna Balian. Illustrated by the author. Abingdon. Unpaged (32 pp.).

Margie's older brother Arthur, asserting that Santa Claus is a big fat humbug, sets out to trap him by concocting a maze of string, balloons, and wind chimes all over the living room. Arthur threatens dire consequences if Margie falls asleep, but soon falls asleep himself. Margie helps Santa through the maze, feeds him milk and cookies, and thanks him for his wonderful presents. A lively tale of the comeuppance of a know-it-all older sibling. The pictures are cheerful, with bright red splashes on dull gold and gray.

Barney Bipple's Magic Dandelions.   Carol Chapman. Illustrated by Steven Kellogg. E. P. Dutton. Unpaged (27 pp.).

Six-year-old Barney Bipple is full of ideas about things he would like to change. His neighbor, Miss Minerva Merkle, has a lawn covered with magic dandelions that grant wishes to those who know their secret. Barney's adventures (courtesy of the magic dandelions) provide some surprises for Barney and his parents. Children chuckle over the story and pore over Steven Kellogg's intricate and humorous drawings.

Big Bad Bruce.   Bill Peet. Illustrated by the author. Houghton Mifflin. 38 pp.

The peace and quiet of Forevergreen Forest was disrupted when Bruce, a rock-tumbling bully of a bear, moved in. But one day he angered a witch who gave him a taste of his own medicine. This unusual tale emphasizes that a partial change isn't necessarily indicative of a total reformation.

The Birthday Trombone.   Margaret A. Hartelius. Doubleday. Unpaged (45 pp.).

The hippos capsize; an elephant's umbrella breaks down; the zebra falls into her washing and the rhino, giraffe, and lion all collapse when a small monkey plays her birthday trombone. But snake comes to the rescue, and all must endure the terrible trombone's tremolo. This orange-and-black wordless book brought instant laughter to its many fans as they told its story from page to page, adding numerous embellishments.

A Birthday Wish.   Ed Emberley. Little, Brown. Unpaged (32 pp.).

This wordless picture book centers around the highly imaginative story of how a little mouse's birthday wish comes true by means of a series of unexpected events. Each of the illustrations is full of detail and action that capture the interest of the young child.

The Bravest Babysitter.   Barbara Greenberg. Illustrated by Diane Paterson. Dial. Unpaged (28 pp.).

A thunderstorm causes a role reversal when the baby-sitter becomes the babysat. Pleasant text and pictures show the many diversions Lisa uses to distract her nervous babysitter from the storm. Readers love the believable chance for a young child to take care of an older one.

Burnie's Hill.   A traditional rhyme illustrated by Erik Blegvad. McElderry/ Atheneum. Unpaged (24 pp.).

The full-page watercolor illustrations portraying the seasons of the year beautifully tell the story of this much-loved cumulative rhyme. They softly capture the child's viewpoint of the chant, the fluency and rhythm of which make it especially appropriate for creative role playing.

The Butterfly.   A. Delaney. Illustrated by the author. Delacorte. Unpaged (27 pp.).

When a butterfly floating through a meadow catches the eye of a playful dog, the dog follows the fluttering butterfly and is soon joined by a group of children. The entire parade enjoys the free frolic on a summer day. The illustrations tell the story.

Carrot Cake.   Nonny Hogrogian. Illustrated by the author. Greenwillow. Unpaged (27 pp.).

In this warm and humorous tale, Mr. and Mrs. Rabbit find out that even the most perfect couple has a lot to learn about each other. Talkative Mr. Rabbit must learn to be silent at times, while Mrs. Rabbit must learn to share her thoughts. The soft and delicate illustrations beautifully complement this realistic theme.

Chasing the Goblins Away.   Tobi Tobias. Illustrated by Victor Ambrus. Warne. Unpaged (32 pp.).

Every night when Jimmy goes to bed, frightening goblins enter his room. Then one night his parents tell him he must face the goblins alone. A mighty battle follows. The pictures of weird, ugly, obese goblins add humor to this story for children who have had frightening nightmares. For reading aloud and to foster discussion.

Come Away from the Water, Shirley.   John Burningham. Illustrated by the author. Crowell. Unpaged (22 pp.).

While Shirley's parents sun themselves at the beach, Shirley slips away and captures a pirate ship, discovers treasure on an island, and pilots her boat back through dark seas. Unaware of all this, her parents take her home quietly at the day's end. Large print and credible drawings give force to the story's contrasts. The discrepancy between quiet speech and wild action pictures did not puzzle young children at all.

Crocus.   Roger Duvoisin. Illustrated by the author. Knopf. Unpaged (29 pp.).

Crocus, the crocodile who lives on the Sweetpeas' farm, is loved, respected, admired, but somewhat feared by the other animals. He is especially proud of his four long rows of sharp teeth. His problems, begin when he develops a terrible toothache, and when he has to lose his teeth, he loses his self-esteem as well. The full-page color illustrations add a special splash of fun.

Daddy.   Jeannette Caines. Illustrated by Ronald Himler. Harper & Row. 32 pp.

This loving picture of fatherhood is reassuring to the child whose parents quarrel or have parted. Wendy, age 7 or 8, tells what she and her daddy do on his Saturday visits, as well as how she feels before he appears each week.

The Elephant's Ball.   Evelyne Johnson. Illustrated by Tien. McGraw-Hill. Unpaged (40 pp.).

All the animals delight in the excitement surrounding the elephant's ball. Text in verse and accompanying detailed black-and-white illustrations are appealing to ear and eye. Perfect to read aloud, but individual children also enjoyed picking it up to study the pictures.

Everett Anderson's 1-2-3.   Lucille Clifton. Illustrated by Ann Grifalconi. Holt, Rinehart & Winston. Unpaged (27 pp.).

Everett's mom explains that even two can be lonely. Everett tries to understand why Mom wants to see so much of Mr. Perry who lives down the hall, but has a difficult time believing that three would not be a crowd. This is a touching and timely story in verse, highlighted by illustrations that carefully capture the emotion.

The Everyday Train.   Amy Ehrlich. Illustrated by Martha Alexander. Dial. Unpaged (27 pp.).

Jane enjoys meeting the train that passes daily not far from her house, fascinated by the rhythm of its movement, its variety of cars, its friendly engineer, and the mystery of its destination. She plays the games all children enjoy of counting the cars and guessing the color of the caboose, always eager for the train's return the following day.

The Family Minus.   Fernando Krahn. Illustrated by the author. Parents' Magazine. Unpaged (32 pp.).

Eight long-nosed, odd-looking animal children drive to school in Mother's latest invention, a caterpillar-like car with an open cab for each. Children laugh at this novel school bus and the adventures of the zany family.

A Flea Story: I Want to Stay Here! I Want to Go There!   Leo Lionni. Illustrated by the author. Pantheon. Unpaged (32 pp.).

An adventurous flea, having convinced a hesitant homebody partner to join it on a journey to see the world, sets off via the backs of a series of animals. The adventurous flea finds life intriguing and continues the exploration, but the other flea is not happy and returns home. Large, colorful animals and scenery done in collage add to the beautiful simplicity of this tale.

The Foundling. Carol Carrick. Illustrated by Donald Carrick. Seabury. Unpaged (29 pp.).

It isn't easy to get over the loss of a pet, even after many weeks. Christopher thought there would never be another dog like Bodger. His dad drove him to an animal shelter hoping he would find a pet he could care for, but not just any dog would do. A book rare in its sensitivity and insight into the feelings of a young child. The detailed illustrations beautifully depict the seacoast town.

Fox Eyes. Margaret Wise Brown. Illustrated by Garth Williams. Pantheon. Unpaged (32 pp.).

As a fox trots through the woods, other animals shiver, feeling that his eyes can detect their secrets. The simple story is heightened by the muted illustrations with glowing fox eyes, done especially for this reissue. Children sympathize with the animals and find the fox's eyes compelling.

Gertie and Gus. Lisl Weil. Illustrated by the author. Four Winds. Unpaged (29 pp.). Paper ed., Scholastic Book Services.

Gus, content catching fish to feed Gertie and himself, is surprised when Gertie pursues her plans for building an elaborate business. Gus, preferring the simple life, returns to his old cottage and way of life, and Gertie soon follows when she discovers she misses Gus and the uncomplicated life they had together. The simple but colorful illustrations give added enjoyment to the story.

The Great Big Elephant and the Very Small Elephant. Barbara Seuling. Illustrated by the author. Crown. Unpaged (36 pp.).

Friendship is the theme of these three stories. The first is about having to say good-bye to a friend, the second shows how friends help each other out of difficult situations, and the last, how friends value each other's companionship.

The Grouchy Ladybug. Eric Carle. Illustrated by the author. Crowell. Unpaged (48 pp.).

Children enjoy this unusual book with pages of varying widths and a clock showing the same time on each page. A grouchy ladybug challenges numerous insects and animals to fight, but they all refuse. A whale's tale finally swishes the hero back home, where a friendly ladybug shares her aphids with the now-chastened traveler.

Harriet Goes to the Circus. Betsy Maestro. Illustrated by Giulio Maestro. Crown. Unpaged (29 pp.).

Harriet the elephant wants to be first in line at the circus but finds that she is last. Disappointedly she enters the tent to discover a pleasant surprise. The story with its bold illustrations in a variety of brilliant colors offers a delightful way of introducing ordinal numbers.

Harry and the Terrible Whatzit. Dick Gackenbach. Illustrated by the author. Seabury. Unpaged (32 pp.). Paper ed., Scholastic Book Services.

After his mother ignores his warnings and goes down into the cellar, Harry arms himself with a broom and descends to find her. There he encounters the terrible Whatzit! Children, many of whom are sure there is a monster hiding somewhere in their homes, easily identify with this story. Gackenbach's animated illustrations depict Harry's heroic determination to conquer the Whatzit and find his missing mother.

Hector and Christina. Louise Fatio. Illustrated by Roger Duvoisin. McGraw-Hill. Unpaged (32 pp.).

"One day Hector Penguin fell off a truck on the way to the zoo." Pupils like that opening sentence with its invitation to freedom and adventure. They follow Hector's good-to-bad-to-good fortune: capture, escape, finding a mate. Above all, they like the happy resolution when the townspeople decide that Hector and his mate must be "free to live in the forest with their friends."

The Hiding Game. Ben Shecter. Illustrated by the author. Parents' Magazine. Unpaged (27 pp.).

Though Henri Hippopotamus and Pierre Rhinoceros are good friends who enjoy playing together, they find that in their game of hide-and-seek they're actually playing apart rather than together. The colorful illustrations and unusual happenings bring this special tale of friendship to life.

How the Rooster Saved the Day. Arnold Lobel. Illustrated by Anita Lobel. Greenwillow. Unpaged (28 pp.).

Clever as ever, the rooster saves himself from a nighttime robber by tricking the robber into crowing to make the sun come up. The simple text is augmented with simple-impact drawings, brightly tinted. "Smart rooster!" was the judgment of primary-level listeners.

If I Could Be My Grandmother. Steven Kroll. Illustrated by Lady McCrady. Pantheon. Unpaged (30 pp.).

A little girl, remembering all the reasons why her grandmother is so special, assumes in her make-believe the role of grandmother and makes her Raggedy Ann her grandchild. The sharing, caring, and love between the girl and her grandmother, evident throughout, are best expressed when Grandma comes for a surprise visit. Soft, colored-pencil drawings enhance the story.

If I Were a Toad. Diane Paterson. Illustrated by the author. Dial. Unpaged (29 pp.).

Glimpses of a child's thought provide an imaginative look at what it would be like to be a toad, a crab, a raccoon, and a variety of other familiar animals. The ending that Papa brings to the story gives it a lovely warmth. The flavor and simplicity of the illustrations appeal to the fantasies of the young child.

I Like the Library. Anne Rockwell. Illustrated by the author. E. P. Dutton. Unpaged (28 pp.).

While visiting a modern public library with his mother, a little boy finds many things he likes. Children enjoy the bright pictures and simple recounting of a happy experience.

Ivan, Divan, and Zariman. Marta Koci. Illustrated by the author. Parents' Magazine. Unpaged (28 pp.).

A boy, a couch, and a mouse make rather unusual playmates, but they happily inhabit an attic together. When the junk man takes everything in the attic to the dump, Ivan rescues Zariman, the mouse, but Divan is beyond help. Unusual, but appealing to young readers.

Jethro's Difficult Dinosaur. Arnold Sundgaard. Illustrated by Stan Mack. Pantheon. Unpaged (26 pp.).

Rhymed couplets and action-packed cartoon drawings tell what happens when Jethro brings home an unusual egg that hatches into a baby dinosaur. Vocabulary-stretchers such as "succinct" and "extinct" increase interest, and listeners find the rhymes memorable.

Keep Out. Noela Young. Illustrated by the author. Collins + World. Unpaged (32 pp.).

Though the urban setting is in Australia, the children are universally recognizable. A group without a playground takes over a cluttered vacant lot marked "Keep out." When the city decides to make it a park, the children insist it is all right as it is. The element of wish fulfillment attracted many readers.

Little One Inch. Barbara Brenner. Illustrated by Fred Brenner. Coward. Unpaged (28 pp.).

Little One Inch, no bigger than a finger, sets off for Kyoto to make his fortune. Along the way he outwits some strange demons and then secures a job as bodyguard for the beautiful Michiko. While protecting her from two Oni demons, Little One Inch is granted a wish. This Japanese folktale ends with an unusual twist.

Love from Uncle Clyde. Nancy Winslow Parker. Illustrated by the author. Dodd, Mead. Unpaged (32 pp.).

Charlie's birthday present from Uncle Clyde is Elfreda, a purple hippopotamus complete with full directions for care. Children love the surprise and wish they had a hippo too.

Martha's Mad Day. Miranda Hapgood. Illustrated by Emily McCully. Crown. Unpaged (29 pp.).

Martha woke up fierce and mean on this Saturday morning. She began by throwing poor piggy across the room and continued by being her loudest most disagreeable self. Only when alone at bedtime did she begin to come out of her mood. The illustrations as well as the text capture a mood children can identify with.

The Most Amazing Hide-and-Seek Alphabet Book. Robert Crowther. Viking. Unpaged (12 pp.).

As the title suggests, the animal illustrations for each letter of the alphabet are cleverly hidden behind the bold black letters. A young child will delight in pulling, pushing and turning each letter to discover an animal whose name starts with that letter. The charming illustrations and the variety of physical manipulations entice children to read this one again and again.

Ms. Klondike. Jessica Ross. Illustrated by the author. Viking. Unpaged (28 pp.).

A picture book depicting a woman in a job usually reserved for men. Ms. Klondike is nervous about her new job, driving a taxi, and has problems with the male drivers until she prevents one from being robbed. The brief text accompanied by large, simple line drawings washed with yellow appeals to the very young.

My Friend, Jasper Jones. Rosamond Dauer. Illustrated by Jerry Joyner. Parents' Magazine. Unpaged (27 pp.).

Teddy was having trouble with his room: a broken bed, leaves in his dresser drawer, and walls painted with peanut butter. When his parents asked who was responsible, Teddy said his friend, Jasper Jones. At first Teddy's parents helped him clean up Jasper's messes. But when they realized Jasper was only make-believe, Teddy had to do all the cleaning up himself. Double-view illustrations allow two stories to be told.

The Mysterious Tadpole. Steven Kellogg. Illustrated by the author. Dial. Unpaged (20 pp.).

When Uncle McAlister sends Louis a tadpole from Loch Ness, it is only a matter of time until the creature grows to amazing proportions. Fortunately, the giant tadpole has a giant brain. Furthermore, it turns out there is a sunken treasure chest to be found. At the end Uncle McAlister brings another present. Children followed the story by means of its lively pictures, and they loved Alphonse, the Lock Ness tadpole-monster.

The Mystery of the Giant Footprints.   Fernando Krahn. E. P. Dutton. Unpaged (32 pp.).
Two children run off to follow some giant footprints in the snow. Panic-stricken, their parents gather a rescue party, and the villagers give chase armed with shotguns, pitchforks, and axes. After following them across a frozen lake and up the side of a mountain, the parents find their children have discovered two unusual animal friends. A wordless picture book with Krahm's usual black-and-white pencil drawings expressing wry humor. Also suitable for middle grades.

Noah's Ark.   Peter Spier. Doubleday. Unpaged (44 pp.).
This wordless picture-book version of the age-old story shows a multitude of details about the animals that climb onto Noah's huge ark, eat, sleep, and have families there, and start a new life after the flood. Children were amazed and impressed by the full-color drawings as was the committee that awarded the book the Caldecott Medal. Suitable for all ages.

Owl's New Cards.   Kathryn Ernst. Illustrated by Diane de Groat. Crown. Unpaged (30 pp.).
This is a warm, original story about a friendship, misunderstanding, and reunion. Owl, Brown Bear, and Rat form a pleasant cast, and Owl's new cards are as appealing to young readers as to the three friends. Children and their teachers considered this to be one of their most prized "finds." The drawings, at once funny and friendly, heighten the characterization.

Pettifur.   Jay Williams. Illustrated by Hilary Knight. Four Winds. Unpaged (35 pp.).
Pettifur is an excellent mouse catcher. He is so good, in fact, that there are no more mice in his house to catch. Subsequently, he spends his time indulging in his favorite pastime, eating, until, becoming so fat he cannot chase mice when they reappear, Pettifur must go on a diet. He leaves all his food for the mice, who become so fat they decide to move away. Children enjoy the humor in this book.

Rodney Peppe's Puzzle Book.   Rodney Peppe. Viking. Unpaged (24 pp.).
Eleven intricate and humorous, full-color picture puzzles encourage young children to look closely at and discuss what they see. Size relationships, simple counting, and naming animals are among the numerous activities teachers can pursue with this book.

Sam Who Never Forgets.   Eve Rice. Illustrated by the author. Greenwillow. Unpaged (30 pp.).
The zoo animals love Sam the Keeper because he never forgets to feed them. One day when he doesn't bring the elephant's food they are tempted to doubt him; but Sam comes back with a whole wagonful of hay! The bright illustrations attract attention and the elephant's plight evokes much sympathy, with sighs of satisfaction at the conclusion.

Sara and the Door.   Virginia Allen Jensen. Illustrated by Ann Strugnell. Addison-Wesley. Unpaged (26 pp.).

While closing the front door, Sara catches her coat. Alone in the house, she is unable to reach the doorknob to free herself, and, after several unsuccessful attempts at escape, she becomes very upset. Then she spies the buttons. One, two, three, and she's free and feeling very proud. Children easily identify with the feeling of helplessness.

The Seeing Stick. Jane Yolen. Illustrated by Remy Charlip and Demetra Maraslis. Crowell. Unpaged (26 pp.).

Set in ancient China, this modern legend about an emperor's blind daughter and a wise old man who, by means of his "seeing stick," helps her (though not in the manner we at first anticipate) to learn to see, offers children an ending they can ponder. The illustrations, with their effective use of line and color, augment the story.

Seven Little Monsters. Maurice Sendak. Harper & Row. Unpaged (16 pp.). Paper ed., Harper & Row.

Seven very distinct, individual monsters emerge from a house, frighten the townspeople, and arouse a row of bumbling soldiers. The counting-rhyme text describes the creatures' brief progress until, chained together, they must return glumly to where they began. As usual, the Sendak drawings—more childlike, less polished than in his previous books—bring complete approval from young listeners and lookers.

Small Rabbit. Miska Miles. Illustrated by Jim Arnosky. Atlantic/Little, Brown. 31 pp.

While looking for a friend, Small Rabbit encounters what she thinks are four enemies. The enemies turn out to be a mouse, two butterflies, and a squirrel. Small Rabbit has no trouble recognizing her friend, who looks just like her. Children find Small Rabbit's mistaken identifications especially fun.

Squeeze a Sneeze. Bill Morrison. Illustrated by the author. Houghton Mifflin. Unpaged (30 pp.).

This lighthearted rhyme will tickle the fancy of every young child. The delightful nonsensical verse can only be matched by the vividly colorful illustrations depicting a W. C. Fields–type character in all of his humorous exploits. The clever use of words will inspire readers to create their own zany, fun-filled verse.

The Strongest One of All. Mirra Ginsburg. Illustrated by Jose Aruego and Ariane Dewey. Greenwillow. Unpaged (32 pp.).

In this Caucasian variation of the common folktale motif about the search for the strongest one of all, a lamb takes a journey and arrives at a reassuring conclusion. Aruego and Dewey's gentle line drawings, colorfully filled in, delight the eye. Their sense of proportion adds a further dimension to the lamb's quest. The repetitive words and pattern of the tale make it a good story-starter for creative writing.

The Substitute. Ann Lawler. Illustrated by Nancy Winslow Parker. Parents' Magazine. Unpaged (32 pp.).

An eccentric substitute teacher urges the class to dance like a series of animals while she plays the piano. Children enjoy the humorous fantasy and especially the pictures of student-animals as they dance around their classroom.

Summer on Cleo's Island. Natalie G. Sylvester. Illustrated by the author. Farrar, Straus & Giroux. Unpaged (37 pp.).

The beauty of summer on a Maine island is seen through the eyes of a Siamese cat. The language is rich, informative, expressive; and the large black-and-white drawings are exquisite—a perfect accompaniment to the text. An excellent choice for reading aloud and discussing with groups of young children. A favorite in kindergarten.

The Tailypo. Joanna Galdone. Illustrated by Paul Galdone. Seabury. Unpaged (30 pp.).

Subtitled "A Ghost Story," the book, derived from the folklore of the backwoods of Tennessee, offers a familiar pattern with a shock ending. An old man eats a varmint's tail. That night when the creature returns to claim its tail—well, that's the story. "It was pretty scary, but I laughed at the pictures." "I wish the dogs had come back at the end, but it was good all the same."

Thorn Rose or The Sleeping Beauty. The Brothers Grimm. Illustrated by Errol Le Cain. Bradbury. Unpaged (32 pp.). Paper ed., Puffin.

Lovely illustrations, reminiscent of French tapestries, illuminate this version of a traditional tale. Children pore over the intricate illustrations and love all the creatures interwoven with the design. An interesting contrast to *The Sleeping Beauty*, also on this list.

The Unexpected Grandchildren. Jane Flory. Illustrated by Carolyn Croll. Houghton Mifflin. 32 pp.

After many years of peace, quiet, and order, the elderly, childless Newtons receive a note announcing the imminent arrival of their grandchildren. They are surprised by the obvious mistake, yet disappointed when no one arrives. Mr. Newton decides to invite the neighborhood children over and a wonderful day results. The warmhearted story, simple and colorfully illustrated, serves to reemphasize everyone's need for love and acceptance regardless of age. Also suitable for middle grades.

The Visit. Diane Wolkstein. Illustrated by Lois Ehlert. Knopf. Unpaged (29 pp.).

An ant makes a long journey to play with a friend, and the friend promises to return the visit next time. Children like the simple presentation of the universal theme of friendship, well conveyed by the bright, bold illustrations.

What's Happening to Daisy? Sandy Rabinowitz. Harper & Row. 32 pp.

Daisy's belly has grown big and round and she can hardly squeeze into her stall. Twenty-two simple sentences tell of the birth of her colt. Illustrations in blue and coral show the process. Many teachers found the three pictures that show the actual birth to be less graphic than photographs, thus perhaps more suitable for very young children.

Where's Mark? Jacquie Hann. Illustrated by the author. Four Winds. Unpaged (34 pp.).

Did the boogeyman get Mark? His youngest sister thinks so as she reluctantly searches the house for him with her older sister. Young children sympathize with Mark's sisters in their fear and subsequent relief when they find no boogeyman. The charming illustrations, seeming almost to step out of the page in their heather-soft tones, give the book its character.

Where's My Hippopotamus? Mark Alan Stamaty. Illustrated by the author. Dial. Unpaged (30 pp.).

Henry ties his pet hippopotamus, Herbert, to a parking meter while he goes to the post office. Enticed by a passing truck full of hay, Herbert jerks loose and follows the truck. Henry finally finds Herbert swimming in a nearby lake having escaped the wrath of the angry truck driver. A good detective story.

Willaby.   Rachel Isadora. Illustrated by the author. Macmillan. Unpaged (30 pp.).
The drawings are a ballet of motion in this story of a Black first-grader who loves to draw but cares little about writing. Many primary children identify with Willaby and her enthusiasm for drawing get-well cards. They also share her love for her teacher, Miss Finney.

Will It Be Okay?   Crescent Dragonwagon. Illustrated by Ben Shecter. Harper & Row. 32 pp.
"But what if snakes come in the night? You keep a flute by your bed and play a song, and the snakes hear, and are quiet, and happy, and love you . . ." The fears and anxieties of a little girl are relieved by a comforting and loving mother who reassures her that in spite of problems everything will be okay. Rare insight and warm sensitivity are beautifully expressed and illustrated in this unique book.

A Worm for Dinner.   Ned Delaney. Illustrated by the author. Houghton Mifflin. Unpaged (32 pp.).
Bird from above and mole from below find the same worm, and both want it for dinner. While they fight over the worm it crawls away. As they search for another, each tries to outwit its rival until they find a "worm" which makes them both lose their appetite. Children were immediately drawn to the bold, colorful illustrations in this tale of trickery.

1979

ABC of Monsters.   Deborah Niland. Illustrated by the author. McGraw-Hill. 30 pp.
Children find these lovable, roly-poly monsters, performing various antics representing each letter of the alphabet, hard to resist. For example, these cuddly comical creatures can be found "eating eggs," "frightening frogs" and "gobbling grandmas." Their delightful facial expressions and bright colors add to the charm that makes this a favorite book for the younger reader.

Albert's Story.   Claudia Long. Illustrated by Judy Glasser. Delacorte. Unpaged (32 pp.).
When do children discover that a story has a beginning, middle, and end? Albert's story: "He put the thing on his back." Who did what and why comprises a very original story indeed. Albert, however, fails to grasp the idea, the audience sharing what the character cannot. Young children clamored to explain to Albert. Unable, many told their own, fuller tales instead.

Alexander, Who Used to Be Rich Last Sunday.   Judith Viorst. Illustrated by Ray Cruz. Atheneum. Unpaged (29 pp.).
Alexander receives a dollar from his grandparents and intends to save it for a walkie-talkie. His intentions go astray in the drugstore, in foolish bets, etc. Whenever he loses the money, the illustration features coins flying away and forlorn Alexander sighing, "Bye bye, eight (or twenty, etc.) cents!" Understated humor is the highlight of the text.

Appelard and Liverwurst.   Mercer Mayer. Illustrated by Steven Kellogg. Four Winds. 34 pp.
Children's ratings on this book were extremely high, but their reasons varied. Certainly Kellogg's sketches of Mr. Appelard and his bed partners (pig, hen, cow, goat, and "rhinosterwurst") were a big factor. But so were Mayer's tall-tale

farm-rags-to-circus-riches climax and ending. Pupils in middle grades also liked this book.

Arion and the Dolphins. Lonzo Anderson. Illustrated by Adrienne Adams. Scribner's Unpaged (32 pp.).
Sparkling prose and sea-green watercolors set the tone for this story based on an ancient Greek legend of friendship. Arion makes friends with the dolphins who later save him from drowning. Discussion, watercolor paintings, stories, and poems were natural classroom extensions after children read this story.

The Bearskinner. Brothers Grimm. Illustrated by Felix Hoffman. McElderry/Atheneum. Unpaged (32 pp.).
An out-of-work soldier bargains with the devil: in exchange for riches, he will live inside a bearskin for 7 years and never bathe. How he survives the ordeal and marries happily at the end makes a satisfying story. The large bold brush drawings splashed with brilliant color enhance the tale. Children loved this strong primitive art, requesting that it be shown for careful examination during successive readings.

A Big Fat Enormous Lie. Marjorie Weinman Sharmat. Illustrated by David McPhail. E. P. Dutton. Unpaged (30 pp.).
A small boy tells a lie to avoid punishment and is followed by a burden of guilt throughout the day. His lie grows with his guilt until it threatens to overpower him, and the boy realizes that the truth must be told. Many children should be able to identify with this young child's problem.

Bill and Pete. Tomie de Paola. Illustrated by the author. Putnam. Unpaged (28 pp.). Paper ed., G. P. Putnam's.
William Evert, a crocodile, purchases a toothbrush—a bird he dubs "Pete"—and they become best friends. Pete enters school with William Evert where they learn crocodile history, reading, and writing. Life is a lark until a thinly moustached villain captures Bill, desiring to transform him into a suitcase. Lotus flowers, pyramids, and mummies help establish the Egyptian setting, and children delight as Pete's beak saves the day.

Bus Ride. Nancy Jewell. Illustrated by Ronald Himler. Harper & Row. Unpaged (32 pp.).
Youngsters undergoing fresh independence identify with Janie, traveling alone by bus to visit her grandfather. Himler's drowsy shading effectively conveys the feeling of night and brings to the fore the reassurance Janie gets from the brief relationship she forms with a fellow traveler. This was a good discussion starter.

Catastrophe Cat. Dennis Panek. Illustrated by the author. Bradbury. Unpaged (31 pp.).
Catastrophe isn't the word for it: mischievous, clever, and truly funny are. Sit back and enjoy this kitty's antics during a whirlwind trip around the big city . . . all caused by just a bit too much curiosity. A treat for older readers as well as a springboard for tell-it-yourself times.

Chester Chipmunk's Thanksgiving. Barbara Williams. Illustrated by Kay Chorao. E. P. Dutton. Unpaged (32 pp.).
It's Thanksgiving Day, and Chester Chipmunk wants to share his blessings with his friends. But his friends are all busy with company of their own. Finally, Oswald Opossum comes to dinner, followed by many unexpected guests, and

Chester realizes that Thanksgiving is indeed a day for sharing. Children enjoy this delightful story with its charming illustrations.

Cloudy with a Chance of Meatballs. Judi Barrett. Illustrated by Ron Barrett. Atheneum. Unpaged (32 pp.).

There *can* be too much of a good thing. In Chewandswallow people didn't have to buy or grow food—their diet rained down from the sky. Suddenly, though, things turned sour. One day there was only broccoli, all overcooked, and eventually huge foodstorms forced evacuation (achieved on oversized peanut butter and jelly sandwich rafts). Teachers and children ate this one up, relishing the happily busy pictures and the imaginative foodtrips it engendered.

Ed Emberley's ABC. Ed Emberley. Illustrated by the author. Little, Brown. Unpaged (62 pp.).

Animals involved in a variety of activities introduce the letters of the alphabet. Bold, black ink drawings with colorful overlays on rich textured paper show the evolution of each letter. Children love finding objects that begin with the featured letter such as "ant," "alligator," and "airplane" on the *A* pages. Producing their own ABC books was another favorite extension activity.

George and Martha One Fine Day. James Marshall. Illustrated by the author. Houghton Mifflin. 46 pp.

In this book, we follow the adventures of George and Martha, two delightful hippos, who seem to enjoy both life and one another. Their days are filled with tightrope walking, stamp collecting, playing practical jokes, and visiting amusement parks. The book is filled with the type of humor which should have great appeal for primary children. The accompanying illustrations are a delight.

George the Babysitter. Shirley Hughes. Illustrated by the author. Prentice-Hall. Unpaged (32 pp.).

Mike, Jenny, and Baby Sue's mother goes to work, and a young man comes to sit. Their day is warmly evoked in simple words and soft watercolors. Children recognized themselves in dramatic play—the shiny part of the floor is the sea, the carpeted area the land. The depiction of a normal, cluttered household provides amusing detail to view and review, as whatever George tries to accomplish rapidly gets undone.

Gregory Griggs and Other Nursery Rhyme People. Selected by Arnold Lobel. Illustrated by the author. Greenwillow. 47 pp.

Arnold Lobel has brought to life some obscure nursery rhyme characters and has captured their particular plights and follies in his evocative illustrations. The strong rhyming patterns and the imaginative use of language in the selection add to the reading-aloud appeal of this book.

His Mother's Dog. Liesel Skorpen. Illustrated by M. E. Mullin. Harper & Row. 46 pp.

He wanted a big dog named Moose. He got a cocker spaniel called Puck—just like the one Mother used to have. Worse, Puck likes his Mother better than him. But, when Mother comes home with a new sister, the boy and his dog find that they *can* have good times together. This is a warm and tender story of growing up and learning to work through problems.

Jamie's Tiger. Jan Wahl. Illustrated by Tomie de Paola. Harcourt Brace Jovanovich. Unpaged (48 pp.).

Jamie suddenly loses his hearing after a bout of German measles. When his problem is recognized, Jamie makes the difficult transition to the world of the deaf. His family and friends aid him with love, encouragement, and understanding, and Jamie learns to live successfully with his handicap. This is a beautiful story, and the illustrations add much to its enjoyment.

Jeremy Isn't Hungry. Barbara Williams. Illustrated by Martha Alexander. E. P. Dutton. Unpaged (30 pp.).

Davey's unsuccessful attempts to pacify a baby brother by feeding him lead to panic and interruptions for mother, who is trying to get ready to attend a school function. The illustrations provide much of the humor for this amusing story. As a read-aloud book it should appeal to the young listener, who will recognize the difficulties of living with a younger sibling.

John Brown, Rose and the Midnight Cat. Jenny Wagner. Illustrated by Ron Brooks. Bradbury. 32 pp.

Dealing with jealousy is the subtle theme of this story as John Brown (a shaggy dog) fears the intrusion of Midnight (a black cat) into his cozy and settled life with Rose (a kindly widow lady). The soft-textured and warm-colored illustrations are so inviting that children occasionally patted the dog as if expecting to feel that shaggy fur.

Mr. and Mrs. Button's Wonderful Watchdogs. Janice. Illustrated by Roger Duvoisin. Lothrop, Lee & Shepard. Unpaged (29 pp.).

Mrs. and Mrs. Button have five watchdogs and two cats; but, they're still afraid of burglars because their pets are friendly to everyone. A suprise ending makes this humorous reading.

Mouse Six and the Happy Birthday. Miska Miles. Illustrated by Leslie Morrill. Unicorn/E. P. Dutton. Unpaged (32 pp.).

Mouse Six goes off to find a birthday present for his mother. He tells no one what he is up to, and the rumor spreads that he has run away from home. When his animal friends visit his parents to cheer them up, they provide an unexpected birthday for Mother Mouse. Young children should respond well to the humor of this delightful tale.

Mousekin's Close Call. Edna Miller. Illustrated by the author. Prentice-Hall. 32 pp.

The tale of Mousekin provides information about how certain animals protect themselves against their enemies by playing dead. Mousekin observes a variety of animals in this situation. He sees no need for this "pretending" behavior until he is caught off guard by an enemy. The thrill and relief of danger met and overcome make this an appealing book for young children.

Nate the Great and the Sticky Case. Marjorie Weinman Sharmat. Illustrated by Marc Simont. Coward, McCann & Geoghegan. 48 pp.

Claude's favorite dinosaur stamp, his Stegosaurus, is missing, And Nate the Great and his detective dog Sludge take the case. Nate's sleuthing turns up lots of laughs and, finally, the missing stamp.

The Pancake. Anita Lobel. Illustrated by the author. Greenwillow. 48 pp.

A peasant woman, her seven children, a farmer, a goose, a cat, a sheep and a goat chase a runaway pancake. But before they can catch it, it is eaten by a clever pig. Pastoral illustrations and an easy-to-grasp moral make this a good choice for young readers.

Pancakes for Breakfast. Tomie de Paola. Illustrated by the author. Harcourt Brace Jovanovich. Unpaged (32 pp.). Paperback, Harcourt Brace Jovanovich.

Imagine having to gather eggs, milk a cow, and churn butter amid all sorts of early morning crises—just to have pancakes for breakfast! This near-wordless book shows it all with gentle humor, and a recipe is included so that primary children can try their own hands at pancake making, an excellent activity for building language and reading readiness skills. "It is a crazy, nice story," declared one first-grader.

Paul's Christmas Birthday. Carol Carrick. Illustrated by Donald Carrick. Greenwillow. Unpaged (32 pp.).

To have a birthday on December 24, when many people are thinking about Christmas, seems a misfortune to Paul, who is 5 years old. But Paul's parents arrange for "someone from outer space" to be the mystery guest at Paul's birthday party. The book, marvelously illustrated in shades of brown and ocher, glows in its rural setting. Paul and his classmates struck a note of recognition in readers everywhere.

A Pocket for Corduroy. Don Freeman. Illustrated by the author. Viking. Unpaged (26 pp.).

Corduroy is Lisa's teddy bear, and he wants a pocket. This is his adventure, from beginning to end (which, I might add, is a purple pocket with his name tucked inside!)

Potato Pancakes All Around: A Hanukkah Tale. Marilyn Hirsh. Illustrated by the author. Bonim. Unpaged (32 pp.).

Samuel the peddler brings a new, delightful recipe for potato pancakes to the village. Set in a Europe of generations ago, warm golds and browns—the very colors of potato pancakes—complement this holiday version of the folktale found in many cultures, one example being Stone Soup. Recipes are appended, as is a brief explanation of the Festival of Lights.

The Quiet House. Otto Coontz. Illustrated by the author. Little, Brown. 39 pp.

Bagsley, a lonely pup, responds to a mysterious advertisement for "eggs for the lonely." His plans for a party are frustrated when he realizes that he has no one to invite to his house. When the eggs arrive, they are accompanied by three totally unexpected and thoroughly delightful party guests. Young readers will enjoy both the story and the illustrations.

Rum Pum Pum. Retold by Maggie Duff. Illustrated by Jose Aruego and Ariane Dewey. Macmillan. 32 pp.

Songs and repetition spark this humorous cumulative tale. The king steals Blackbird's wife, so Blackbird declares war. Cat, Stick, and Ant jump in Blackbird's ear to help pay back the king for his evil to them as well. Children loved hearing this story and joined in on the *Rum Pum Pum* drum chorus. Lavishly colorful illustrations caused comments, too.

The Snake: A Very Long Story. Bernard Waber. Illustrated by the author. Houghton Mifflin. Unpaged (48 pp.).

Large capital letters, a long green traveling snake, and collages of labeled scenery breathe life into this around-the-world adventure—a novelty book that inspired primary pupils to create and dramatize very long snake stories of their own. The collages themselves deserve special attention. They add substance to the snake's journey and can stimulate fruitful discussion.

The Snowman. Raymond Briggs. Illustrated by the author. Random House. Unpaged (32 pp.).

The filmstrip-like illustrations in muted pastels tell a wordless story of a poignant relationship between a small boy and a snowman he has made. The highly detailed pictures show how the snowman magically comes to life, and how the snowman and the boy each demonstrate the perils and pleasures of his respective world. This book can be enjoyed by any child old enough to give attention to the meaning conveyed by pictures.

Socks for Supper.　Jack Kent. Illustrated by the author. Parents' Magazine. Unpaged (32 pp.).

An elderly couple are tired of living on nothing but turnips so they begin to trade with their neighbors. They give socks, and receive milk and cheese in return. After several such exchanges, their socks are returned to them in a most unexpected way. This is a thoroughly enjoyable story, with colorful and entertaining illustrations.

The Stupids Have a Ball.　Harry Allard and James Marshall. Illustrated by James Marshall. Houghton Mifflin. 31 pp.

The Stupid children have flunked every course at school. And, Mr. and Mrs. Stupid have a costume party to celebrate. The book is a wonderful combination of tongue-in-cheek dialogue ("You sure can polka, Dot.") and equally wacky cartoonish illustrations (can you imagine a dog dressed as the Bone Ranger!).

The Tortoise and the Tree.　Janina Domanska. Illustrated by the author. Greenwillow. Unpaged (32 pp.).

This African folktale tells of a tortoise who appealed to the High God during a time of great famine. Because the High God heard him, he was able to lead his friends to food. When they killed him in their greed, he was restored to life by some tiny ants. To this day, we are told, the tortoise bears the mark of this adventure upon his shell. The beautiful illustrations add to the appeal of this fable.

The Trip.　Ezra Jack Keats. Illustrated by the author. Greenwillow. Unpaged (32 pp.). Paper ed., Scholastic Book Services.

Homesick, Louis builds a diorama representing his old neighborhood. In imagination he walks into the scene and into a scary adventure. Called back to reality, he joins trick-or-treaters in his new neighborhood. Every space in the book is alive with color. Children responded to the display and to Louis's "trick" to avert loneliness.

What the Moon Saw.　Brian Wildsmith. Illustrated by the author. Oxford. Unpaged (32 pp.). Paper ed., Oxford, Univ. Press.

Patterned and plain, feathered and furry, fierce and timid—such contrasts form the simple text to tell what the sun shows the moon on her holiday. As always, the artist's paintings provide a colorful stylized view of single objects and animals against bright textured backgrounds. Pupils responded most to the animals' quizzical expressions, the touch of humor in a book with gentle tone.

Where Did My Mother Go?　Edna Mitchell Preston. Illustrated by Chris Conover. Four Winds. Unpaged (29 pp.).

Little Cat tricycles off to town looking for his mother but somehow fails to notice her tail as she leaves shops or her back as she browses in the library. Children responded to the loss-and-recovery theme while enjoying humorous picture details—a Varminton map, for instance, showing Gojumpina Lake and Bow-Wow Boulevard.

The Wobbly Tooth.　Nancy Evans Cooney. Illustrated by Marylin Hafner. G. P. Putnam's. Unpaged (32 pp.).

Elizabeth Ann has a problem; her wobbly tooth will not come out. After the usual methods for dislodging a tooth have failed, she decides to forget about it, and goes out for a game with her friends. Naturally, the tooth comes out when Elizabeth Ann least expects that it will. Most primary children should be able to identify with this little girl and her stubborn tooth.

The Worst Person In the World.   James Stevenson. Illustrated by the author. Greenwillow. 32 pp. Paperback, Puffin.

Aided by a visiting monster called Ugly, a grouch reluctantly mends his ways. Ugly cleans Worst's house and readies it for a party. As the man's mood changes, one assumes the guy will no longer trample on flowers or eat lemons to maintain a sour disposition. Stevenson's jaunty cartoons underscore the character change and give new life to an old idea.

The Wounded Wolf. Jean Craighead George. Illustrated by John Schoenherr. Harper & Row. 32 pp.

Wounded Roko is trailed across the Alaskan landscape by ravens, a fox, a snowy owl, and a grizzly. Why this death march does not end in death is vividly described in the author's spare prose and the illustrator's descriptive etchings. After one listening, many primary pupils proudly read the book on their own.

Wriggles, The Little Wishing Pig. Pauline Watson. Illustrations by Paul Galdone. Seabury. Unpaged (32 pp.).

Wriggles' Uncle Oinkie tells him how to make wishes come true, and Wriggles uses this new-found power to turn himself into an unrecognizable member of his family by wishing for the legs of a crane, a tail like a kite, etc. The colorful illustrations add to the appeal of this story for young children.

1980

Beany. Jane Feder. Illustrated by Karen Gundersheimer. Pantheon. Unpaged (32 pp.).

All cat lovers will enjoy this warm, tender story about a little boy's love for his cat, Beany. The small size of the book and of the characters add a dimension children enjoyed.

Bert and Barney. Ned Delaney. Illustrations by the author. Houghton Mifflin. 32 pp.

An alligator and a frog are the best of friends until they have a disagreement. They try to be happy alone, but eventually make up and become better friends than before. Bright, happy pictures convey the warmth of the story.

Bumps in the Night.   Harry Allard. Illustrated by James Marshall. Doubleday. 32 pp.

A friendly, humorous ghost story for the read-aloud group. Dudley the stork is frightened by a bumping noise and something wet touching his cheek. Best friend Trevor Hog advises having Madam Kreepy preside at a séance, at which a ghost horse named Donald appears.

Catastrophe Cat at the Zoo. Dennis Panek. Illustrations by the author. Bradbury. Unpaged (34 pp.).

Lively Catastrophe Cat is pursued by trouble. Even on an outing to the zoo, trouble follows as our hero is bounced from one animal to the next before finally escaping to the roof of a bus for the ride home.

The Cloud over Clarence. Marc Brown. Illustrated by the author. Unicorn/ E. P. Dutton. Unpaged (32 pp.).

The reader weaves through a day of misadventures leading to Clarence's birthday party. His friends give him a letter pleading with him to think first so that he will have fewer accidents and be less forgetful. Colorful pictures portray the "personality" of each cat character.

Cora Copycat.   Helen Lester. Illustrations by the author. E. P. Dutton. Unpaged (32 pp.).

The snappy, cartoon-type illustrations contribute as much to the popularity of this book as the simple text. Cora is a terrible copycat who copies everything anyone says. She learns a lesson when her family leaves her alone in the house and she is visited by a Wild Woolly Wurgal escaped from the zoo.

Cowardly Clyde.   Bill Peet. Illustrated by the author. Houghton Mifflin. 40 pp.

Brave Sir Galavant and his cowardly steed Clyde take up the challenge to rid the farmers of the terrible "giant owl-eyed ox-footed ogre." Clyde, who quivers at a scarecrow, is terrified, but finds that by acting brave, you become brave.

Crackle Gluck and the Sleeping Toad.   Dick Gackenbach. Illustrated by the author. Houghton/Clarion. Unpaged (32 pp.).

Crackle Gluck becomes suspicious of the pampered toad that has supposedly brought her family generations of good luck. She skillfully devises tests to confirm the trickery of the toad and finally exposes the toad as a fraud.

Cross-Country Cat.   Mary Calhoun. Illustrations by Erick Ingraham. Morrow. Unpaged (42 pp.).

In a story told from Henry the Siamese cat's point of view, the reader meets an animal with the uncanny ability to walk on two legs. When Henry is lost in the mountains, he finds his way home on cross-country skis. Children were especially impressed by the realistic pictures.

Fog in the Meadow.   Joanne Ryder. Illustrated by Gail Owens. Harper & Row. 32 pp.

Lost in the fog! The animals in the meadow were frightened when the fog began to roll in. Illustrations are soft, delicate, three-colored presentations that fit the story very well and enhance the mood of the narrative.

Frederick's Alligator.   Esther Allen Peterson. Illustrations by Susanna Natti. Crown. Unpaged (32 pp.). Paper ed., Scholastic.

Prodded by imagination, Frederick always said he had wild animals in his house. Then when he really does have a baby alligator, no one is willing to believe him.

Friends Are Like That!   Selected by The Child Study Children's Book Committee at Bank Street. Illustrated by Leigh Grant. Crowell. 114 pp.

This varied collection of carefully selected stories and poems for the young reader takes a close look at friendship in its various forms. A friend is someone who never laughs at your nose; someone who moves away but whom you still remember; or someone who comes from another country or another generation.

Hester in the Wild.   Sandra Boynton. Illustrations by the author. Harper. Unpaged (32 pp.). Paper ed., Harper & Row.

Hester the pig's solution to her first problem causes another. This cause-effect pattern humorously snowballs, but Hester's perseverance and determination to deal with each frustration set a fine example for young readers.

Hippos Go Berserk.   Sandra Boynton. Illustrations by the author. Little, Brown. Unpaged (32 pp.). Paper ed., Little, Brown.

If you're a hippo and all alone, invite some friends (forty-five in fact) and let the party start. But all good times must end and the hippos go home, leaving a lonely hippo behind once more. The children enjoyed the rhyme of this counting book.

How to Dig a Hole to the Other Side of the World. Faith McNulty. Illustrations by Marc Simont. Harper & Row. 32 pp.

A funny but careful scientific description of a small boy's journey to the other side of the world. Lively, amusing illustrations complement the text.

I Am Not a Pest. Marjorie Weinman Sharmat and Mitchell Sharmat. Illustrations by Diane Dawson. E. P. Dutton. Unpaged (32 pp.).

"Here's how I, Alicia, am not a pest," this book begins. Curious Alicia continues by listing ways in which a person could be a pest, none of which apply to her.

I Want to Be Big. Genie Iverson. Illustrated by David McPhail. Unicorn/E. P. Dutton. Unpaged (32 pp.).

It's fun to be grown up, but not all the time. One child wants to be big enough to dress herself, walk to school alone, and reach the cereal at the supermarket, but not big enough to stay overnight and not too big for her fuzzy bathrobe.

It's Time to Go to Bed. Joyce Segal. Illustrated by Robin Eaton. Doubleday. Unpaged (32 pp.).

This book presents the most familiar but often unsuccessful excuses for delaying bedtime. Different animals present each excuse. Young goldfish, for instance, would not ask for a drink of water. The text is cleverly split with the admonition on one page and the excuse facing it.

Jill the Pill. Julie Castiglia. Illustrations by Steven Kellogg. McElderry/Atheneum. 32 pp.

Jill is nine years older than her brother, Pat the Brat. Text and illustrations combine to present a familiar situation to all those living under the thumb of an older sibling.

The King at the Door. Brock Cole. Illustrated by the author. Doubleday. Unpaged (32 pp.).

Dressed like a beggar while surveying his kingdom on foot, the exhausted king asks a servant boy, Baggit, for a drink. Baggit's master refuses and Baggit unselfishly furnishes his personal share. Baggit's goodness is rewarded and the master's mistrust ridiculed in a climactic final page.

The King's Flower. Mitsumasa Anno. Illustrations by the author. Philomel. Unpaged (32 pp.).

"Biggest is best" thought the king, and so everything in the kingdom was larger than life. Not until the king tried in vain to grow a giant tulip did he realize the beauty of small things. The colorful illustrations helped children write stories of what might happen if things in their environment became gigantic.

Kittymouse. Sumiko. Illustrated by the author. Harcourt Brace Jovanovich. Unpaged (30 pp.).

The full-sized, detailed, earth-colored illustrations add much to this story, told from the animals' perspective, of a kitten who was raised by a mouse family. The kitten is perfectly content until the decision to move the mouse family to a big house reveals her true origin.

Laura's Story. Beatrice Schenk de Regniers. Illustrations by Jack Kent. Atheneum. 32 pp.

"When I was big and you were little," begins Laura when her mother asks for a story. Laura imagines losing her tiny mother through a hole in her pocket and, after a series of adventures, rescuing her and bringing her home to safety.

Little Koala.   Suzanne Noguere and Tony Chen. Illustrated by Tony Chen. Holt, Rinehart & Winston. Unpaged (32 pp.). Paper ed., Random House.

An animal story especially for young children. The details of the koala's life are presented simply, showing the female nursing and carrying the baby in its pouch. A little excitement occurs as a dingo chases the mother koala up a tree.

Maggie and the Goodbye Gift.   Sue Milord. Illustrated by Jerry Milord. Lothrop, Lee & Shepard. 40 pp.

Moving seems fun to Maggie until she arrives in her new home, only to realize her old friends have been replaced by strangers. She tests the goodbye gift, a can opener, and thus engenders a neighborhood feast.

The Magic Meatballs.   Alan Yaffe. Illustrations by Karen Born Andersen. Dial. 38 pp.

Marvin is tired of having his parents and siblings nagging him and ordering him around. He sees his opportunity for revenge when a stranger offers him some magic meat—one bite and his wishes come true!

Messy.   Barbara Bottner. Illustrations by the author. Delacorte. Unpaged (32 pp.).

Harriet (alias Harry) is the messiest 6-year-old in town. However, being chosen to be the princess in her dance recital motivates her to become neat, a condition that lasts only as long as the performance.

Miss Kiss and the Nasty Beast.   Lady McCrady. Illustrated by the author. Holiday House. Unpaged (32 pp.).

Miss Kiss tells of the happy life in Kiss City until the Nasty Beast begins to steal everyone's favorite things. Even her best friends, Twinkletoes and Monkeyface, are missing. The city is in a panic until Miss Kiss tames the Nasty Beast with a kiss.

Mooch the Messy Meets Prudence The Neat.   Marjorie Weinman Sharmat. Illustrations by Ben Shecter. Coward, McCann & Geoghegan. 64 pp.

Mooch the Messy lives happily in his messy hole under a hill in Boston until his new neighbor Prudence moves next door and becomes determined to clean things up. Charcoal drawings accented with red humorously depict the contrasting life-styles of the bright-eyed rats.

Mr. Goat's Bad Good Idea.   Marileta Robinson. Illustrated by Arthur Getz. Crowell. 46 pp.

The animal characters in these three humorous tales are courteous and helpful to each other. Their clothing, food and shelter reflect the rural Navajo tradition. Mr. Goat tries to build his roof the "easy" way and Grandfather Sheep keeps his old hat because "two hats are better than one."

Mrs. Gaddy and the Ghost.   Wilson Gage. Illustrations by Marilyn Hafner. Greenwillow. 60 pp.

Mrs. Gaddy tries to get rid of the ghost in her kitchen with a broom, bug spray, fire, and a mousetrap, but the ghost doesn't leave. She finally writes a letter requesting the ghost to depart, but his sobs cause her to reconsider and decide that his noisy night presence is very good company.

My Brother Never Feeds the Cat.   Reynold Ruffins. Illustrated by the author. Scribner's. Unpaged (32 pp.).

Four-year-old Anna complains of having to do all the work while brother Barney never does anything. In one scene Anna is told "a job gets done by anyone who can do it. There's no boy or girl about it." The last page shows Anna hugging cuddly infant Barney.

The New Girl at School. Judy Delton. Illustrations by Lillian Hoban. E. P. Dutton. Unpaged (32 pp.).

"Give it time, it'll get better" is the theme of this story about a girl's first week at a new school. Marcia has negative feelings when her work is not put on display but is elated when befriended.

Oliver Button Is a Sissy. Tomie de Paola. Illustrated by the author. Harcourt Brace Jovanovich. Unpaged (48 pp.). Paper ed., Harcourt Brace Jovanovich.

Although Oliver is a boy with many talents, none of them are considered masculine—hence his "sissy" nickname. Failure in the popularity department causes Oliver to dread going to school. The triumphant ending elicited smiles of satisfaction from the children.

One-Eyed Jake. Pat Hutchins. Illustrations by the author. Greenwillow. Unpaged (32 pp.).

The brilliantly illustrated double-page spreads enhance a rather simple story. The three members of One-Eyed Jake's pirate crew are a cook who wishes he were on a passenger ship, a bosun who wants to steer a cargo boat, and a small black cabin boy who wishes he were on a fishing boat. As the story develops, each gets his wish.

Portly McSwine. James Marshall. Illustrations by the author. Houghton Mifflin. 40 pp.

Portly McSwine is planning a huge party to celebrate National Snout Day. Being a pessimist, he becomes worried about every detail of the event. Of course, his concerns are unnecessary because his party is a grand success.

Robot-Bot-Bot. Fernando Krahn. Illustrated by the author. E. P. Dutton. Unpaged (32 pp.).

This popular story without words is told with action-filled, cartoon-style, black-and-white drawings. Father brings home a robot to do housework. His curious little girl investigates the robot's innards, causing it to go haywire. The final scene shows robot playing Ping-Pong with the girl.

Ruby. Amy Aitken. Illustrations by author. Bradbury. Unpaged (32 pp.).

Ruby is tired of her humdrum life and decides to be a famous writer. While her friend Axel waits to help her, she decides to become a famous artist; while Axel goes home for blue paint, Ruby decides to become a famous movie star. "Even the President will want an autograph," so she decides to campaign for the presidency.

There's an Elephant in the Garage. Douglas F. Davis. Illustrated by Steven Kellogg. E. P. Dutton. Unpaged (32 pp.).

After Zelda the cat is banished from the house, April Janice Jones decides to leave home with Zelda and hunt wild animals. The book records their safari.

Three Ducks Went Wandering. Ron Roy. Illustrations by Paul Galdone. Clarion. Unpaged (32 pp.). Paper ed., Scholastic Book Services.

In this simple tale of an exploring trip taken by three ducklings, there is a great deal of humor, suspense and surprise. Once the ducklings leave the barnyard, they manage to evade the charge of a bull, the jaws of a fox, and several other hungry predators.

The Tiger-Skin Rug. Gerald Rose. Illustrated by the author. Prentice-Hall. Unpaged (32 pp.).

A humorous and enjoyable story about a not-too-ferocious tiger who finds a home in the Rajah's palace. His problem is how to keep anyone from realizing he is alive and not just a rug.

A Treeful of Pigs. Arnold Lobel. Illustrations by Anita Lobel. Greenwillow. Unpaged (32 pp.).

A tree full of *pigs*? That's just one of the pranks the farmer's wife must resort to in her attempts to get her lazy husband to help around the farm. Children of all ages appreciate the humor in this folktale and the charming, colorful illustrations which help to bring it to life.

A Very Young Circus Flyer. Jill Krementz. Photographs by the author. Knopf. Unpaged (110 pp.).

Nine-year-old Tato, youngest member of the famous Flying Farfans, conducts a tour of the circus. Splendid photographs, both in black and white and color, help the reader learn about riding elephants, costume design, the clown workshop, and many other facets of the Greatest Show on Earth.

We Hide, You Seek. Jose Aruego and Ariane Dewey. Illustrated by the authors. Greenwillow. Unpaged (32 pp.).

When the animals of the jungle decide to play hide-and-seek, the red rhino has quite a job finding them all. Aruego and Dewey's brilliantly colored, crowded, double-page spreads tell without words of the camouflaged hiding places of jungle creatures.

What Should a Hippo Wear? Jane Sutton. Illustrated by Lynn Munsinger. Houghton Mifflin. 32 pp.

When Bertha the Hippo tries to dress for the jungle ball, her giraffe date doesn't even recognize her. Bertha's attempts at dressing up are humorous enough to cause children to laugh out loud, while the story's happy ending is wonderfully satisfying.

Where Can an Elephant Hide? David McPhail. Illustrated by the author. Doubleday. Unpaged (30 pp.).

The pale, cartoon-style illustrations combined with humorous dialogue tell how some animals of the jungle protect themselves. When hunters appear, all the elephants hide, but Morris doesn't know how. Finally, a bird suggests Morris hide in water with only his trunk protruding.

Which Is the Witch? W.K. Jasner. Illustrated by Victoria Chess. Pantheon. Unpaged (48 pp.).

After being teased by brother Nick for liking "witchy things," Jenny, in Halloween witch garb, decides to trade places with real witch Peckity Hecate. But once in the witch's haunt, Jenny shudders at demands for toads and bats' wings while Hecate the witch shudders also as dad pats her on the back and suggests she take off her mask.

Middle Grades (Over 10 Years)
1975

Ben and Annie. Joan Tate. Illustrations by Judith Gwyn Brown. Doubleday. 80 pp.

Annie, a 13-year-old cripple, and Ben, an 11-year-old boy who lives in the duplex above her, communicate on an intercom. Eventually Ben gets permission from Annie's mother to wheel her to the dime store, but the events that follow are not all happy. Easy reading and a short story.

A Billion for Boris. Mary Rodgers. Harper & Row. 216 pp.
Boris and Ann find out the hard way that it really would not be good to know what is going to happen tomorrow. Funny, with characters who talk so the reader hears them. Great potential for discussing the variety of responses readers will express. Contemporary with a happy ending.

Blubber. Judy Blume. Bradbury. 158 pp.
Here is another favorite from Judy Blume. The book never rests. It talks about childhood cruelty and how it can feel (and how it can backfire). Boys and girls who usually do not read on their own want to read *Blubber.* Children laugh out loud when it's read to them.

Blue Fin. Colin Thiele. Harper & Row. 248 pp.
Action and danger combine with a boy's struggle to prove himself in the eyes of his father so that he can earn a place on the fishing crew of the *Blue Fin.* This 1970 Australian Book of the Year deals with development of courage and self-reliance.

Bright Sunset: The Story of an Indian Girl. Ruth Wheeler. Illustrations by Dorothy Matteson. Lothrop, Lee & Shepard. 127 pp.
Sensitive account of a young girl's struggle to pass the tribal ritual into womanhood and learn to face fear. Oral tales of an Indian named Sunset inspired the authentic lore.

A Dance to Still Music. Barbara Corcoran. Illustrations by Charles Robinson. Atheneum. 184 pp.
This is a sensitive story of a young girl coping with her feelings of isolation when she loses her hearing. Feeling rejected, she runs away from home and finds refuge with Josie, who helps her gain confidence to handle her handicap.

The Devil's Storybook. Story and illustrations by Natalie Babbitt. Farrar, Straus & Giroux. 105 pp.
Children laugh at the unique situations—the devil coming and going from his place in Hell and causing all sorts of trouble for good and bad people alike. It's great to read aloud during those short empty spaces in a day, a chapter at a time. Children read it to each other or silently.

Dr. Elizabeth: A Biography of the First Woman Doctor. Patricia Clapp. Lothrop, Lee & Shepard. 155 pp.
A diary-style account of the first woman doctor in the United States, reporting the challenges, victories and bitter disappointments in Elizabeth Blackwell's life. She pioneered in fighting for women's right to serve humanity.

Greenwitch. Susan Cooper. McElderry/Atheneum. 153 pp.
In a sequel to *A Dark Is Rising,* Will and Merriman meet again to ward off attacks of evil. Strong characterization is developed through action and dialogue. Higher-level reading skills of inference and hypothesizing can be developed here.

Laws and Trials That Created History. Brandt Aymar and Edward Sagarin. Crown. 222 pp. Introduction, bibliography.
The topic is appealing. A teacher can help children gain a perspective about American history by considering a motif like trials and tracing it though the years. The Salem witchcraft trials and that of Angela Davis were most appealing.

Midnight Is a Place. Joan Aiken. Viking. 286 pp.
Aiken's tongue-in-cheek story of two English orphans reflects Dickens and

1840 England. Fourteen-year-old Lucas's life with his unpleasant guardian is enriched when an unusual girl enters to change things. Strong plot and characterization.

Modern Football Superstars.   Bill Gutman. Illustrated with photographs. Dodd, Mead. 127 pp.

Much appeal for both boys and girls in stories that are relatively short and easy to read. May lead to more reading about certain individuals or to seeking related sources of material about the stars.

My Black Me: A Beginning Book of Black Poetry.   Edited by Arnold Adoff. E. P. Dutton. 95 pp. Introduction, author and first-line indices.

A collection of poetry written by recognized Black poets. A sense of the Black experience springs through the work.

Philip Hall Likes Me. I Reckon Maybe.   Bette Green. Illustrations by Charles Lilly. Dial. 141 pp.

This is a warm story of a black family in Arkansas and a school girl's universal escapades with clubs, parties and competition. Upper-grade Black girls become attached to the book and claim it as their own.

Rosie and Michael.   Judith Viorst. Illustrations by Lorna Tomei. Atheneum. 40 pp.

Although it looks "younger," this book appeals mostly to upper elementary children because they remember friendships and feelings like those Rosie and Michael share. Children read it silently and share it with a friend.

Street Gangs, Yesterday and Today.   James Haskins. Illustrated with prints and photographs. Hastings House. 154 pp. Introduction, glossary of slang, index.

The boys loved it for its great detail about gangs in history and in the modern era. Photographs and a glossary of slang terms help to sell the book to children. They read parts of the book and share it constantly.

The Tiger's Bones and Other Plays for Children.   Ted Hughes. Illustrations by Alan E. Cober. Viking. 141 pp.

Five unusual poetic plays to be read aloud or to be staged. Could best be used by an interested group of better students who already have done the usual plays for reading aloud.

The Way Things Are and Other Poems.   Myra Cohn Livingston. Illustrations by Jenni Oliver. McElderry/Atheneum. 45 pp.

Poetry depicts a wide variety of moods. Applicable to modern, everyday living to which the kids can easily relate. Used in language classes for promoting discussion and giving a bird's-eye view of individual values.

Whistle in the Graveyard: Folktales to Chill Your Bones.   Maria Leach. Illustrations by Ken Rinciari. Viking. 131 pp. notes and bibliography.

Fourth graders especially loved these mysteries. Recommended for below-grade-level readers in upper grades because of high interest, easy readability and brevity.

Wildfire.   Mavis Thorpe Clark. Macmillian. 219 pp.

A fire in the Australian grasslands brings about heroism among the members of the "mob." Suspense, fear and terror ring through strong dialogue, action and characterization.

The Winds of Time.   Barbara Corcoran. Illustrations by Gail Owens. Atheneum. 169 pp.

Emotional tale of a young girl's effort to free herself from a domineering uncle and learn to trust adults again. Action-packed and suspenseful story shows that kindness often comes where least expected.

1976

The Baron's Hostage. Geoffrey Trease. Nelson. 160 pp.

The Baron's War in thirteenth-century England is used as the intriguing background for this story of two young people. Michael is chosen to serve Henry III's son Edward who is held as a hostage by the cruel leader of the barons. Arlette, a 14-year-old orphaned heiress, is a ward of the baron's wife and she joins Edward's party before the battle of Evesham. The wholesome romance of Michael and Arlette is woven skillfully into authentic historic facts.

The Borrowed House. Hilda van Stockum. Farrar, Straus & Giroux. 215 pp.

This World War II story is not only a good presentation of an important historical period but provides material for discussions concerning courage, prejudice and the danger of unquestioning acceptance of an ideology. The adventure and mystery interwoven with serious themes will lure even reluctant readers to this book.

Bruno. Achim Bröger. Illustrations by Ronald Himler. Morrow. 160 pp.

Seventeen stories tell about a timid, imaginative man whose dreams and wishes come true in the funniest ways. Subtle satire; stories work for oral reading and for language study.

The Code & Cipher Book. Jane Sarnoff and Reynold Ruffins. Illustrations by Reynold Ruffins. Scribner's. 40 pp.

An attractive and varied set of ciphers and codes has been selected for the book. Historical episodes and events and ways of using codes in Elizabethan England and the Middle Ages are depicted in witty illustrations. The title makes this one a self-starter.

The Dark Didn't Catch Me. Crystal Thrasher. Atheneum/McElderry. 182 pp.

A superb book depicting life in the hills of southern Indiana during the depression of the '30s. Seely and her younger brother Jamie adjust to a life that their mother openly and bitterly despises. They face deep despair and grim realities with strength and courage beyond their years. A compassionate story that older readers recommend to their friends.

Dorrie's Book. Marilyn Sachs. Illustrations by Anne Sachs. Doubleday. 144 pp.

This is a very funny, appealing book for middle readers. Dorrie is 11, an only child who lives what she considers to be the perfect life, in a lovely apartment, with parents who are perfect companions. Then her mother has triplets, an event that abruptly shatters Dorrie's idyll. Dorrie's attempts to cope with life among the babies are easily appreciated by any child who has either younger or older siblings. A springboard into talking and writing about "the baby at my house," or "I was a baby."

Dragonwings. Laurence Yep. Harper & Row. 248 pp.

Well-researched historical novel set in early 20th century San Francisco Chinatown, giving vivid details of Chinese folklore, racial relationships, the 1906 earthquake and a fictionalized account of a Chinese man who built a flying machine with help from the Wright brothers. Excellent discussion material countering Chinese-American stereotypes. Received 1976 IRA Children's Book Award.

Fast Sam, Cool Clyde and Stuff. Walter Dean Myers. Viking. 190 pp.

A funny, fast-paced story of teenagers in the ghetto. The characters are memorable: amusing, troubled, embarrassed, triumphant, angry—they run the gamut of adolescent emotions. The plot is an exciting one revolving around a dope ring; the day-to-day episodes of life at school and at home are done well. This is an excellent portrayal of warm relationships of family and friends, and a fine stimulus to discussion and personal writing.

The Figure in the Shadows. John Bellairs. Illustrations by Mercer Mayer. Dial. 155 pp.
Orphaned Lewis lives with Uncle Jonathan and finds a good friend in courageous Rose Rita. When he finds an old coin in a trunk, he hopes it is an amulet that will ward off evil. Instead, Lewis brings forth the shadowed figure of a ghost and finds himself in great danger. Good for discussion of techniques used to build suspense.

The Ghost Belonged to Me. Richard Peck. Viking. 183 pp.
This tale is truly humorous, even witty at times. The story holds together with no lapses into contrivance. Set in 1900 in the area from the upper Mississippi Valley to New Orleans, it satisfies requests for mystery and adventure.

The Glad Man. Gloria Gonzalez. Knopf. 160 pp.
This is a good story about how the law applies to everyone even when it might seem better if a law were overlooked. Kids like the way children worked out a plausible solution to a problem and got a job done against many odds.

Going Back. Penelope Lively. E. P. Dutton. 128 pp.
The present is never lost in telling of village life in England during World War II. Skillful technique results in reconstructing without being nostalgic. Many possibilities for working with children in literature and in social studies. The author writes superbly.

Good-By to Stony Crick. Kathryn Borland and Helen Speicher. Illustrations by Deanne Hollinger. McGraw-Hill. 138 pp.
Children can identify with Jeremy as he bears the taunts of new classmates and poor treatment from a teacher who has little patience with a mountain child new to the city. A good book for showing how self-respect can endure even amid harsh living conditions when neighbors and friends look out for one another.

Ladies of the Gothics: Tales of Romance and Terror by the Gentle Sex. Selected by Seon Manley and Gogo Lewis. Lothrop, Lee & Shepard. 224 pp.
This collection of sinister short stories provides a unique look at women's writings of the last two centuries. Suited for teacher read-aloud or individual pupil use, it is a fine addition to a literature class.

Mr. McFadden's Hallowe'en. Rumer Godden. Viking. 127 pp.
Touching and involving story of a young Scottish girl's friendship and dedication to a lonely old man. Read the first chapter to your fifth- or sixth- graders today. Tomorrow you will need several copies. A combination of sophistication for the 12-year-old-going-on-19 and the fantasy needed for the 12-year-old-still-6. It's thought provoking, simple, refreshing, and as one sixth-grade class put it, "It's really neat!"

A Present for Yanya. Peggy Mann and Katica Prusina. Illustrations by Douglas Gorsline. Random House. 119 pp.
Life is difficult and lonely for Yanya in post–World War II Yugoslavia until she ingeniously earns the money to buy a beautiful and extravagant doll. An involving story as well as an excellent background to Europe's change of life style after a war. Good for social studies.

A Second Springtime. Gordon Cooper. Nelson. 223 pp.
An authentic story of one of six girls to be transported from an orphanage in

England to adoptive families in Nova Scotia in the 1870s. Hester's adjustment to her new life and problems makes this an appealing story. Her friend Bethanne, also placed in an adoptive home, did not fare as well as Hester and this adds flavor to the story. Relatively easy reading.

Teetoncey and Ben O'Neal.   Theodore Taylor. Illustrations by Richard Cuffari. Doubleday. 184 pp.

This is the second volume of a trilogy about an English girl who is shipwrecked on Cape Hatteras and cared for by a Hatteras family. The vivid detail of the unusual setting and the well-drawn characters make this a good novel of interpersonal relationships for older readers. Excellent supplement for social studies and geography.

The Transfigured Hart.   Jane Yolen. Illustrations by Donna Diamond. Crowell. 86 pp.

Depending on the interest of the group, this book fosters many discussions about legends, because of the unicorn; about ecology, because of the beautiful woods and pool; about hunting, because of the two different factions in the book; and about boy-girl relations, because of Richard and Heather.

Tuck Everlasting.   Natalie Babbitt. Farrar, Straus & Giroux. 139 pp.

The promise of everlasting life from a magical spring of water is used as a unifying thread in this story of the Tuck family. A 10-year-old neighbor, Winnie, discovers the spring and nearly drinks from it without knowing of its power. Strong characterization and flawless prose qualify this book for literary study.

The Way It Was–1876.   Suzanne Hilton. Illustrated with old prints and photographs. Westminster. 216 pp.

Children love it for its great detail about everyday life 100 years ago. Old prints, photographs and diary excerpts were read and shared constantly. In great demand as a fine source for unusual historical information.

Weakfoot.   Linda Cline. Lothrop, Lee & Shepard. 160 pp.

Continuing excitement makes this book one in which the reader is compelled to go on. Superb writing causes the reader to experience the danger and suspense throughout the text. Definitive characterization provides numerous possibilities for sharing the book creatively. One child remarked enthusiastically, "It should belong in a book section with *Savage Sam* and *Old Yeller!*"

Winter Wheat.   Jeanne Williams. G. P. Putnam's. 157 pp.

Exciting and realistic story of a Mennonite family's settlement in Kansas in the 1800s and how people share work and become friends. A good period piece for those children who have devoured *The Little House on the Prairie* series. Good to use for comparing accounts of historical periods.

1977

The Accident.   Carol Carrick. Illustrations by Donald Carrick. Seabury. Unpaged (32 pp.).

An understanding father helps Christopher master his grief at his dog's death. A warm, realistic story that evokes much heated response from readers. A fine book to stimulate class discussion of death and responsibility.

The Against Taffy Sinclair Club.   Betsy Haynes. Nelson. 125 pp.

Five girls form a club to organize their jealousy of and disdain for Taffy

Sinclair, who is intelligent, pretty, and the first in their class to develop breasts. Eventually the girls decide that self-improvement is more productive and "a lot more fun than hating someone." Realistic scenes of childhood hostility. Also appropriate for older readers.

All the Children Were Sent Away. Sheila Garrigue. Bradbury. 171 pp.

At the age of 8, Sarah is sent away from her home and parents in England. She is an evacuee, fleeing the bombings of 1940. Aboard the ship bound for Canada she finds other problems: a disapproving guardian and a torpedo scare. The book has an autobiographical tone and shows appealing characters living in a troubled time.

Beat the Turtle Drum. Constance C. Greene. Illustrated by Donna Diamond. Viking. 119 pp.

Constance Greene has written a touching story about a family facing tragedy. Kate learns the supportive value of friendship and develops an understanding of how people cope with grief. The book is useful in classroom discussions of human relationships.

The Big Cats. Herbert S. Zim. Illustrated by Dot Barlowe. Morrow. 64 pp.

A revised edition of Herbert Zim's 1955 *Big Cats*. Detailed factual information provides supplemental material for a social studies/science unit on big cats and their habitats as well as providing a basis for discussing population growth and human needs in relation to endangering the cat species.

The Case of the Nervous Newsboy. E. W. Hildick. Illustrations by Lisl Weil. Macmillan. 106 pp.

Jack McGurk is the leader as he and his friends solve this mystery. The story does not make great demands on reading ability, yet there is enough action to hold the interest of students who are often reluctant to stay with a book.

A Chocolate Moose for Dinner. Written and illustrated by Fred Gwynne. Windmill. 64 pp. Paper ed., Windmill.

Vivid illustrations picture thirty-two examples of a child's misinterpretations of words. "Mommy says she had a chocolate moose for dinner" shows a huge brown moose sitting at a table. "Daddy says there should be more car pools" features cars diving and swimming in a huge swimming pool. Children found the pictures of "on the lamb," "in the pen," "gorilla war," and others hilarious.

The Church Mice Spread Their Wings. Graham Oakley. Atheneum. 32 pp.

Sampson the church cat is pressured into escorting a party of church mice into the country for fresh air. Numerous adventures culminate in an owl's capture of Humphrey and Arthur. Deposited in the church tower, the two mice escape via airplanes made of hymnal pages. The humorous tale and intricately detailed color illustrations invite and delight readers.

Clyde Monster. Robert L. Crowe. Illustrated by Kay Chorao. E. P. Dutton. Unpaged (27 pp.).

If you've ever been afraid of the dark, *Clyde Monster* will bolster your courage and help you laugh at yourself as you learn to see the situation from the monster's viewpoint. One child summarized, "Clyde was scared like I am sometimes." Kay Chorao's illustrations enhance the story. This is a great read-aloud book for young readers.

Danbury's Burning! The Story of Sybil Ludington's Ride. Anne Grant. Illustrated by Pat Howell. Walck, 47 pp.

This fast-paced retelling of an exciting ride in 1777 to warn American colonists of the approach of British soldiers jogged the interest of boys and girls. "Short," "good pictures," "fun to read," said the students.

The Difference of Ari Stein.   Charlotte Herman. Illustrated by Ben Shecter. Harper & Row. 150 pp.

Jewish Ari moves to a mixed neighborhood and tries to be one of the boys. He discovers that, while he needs friends, he can't give up all the things that make him an individual. This was enjoyed for its insight into Jewish customs and beliefs. Good for social studies and comparative religion discussions.

Everyone Knows What a Dragon Looks Like.   Jay Williams. Illustrations by Mercer Mayer. Four Winds. Unpaged (28 pp.).

The leaders of the city of Wu are faced with the destruction of their town by the Wild Horsemen of the North. Their only hope is to be saved by a dragon. While the leaders argue about what a dragon looks like, humble Han treats a short, fat, bald old stranger kindly and saves the city. A traditional tale illustrated beautifully and with humor.

Getting Along in Your Family.   Phyllis Reynolds Naylor. Illustrated by Rick Cooley. Abingdon. 107 pp.

This book, which explores various aspects of living in a family, helps children understand the dynamics of human relationships. The discussions of common family problems let the child see how others have faced difficult situations and learned to accept or adapt to the needs of others.

Ghosts.   Seymour Simon. Drawings by Stephen Gammell. Lippincott. 76 pp. Paper ed., J. B. Lippincott.

Children enjoy the realism of these nine ghost stories and the fact that they remain unsolved. This is an excellent book to use by reading the first chapter and then watching the children enjoy the rest independently.

Good Work, Amelia Bedelia.   Peggy Parish. Pictures by Lynn Sweat. Greenwillow. Unpaged (56 pp.).

Amelia Bedelia continues her escapades as housekeeper in this latest book by Peggy Parish. Children enjoy anticipating Amelia's mistakes. "Amelia didn't know the meaning of words it's important to know," observed one child. The text lends itself to a study of word play and puns.

The Goof That Won the Pennant.   Jonah Kalb. Illustrated by Sandy Kassin. Houghton Mifflin. 103 pp.

Based on an actual goof in professional baseball, this fictional baseball story is especially popular with young boys. The action is fast and the characters are developed with humor and realism. Baseball skills and physical fitness are emphasized throughout the book.

Horatio's Birthday.   Eleanor Clymer. Illustrated by Robert Quakenbush. Atheneum. 60 pp.

Horatio, a large, striped, middle-aged cat, is displeased during preparations to celebrate his birthday. He sneaks a night out, keeping up with the younger cats with some difficulty. Experience helps him rout a fearsome dog, and he takes home his own birthday present—a small lady cat. Cat lovers loved this.

It's Not Fair.   Charlotte Zolotow. Illustrations by William Pène du Bois. Harper & Row. 32 pp.

Red curly hair, a tendency to get fat, and a teacher who insists on Absolute Silence: those are the problems of the heroine in this lyrical, meaningful book. But her basic difficulty is that she envies Martha, who suffers none of these encumbrances. The author and illustrator give the theme of envy just the right tone for pleasant but thoughtful consideration by the envy-prone reader.

Kickle Snifters and Other Fearsome Critters. Alvin Schwartz. Illustrations by Glen Rounds. J. B. Lippincott. 64 pp.

The snawfus, the squonk, and the whing-whang join kickle snifters (small fellows who live inside old men's beards) in this well-composed, carefully documented description of twenty-six American folklore creatures.

Knock Knocks: The Most Ever. William Cole. Illustrations by Mike Thaler. Watts. Unpaged (96 pp.). Paper ed., Dell.

The author points out that knock knock jokes "stimulate a child's imagination and interest in the language. They are an introduction to punning and to the delights of English." That seems justification enough for this pleasant, easily read trip through knock knock land.

Lizzie Lies a Lot. Elizabeth Levy. Illustrated by John Wallner. Delacorte. 102 pp. Paper ed., Dell Yearling.

Lizzie finds lying very easy until she realizes it is harder and harder to go back and erase the lies. Her self-image and her relationship with her best friend suffer. Students enjoyed this book both as independent and oral reading. Excellent discussions on values ensue.

McBroom Tells a Lie. Sid Fleischman. Illustrated by Walter Lorraine. Atlantic/Little, Brown. 48 pp.

Sid Fleischman presents another easy-to-read McBroom tall tale so outlandish that even young children love to have it read to them. Though Josh McBroom begins his story by admitting he once told a lie, not until the last page does the reader learn what the lie was.

The Most Delicious Camping Trip Ever. Alice Bach. Illustrated by Steven Kellogg. Harper & Row. 46 pp.

Children fully appreciated the problems of packing for a camping trip, whether they sided with Oliver, the gourmet bear cub, or Ronald, the scientific cub. And accommodation, as practiced by Aunt Bear, struck a responsive chord. Not only funny, with especially humorous illustrations, but a discussion-sparker.

Periwinkle. Written and illustrated by Roger Duvoisin. Knopf. Unpaged (28 pp.).

Every child who has ever felt like an outsider can identify with Periwinkle, the giraffe, as he learns to communicate with someone as unique as himself. One child summarized, "This book taught us a good lesson—how to make friends."

The 17 Gerbils of Class 4A. William H. Hooks. Illustrated by Joel Schick. Coward, McCann & Geoghegan. 56 pp.

Taking care of a pair of gerbils in a classroom can lead to knowledge and humor. It also results in more gerbils. A very popular animal book, good for any class that studies animals. Children love the story and accompanying sketches. The book integrates all areas of the curriculum.

Somebody Else's Child. Roberta Silman. Illustrated by Chris Conover. Warne. 64 pp. Paper ed., Dell.

When the school bus driver first called Peter "Smiley," he had no idea how much Peter would idolize him—nor how much he would hurt Peter when he said adoption was "bringing up somebody else's child." A sensitive, effective treatment of why adopted children "belong" in a family.

Warton and Morton. Russell E. Erickson. Illustrated by Lawrence Di Fiori. Lothrop, Lee & Shepard. 64 pp.

Two toad brothers set out on a vacation trip. After having been separated by a sudden storm, Warton is entertained by muskrats, Morton by beavers. When they're united, they settle the feud between their hosts. Humor and action make this excellent for reading aloud as well as for reading by individual chucklers.

The Well-Mannered Balloon. Nancy Willard. Illustrated by Haig and Regina Shekerjian. Harcourt Brace Jovanovich. Unpaged (28 pp.).

James's balloon comes to life as a demanding, insatiable pirate. Children approve of the way James handles the problem and enjoy the humor as they anticipate the satisfying conclusion. Younger readers like this story when read aloud.

What's the Big Idea, Ben Franklin? Jean Fritz. Illustrated by Margot Tomes. Coward, McCann & Geoghegan. 48 pp.

Jean Fritz again presents a fine upper-primary biography on an early American—Ben Franklin—and his many inventions. The author's detailed factual "notes" as well as the illustrator's accurate drawings of inventions stimulate further search for information about the man with "a twinkle in his eye and a new idea always in his mind."

When Lucy Went Away. G. Max Ross. Illustrated by Ingrid Fetz. E. P. Dutton. Unpaged (26 pp.).

A sensitive treatment of a common problem: a boy relates experiences shared with his pet cat and fantasizes explanations for her disappearance. The pen-and-ink drawings fit the mood of the text.

Will You Sign Here, John Hancock? Jean Fritz. Illustrations by Trina Schart Hyman. Coward, McCann & Geoghegan. 47 pp.

John Hancock's life and accomplishments are pictured in a human and humorous manner. Children enjoy reading about the feats and failures of a famous person. This biography encourages further reading about other famous people.

Zag: A Search through the Alphabet. Written and illustrated by Robert Tallon. Holt, Rinehart & Winston. 64 pp.

A zany search for Zag starts on an airplane flown by an apple and in a boat with bread, continues in a frying pan with three furious frankfurters; an old teabag on a telephone refuses to help, but a yo-yo over yonder finally locates him. For the zany of any age. Middle-grade children appreciate the humor; older children use the pattern as a writing starter.

1978

The Big Orange Splot. Daniel Manus Pinkwater. Illustrated by the author. Hastings House. 32 pp. Paper ed., Scholastic Book Services.

When his neighbors ask Mr. Plumbean to remove the big orange splot from his roof, Plumbean constructs a jungle scene instead. Gradually his neighbor's horror gives way to self-expression and they decorate their own houses. Children love the bright colors and original designs.

Charles Bear and the Mystery of the Forest. Douglas Adamson. Illustrated by the author. Houghton Mifflin. 87 pp.

During his vacation in the mountains, Charles Bear tries to locate wild bears, but instead he meets an enigmatic bear named Willy and an even more puzzling, nonspeaking bear who rides around in a balloon. There are mysterious happenings, never explained. Middle-grade readers called the book a winner, agreeing with Charles Bear that the events were exciting despite (or because of) their strangeness.

The Frog Band and the Onion Seller. Jim Smith. Illustrated by the author. Little, Brown. Unpaged (32 pp.).
Hilarious adventures, akin to those of the Pink Panther, befall Alphonse le Flic as he rides his bicycle atop a submarine across the English Channel into the English countryside to locate a hidden treasure. Disguised as an onion seller, he is pursued by a band of frogs. There are underground scenes in a monastery and all sorts of absurd details, documented by lively drawings. Young readers love the author's ability to spin a wild yarn.

Guess Who My Favorite Person Is. Byrd Baylor. Illustrated by Robert Andrew Parker. Scribner's. Unpaged (32 pp.).
A chance meeting of a man and a girl in an alfalfa field leads to a game of "tell-what-your-favorite-thing-is." From kitten fur to falling stars, things to touch, see smell, etc., are explored. Readers respond to the quiet affection and immediately begin their own game.

Half a Kingdom. Ann McGovern. Illustrated by Nola Langner. Warne. Unpaged (38 pp.).
Icelandic folklore often contains active, clever heroines. This version of an Icelandic folk story also contains up-to-date humor, which adds substantially to students' enjoyment. When Prince Lini refuses for the ninety-ninth time to marry a troll, he is warned, "The end is near for you," but it isn't. Signy, his rescuer and the book's practical-minded heroine, has much better things in store for him.

Harriet and the Runaway Book. Johanna Johnston. Illustrated by Ronald Himler. Harper & Row. 80 pp.
As a young girl, Harriet Beecher Stowe wrote stories and dreamed of freedom for Negro slaves. Her later novel, *Uncle Tom's Cabin*, became famous and was even said to have helped start the Civil War. This is an inspiring story about a woman who had tremendous impact during a time when most women had little influence.

Helga's Dowry: A Troll Love Story. Tomie de Paola. Illustrated by the author. Harcourt Brace Jovanovich. Unpaged (32 pp.). Paper ed., Harcourt Brace Jovanovich.
Helga, lovely by troll standards, is an orphan with no dowry to seal a marriage contract with the handsome gold-digging Lars. She works like a whirlwind to earn a dowry of cows and gold and land, only to discover that moonstruck Lars is fickle. In the end a liberated Helga has outgrown Lars and moves on to a bigger and better life. The magic of Troll-land and the humorous de Paola style in word and picture are wonderfully combined in this funny tale of human foibles.

Jane, Wishing. Tobi Tobias. Illustrated by Trina Schart Hyman. Viking. Unpaged (48 pp.).
Jane wishes that everything about herself—her home, her pets, everything— were different. Finally, with the help of her family, she learns to live with what

she has. A universal problem that is realistically handled. Children sympathize with Jane and enjoy the full-color illustrations of her dream world.

The Juice: Football's Superstar O. J. Simpson. Dick Belsky. Walck/McKay. 58 pp.
O. J. Simpson was one of the University of South California's finest running backs when he won the Heismann trophy in 1968. Although his career with the Buffalo Bills began poorly, he soon became the highest paid professional football player as well as a successful sportscaster and actor. This exciting, fast-paced account will appeal even to those who aren't sports fans. Illustrated with photogaphs.

The Mariah Delany Lending Library Disaster. Sheila Greenwald. Illustrated by the author. Houghton Mifflin. 123 pp.
Mariah learns the library profession the hard way: she lends her parents' books for a fee and then discovers that neither the books nor the fees are easily collected. In its truly comic way, the story tells quite a bit about the joys of reading, if not of lending. "Super! Loved it!" responded readers.

Mary McLeod Bethune. Eloise Greenfield. Illustrated by Jerry Pinkney. Crowell. 32 pp.
As a young Black girl working on a farm, Mary could not begin school until she was eleven. No one in her family could read, but Mary finished school and became a teacher. After she married and had a son, she fulfilled a lifelong dream of starting her own school. This is an appealing biography about an important Black woman.

Merry Merry FIBruary. Doris Orgel. Illustrated by Arnold Lobel. Parents' Magazine. Unpaged (28 pp.).
A zany look at the days of the month of February, renamed FIBruary. Each day is a glorious fib, told in rhyme, that is humorously depicted by Lobel's drawings. This book generated many additional fibs on paper by its delighted readers.

Mice on My Mind. Bernard Waber. Illustrated by the author. Houghton Mifflin. 48 pp.
A cat dressed like a man soliloquizes on the problem of getting mice off his mind. When he visits a psychiatrist, it turns out the doctor has the same difficulty. A newspaper account of a mouse problem in foreign parts sends our hero off on the first plane. Children found this hilarious.

Miss Nelson Is Missing. Harry Allard. Illustrated by James Marshall. Houghton Mifflin. 32 pp. Paper ed., Scholastic Book Services.
The kids in Room 207 are the worst-behaved class in the whole school. One day sweet Miss Nelson does not come to school and is replaced by Miss Viola Swamp who means business. After the class is whipped into shape, Miss Nelson reappears, and all that is left of Miss Viola Swamp is an ugly black dress and a wig in Miss Nelson's closet. The odds-on favorite funny book of the year had children exploding with laughter at the misbehavior in Room 207 and Miss Nelson's dramatic solution. Also suitable for younger and older children.

Never Tickle a Turtle! Mike Thaler. Illustrated by the author. Watts. 96 pp. Paper ed., Avon.
Mike Thaler has written delightful new puns, riddles, and jokes about familiar subjects such as the ant, the mouse, and the pig. The black-and-white illustrations and pictorial jokes make this book difficult to put down.

The Old Joke Book. Janet and Allan Ahlberg. Illustrated by the authors. Viking. Unpaged (30 pp.).

This book of jokes, riddles, and poems done in a cartoon-strip format will appeal to the child who is quick-witted and familiar with British humor. The illustrations are appropriate and well done.

Oliver Hyde's Dishcloth Concert. Richard Kennedy. Illustrated by Robert Andrew Parker. Atlantic/Little, Brown. 47 pp.

Though "You can't have any fun with a dishcloth over your head," Oliver has worn a dishcloth over his head since the death of his bride. This is the tale of how Oliver and his wonderful fiddle music were coaxed back into the farm community. When the story was read aloud to classrooms, pupils gave it their hearty approval. They also praised its moody gray-washed drawings.

The Painter's Trick. Piero and Marisa Ventura. Illustrated by the authors. Random House. Unpaged (34 pp.).

A hungry painter working on a mural in a monastery tricks the monks into feeding him. Children enjoy the double surprise at the end and the brightly colored illustrations.

The Quicksand Book. Tomie de Paola. Illustrated by the author. Holiday House. Unpaged (32 pp.).

When Jungle Girl falls into the quicksand, Jungle Boy lectures her on its physical properties, explains safety rules, and chides her for her carelessness before he helps her out. Later, when Jungle Boy falls in the quicksand, Jungle Girl slowly sips her tea and rescues him at the last possible minute. Youngsters love her sweet revenge. The pictures of jungle greens and quicksand tans provide illustrations of the science concepts and set a merry mood for the lighthearted story.

Ramona and Her Father. Beverly Cleary. Illustrated by Alan Tiegreen. Morrow. 186 pp.

When Ramona's father loses his job, Ramona's well-meaning attempts to help during the family crisis are both humorous and touching. An antismoking campaign is almost more than Mr. Quimby can bear on top of his other problems. This book was read repeatedly by the children.

The Rascals from Haskell's Gym. Frank Bonham. E. P. Dutton. 119 pp.

"Gymnastics is practice and inspiration," the coach instructs the young women of the Butterflies Gymnastics Club. In their encounters with a rival club, the Rascals, the Butterflies learn what she means. Sissy, the book's busy heroine, uses mind and muscle to unmask a cheater and solve a mystery of missing money. Readers like the specifics about gymnastics training and performance.

The Sleeping Beauty. Retold by Trina Schart Hyman. Illustrated by the author. Little, Brown. Unpaged (43 pp.).

An exquisitely illustrated, powerfully retold version of one of the great fairy tales. It draws the reader into the emotions evoked by the beautiful young woman who waits for a sign of love to awaken her. A book for all children, with strong, full-colored illustrations.

Sums: A Looking Game. Diane Vreuls. Viking. Unpaged (48 pp.).

A wordless picture puzzle book in which familiar objects have been divided into pieces (addends) and presented in the format of addition problems. The addends appear on the right-hand page, the whole (sum) appears on the left when the page is turned. Clear, simple black-and-white drawings of the objects and their sums challenge eager children to try each puzzle and then check their answers.

The Upside-Down Man. Russell Baker. Illustrated by Gahan Wilson. McGraw-Hill. 48 pp.

In the Kingdom of Delirium, Dr. Frankenstein, with the help of his bungling assistant Lazlo, attempts to create a man. The results are the upside-down man and a girl with cow's ears. Insanely imaginative, the book makes great fun out of the story of the mad scientist and his creations.

A Very Young Rider. Jill Krementz. Photographs by the author. Knopf. Unpaged (119 pp.).

What is it really like to own, care for, and show a pony in competition? Ten-year-old Vivi Malloy demonstrates in a simple manner what is involved in feeding, grooming, teaching and loving a pony. The clear, sharp photographs on every page add excitement and realism.

1979

Bad Luck Tony. Dennis Fradin. Illustrated by Joanne Scribner. Prentice-Hall. 40 pp.

Tony finds a pregnant dog, but as pets are prohibited in his apartment house he sadly tries to place the dog in an adequate home, searching in the cold. A second plotline involves his visiting grandfather, a wanderer who assists in the situation and helps make Christmas a joy. Quiet drawings complement a subdued story which, in spite of elements which have been used many times before, works well.

The Best Burglar Alarm. Brenda Seabrooke. Illustrated by Loretta Lustig. Morrow. Unpaged (30 pp.).

A green parrot, an orange cat and a black dog make the best burglar alarm. This is the story of how three animal friends outwit a burglar after he sneaks through the fancy electronic system their owners have installed.

Captain Toad and the Motorbike. David McPhail. Illustrated by the author. McElderry/Atheneum. Unpaged (29 pp.).

From his youth, Captain Toad was a daredevil and a winner. Upon retirement, he encounters a new challenge—the motorbike. In this all's-well-that-ends-well tale, the Captain rides a motorbike and saves his neighborhood. Delightful full-color illustrations enhance the story.

Cinderella. Retold by Paul Galdone. Illustrated by the author. McGraw-Hill. Unpaged (40 pp.).

Over half the illustrations in this retelling of Perrault's story are double-page spreads which invite children's leisure inspection. Children enjoyed comparing text and illustrations of this version with those of others.

The Clown of God. Tomie de Paola. Illustrated by the author. Harcourt Brace Jovanovich. Unpaged (47 pp.). Paper ed., Harcourt Brace Jovanovich.

Detailed paintings graphically illustrate the scenery and customary garb of Renaissance Italy in de Paola's rendition of an old French legend. Orphaned Giovanni exists on begged food and doorway sleeping, but his exceptional talent—juggling—provides him with a job and adoration by royalty and commoner alike. Age takes its toll, however, and Giovanni's ability to kindle smiles is forgotten until a miracle immortalizes him in a tale.

The Door. Jacklyn O'Hanlon. Dial. 88 pp.

Fantasy and realism both thread their way through this novel of terror and mystery. A neighborhood peddler encourages Rachel to walk through a door. Beyond it lies a group of kidnapped children who try to beckon her into their misery. "I tingled when I read this," wrote one student. Many indicated they couldn't put it down.

Dracula's Cat. Jan Wahl. Illustrated by Kay Chorao. Prentice-Hall. Unpaged (28 pp.)

Dracula's best friend, his cat, narrates this tale of nighttime revels. The twist . . . Dracula isn't a bad fellow at all; he loves his kitty, and can't even scare old Mistress Agatha. Pen-line drawings in Halloween colors, plus a text that's spine-tingling and rib-tickling at once make this a favorite.

Four Scary Stories. Tony Johnston. Illustrated by Tomie de Paola. G. P. Putnam's. Unpaged (30 pp.).

Now what do you think would scare an imp, a goblin and a scalawag? A boy, of course! But these three little creatures find out that boys aren't all bad—they're just different. Whimsical illustrations and an almost poetic text make this a delightful reading experience.

The Frog Band and Durrington Dormouse. Jim Smith. Illustrated by the author. Little, Brown. Unpaged (32 pp.).

A "journey through time" befalls Durrington Dormouse as he and the Frog Band encounter one unusual situation after another. This adventurous, fun-filled tale captured children's interest—from one surprise to another. Full-color, lively illustrations with intriguing details catch viewers' attention. Frequently heard from children was "When will there be another Frog Band story?"

The Girl Who Loved Wild Horses. Paul Goble. Illustrated by the author. Bradbury. Unpaged (32 pp.).

A mystical bond unites a Native American girl and wild horses led by a marvelous spotted stallion. The sweep of the story is more than matched by the choreography of the paintings. Pupils commented most often on the language: "I liked the words, such as the ones about the horse: 'His eyes shown like cold stars.'"

Grandpa's Ghost Stories. James Flora. Illustrated by the author. McElderry/Atheneum. Unpaged (32 pp.).

During a stormy night, a grandfather tells scary stories, his grandson cozily cuddled on his knee. Skeletons in sacks surface, apparitions appear. In the manner of Scheherazade, the older keeps the younger hanging on, "But that's another story, too terrible to tell." Humorous touches in the nighttime-blue illustrations mitigate any fears.

I, Heracles. Elizabeth Siverthorne. Illustrated by Billie Jean Osborne. Abingdon. 128 pp.

The ten labors of the half-god Heracles comprise exciting episodes, including the lyrical tale of the Golden Hind. There is a helpful glossary and pronunciation guide of names. The first-person telling lends credibility and oral tone to the account. "This book is for people that love myths," wrote one reader, and apparently many people did.

Mouse and Tim.   Faith McNulty. Illustrated by Marc Simont. Harper & Row. 48 pp.
Tim finds a gumdrop-sized baby mouse during the spring barn cleaning and keeps it until August. Tim's narrative faces the mouse's thoughts so that both sides of the story are told. The artist's charcoal pencil drawings, shaded in soft turquoises and oranges, add warmth and humor to the text.

Ms. Glee Was Waiting.   Donna Hill. Illustrated by Diane Dawson. Atheneum. Unpaged (29 pp.).
Every excuse in the book, you might say. A delightfully breathless recounting of *exactly* why Laura missed her piano lesson. Wonderful pen-and-ink and watercolor illustrations are spellbinding, in themselves, amusing and accurate to the last detail. Suited to all ages.

The Rainbow-Colored Horse.   Pura Belpré. Illustrated by Antonio Martorell. Warne. Unpaged (44 pp.).
Who can resist a magic seven-color horse who comes to help you when you call him and then disappears in a cloud of smoke? Impressionistic woodcuts adorn the pages, and the rather complex folktale of Pio and his horse is told in rich read-aloud language. One class dramatized the story, appropriately converting its direct quotes into Spanish.

Taxi Dog.   Svend Otto. Illustrated by the author. Parents' Magazine. Unpaged (29 pp.).
What could make a big-city dog like Jasper give up his life of intrigue (his narrow escape from a farmer), excitement (his near-accident with a bus) and travel (what else would a "taxi dog" do!)? The answer will surpise your readers as much as it did Jasper.

Tracy Austin.   Nancy Robison. Illustrated with photographs. Harvey House. 60 pp.
People who have known or worked with Tracy Austin give their impressions of her, and praise her tennis ability. Non-buffs will benefit from the explanations of tennis terms and the concise histories of other greats (Chris Evert, Yvonne Goolagong, Billie Jean King) and how their careers parallel Tracy's. Photographs feature Tracy's determination and concentration on court and the fresh teenager who is "just like other kids" off court.

A Very Young Gymnast.   Jill Krementz. Illustrated with photographs by the author. Knopf. Unpaged (125 pp.).
Torrance York, 10 years old and devoted to gymnastics, relates her daily routine of training and competing. York's exploration of her feelings about gymnastics and her dreams for the future help students become more aware of the demands of gymnastics and of the enormous amount of dedication required to excel. Krementz's pictures (at least one per page) accompany the large type to produce an easily read story for ages ten and above.

1980

Aldo Applesauce.   Johanna Hurwitz. Illustrated by John Wallner. Morrow. 128 pp.
Aldo, a shy fourth-grader, finds moving from the city to the suburbs brings many challenges, especially making friends in a new school. This warm story of friendship is a great read-aloud to younger children or just right for those beginning to read chapter books on their own.

All the Money in the World.   Bill Brittain. Illustrations by Charles Robinson. Harper & Row. 160 pp. Paper ed., Random House.

The consequences of having all the money in the world deposited in your backyard include a humorous encounter with the army, a kidnapping and an interview with the President of the United States. A delightful fantasy with some hilarious moments shared by an interracial group of friends.

Anastasia Krupnik.   Lois Lowry. Houghton Mifflin. 160 pp.

Not only is 10-year-old Anastasia Krupnik's name too long to fit on a T-shirt, but it does not end with an "i" like Judi or Terri. She keeps lists in her notebook of "Things I Love" and "Things I Hate." These help her to deal with the impending birth of a baby brother, a grandmother who lives in a nursing home and can never remember Anastasia's name, and her romance with a cool, sixth-grade boy with an Afro.

Big Anthony and the Magic Ring.   Tomie de Paola. Illustrated by the author. Harcourt Brace Jovanovich. Unpaged (32 pp.). Paper ed., Harcourt Brace Jovanovich.

When bumbling Big Anthony borrows Strega Nona's magic ring to turn himself into a handsome fellow, he finds more trouble than pleasure. Wise Strega Nona sets Big Anthony down the right path, with love just around the corner in the form of Bambolona, the baker's daughter.

Bunnicula.   Deborah and James Howe. Illustrations by Alan Daniel. Atheneum. 112 pp.

Harold, the family dog, narrates this hilarious tale of a bunny who was found by the Monroe family in a Dracula movie. The well-read pet cat, Chester, observes strange nighttime behavior by the bunny. Humorous adventures result as Chester and Harold attempt to "save" the family from a suspected vampire.

The Case of the Phantom Frog.   E. W. Hildick. Illustrated by Lisl Weil. Macmillan. 122 pp. Paper ed., Archway/Pocket.

The McGurk Organization takes on the task of babysitting for a 7-year-old Hungarian boy named Bela. The real motive is to investigate the incredibly loud frog noises that are frightening Bela's aunt, Mrs. Kranz. At first the kid detectives are convinced that Bela is a "werefrog," but at last the McGurk gang exposes the presence of Bela's smuggled-in best "friend."

The Case of the Vanishing Boy.   Alexander Key. Archway/Pocket. 212 pp.

Jan and Ginny use their supernatural powers to overcome the forces of evil in a science fiction story of excitement and intrigue. Characters are well drawn, and the story moves along at a brisk pace. The friendship between the hero and heroine is sensitively depicted.

Good-Bye, Chicken Little.   Betsy Byars. Harper. 112 pp. Paper ed., Scholastic Book Services.

Though death, guilt, and feelings of abandonment haunt this fine study of Jimmie Little's coming of age, the reader still experiences a sense of hopefulness and faith in the future. Jimmie wrestles with the question of how he might have prevented his Uncle Pete's death and, through the understanding and acceptance of his unconventional and extended family, begins to see the positive side of life.

The Great Pete Penney.   Jean Bashor Tolle. McElderry/Atheneum. 112 pp.

"Even if you do not like baseball, you will like this book," wrote a young reader. An 11-year-old, Little League, girl pitcher and a tiny, invisible man combine to make a memorable baseball season.

The Hocus-Pocus Dilemma. Pat Kibbe. Illustrated by Dan Jones. Knopf. 124 pp. Paper ed., Scholastic Book Services.

Books and magazines about superstition, magic, and evil spirits are the reading diet of 10-year-old B. J. Pinkerton, who believes that she has a special talent for ESP. And, indeed, there are times when events conspire to give credibility to her notion.

How Lazy Can You Get? Phyllis Reynolds Naylor. Illustrated by Alan Daniel. Atheneum. 64 pp.

The "straw person" in this humorous book is Hildegarde Brasscoat, a housekeeper who lives up to her name. During the one week that she cares for the three Megglethorp children, a series of fractious events occur which test everyone's resilience.

In the Circle of Time. Margaret J. Anderson. Knopf. 182 pp. Paper ed., Scholastic Book Services.

This intriguing and exciting trip into the future, 2179 to be exact, is set on the Scottish moors. A time warp plunges two children into the struggle between peace-loving and barbaric, mechanized people.

The Land Where the Ice Cream Grows. Anthony Burgess. Illustrated by Fulvio Testa. Doubleday. Unpaged (32 pp.).

The magic in this adventure in a fantasy land is in the creative manipulation of the sounds and words of the English language. The days of the week, for instance, include Munchday and Chewsday.

Latki and the Lightning Lizard. Betty Baker. Illustrated by Donald Carrick. Macmillan. Unpaged (52 pp.).

Latki's father, a woodcutter, chops into a tree stump and unleashes a giant magical lizard. In payment for destroying his home, the lizard demands that Latki's favorite sister Seri become his housekeeper. Latki can communicate with animals and is able to rescue Seri.

Meet the Vampire. Georgess McHargue. Illustrated with drawings and photographs. J. B. Lippincott. 80 pp. Paper ed., Dell.

All you ever wanted to know about vampires and more, this book includes myths and legends, information about the real Dracula, and tells how to recognize and banish vampires.

More Science Experiments You Can Eat. Vicki Cobb. Illustrations by Giulio Maestro. J. B. Lippincott. 126 pp.

Simple scientific processes can be observed in changes in food. The majority of the experiments can be performed in a typical classroom with ordinary kitchen utensils. Each chapter includes a short explanation of what will be proved, a list of materials needed, and a detailed procedure. But best of all, everybody gets to taste the results!

Mummies Made in Egypt. Aliki. Illustrated by the author. Crowell. Unpaged (32 pp.).

This informative book begins with an explanation of why the Egyptians mummified their dead and continues to describe the process of mummification, burial rites, and construction of pyramids. Many of the colorful illustrations are drawn from ancient Egyptian art.

North American Legends. Selected by Virginia Haviland. Illustrated by Ann Strugnell. Philomel. 214 pp.

A broad collection of stories from different cultures found in North America.

Young readers were particularly interested in the sections relating to Indian and Eskimo legends. Attractive black-and-white illustrations fittingly reflect the cultures and peoples represented.

An Orphan for Nebraska.   Charlene Joy Talbot. Atheneum. 216 pp.

During the 1870s, Kevin arrives in New York City from Ireland only to discover he is alone. He journeys west with a group of children seeking adoption and finds a home with the publisher of a small Nebraska newspaper.

The Queen and Rosie Randall.   Helen Oxenbury (from an idea by Jill Buttfield-Campbell). Illustrations by the author. Morrow. Unpaged (40 pp.).

The queen is in a panic about how to entertain her guest, the King of Wottermazzy. Rosie, the queen's young friend, involves the king and royal court in various children's games that lead everyone from one messy disaster to another.

Ramona and Her Mother.   Beverly Cleary. Illustrations by Alan Tiegreen. Morrow. 208 pp. Paper ed., Dell.

When Mrs. Quimby goes to work, domestic tensions rise and the usual order of home life is interrupted. Ramona wonders, "Does my mother love me as much as my sister?" and she decides to run away. Mrs. Quimby helps Ramona pack and the shared activity allows Ramona to discover that she had never really doubted her mother's love and that her mother certainly does not want her to run away.

Samantha on Stage.   Susan Clement Farrar. Illustrated by Ruth Sanderson. Dial. 164 pp.

Samantha, the best dancer in her ballet class, gets to go "en pointe" this year. Samantha's stellar performance is challenged, however, when the daughter of a Russian diplomat joins the class. Following the changing relationship between these two 11-year-olds is a delightful excursion into the world of ballet and into the meaning of friendship.

Sandy and the Rock Star.   Walt Morey. E. P. Dutton. 190 pp. Paper ed., Scholastic Book Services.

A teenage rock star runs to an island to escape a life over which he seems to have lost control. Through an unusual friendship with Sandy, a trained Cougar, Paul is able to give his own life more meaning. A sympathetic treatment of adolescent rebellion that suggests dignified alternatives.

Secrets.   Nancy J. Hopper. Elsevier/Nelson. 138 pp.

Lenore hears secrets because she doesn't speak and people talk freely around her, labeling her as a looney. When one secret she hears turns out to be a kidnapping plot against a fellow student, Lenore encounters too much adventure to remain silent.

Seven Spells to Sunday.   Andre Norton and Phyllis Miller. McElderry/Atheneum. 144 pp. Paper ed., Archway/Pocket.

The story delineates the relationship between two children and how they learn to work together and to cope with their problems during the strangest week of their lives. Appealing to those who seek a little magic or fantasy in books.

The Sisters Impossible.   James David Landis. Knopf. 174 pp. Paper ed., Bantam.

Two sisters learn to trust and help each other when a reversal of roles makes the younger, Lily, become "big sister" to Saundra. The humorous characters are very real and the detailed use of the ballet world setting helps make an exciting and enjoyable story.

Soonie and the Dragon.   Shirley Rousseau Murphy. Illustrations by Susan Vaeth. Atheneum. 96 pp.

Sixteen-year-old Soonie embarks on a journey to seek her fortune and meets a griffin and a young man who help her to understand that her quest is really for the meaning of life. Soonie is a believable character and a model of a resolute, independent, and sympathetic young woman.

The Sorcerer's Apprentice.   Wanda Gág. Illustrations by Margot Tomes. Coward, McCann & Geoghegan. 32 pp.

This newly illustrated version of a dearly beloved old tale weaves pictures and text into a powerful literary experience for children. As the story of the sorcerer's misdeeds reaches a crescendo, so do the accompanying illustrations.

The Star Child.   Oscar Wilde. Illustrated by Fiona French. Four Winds. Unpaged (32 pp.).

Typical of Oscar Wilde's other stories, this literary fairy tale spotlights a moral: the price paid for unreasonable vanity. The Star Child is seen growing from a baby found in a forest to a young boy with a hard heart to a just and merciful Prince. The beautiful illustrations clearly illuminate the medieval world.

Summer of the Stallion.   June Andrea Hanson. Illustrated by Gloria Singer. Macmillan. 108 pp.

Janie's uneventful summer at her grandparents' ranch is enlivened by the sudden appearance of a beautiful wild stallion. Her grandfather's efforts to tame the stallion by brute force lead Janie to a new understanding of herself and of her grandfather.

Thumbelina.   Hans Christian Andersen. Retold by Amy Ehrlich. Illustrated by Susan Jeffers. Dial. Unpaged (32 pp.).

Delicate, finely etched drawings embellish this classic tale. The magical story tells of a woman who wanted a child more than anything in the world. When her wish was granted, the child was so small she could fit in a walnut shell.

A Time to Keep Silent.   Gloria Whelan. G. P. Putnam's. 128 pp.

Clair, struck into silence by her mother's death, is taken by her minister father to the northern Michigan woods where he hopes a new life-style will heal her. Clair meets another girl in the woods whose life is the antithesis of her own, and through this association, Clair and her father both experience emotional growth.

The Trouble with Thirteen.   Betty Miles. Knopf. 108 pp. Paper ed., Avon.

Thirteen is frequently an age of upheaval, so if you're like 12-year-olds Annie and Rachel, you get pretty anxious about this beginning metamorphosis. Many children expressed their identification with this honest presentation of the ambivalent feelings of two friends as their bodies and life-styles undergo many changes.

Where Are You, Angela von Hauptmann, Now That I Need You?   Barbara Williams. Holt Rinehart & Winston 192 pp.

Woody Jones and the graduating seventh-graders at Walt Whitman Elementary School in 1939 are never the same after their experiences with Angela von Hauptmann. Angela, a new student, creates turmoil and curiosity.

Words by Heart.   Ouida Sebestyen. Atlantic/Little, Brown. 162 pp. Paper ed., Bantam.

Lena, who memorizes Bible verses, quickly discovers the dangers of excelling when a raid on her Reconstruction home follows her defeat of a White classmate in a Bible-quoting contest. After fears, heartache, and tragedy, Lena learns through her father's example to live the words she knew by heart.

Older Readers
1977

Alvin's Swap Shop.   Clifford B. Hicks. Illustrations by Bill Sokol. Holt. 143 pp. Paper ed., Scholastic Book Services.
> This story of Alvin Fernald, the Magnificent Brain, begins simply enough with a summer Swap Shop and turns into a truly frightening adventure as he and his friends help Pim, a Bahamian boy, to escape from a criminal. Students liked the mysterious elements of the story as well as the humorous episodes that they have come to associate with stories of Alvin.

Connie.   Anne Alexander. Illustrated by Gail Owens. Atheneum. 179 pp.
> Connie's troubles begin when her father loses his job and are compounded when she is falsely accused of being an informer, but they're all solved by the end of this story. Connie's difficult but exciting life enables more sheltered students to test their own abilities to deal with a harsher reality. Can spark discussion of school problems and relationships.

Deborah Sampson: Soldier of the Revolution.   Harold W. Felton. Illustrated by John Martinez. Dodd, Mead. 111 pp.
> The story of the first woman to bear arms in the U.S. Army appealed to both boys and girls, but girls especially liked to know that "girls can do things too." Useful for social studies.

Father's Arcane Daughter.   E. L. Konigsburg. Atheneum. 118 pp.
> Each chapter of this fascinating mystery begins with part of a continuing conversation before flashing back twenty-five years to the story. Students respond to the underlying message about freedom and human concern.

The Giant Book of Strange but True Sports Stories.   Howard Liss. Illustrated by Joe Mathieu. Random House. 147 pp. Paper ed., Random House.
> Both boys and girls will enjoy this book of short sketches of unique and humorous happenings in sports. Baseball buffs, rodeo fans, and hockey enthusiasts will find strange tales about their favorite sport in this book.

Jaguar, My Twin.   Betty Jean Lifton. Illustrations by Ann Leggett. Atheneum. 114 pp.
> The Zinacantecs of Mexico believe that each person has a twin spirit from the animal world. In Shun's village, where the coming of electricity is looked on by some as evil, Shun's father stands out as a progressive man who recognizes the good it can do. The book reflects the pull between ancient and modern cultures as Shun's Jaguar spirit saves him from a spell cast by a shaman. The book is a good resource for a unit on Mexico.

The Journey Back.   Johanna Reiss. Crowell. 212 pp.
> This sequel to *The Upstairs Room* gives a realistic picture of the period just after World War II, showing the difficult adjustment of family members who had become strangers through separation. This ties in well with social studies units on postwar Europe, especially Holland.

The Letter, the Witch, and the Ring.   John Bellairs. Illustrated by Richard Egielski. Dial. 188 pp. Paper ed., Dell Yearling.

Witches promise excitement and trigger mystery, and children sympathize with Lewis' and Rose Rita's problems in dealing with both. Shivery, suspenseful, and hard to put down.

Lizard Music. Written and illustrated by D. Manus Pinkwater. Dodd, Mead. 157 pp.

Left alone when his parents go on a vacation, Victor discovers, through late-night TV, a community of intelligent lizards and the Chicken Man. The succeeding adventures take Victor through some strange but thought-provoking escapades. Children associate with the ending—a return to normal but dull life when the rest of the family returns. A good read-aloud book.

The Man with the Silver Eyes. William O. Steele. Harcourt Brace Jovanovich. 147 pp.

William Steele's story of frontier life is useful for studying the Revolutionary War period. Information about the era, Cherokee life, and becoming an adult are a part of an exciting plot that involves the reader.

Merry Ever After: The Story of Two Medieval Weddings. Written and illustrated by Joe Lasker. Viking. 48 pp. Paper ed., Puffin.

The story tells of two couples who marry in medieval times: one in a noble wedding, one in a peasant. As the couples prepare for the weddings and the social customs unfold, information about life in the Middle Ages is conveyed. Much of the information was gleaned from medieval and early Renaissance paintings; many of the illustrations show the influence of the great painters from the period. A handsome picture book for older children.

The Missing Persons League. Frank Bonham. E. P. Dutton. 157 pp. Paper ed., Scholastic Book Services.

In this fast-paced science fiction suspense story, a young man, attempting to discover why people are disappearing from Earth, is led into dangerous circumstances. Plausible and exciting writing holds students' interest. The ending is especially fine.

Showboat in the Backcourt. William Campbell Gault. E. P. Dutton. 122 pp.

A sports story with plenty of action and a good pace that holds the attention of reluctant readers. Young athletes compare their own on-court experiences with those in the story.

The Turning Place. Jean E. Karl. E. P. Dutton. 213 pp. Paper ed., Dell.

Nine science fiction stories about adolescents transport the reader into the future. These fascinating projections concentrate on human relationships and hold students' interest throughout. Even students who don't usually like science fiction enjoy this book, since it is the characters who are important.

1978

Alan and the Animal Kingdom. Isabelle Holland. J. B. Lippincott. 192 pp.

After the death of Great-aunt Jessie, Alan tries to live alone in New York City with his five animal pets. Readers enjoy Alan's pluck and ingenuity in attending school, caring for sick pets, finding money for food, and misleading his not-very-concerned neighbors and landlord. A modern survival story.

Bargain Bride. Evelyn Sibley Lampman. McElderry/Atheneum. 180 pp.

On Ginny's fifteenth birthday, Mr. Mayhew, a much older man to whom she has been sold into marriage, comes to get his bride. When Mr. Mayhew unexpectedly dies of a stroke, Ginny, refusing to be taken advantage of again, strives to make it on her own. A warm and realistic story of a unique time in history.

Dogsbody.   Diana Wynne Jones. Greenwillow. 242 pp.

The Dog Star, Sirius, has been sent to earth in the body of a dog as a punishment for his misdeeds. If he can recover the mysterious Zoi in his lifetime as a dog, he will be reinstated in the heavens. His dog nature wars with his stellar nature, almost to his destruction. This fantasy includes allusions to cosmic beings and to the mythology concerning Arawn, Master of the Hunt.

Foster Child.   Marion Dane Bauer. Seabury. 155 pp. Paper ed., Dell.

Twelve-year-old Rennie is one of four children in a foster home where the foster father, outwardly religious, is a child molester. The grimness of the situation is partially softened by the young people's kindness to each other. Many readers cited the book's fast pace as their reason for liking it.

Frozen Fire.   James Houston. McElderry/Atheneum. 149 pp.

When Matt Morgan's prospector father fails to return from a helicopter flight over the Canadian Arctic, Matt and a new Eskimo friend set out to find him, almost losing their lives in the attempt. Traditional knowledge proves superior to technology in an exciting race against the cold. Highly satisfying to the ecology-minded and the adventure-loving.

Ghosts I Have Been.   Richard Peck. Viking. 214 pp.

This wise, wonderful, witty story ("Too good to be true," wrote one reader) tells how 14-year-old Blossom Culp of Bluff City, U.S.A., develops second sight and "sees" the Titanic in its final moments. Readers like the way Blossom "takes charge of things."

The Girl Who Had No Name.   Berniece Rabe. E. P. Dutton. 149 pp. Paper ed., Bantam.

When Girlie's mother dies, Papa sends her off to live with sister after sister. But Girlie (for "girl baby"—Papa had refused to name her) wants to discover why Papa feels different toward her than he does toward her sisters. Set in the Midwest during the depression.

Hangin' Out with Cici.   Francine Pascal. Viking. 152 pp. Paper ed., Archway.

Victoria, perpetually misunderstood by her mother, finds herself back in 1944 with a new friend named Cici. Cici is Victoria's mother, of course, and their experiences ultimately lead to harmony in Victoria's time. Youngsters love this glimpse into their mothers' school days.

The Haunting of Julie Unger.   Valerie A. Lutters. Atheneum. 193 pp.

Julie, inconsolable over her father's death, continues with her photography, during which she seems to sense his presence. Shocked by the killing of some geese she has lured for her work, she begins to surmount her sorrow. Readers were attracted by the combination of a realistic problem and a ghost-like presence.

Konrad.   Christine Nostlinger. Translated by Anthea Bell. Illustrated by Carol Nicklaus. Watts. 135 pp.

One day Mrs. Bartolotti receives a mysterious package containing a factory-produced, 7-year-old boy. Perfect in every way, Konrad tries to adapt to living in an imperfect world. Further complications arise when the factory wants him back. This hilarious and thought-provoking fantasy includes innocent questioning of traditionally accepted behavior.

The Luck of Brin's Five.   Cherry Wilder. Atheneum. 230 pp.

Torin is an ancient world populated mostly by craftsmen. When an Earthman, Scott Gale, parachutes in, he becomes the focus of a struggle between the powers seeking change and those wanting life to remain as it is. Gale becomes the "luck" of the family group who rescues him. The changes in characters are fascinating and believable.

The Pinballs. Betsy Byars. Harper & Row. 136 pp. Paper ed., Scholastic Book Services.

Placed in the same foster home, three victims of child abuse learn to help and care for each other, thus making a start toward self-determination and independence. The sympathetic portrayal of these luckless children evokes sympathy and compassion. A good discussion starter.

Refugee. Anne Rose. Dial. 118 pp.

When the Nazi threat begins to spread across Europe, Elke is forced to leave her family in Belgium and go to New York to live with relatives. Her search for a new identity, fears for friends and relatives left behind, and final reunion with her parents are captured in her own diary. The story is based on the author's personal experiences.

The Saving of P.S. Robbie Branscum. Illustrated by Glen Rounds. Doubleday. 127 pp. Paper ed., Dell.

P.S., whose mother died at her birth, is the youngest child in a hill preacher's family, and, at 12, she doesn't fit in. She is dark in a family of blue-eyed blondes, she's the only "sinner" in a preacher's family, and she resents the new woman in her father's life. In the end, P.S. finds herself and becomes "saved" in the bargain. This was read over and over by middle-schoolers who wouldn't read other books.

The Solid Gold Kid. Norma Fox Mazer and Harry Mazer. Delacorte. 219 pp. Paper ed., Dell.

Derek, son of a millionaire, and four other teenagers are kidnapped and undergo a six-day ordeal before they are released. The gradual revelation of the true nature of each teenager combined with the life-and-death suspense make this irresistible.

A Summer to Die. Lois Lowry. Illustrated by Jenni Oliver. Houghton Mifflin. 154 pp. Paper ed., Bantam.

Meg is sometimes envious of her older sister Molly who is pretty, enthusiastic, poised, and sure of her goals for the future. When Molly develops an incurable disease and Meg must watch her slowly die, Meg's emotions are torn apart, then reconstructed through the help of understanding parents and exceptionally helpful adult friends. Winner of the 1978 International Reading Association's Children's Book Award.

Trial Valley. Vera and Bill Cleaver. J. B. Lippincott. 158 pp. Paper ed., Bantam.

This sequel to *Where the Lilies Bloom* finds Mary Call Luther at sixteen taking care of her brother and sister as well as an affectionate foundling named Jack Parsons. Mary Call longs for a different life, but the book's dramatic climax brings a change of heart. The Appalachian conversation and the book's graceful style appeal to readers, who remark that the book should be read aloud to be fully appreciated.

1979

Absolute Zero. Helen Cresswell. Macmillan. 174 pp. Paper ed., Avon.

The world of advertising moves in on the warm and funny Bagthorpe family. Those who have read the first book in the series, *Ordinary Jack,* will not be surprised to learn that the resulting competition among family members leads to an "All Out Furor." And the winner is Zero, the "untrainable" mongrel dog! In one school students selected favorite episodes to share in a readers theater format.

Bagthorpes Unlimited.   Helen Cresswell. Macmillan. 180 pp. Paper ed., Avon.

The book begins with a wacky burglary and ends with the Bagthorpe family threading the longest daisy chain in the world. It's a joyful tribute to family living with old, young, and middle-aged members engaged in hilarious endeavors. Pleased readers commended the family warmth along with the comedy in this welcome third volume of the "Bagthorpe Saga." As one reader characterized the humor: "The author explained things right."

Beauty and the Beast.   Retold by Marianna Mayer. Illustrated by Mercer Mayer. Four Winds. Unpaged (44 pp.).

Beauty is no less compassionate and lovely, and the Beast no less ferocious and magical in this superb retelling of an age-old favorite. The beautiful full-color illustrations are sure to capture the imagination.

The Case of the Baker Street Irregular.   Robert Newman. Atheneum 216 pp.

Sherlock Holmes solves the case, but it takes Andrew, age 14, and his female cohort, Screamer, to provide the real action in this complex yarn about art theft, disguise, bombing, and kidnapping. The author opts for suspense and authentic London setting instead of comic effect—and avid mystery fans heartily approved. This book makes a fine lead-in to Conan Doyle.

How I Came to Be a Writer.   Phyllis Reynolds Naylor. Illustrated with memorabilia. Atheneum. 133 pp.

Through this autobiographical account, Naylor traces the process of becoming a professional writer from her family's early love of literature to the complexities of writing and publishing a book. Photographs of her life along with previous book illustrations are presented in sequence with the text. Examples of Naylor's own writings, from kindergarten to recently published books, prove most intriguing to children.

It Can't Hurt Forever.   Marilyn Singer. Illustrated by Leigh Grant. Harper & Row. 192 pp.

Ellie's twelve-day experience as a young heart patient in the hospital is both humorous and poignant. At times Ellie is sure she will die, but with the help of wise parents, a special nurse, and a few veteran patients, she survives. The story is believable and lively. Leigh Grant's crisp black-and-white illustrations support and extend the story.

Journey Home.   Hoshiko Uchida. Illustrated by Charles Robinson. McElderry/ Atheneum. 131 pp.

Realistically told from the point of view of 12-year-old Yuki, an American-born Japanese girl, this moving story reveals a family's readjustment to society after their imprisonment in a Japanese concentration camp during World War II. While rebuilding a life in an atmosphere of fear and distrust, Yuki becomes painfully aware of prejudice as she also discovers inner strength and hope.

The Lines Are Coming, A Book about Drawing.   Hans-Georg Rauch. Illustrated by the author. Scribner. 56 pp.

Through black-and-white illustrations along with a simple text, Rauch shows visual images that can be created by the arrangement of lines on a page; thin lines make skyscrapers; curly lines make the blowing wind. This picture book encourages children to experiment with various lines as a technique for drawing that proves successful as well as enjoyable.

The Pistachio Prescription.   Paula Danziger. Delacorte. 160 pp. Paper ed., Dell.
Cassie is an asthmatic, hypochondriacal girl with a poor self-image. Her family, too, is troubled. Each member has virtues and faults, but together they don't function well. When, inevitably, Cassie must suffer her parents' separation, she manages because she has gradually come to see her own likability and leadership potential. Strong characterization and laugh-out-loud dialogue are highlights.

Robbers, Bones and Mean Dogs.   Compiled by Barry and Velma Berkey. Illustrated by Marylin Hafner. Addison-Wesley. Unpaged (25 pp.).
This collection of kids' essays shows young readers they're not alone in their fears and, that no matter how silly, other people are scared of the same things they are. The important thing is, "most of my fears, I get over them." Amusing, pertinent illustrations.

Runaway to Freedom: A Story of the Underground Railway.   Barbara Smucker. Illustrated by Charles Lilly. Harper & Row. 160 pp.
The underground railway, as seen through Julilly's adolescent eyes, is given taut description. Julilly's escape to Canada and the reunion with her mother make for exciting reading. This book proved so gratifying that urban readers vied for a turn, and many were unhappy that time didn't permit a second go-around.

Sideways Stories from Wayside School.   Louis Sachar. Illustrated by Dennis Hockerman. Follett. 139 pp.
The architectural error of constructing a thirty story school with one classroom on each floor begins the humorous story of Wayside School. Each of thirty chapters features one particular student or teacher in a ridiculously funny situation. Hilarious episodes included Mrs. Gorf's changing students into apples and John's ability to read only upside-down material.

Superstars of the Sports World.   Bill Gutman. Illustrated with photographs. Messner. 96 pp.
To be dubbed a "superstar," you must be tops in your field. Gutman chose five outstanding athletes to examine: Chris Evert, Franco Harris, Pete Rose, Julius Erving, and Bobby Clarke. He relates their statistics, their upbringing, and their confident attitudes. Each had to overcome some obstacle—injury, self-doubt, small size, poverty, etc.—to be successful. Gutman's humanistic writing portrays "real people" worthy of our admiration.

A Swiftly Tilting Planet.   Madeleine L'Engle. Farrar, Straus & Giroux. 278 pp.
Charles Wallace, 15, must undergo a harrowing series of adventures in strange warps of time and space in order to avert Earth's destruction. From Wales to South America to mystical outer space on the back of a magnificent unicorn, the novel travels brilliantly on its own profound theme. "Not many writers can make it seem so real," wrote one reader, and many put the book on an equal plane with its forerunner, the ingenious *A Wrinkle in Time.*

Tawny.   Charles Carner. Illustrated by Donald Carrick. Macmillan. 160 pp.
If, as some psychologists believe, life is a series of losses, then we're called upon to say good-bye frequently, as protagonist Trey must do. His twin brother has died, and now he must allow Tawny, a beloved doe, to return to the wild. In letting go of the animal, Trey also comes to terms with grief felt for his brother.

The Whole Mirth Catalog.   Michael Scheier and Julie Frankel. Illustrated by the authors. Watts. 96 pp. Paper ed., Watts.
Open this big book (8½″ × 11″) anywhere and turn the pages in either direction and you'll experience "a regular riot," as stated by a seventh-grader. Packed full of puns, jokes, and things to make and do, it is organized into a hodgepodge of humorous illustrations and how-to sketches in red, white, and black, easily read graphics. No subject is sacred: parents, teachers, food, habits, and writing about "My Summer Vacation" all go down laughing.

1980

Alan Mendelsohn, The Boy from Mars.   Daniel M. Pinkwater. E. P. Dutton. 240 pp. Paper ed., Bantam.
Leonard Neeble, new at Bat Masterson Junior High, is "a short, portly, wrinkled kid with glasses." He soon makes friends with Alan Mendelsohn, another weird kid who causes a riot at school by claiming he is a Martian. A humorous, exaggerated lampooning of psychic powers, con men, quack medics, and natural food faddists.
Can You Sue Your Parents for Malpractice?   Paula Danziger. Delacorte. 152 pp. Paper ed., Dell.
Fourteen-year-old Lauren feels life is the pits when her boyfriend jilts her, her beautiful older sister seems to get everything she wants, and she has to share a room with her 10-year-old sister. Solutions to her problems seem to appear when she takes a course in "Law for Children and Young People" and meets Zack, an eighth-grader.
Does Anybody Care about Lou Emma Miller?   Alberta Wilson Constant. Crowell. 278 pp.
Lou Emma Miller lives in Gloriosa, Kansas, at the turn of the century. This "well-behaved young lady" who never causes any trouble is tired of being unnoticed and enthusiastically campaigns for the election of her town's first woman mayor.
Fridays.   Patricia Lee Gauch. G. P. Putnam's 160 pp. Paper ed., Archway/Pocket.
Carey Martin is aware of a puzzling undercurrent at Calvin Junior High, but she is unable to identify it. Finally, the tension surfaces and explodes on a Friday. This story depicts Carey's struggles with adolescence, peer pressure, and personal and familial conflicts.
The Girl Who Lived on the Ferris Wheel.   Louise Moeri. E. P. Dutton. 118 pp. Paper ed., Avon.
Sixth-grader Til rides the ferris wheel every Saturday with her divorced father. The outing is Til's one escape from a terrifying situation at home. A powerful statement on child abuse for older readers.
The InnKeeper's Daughter.   Barbara Cohen. Lothrop, Lee & Shepard. 160 pp.
Lonely, shy Rachel Gold is 16 years old in the summer of 1948. Restless and dissatisfied with life, she wishes she were someone other than an innkeeper's daughter in northern New Jersey. Sudden tragedy provides her with an opportunity to reassess her feelings about herself and her family, and an unexpected discovery enables her to be of assistance to them.
Into the Dream.   William Sleator. Illustrated by Ruth Sanderson. E. P. Dutton. 144 pp. Paper ed., Scholastic Book Services.

Elements of ESP and psychokinesis thrill the reader as an adolescent couple seek the transmitter of their mental messages to decode their prophetic dream of doom. Intricate black-pencil illustrations add substance to the eerie, nebulous content of this dream.

Lori. Gloria Goldreich. Holt, Rinehart & Winston. 182 pp. Paper ed., Dell.
Sixteen-year-old Lori has been caught smoking pot at school and is suspended for a year. Her grandfather decides she is to spend a year in Israel with an old friend of his. There Lori makes new friends and gains self-confidence and compassion.

The Magic of the Glits. C. S. Adler. Illustrations by Ati Forberg. Macmillan. 132 pp.
Jeremy is sure his summer at Cape Cod is ruined by his broken leg and the presence of a 7-year-old house visitor for whom he must babysit. But Jeremy and Lynette, who has just lost her mother, become true friends, and he invents magical creatures called Glits to entertain her.

Nightmare Town. T. Ernesto Bethancourt. Holiday House. 158 pp.
Jimmy Hunter runs away from an unloving guardian uncle and hitches a ride with a family who befriends him. An accident leaves only him and the daughter, Liz, alive in the Arizona desert, where Jimmy meets a hermit and Liz is kidnapped by a cult. Her rescue forms part of an extraordinary conclusion.

Secret Lives. Berthe Amoss. Atlantic/Little, Brown. 192 pp. Paper ed., Dell.
Addie tries to discover the truth about the legends surrounding her mother, who died when she was 5. By inquiring about her mother, Addie is freed to come into her own in this moving and humorous story.

The Story of American Photography. Martin W. Sandler. Illustrated with photographs. Little, Brown. 318 pp.
This beautifully illustrated book traces the development of photography since its invention in 1839. The photographs cover a wide variety of themes, with particular emphasis given to the 19th century. Various American artists are also discussed in some detail.

The Swing. Emily Hanlon. Bradbury. 210 pp. Paper ed., Dell.
Eleven-year-old Beth is deaf and feels that the swing near her family's summer home is her private possession. Danny, three years older, hates his stepfather and resents Beth's use of the swing and her intrusion into his private place. The two become friends as they soothe each other's pain.

There Are Two Kinds of Terrible. Peggy Mann. Avon. 132 pp.
The first kind of terrible was when Robbie broke his arm. The second was when his mother went to the hospital for "tests." A moving account of how death brings changes to a family.

We Interrupt This Semester for a Very Important Bulletin. Ellen Conford. Little, Brown. 176 pp.
Carrie Wasserman is in trouble for trying to expose a school scandal in the school newspaper, but her relationship with the editor of the paper provides an old-fashioned flavor of romance to this funny and fast-paced novel.

Wonder Wheels. Lee Bennett Hopkins. Knopf. 172 pp. Paper ed., Dell.
A skillfully written story set in a contemporary roller rink. The development of the relationships between the teenage characters is so strong that when Kitty dies the reader is emotionally involved.

Your Old Pal, Al. Constance C. Green. Viking. 156 pp. Paper ed., Dell.
Twelve-year-old Al checks the mail every day for letters from her father and

stepmother and from Brian, the boy she met at her father's wedding. Al's best friend has a house guest for two weeks and Al feels left out. All ends well when Al gets an invitation to visit from her father, receives a letter from Brian, and has a jubilant celebration with her friend, with wise talk about the strains of true friendship.

All Ages
1975

Arrow to the Sun: A Pueblo Indian Tale. Adapted and illustrated by Gerald McDermott. Viking. Unpaged (42 pp.).
McDermott has created a book with graphic appeal for all. The Pueblo Indian tale is told first in bold oranges and black with pictures speaking for some of the text. Later "power" is shown through use of other colors. Children turn the pages slowly and absorb the feeling of mystery and magic.

Best Wishes, Amen: A New Collection of Autograph Verses. Compiled by Lillian Morrison. Illustrations by Loretta Lustig. Crowell 208 pp.
Favorite with fourth- and fifth- graders. Excellent for free reading. Promotes rhyme writing. Light, humorous.

Dawn. Story and illustrations by Uri Shulevitz. Farrar, Straus & Giroux. Unpaged (32 pp.).
A special book for a quiet corner in any classroom. *Dawn* is well liked by children of all ages. The colors create a mood of stillness that older children can recall from a similar fishing trip—watching the sunrise.

Don't Feel Sorry for Paul. Bernard Wolf. Photographs by the author. J. B. Lippincott. 96 pp.
A heroic child adjusts to the use of an artificial arm and asks no quarter from those around him. This book creates an intense emotional experience for the reader, especially valuable in schools with mainstreaming.

Farmer Palmer's Wagon Ride. Story and illustrations by William Steig. Farrar, Straus & Giroux. Unpaged (32 pp.).
A beautifully illustrated story showing the courage and resourcefulness of Farmer Palmer, all done with an underlying sense of humor which is largely whimsical. Good for reading aloud if pictures are shown to listeners.

Frog Goes to Dinner. Story and illustrations by Mercer Mayer. Dial. Unpaged (32 pp.).
This one inspires laughter and "reading" and writing. In this book without words, the story is told through the pictures. Children sometimes like to tell it or tape it or write it in great detail. High interest for those otherwise not interested in books.

Hand Talk: An ABC of Finger Spelling & Sign Language. Remy Charlip, Mary Beth, and George Ancona. Parents' Magazine. Unpaged (46 pp.).
A suitably nonverbal manual for communicating through finger spelling and signing. Children will try this "new language" on their friends. An excellent introduction to the communication problems deaf people face and the means by which they overcome barriers imposed by silence.

Jack-O'-Lantern. Edna Barth. Illustrations by Paul Galdone. Seabury. Unpaged (48 pp.).

A spooky Halloween legend tells how the first jack-o'-lantern might have originated. Paul Galdone's illustrations of Mean Jack and the devil add to the appeal of the book.

Jambo Means Hello: Swahili Alphabet Book.   Muriel Feelings. Illustrations by Tom Feelings. Dial. Unpaged (60 pp.).

The fine illustrations add a dimension to the simple definitions given for each word in this Swahili alphabet book. A good book for initiating interest in anthropology and comparative linguistics.

My Grandson Lew.   Charlotte Zolotow. Illustrations by William Pène du Bois, Harper & Row. 131 pp.

Charlotte Zolotow creates a mood that is not too sophisticated for young children and older ones respond to the book's small size and big meaning. It speaks of memories, those wispy ones, easily lost but remembered here.

With a Deep Sea Smile: Story Hour Stretches for Large or Small Groups.   Selected by Virginia A. Tashjian. Illustrations by Rosemary Wells. Little, Brown. 140 pp. Title index.

A collection of poetry, prose and verse with subtle humor and well-stated themes. In the mode of *Juba This, Juba That,* by the same author, it is a good stimulus for creative writing, dramatization and independent reading.

1976

Alligator Pie.   Dennis Lee. Illustrations by Frank Newfield. Houghton Mifflin. 64 pp.

Repeatedly, children chose to pick up and read aloud this funny, rhythmic collection of poems. They pointed at the pictures and laughed at the ridiculous combinations of words and ideas. Excellent for introducing poetry, teaching Canadian geography, read-aloud, or pure personal pleasure reading.

The Desert Is Theirs.   Byrd Baylor. Illustrations by Peter Parnall. Scribner's. Unpaged (32 pp.).

Poetic interpretation of Papago Indians' ecological and spiritual relationships with desert resources. Distinguished, imaginative illustrations add to the usefulness of this mood piece for sensitizing children to respect for nature, reading aloud, and studying Indian cultures and techniques of using line, space, and color.

Ed Emberley's Drawing Book of Faces.   Written and illustrated by Ed Emberley. Little, Brown. 32 pp.

A book to fascinate a child who likes to draw. Index is helpful and youngest children will show they can use it. With this book, they will also show how well they follow directions but, at least to the children, the drawing will be the important reason for having the book.

The Gobble-Uns'll Git You Ef You Don't Watch Out!   James Whitcomb Riley. Illustrations by Joel Schick. J. B. Lippincott. Unpaged (42 pp.).

The "Little Orphan Annie" story has been brought back in excellent taste by the illustrator. It is a fun reading book that was labeled as one most reread. The pupils enjoy writing their own scarey stories as a follow-up. The story holds the attention of all children regardless of age. The dialect is interesting and easy to read, leading to oral interpretation and the study of dialects.

The I Hate Mathematics! Book.   Marilyn Burns. Illustrations by Martha Hairston. Little, Brown. 127 pp.

This book proves to be an all-purpose amusement center for children of all ages (6 to adult). A fourth-grader used it for his birthday party games; his 19-year-old sister used it to stump her dates; his mom loves it for rainy-day assistance. It presents math as the most useful tool that it really is.

Is There an Actor in the House?   Virginia Bradley. Dodd, Mead. 298 pp.

A collection of plays for reading aloud, acting out, pantomiming or just enjoying. Excellent for stimulating creative dramatics, creative writing, oral interpretation and storytelling. Reading plays has motivated many reluctant readers, and this collection serves well for that purpose.

The Monster Riddle Book.   Written and illustrated by Jane Sarnoff and Reynold Ruffins. Scribner's. Unpaged (30 pp.).

Children waited eagerly for the copy to be available and enjoyed trying to stump each other with the riddles. The book can be used to interest reluctant readers and also to develop awareness of play on words and clever use of double meanings.

Motorcycle Moto Cross School.   Written and illustrated with photographs by Ed and Dan Radlauer. Watts. 44 pp.

Children who like the book show interest in the photographs and in the detailed information about motorcycles and racing. The writing style is informal, especially the dialogue sections. High-interest materials for readers who may not be reached through other kinds of books.

Naughty Nancy.   Story and illustrations by John S. Goodall. Atheneum/McElderry. 32 pp.

Children's responses to this book showed delight at Nancy's antics as she all but ruins a wedding and reception. This excellent wordless picture book gives children experience with storytelling from pictures. They also like to look at it independently in order to enjoy the many details in the illustrations. Fine for developing inference skills.

Pets in a Jar.   Seymour Simon. Illustrations by Betty Fraser. Viking. 96 pp.

When the garter snakes, salamanders, snails, skunks and others are in season, this book is indispensable for children. It's a "how-to" manual on capturing and caring for small animals. Profuse, informative illustrations. Reading level is definitely intermediate. An excellent science aid.

Pyramid.   Written and illustrated by David Macaulay. Houghton Mifflin. 80 pp.

Richly detailed pictures, explanatory diagrams, and lucid expository writing bring to life the story of a great pyramid and the ancient culture that produced it. Fascinating supplementary material for social studies. Spurs interest in further study of relationships between society and architecture, collecting, discussing, and writing about pictures of great contemporary architecture.

See My Lovely Poison Ivy.   Lilian Moore. Illustrations by Diane Dawson. Atheneum. 42 pp.

A poetry book about spooky things that is popular in the classroom all year round. The humor of a ghost at the Laundromat or in an elevator and a poem from the point of view of a jack-o'-lantern start children thinking of unique approaches to creating poetry.

The Stonecutter.   Story and illustrations by Gerald McDermott, Viking. Unpaged (28 pp.).

Ancient Japanese folktale of man's foolish longing for power, portrayed in vibrantly colored, dramatic contemporary collages, can be enjoyed as a read-aloud. The ironic, thought-provoking ending on the theme of humility leads older children to discuss the value of contentment and the setting of realistic goals in life.

Thirteen. Written and illustrated by Remy Charlip and Jerry Joyner. Parents' Magazine. Unpaged (28 pp.).

Children as young as 6 delight in figuring out the puzzle of the thirteen stories in this brilliantly designed picture book. Intrigued with the many ways of interpreting this complex book, older readers were challenged to apply the concepts by writing their own, entitled *Twelve*.

Whoppers: Tall Tales and Other Lies. Alvin Schwartz, Illustrations by Glen Rounds. J. B. Lippincott. 128 pp.

According to the author in his introduction, ". . . . this book is a pack of lies." This collection of stories is good to use for the art of storytelling, for the history of the frontier "gallyfloppers," and for inspiration in writing stories.

Why Mosquitoes Buzz in People's Ears. Verna Aardema. Illustrations by Leo and Diane Dillon. Dial. Unpaged (32 pp.).

Children respond to the color and rhythm in the pictures as well as to the storytelling style. Descriptive language used to depict the movements of the animals (python: *wasawusu, wasawusu, wasawusu*) adds to the story's effectiveness for reading aloud and for story theater activities.

References: Children's Choices

"Classroom Choices: Children's Trade Books, 1974." *The Reading Teacher,* **29**:122–132 (1975).

"Classroom Choices: Children's Trade Books, 1975," *The Reading Teacher,* **30**:50–63 (1975).

"Classroom Choices for 1977: Books Chosen by Children." *The Reading Teacher,* **31**:6–23 (1977).

"Classroom Choices for 1978: Books Chosen by Children." *The Reading Teacher,* **32**:28–46 (1978).

"Children's Choices." *The Reading Teacher,* **33**:33–52 (1979).

"Children's Choices." *The Reading Teacher,* **34**:37–56 (1980).

BIBLIOTHERAPY: HELPING CHILDREN COPE

In recent times, a number of children's books have been published that deal with life problems. Reading about characters with similar problems helps children to cope with their own life situations. This process is entitled bibliotherapy. The following pages list recommended picture books for children in the early grades and books for intermediate-grade students.

TABLE B-1 Bibliotherapy for Young Children

AUTHOR ILLUSTRATOR	TITLE	PUBLISHER	GRADE LEVEL	THEME
Alexander, M.*	*Nobody Asked Me If I Wanted a Babysitter*	Dial	PS–1	Sibling rivalry
Arnold, A. McCully, E. A.	*Black Is Brown Is Tan*	Harper & Row	K–3	Interracial family
Babbitt, N.*	*The Something*	Farrar, Straus & Giroux	PS–3	Fear of the dark
Baylor, B. Marshall, J.	*Plink, Plink, Plink*	Houghton Mifflin	K–3	Fear of night sounds
Bernstein, J. E. Gullo, S. V.	*When People Die*	E. P. Dutton	K–3	Death
Blaine, M. Walner, J.	*The Terrible Thing That Happened at Our House*	Parents Magazine	K–2	Working mother
Brandenberg, J. Aliki	*I Wish I Was Sick Too!*	Greenwillow	K–3	Sibling conflict
Bunin, C.* Bunin, S.*	*Is That Your Sister? A True Story of Adoption*	Pantheon	K–3	Interracial adoption
Caines, J. F. Kellog, S.	*Abby*	Harper & Row	PS–1	Adoption
Carrick, C. Carrick, D.	*The Accident*	Seabury	K–3	Death of a pet
Clifton, L. Grifalconi, A.	*Everette Anderson's 1-2-3*	Holt, Rinehart & Winston	K–3	New father

*Illustrated by the author.

383

TABLE B-1   Bibliotherapy for Young Children (*Continued*)

AUTHOR ILLUSTRATOR	TITLE	PUBLISHER	GRADE LEVEL	THEME
Clifton, B. Barnett, M.	My Brother—Fine With Me	Holt, Rinehart & Winston	K–3	Running away
De Paola, T.*	Andy: (That's My Name)	Prentice-Hall	PS–K	Teasing
De Paola, T.*	Nana Upstairs and Nana Downstairs	G. P. Putnam's	PS–K	Death of a grandparent
Dragonwagon, C.	Will I Be Okay?	Harper & Row	K–2	Fears
Fassler, J. Lasker, J.	Howie Helps Himself	Whitman	1–3	Handicapped child
Genevieve, G. Shimin, S.	Send Wendell	McGraw-Hill	K–3	Sibling conflict
Goffstein, M. B.*	My Crazy Sister	Dial	K–3	Sibling conflict
Greenfield, E. Steptoe, J.	She Came Bringing Me That Little Baby Girl	J. B. Lippincott	K–2	Sibling conflict
Hutchins, P.*	Titch	Macmillan	K–3	Sibling conflict
Jerrold, B. Wohlberg, M.	The Smallest Boy in the Class	Morrow	1–3	Being the smallest
Keats, E. J.*	Peter's Chair	Harper & Row	PS–1	Sibling conflict
Lapsley, S. Charlton, M.	I Am Adopted	Bradbury	PS–K	Adoption
Lexan, J. M. Weaver, R.	Me Day	Dial	K–3	Divorce
Peterson, J. W. Ray, D.	I Have a Sister: My Sister Is Deaf	Harper & Row	PS–2	Deaf sister

Author	Title	Publisher	Level	Topic
Schick, E.*	Peggy's New Brother	Macmillan	K–2	Sibling conflict
Sharmat, M. W. Hoban, L.	I Want Mama	Harper & Row	K–2	Mother's trip to hospital
Shortall, L.*	Tony's First Dive	Morrow	1–3	Fear of the water
Simon, N. Leder, D.	I Was So Mad!	Whitman	K–3	Anger
Tobias, T. du Bois, W. P.	Moving Day	Knopf	PS–K	Moving
Viorst, J. Cruz, R.	Alexander and the Terrible, Horrible, No Good, Very Bad Day	Atheneum	K–3	Having an off day
Viorst, J. Bleguad, I.	The Tenth Good Thing About Barney	Atheneum	K–2	Death of a pet
Waber, B.*	But Names Will Never Hurt Me	Houghton Mifflin	PS–1	Teasing
Wasson, V. P. Coalson, G.	The Chosen Baby	J. B. Lippincott	PS–K	Adoption
Zolotow, C. Shecter, B.	A Father Like That	Harper & Row	K–2	Not having a father
Zolotow, C. Shecter, B.	If It Weren't For You	Harper & Row	1–3	Sibling conflict
Zolotow, C. du Bois, W. P.	My Grandson Lew	Harper & Row	K–3	Death of a grandparent
Zolotow, C. Lobel, A.	The Quarreling Book	Harper & Row	K–2	Family conflicts
Zolotow, C. du Bois W. P.	William's Doll	Harper & Row	PS–3	Sex roles

*Illustrated by the author.

385

TABLE B-2   Bibliotherapy for Intermediate-Grade Children

AUTHOR ILLUSTRATOR	TITLE	PUBLISHER	GRADE LEVEL	THEME
Aaron, C.	*Better Than Laughter*	Harcourt Brace Jovanovich	5–7	Running away
Albert, L.	*But I'm Ready to Go*	Bradbury	6–9	Learning disabilities
Alcock, G.	*Run, Westy, Run*	Lothrop, Lee & Shepard	4–6	Running away
Alexander, A.	*To Live a Lie*	Atheneum	4–6	Runaway mother
Bauer, M. D.	*Foster Child*	Seabury	5–7	Foster child
Blue, R.	*Grandma Didn't Wave Back*	Watts	3–5	Senility
Blue, R.	*A Month of Sundays*	Watts	3–4	Divorce
Blume, J.	*Are You There God? It's Me, Margaret*	Bradbury	4–6	Religious identity
Blume, J.	*Blubber*	Bradbury	4–6	Defending a friend
Blume, J.	*Deenie*	Bradbury	5–7	Scoliosis
Blume, J.	*It's Not the End of the World*	Bradbury	4–7	Divorce
Blume, J.	*Tales of a Fourth-Grade Nothing*	Dell	3–4	Sibling conflict
Blume, J.	*Then Again, Maybe I Won't*	Bradbury	5–7	Moving
Brandon, B.	*Luther Raps*	Eriksson	2–4	Black awareness
Branfield, J.	*Why Me?*	Harper & Row	5–7	Diabetes

386

Author	Title	Publisher		Topic
Brooks, J.	*Uncle Mike's Boy*	Harper & Row	5–7	Divorce; Death of a sister
Byars, B.	*The Summer of the Swans*	Avon	5–7	Mentally retarded brother
Cameron, E.	*A Room Made of Windows*	Dell	5–7	Loneliness
Carlson, N. S.	*Marchers for the Dream*	Harper & Row	4–5	Poor and Black
Cavanna, B.	*Going on Sixteen*	Scholastic Book Services	6–9	Motherless girl
Cleaver, V. Cleaver, B.	*Grover*	J. B. Lippincott		Mother's suicide; Father's nervous breakdown
Cleaver, V. Cleaver, B.	*Me Too*	J. B. Lippincott	5–7	Mentally retarded twin
Cohen, B.	*Bitter Herbs and Honey*	Lothrop, Lee & Shepard	6–9	Jewish prejudice
Coles, R.	*Dead-End School*	Dell	4–6	Busing
Conford, E.	*Dreams of Victory*	Dell	4–6	Shy, social misfit
Corcoran, B.	*A Dance to Still Music*	Atheneum	6–9	Deafness
Corcoran, B.	*Make No Sound*	Atheneum	5–7	Guilt
Donovan, J.	*Wild in the World*	Avon	6–9	Death of family
Duncan, L.	*A Gift of Magic*	Little, Brown	5–8	ESP; Divorce
Ellis, E. T.	*Celebrate the Morning*	Atheneum	5–9	Mentally ill mother
Ewing, K.	*A Private Matter*	Harcourt Brace Jovanovich	4–5	Divorce
Farley, C.	*The Garden Is Doing Fine*	Atheneum	5–7	Death of father

TABLE B-2 Bibliotherapy for Intermediate-Grade Children (*Continued*)

AUTHOR ILLUSTRATOR	TITLE	PUBLISHER	GRADE LEVEL	THEME
Fassler, J.	*Howie Helps Himself*	Whitman	2-4	Cerebral palsy
Gardam, J.	*The Summer after the Funeral*	Macmillan	6-9	Death of father
Gersten, I. F.	*Ecidujerp, Prejudice: Either Way, It Doesn't Make Sense*	Watts	5-7	Prejudice
Gordon, S.	*Girls Are Girls and Boys Are Boys: So What's the Difference?*	Day	3-4	Sex roles
Greene, C. C.	*Beat the Turtle Drum*	Viking	4-6	Death of sister
Greenwald, S.	*The Secret in Miranda's Closet*	Houghton Mifflin	3-5	Sex roles
Griffin, J. H.	*A Time to Be Human*	Macmillan	5-7	Prejudice
Hooks, W. H.	*Doug Meets the Nutcracker*	Warne	4-6	Sex roles
Hunt, I.	*Lottery Rose*	Scribner's	6-8	Child abuse
Karp, N. J.	*Turning Point*	Harcourt Brace Jovanovich	5-8	Jewish prejudice
Kelley, S.	*Trouble with Explosives*	Bradbury	5-7	Stuttering
Klein, N.	*Taking Sides*	Pantheon	5-7	Divorce
Le Shan, E.	*Learning to Say Good-by: When a Parent Dies*	Macmillan	5-7	Death of parents

Little, J.	*Home From Far*	Little, Brown	4–6	Death of brother; Foster siblings
Little, J.	*Kate*	Harper & Row	5–8	Jewish prejudice
Little, J.	*Mine for Keeps*	Little, Brown	4–6	Cerebral palsy
Little, J.	*Take Wing*	Little, Brown	5–7	Mentally retarded brother
Madison, W.	*Maria Luisa*	J. B. Lippincott	4–6	Chicano prejudice
Mann, P.	*There Are Two Kinds of Terrible*	Doubleday	5–7	Illness and death of mother
Mathis, S. B.	*Sidewalk Story*	Viking	3–5	Eviction
Mathis, S. B.	*Teacup Full of Roses*	Viking	6–9	Drug addiction
Newfield, M.	*A Book for Jodan*	Atheneum	3–4	Divorce
Orgel, D.	*The Mulberry Music*	Harper & Row	4–6	Death of grandparent
Parker, R.	*He Is Your Brother*	Scholastic Book Services	5–6	Autistic brother
Perl, L.	*Dumb Like Me, Olivia Potts*	Seabury	4–6	Superintelligent siblings
Pollowitz, M.	*Cinnamon Cane*	Harper & Row	5–7	Death of grandfather
Reynolds, P.	*Different Kind of Sister*	Lothrop, Lee & Shepard	5–6	Mentally retarded sister
Richards, A. Willis, I.	*How to Get It Together When Your Parents Are Coming Apart*	McKay	6–9	Divorce
Roberts, W. D.	*Don't Hurt Laurie*	Atheneum	4–6	Child abuse

TABLE B-2 Bibliotherapy for Intermediate-Grade Children (*Continued*)

AUTHOR ILLUSTRATOR	TITLE	PUBLISHER	GRADE LEVEL	THEME
Rodowsky, C. F.	*What About Me?*	Watts	6–9	Death of mongoloid brother
Sachs, M. A.	*A December Tale*	Doubleday	5–7	Child abuse
Slote, A.	*Hang Tough, Paul Mather*	J. B. Lippincott	4–7	Leukemia
Smith, D.	*A Taste of Blackberries*	Crowell	4–6	Death of a friend
Synder, A.	*First Step*	Holt, Rinehart & Winston	5–8	Divorce; Alcoholic parent
Sobol, H. L.	*My Brother Stephen Is Retarded*	Macmillan	2–4	Mentally retarded brother
Spence, E.	*The Devil Hole*	Lothrop, Lee & Shepard	6–9	Autistic brother
Stolz, M.	*The Edge of Next Year*	Harper & Row	5–8	Death of mother
Stolz, M.	*Leap Before You Look*	Harper & Row	6–9	Divorce
Vogel, I.	*My Twin Sister Erika*	Harper & Row	5–7	Death of twin

TABLE B-3 High-Interest, Low-Vocabulary Magazines (These magazines are designed for intermediate-grade students reading at the primary-grade levels.)

TITLE	Interest Level (GRADE)	Reading Level (GRADE)	ISSUES per year	PUBLISHER	COMMENTS
Action	7–9	2.0–2.9	14	Scholastic Book Services	Minimum 10 subscriptions to one address; free teacher's edition
Know Your World	4–10	2–3	28	Xerox Education Publications	Minimum 10 subscriptions to one address; free teacher's edition
Sprint	4–6	2.0–2.9	14	Scholastic Book Services	Minimum 10 subscriptions to one address; free teacher's edition

TABLE B-4 Children's Magazines

TITLE	AUDIENCE	ISSUES Per Year	PUBLISHER	COMMENTS
Boys' Life	ages 11–16	12	Boy Scouts of America	
Career World I	ages 9–13	9	Curriculum Innovations	Minimum 15 subscriptions to one address; free teacher's edition
Child Life	ages 7–14	10	Saturday Evening Post	
Children's Digest	ages 7–12	10	Parents' Magazine	
Children's Express	ages 7–14	12	Cheshire Communications Company	Written by children 13 years and younger; assistant editors 14–17 years
Children's Playcraft	ages 7–12	10	Parents' Magazine	
Children's Playmate	ages 3–8	10	Saturday Evening Post	
Cricket	ages 6–12	12	Open Court	
The Curious Naturalist	ages 6–12	4	Massachusetts Audubon Society	
Current Health	ages 9–13	9	Curriculum Innovations	Minimum 15 subscriptions to one address; free teacher's edition
Daisy	age 9	9	Girl Scouts of U.S.A.	Intended for Brownie Girl Scouts
Dynamite	ages 9–14	12	Scholastic Book Services	

Magazine	Age		Publisher	Notes
Ebony Jr.	ages 6–12	10	Johnson	
Electric Company Magazine	graduates of *Sesame Street*	12	Children's Television Workshop	
Highlights for Children	preschool and elementary school children	11	Highlights for Children	
Humpty Dumpty's Magazine for Little Children	ages 3–7	10	Parents' Magazine	
Jack and Jill Magazine	ages 5–12	10	Saturday Evening Post	
Pack-O-Fun	ages 7–12	10	Clapper	"The only scrapcraft magazine"
Pizzazz	ages 10–14	12	Marvel Comics	
Ranger Rick's Nature Magazine	ages 5–12	12	National Wildlife Federation	
Sesame Street	preschool children	10	Children's Television Workshop	Spanish edition available
Stone Soup	ages 6–12	5	Children's Art Foundation	Composed of children's work
World, National Geographic	ages 8–12	12	National Geographic Society	
Wow	ages 4–8	9	Scholastic Book Services	
Young World Magazine	ages 10–14	10	Saturday Evening Post	Formerly *Golden Magazine*

Prepared by Dr. Margaret Corboy, Reading Department, University of South Carolina, Columbia, SC 29208. For additional information on children's magazines consult B. Katz and B. G. Richards, *Magazines for Libraries*, 3rd ed., R. R. Bowker, New York, 1978.

Informal Techniques for Assessing Readability

APPENDIX C

Raygor Graph for Estimating Readabililty   396
Singer Eyeball Estimate of Readability   397

RAYGOR GRAPH FOR ESTIMATING READABILITY

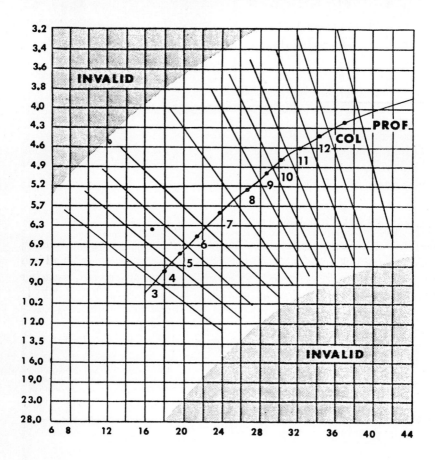

Directions

Count out three 100-word passages at the beginning, middle, and end of a selection or book. Count proper nouns but not numerals.

1. Count sentences in each passage, estimating to nearest tenth.
2. Count words with six or more letters.
3. Average the sentence length and word length over the three samples and plot the average on the graph.

For example:

For more information, see R. S. Baldwin and R. K. Kaufman, "A Concurrent Validity Study of the Raygor Readability Estimate," *Journal of Reading*, **23**: 148–153 (1979).

PASSAGE	NUMBER OF SENTENCES	WORDS OF 6+ LETTERS
A	6.0	15
B	6.8	19
C	6.4	17
Total	19.2	51
Average	6.4	17

Note mark on graph. Grade level is about 5.

This graph is not copyrighted. It may be reproduced. Also, copies can be obtained from Dr. Alton L. Raygor, University of Minnesota, 192 Pillsbury Drive SE, Minneapolis, MN 55455.

SINGER EYEBALL ESTIMATE OF READABILITY

Research confirms that the Singer Eyeball Estimate of Readability (SEER) technique is a quick and simple method of determining readability and is as valid as the Fry graphed procedure. Using the SEER technique, a teacher estimates readability levels by comparing passages of unknown difficulty to a set of graded sample passages. Since this procedure requires a visual comparison of passages, it is called an *eyeball technique*. A set of graded passages from a basal series may be used as a sample in making comparisons.

For more information, see H. Singer, "The SEER Technique: A Non-Computational Procedure for Quickly Estimating Readability Level," *Journal of Reading Behavior*, **7**: 255–267 (1975).

Assessing Reading Interests

D APPENDIX

Interest Inventory   400
Incomplete Sentences   401
A Procedure for Developing an Inventory of Student
    Reading Selections   402

INTEREST INVENTORY

For beginning readers, this inventory must be administered orally. Better readers may be encouraged to complete it independently. Urge the students to mark what intersts *them*, as students occasionally mark responses which they believe will please the teacher.

Name _____ Age _____

1. What do you like to do after school?_____

_____

2. What do you like to do in the evenings, after dinner? _____

_____

3. Are you a member of any club (Boy Scouts, YWCA, etc.)? _____

_____

4. What are your favorite sports? _____

_____

5. Do you play any sports on an organized team? _____

_____

6. Outside of school, do you take any additional lessons (karate, music, dancing)? _____

_____

7. What chores do you do at home? Do you have a job? _____

_____

8. What is your favorite TV show? _____

_____

9. What is your favorite movie? _____

_____

10. What books and magazines do you have at home? _____

_____

11. How often do you visit the library? _____

_____

12. What is your favorite book? _____
13. What is your favorite magazine? _____
    comic? _____
14. What famous person do you admire the most? _____

_____

15. Which of the following subjects interest you the most?

_____ animals	_____ romance	_____ fantasy
_____ fairy tales	_____ growing up	_____ humor
_____ science	_____ history	_____ famous men
fiction	_____ geography	and women
_____ adventure	_____ family life	_____ unusual
_____ sports		facts

Prepared by Dr. Margaret Corboy, Reading Department, University of South Carolina, Columbia, SC 29208.

INCOMPLETE SENTENCES*

Directions

Complete the following sentences to express how you really feel. There are no right answers or wrong answers. Put down what first comes into your mind. Work as quickly as you can.

1. Today I feel ____
2. When I have to read, I ____
3. I get angry when ____
4. To be grown up ____
5. My idea of a good time ____
6. I wish my parents knew ____
7. School is ____
8. I can't understand why ____
9. I feel bad when ____
10. I wish teachers ____
11. I wish my mother ____
12. Going to college ____
13. To me, books ____
14. People think I ____
15. I like to read about ____
16. On weekends, I ____
17. I don't know how ____
18. To me, homework ____
19. I hope I'll never ____
20. I wish people wouldn't ____
21. When I finish high school ____
22. I'm afraid ____
23. Comic books ____
24. When I take my report card home ____
25. I am at my best when ____
26. Most brothers and sisters ____
27. I'd rather read than ____
28. When I read math ____
29. The future looks ____
30. I feel proud when ____
31. I wish my father ____
32. I like to read when ____
33. I would like to be ____
34. For me, studying ____
35. I often worry about ____
36. I wish I could ____

*Ruth Strang, *Diagnostic Teaching of Reading*, McGraw-Hill, New York, 1969, pp. 262–263. Copyright © 1969 by McGraw-Hill, Inc. All rights reserved. Reprinted by permission from the McGraw-Hill Book Company.

37. Reading science _____
38. I look forward to _____
39. I wish someone would help me _____
40. I'd read more if _____
41. Special help in reading _____
42. Every single word is _____
43. My eyes _____
44. The last book I read _____
45. My mother helps _____
46. Reading in junior high school _____
47. My father thinks reading _____
48. I read better than _____
49. My father helps _____
50. I would like to read better than _____

A PROCEDURE FOR DEVELOPING AN INVENTORY OF STUDENT READING SELECTIONS

Frequently, the books that are most popular among students are those recommended by their peers, rather than those recommended by teachers, parents, and librarians. The following procedure was designed to allow students the opportunity to share titles of favorite books:

1. Ask students to write down the titles of several of their favorite books.
2. Compile their selections and list the book titles on a worksheet, using a format similar to the one below.

RECREATIONAL READING SURVEY
Student Selections

In the first column, put a check next to any books you have read. If you have not read a book but you have heard of it, place a check in the second column. In the third column, put a check next to any books you would like to read.

BOOK TITLES	BOOKS I HAVE READ	BOOKS I RECOGNIZE	BOOKS I WOULD LIKE TO READ
Star Wars	_____	_____	_____
UFO	_____	_____	_____
Cars Against the Clock	_____	_____	_____
Riddles and Jokes	_____	_____	_____
Martin L. King, Jr.	_____	_____	_____
The Army Bear	_____	_____	_____
Little House in the Big Woods	_____	_____	_____

NOTE: These titles are some of the favorites listed by a group of sixth graders.

3. Collect the surveys and direct a committee of students in tallying the results.
4. Provide feedback on the results of the survey in one of the following ways:
    (a) Distribute a duplicated copy of the results to the class; for example; "20 percent of the class has read *Star Wars* and 100 percent of the class is familiar with it."
    (b) Direct the students in constructing posters and bulletin boards publicizing the results of the study.
    (c) Provide students with graph paper and assist them in plotting the number of students who read each book, etc.
    (d) Submit the information for publication in the school newspaper.
5. Obtain from the library those books that the students indicated they would like to read.
6. Apply your findings to future book orders. Share the results with the librarian and other teachers.

Prepared by Dr. Margaret Corboy, Reading Department, University of South Carolina, Columbia, SC 29208.

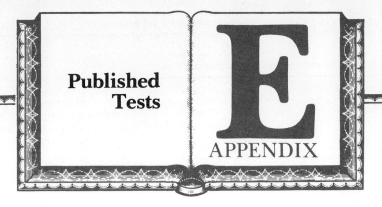

Published Tests

APPENDIX E

Group Reading Readiness Tests 406
Informal Individual Reading Inventories 406
Group Reading Achievement Tests 407
Individual Diagnostic Tests 408
Group Diagnostic Tests 409
Individual Intelligence Tests 410
Group Intelligence Tests 412

TABLE E-1 Group Reading Readiness Tests

TITLE AND PUBLISHER	TIME	ABILITIES MEASURED
Clymer Barrett Prereading Battery Personnel	90 minutes	letter knowledge, shape completion, sentence copying, auditory discrimination, word matching
Gates MacGinitie Reading Tests: *Readiness* Riverside	untimed	listening, auditory and visual discrimination, following directions, letter recognition, visual-motor coordination, auditory blending, word recognition
Harrison-Stroud Reading Readiness *Test* Houghton Mifflin	76 minutes	visual and auditory discrimination, letter identification, use of context clues
Lee Clark Reading Readiness Test California Test Bureau	15 minutes	vocabulary, letter symbols, word symbols
Macmillan Reading Readiness Test Macmillan	90 minutes	visual and auditory discrimination, visual-motor skills, letter names, vocabulary, following directions
Metropolitian Readiness Test Harcourt Brace Jovanovich	60 minutes	letter and number knowledge, motor skills, following directions
Murphy-Durrell Reading Readiness *Analysis* Harcourt Brace Jovanovich	72 minutes	visual and auditory discrimination, learning rate

INFORMAL INDIVIDUAL READING INVENTORIES

The following reading inventories are designed to determine a student's level of independence, instruction, and frustration. Each inventory includes word lists and graded passages with reading comprehension questions. Typically, a student's oral reading and comprehension are assessed. However, these inventories may also be used to measure silent reading and listening comprehension. The administration time varies from 10 to 45 minutes, depending on the performance of the child and the extent of the testing done.

TABLE E-2 Informal Reading Inventories

TITLE	AUTHOR	PUBLISHER
Analytical Reading Inventory	Woods and Moe	Merrill
Classroom Reading inventory	Silvaroli	Brown
Ekwall Reading Inventory	Ekwall	Allyn and Bacon
*Reading Diagnosis Kit**	Miller	Center for Applied Research in Education
Reading Placement Inventory	Sucher and Allred	Economy
Standard Reading Inventory	McCracken	Klamath Printing

*This reference also includes inventories to assess phonics, structural analysis, use of context clues, reading attitudes, and interests.

TABLE E-3   Group Reading Achievement Tests

TITLE AND PUBLISHER	TIME	LEVEL	GRADE EQUIVALENT	ABILITIES MEASURED
California Achievement Tests:	35–80	1	1–2	vocabulary,
Reading	minutes	2	2–4	comprehension
California Test Bureau		3	4–6	
		4	6–9	
Comprehensive Tests of Basic Skills:	40–45	1	2.5–4	vocabulary,
Reading	minutes	2	4–6	comprehension
California Test Bureau		3	6–8	
Gates-MacGinitie Reading Tests	40–60	A	1	vocabulary,
Riverside	minutes	B	2	comprehension
		C	3	
		CS	2–3	vocabulary, com-
		D	4–6	prehension,
		E	7–9	speed and ac-
				curacy
Iowa Tests of Basic Skills	60–85	1	1.7–3.5	vocabulary,
Riverside	minutes	2	3–8	comprehension,
				word analysis,
				work-study
				skills
Metropolitan Achievement Tests:	42–60	P	K.7–1.4	word knowledge,
Reading	minutes			comprehension,
Harcourt Brace Jovanovich		P1	1.5–2.4	sounds
		P2	2.5–3.4	word knowledge,
		E	3.5–4.9	word analysis,
				comprehension
		I	5–6.9	word knowledge,
		A	7–9.5	comprehension
SRA Achievement Series:	60	P1	1–2.5	vocabulary,
Reading	minutes	P2	2–3.5	comprehension
Science Research Associates		Blue	4–5	
		Green	6–7	
		Red	8–9.5	
Stanford Achievement Tests:	35–95	P1	1.5–2.4	vocabulary,
Reading	minutes	P2	2.5–3.4	comprehension,
Harcourt Brace Jovanovich		P3	3.5–4.4	word-study
		I1	4.5–5.4	skills
		I2	5.5–6.9	

TABLE E-4 Individual Diagnostic Tests

TITLE AND PUBLISHER	TIME	LEVEL	GRADE EQUIVALENT	ABILITIES MEASURED
Diagnostic Reading Scales California Test Bureau	45 minutes	1	1–8	word recognition, oral reading, silent reading rate, listening comprehension, phonics
Durrell Analysis of Reading Difficulty Harcourt Brace Jovanovich	30–90 minutes	1	1–6	comprehension, oral reading, silent reading, listening, word recognition, phonics, visual memory, spelling, handwriting
Gates-McKillop Reading Diagnostic Test Teachers College	30–60 minutes	1	2–6	vocabulary, oral reading, knowledge of word parts, auditory blending, spelling, syllabication, auditory discrimination
Gilmore Oral Reading Test Harcourt Brace Jovanovich	20 minutes	1	1–8	oral reading and comprehension rate
Goodman-Burke Reading Miscue Inventory Macmillan	15–20 minutes	1	1–8	oral reading

Test / Publisher	Grade		Time	Skills Measured
Gray Oral Reading Test Bobbs-Merrill	1–12	1	15 minutes	oral reading, rate
Peabody Individual Achievement Test American Guidance Service	K–12	1	30–40 minutes	comprehension, information, letter names and sounds, visual discrimination
Roswell-Chall Auditory Blending Test Essay Press	1–4	1	5 minutes	sound blending
Roswell-Chall Diagnostic Test of Word Analysis Skills Essay	2–6	1	5 minutes	word recognition, phonics
Slosson Oral Reading Test Slosson Educational Publications	1–12	1	5–10 minutes	word recognition
Stanford Diagnostic Reading Test Harcourt Brace Jovanovich	2–4	1	113–165 minutes	vocabulary, comprehension, syllabication, auditory skills, phonics skills; plus rate on level 2
Woodcock Reading Mastery Tests American Guidance Service	K–12	1	20–30 minutes	comprehension, letter knowledge, word recognition, word attack

TABLE E-5 Group Diagnostic Tests

TITLE AND PUBLISHER	TIME	LEVEL	GRADE EQUIVALENT	ABILITIES MEASURED
Botel Reading Inventory Follett	untimed	1	1–8	word recognition, word opposites, phonics, spelling
California Phonics Survey California Test Bureau	40 minutes	1	2–12	word analysis
Doren Diagnostic Reading Test of Word Recognition Skills American Guidance Service	untimed	1	3–8	word recognition, letter recognition, phonics
McCullough Word-Analysis Tests Personnel	untimed	1	4–8	phonics, structural analysis
Prescriptive Reading Inventory California Test Bureau	150 minutes	1 2 3 4	1.5–2.5 2.0–3.5 3.0–4.5 4.0–6.5	vocabulary, comprehension, phonics, structural analysis

TABLE E-6   Individual Intelligence Tests

TITLE AND PUBLISHER	TIME	AGE LEVEL	ABILITIES MEASURED
Peabody Picture Vocabulary Test American Guidance Service	untimed	2.5–19	receptive vocabulary
Slosson Intelligence Test Slosson Educational Publications	10–20 minutes	infant to adult	general information
Stanford Binet Intelligence Scales* Houghton Mifflin	untimed	2 to adult	vocabulary, general information
Wechsler Intelligence Scale for Children* Psychological Corporation	40–60 minutes	5–15	verbal: information, vocabulary, comprehension, arithmetic, digit span, similarities; performance: picture completion, picture arrangement, block design, object assembly, coding, mazes

*Only a specially trained examiner may administer and score these tests.

TABLE E-7 : **Group Intelligence Tests**

TITLE AND PUBLISHER	TIME	LEVEL	GRADE EQUIVALENT	ABILITIES MEASURED
California Test of Mental Maturity California Test Bureau	90 minutes	0 1 2 3	K-1 1.5-3 4-6 7-9	language, memory, spatial relationships, reasoning vocabulary
Kuhlman-Anderson Test Personnel	40-45 minutes	1 2 3 4 5 6 7 8	K 1 2 3 4 5 6 7-8	verbal, quantitative
Lorge-Thorndike Intelligence Test Houghton Mifflin		1 2 3 4	K-1 2-3 4-6 7-9	verbal verbal and nonverbal
Otis Quick Scoring Test of Mental Ability Harcourt Brace Jovanovich	25-30 minutes	1 2	1-4 4-9	general mental ability
SRA Short Test of Educational Ability Science Research Associates		1 2 3 4	K-1 2-3 3-6 6-9	verbal, quantitative

Organizations and References for Reading Professionals

APPENDIX F

Professional Organizations and Periodicals   414

Recommended Textbooks   415

PROFESSIONAL ORGANIZATIONS AND PERIODICALS

Association for Childhood Education
International (ACEI)
  3615 Wisconsin Avenue NW
  Washington, DC 20016
    Membership: teachers, parents,
    and adults (15,000)
    Journal: *Childhood Education*, 5 is-
    sues per year.

American Association of School Librarians (AASL)
  50 East Huron St.
  Chicago, IL 60611
    Membership: elementary-and
    secondary-school librarians and
    media specialists (7500)
    Journal: *School Media Quarterly*, 4
    issues per year.

Association for Supervision and Curriculum Development (ASCD)
  1701 K Street NW
  Suite 1100
  Washington, DC 20006
    Membership: teachers, school
    administrators, teacher-trainers
    (35,000)
    Journal: *Educational Leadership*, 8
    issues per year.

Children's Book Council (CBC)
  61 Irving Place
  New York, NY 10003
    Membership: reviewers of chil-
    dren's trade books (60)
    Publications: children's booklists,
    promotional materials (book-
    marks, posters, mobiles, etc.) to
    encourage children's recrea-
    tional reading

College Reading Association (CRA)
  James R. Layton
  Southwest Missouri State University
  3340 S. Danbury Avenue
  Springfield, MO 65807
    Membership: teachers, school
    administrators, teacher-trainers

    interested in college and adult
    reading (575)
    Journal: *Reading World*, 4 issues
    per year.

International Reading Association
(IRA)
  800 Barksdale Road
  PO Box 8139
  Newark, DE 19711
    Membership: teachers, teacher-
    trainers, school administrators,
    parents, and individuals in-
    terested in the teaching of
    reading at all levels (70,000)
    Journals: *The Reading Teacher*, 8
    issues per year
    Journal of Reading, 8 issues per
    year
    Reading Research Quarterly, 4 is-
    sues per year

National Council of Teachers of English (NCTE)
  1111 Kenyon Road
  Urbana, IL 61801
    Membership: teachers of English
    at all levels (100,000)
    Journals: *Language Arts*, 9 issues
    per year.
    English Journal, 8 issues per year.

National Education Association
(NEA)
  1201 16th Street NW
  Washington, DC 20036
    Membership: teachers, teacher-
    trainers, school administrators
    (1,600,000)
    Journal: *Today's Education*, 4 is-
    sues per year.

National Reading Conference (NRC)
  1230 Seventeenth Street NW
  Washington, DC 20036
    Membership: teacher-trainers,
    school administrators (700)
    Journal: *Journal of Reading Be-
    havior*, 4 issues per year.

RECOMMENDED TEXTBOOKS

In a national study, reading educators were asked to name the professional books and materials they would recommend to the first-year elementary-school teacher who wanted to begin a professional library in reading. The five most frequently recommended book titles are listed below and ranked in descending order.

Spache, G, and Spache, E.: *Reading in the Elementary School*, Allyn and Bacon, Boston, 1974.

Harris, A. J., and Sipay, E.: *How to Increase Reading Ability*, Longmans, New York, 1980.

Heilman, A. W.: *Principles and Practices of Teaching Reading*, Merrill, Columbus, Ohio, 1977.

Ekwall, E.: *Locating and Correcting Reading Difficulties*, Merrill, Columbus, Ohio, 1977.

Zintz, M. V.: *The Reading Process: The Teacher and the Learner*, Brown, Dubuque, Iowa, 1980.

Other frequently mentioned book titles are listed below in alphabetical order.

Aukerman, R. C.: *Approaches to Beginning Reading*, Wiley, New York, 1971.

Durkin, D.: *Teaching Them to Read*, Allyn and Bacon, Boston, 1978.

Ekwall, E. E.: *Diagnosis and Remediation of the Disabled Reader*, Allyn and Bacon, Boston, 1976.

Guszak, F. J.: *Diagnostic Reading Instruction in the Elementary School*, Harper & Row, New York, 1978.

Heilman, A. W.: *Phonics in Proper Perspective*, Merrill, Columbus, Ohio, 1976.

McCracken, R. A., and McCracken M.: *Reading Is Only the Tiger's Tail*, Leswing, San Rafael, Calif., 1972.

Ruddell, R. B.: *Reading Language Instruction: Innovative Practices*, Prentice-Hall, Englewood Cliffs, N.J., 1973.

Silvaroli, N. J.: *Classroom Reading Inventory*, Brown, Dubuque, Iowa, 1976.

Smith, F.: *Understanding Reading: A Psycholinguistic Analysis of Reading and Learning to Read*, Holt, Rinehart & Winston, New York, 1978.

Spache, E. B.: Reading Activities for Child Involvement, Allyn and Bacon, Boston, 1976.

Stauffer, R. G.: *Directing the Reading-Thinking Process*, Harper & Row, New York, 1975.

Van Allen, R.: *Language Experiences in Communication*, Houghton Mifflin, Boston, 1976.

K. A. Koenke, "A Minimal Professional Reference Library in Elementary Reading Instruction: A Survey," National Reading Conference, New Orleans, 1977 (ERIC/RCS Report No. ED 151 761). Reprinted by permission from the author.

Materials and Suggestions for Working with Parents

G

APPENDIX

A Bibliography for Teachers on Parent Involvement
in Reading   418
Parental Involvement Letter   419
Suggestions for Conducting Parent-Teacher Conferences   420
Parent Checklist for Encouraging Reading   420

A BIBLIOGRAPHY FOR TEACHERS ON PARENT INVOLVEMENT IN READING

The Reading Teacher

Baker, I.: "Children's Literature at Home Base," *The Reading Teacher*, **28**:770–772 (1975).

Duncan, L. J. and Von Behren, B.: "Pepper—A Spicy New Program," *The Reading Teacher*, **28**:180–183 (1974).

Freshour, F. W.: "Parent Education and Reading Readiness and Achievement," *The Reading Teacher*, **24**:763 (1971).

———— : "Parents Can Help," *The Reading Teacher*, **25**:513–516 (1972).

Lange, R.: "P.R.: Public Relations; Parents and Reading," *The Reading Teacher*, **31**:858–861 (1978).

Swift, M. S.: "Pre-School Books and Mother-Child Communication," *The Reading Teacher*, **25**:236–238 (1971).

Todd, C. C., Jr.: "Should Reading Be Taught At Home?" *The Reading Teacher*, **26**:814–816 (1973).

Vukelich, C.: "Parents are Teachers: A Beginning Reading Program: Preschool Readiness Outreach Program," *The Reading Teacher*, **31**:524–527 (1978).

———— : "Survival Reading For Parents and Kids: A Parent Education Program," *The Reading Teacher*, **31**:638–641 (1978).

Other Selected Readings

Cramer, W.: "My Mommy Can Teach Reading Too!" *Elementary School Journal*, **72**:72–75 (1971).

Criscuolo, N. P.: "Meaningful Parental Involvement in the Reading Program," *National Elementary Principal*, **51**:64–65 (1972).

DeFranco, E. B.: "Parental Education As an Aid to Improving Children's Reading," *Adult Leadership*, **21**:320–323 (1973).

Hoskissen, K.: "Should Parents Teach Their Children to Read?" *Education Digest*, **39**:44–47 (1974).

Larrick, N.: "Home Influence on Early Learning," *Today's Education*, **64**:77– (1975).

Merrick, H. U.: "An Open Letter to Parents," *Contemporary Education*, **46**:264–265 (1975).

Niedermeyer, F. E.: "Parents Teach Kindergarten Reading at Home," *Elementary School Journal*, **70**:438–445 (1970).

Rossman, J. F.: "Remedial Readers: Did Parents Read to Them at Home?" *Journal of Reading*, **17**:622–625 (1974).

Sullivan, H. J.: "Parents: Summer Reading Teachers." *Elementary School Journal*, **71**:279–285 (1971).

Weisner, M. G.: "Parental Responsibility in the Teaching of Reading." *Young Child*. **29**:225–230 (1974).

Prepared by Richard C. Ingram, Reading Department, Winthrop College, Rock Hill, SC 29730.

REFERENCES FOR PARENTS

Books

Arbuthnot, M. H.: *Children's Reading in the Home*, Scott, Foresman, Glenview, Ill., 1969.

Buskin, M.: *Parent Power: How to Deal with Your Child's School*, Walker, New York, 1975.

Chess, S.: *How to Help Your Child Get the Most out of School*, Doubleday, New York, 1974.

Larrick, N.: *A Parent's Guide to Children's Reading*, Doubleday, New York, 1975.

Smith, C.: *Parents and Reading*, International Reading Association, Newark, Del., 1971.

Micromonographs

For a charge of 50 cents each, the following micromonographs may be obtained from the International Reading Association, 800 Barksdale Road, PO Box 8139, Newark, DE 19711.

Baghban, M.: *How Can I Help My Child Learn to Read English As a Second Language?* (Also available in Spanish.)

Chan, J.: *Why Read Aloud to Children?*

Eberly, D. W.: *How Does My Child's Vision Affect His Reading?*

Ransbury, M. K.: *How Can I Encourage My Primary-Grade Child to Read?*

Rogers, N.: *How Can I Help My Child Get Ready to Read?*

Rogers, N.: *What Books and Records Should I Get for My Preschooler?*

Rogers, N.: *What is Reading Readiness?*

U.S. Government Publications

The following publications are available free or at a small charge from the U.S. Government Printing Office, North Capitol and H Streets, NW, Washington, DC 20401.

Children and Television. Free

Dyslexia. $1.00

Parents and Beginning Readers. Free

Plain Talk about Learning Disabilities. Free.

PARENTAL INVOLVEMENT LETTER

Dear Moms and Dads,

You are your child's first and most important teacher, and I would like to suggest how you can continue to help at home if you wish. I've planned this program because many parents, in the past, have expressed an interest in supporting their child's education by engaging them in activities at home. These are a few suggestions that you might like to try with your child when you have a few minutes together.

I will be sending an activity home each Friday. As you complete the activity with your child, please sign the railroad car so that your child may return it to school. There he will color it, cut it out, and add it to his "train" at school. We hope he will enjoy seeing his train grow, but most of all the interaction and enjoyment he will receive from your time and interest will be invaluable to his academic achievements.

If this will not fit into your schedule, which indeed is understandable at these busy times, please let me know, and I will be happy to arrange another program whereby your child will receive a similar experience.

Most sincerely,

Carolyn M. Long

Reprinted by permission of the author.

SUGGESTIONS FOR CONDUCTING PARENT-TEACHER CONFERENCES

1. Review your files prior to the conference in order to avoid asking unnecessary questions.
2. Arrange to meet in a private place where parents will feel comfortable in talking freely.
3. Avoid questions that encourage yes-no answers. Open-ended questions will provide you with more information.
4. Emphasize the positive. Rather than reporting that a student missed 40 percent of the words on a list, report that he recognized 60 percent correctly.
5. Limit your discussion to the performance of the child, and avoid discussion in which he is compared to his siblings, neighbors, and classmates.
6. Give a realistic assessment of the student's progress in relationship to his ability.
7. Share with parents any notes taken during the conference.
8. Invite parents to the classroom to observe the student's performance during the school day.
9. If a problem requires additional professional assistance, refer the parents to the appropriate personnel.
10. Provide examples of student work.
11. Maintain confidentiality of all matters discussed.

PARENT CHECKLIST FOR ENCOURAGING READING

_____ 1. Do you have children's books and magazines available in your home?
_____ 2. Do you set aside a quiet time each day (without the distractions of the television) in which you and your child read?
_____ 3. Do you have a library card and use it?

_____ 4. Do you take your child to the library frequently and assist him in locating books relating to his interests?

_____ 5. Do you subscribe to magazines and newspapers?

_____ 6. Do you share sections of the newspaper (sports, weather, comics, etc.) with your child?

_____ 7. Do you provide your child with a place to keep his books (a bookcase, bookshelf, or a cardboard box)?

_____ 8. Do you have reference books in your home (dictionary, atlas, almanac, encyclopedia)?

_____ 9. Do you guide your child in using reference books to locate answers to questions he asks?

_____ 10. Do you give books and magazines to your child as gifts on special occasions?

_____ 11. Do you develop your child's background by taking him on trips to the zoo, park, airport, museum, post office, etc.?

_____ 12. Do you discuss with your child his experiences on such trips?

_____ 13. Do you watch television with your child and discuss the programs he views?

_____ 14. Do you read aloud to your child regularly?

_____ 15. Do you provide your child with a quiet, comfortable, well-lighted place for reading?

Prepared by Dr. Margaret Corboy, Reading Department, College of Education, University of South Carolina, Columbia, SC 29208.

Names and
Addresses of
Publishers

H

APPENDIX

NAMES AND ADDRESSES OF PUBLISHERS

Academic Press, Inc.
 111 Fifth Avenue
 New York, NY 10003
Academic Therapy Publications
 20 Commercial Boulevard
 Novato, CA 94947
Addison-Wesley Publishing Co., Inc.
 2725 Sand Hill Road
 Menlo Park, CA 94025
Aladdin Books
 Atheneum Publishers
 597 Fifth Avenue
 New York, NY 10017
Allyn and Bacon, Inc.
 470 Atlantic Avenue
 Boston, MA 02210
American Book Company
 135 West 50 Street
 New York, NY 10020
American Council on Education
 1 Dupont Circle NW
 Washington, DC 20036
American Guidance Service, Inc.
 Publishers' Building
 Circle Pines, MN 55014
American Library Association
 50 East Huron Street
 Chicago, IL 60611
Ann Arbor Science Publishers
 230 Collingwood Avenue
 Ann Arbor, MI 48106
Arlington House, Inc.
 165 Huguenot Street
 New Rochelle, NY 10801
Atheneum Publishers
 597 Fifth Avenue
 New York, NY 10017
Avon Books
 959 Eighth Avenue
 New York, NY 10019
Ball-Stick-Bird Publications
 P. O. Box 592
 Stony Brook, NY 11790
Bantam Books, Inc.
 666 Fifth Avenue
 New York, NY 10019

Barnell Loft, Ltd.
 958 Church Street
 Baldwin, NY 11510
Basic Books, Inc., Publishers
 10 East 53 Street
 New York, NY 10022
Beginner Books
 201 East 50 Street
 New York, NY 10022
Behavioral Research Laboratories
 P. O. Box 577
 Palo Alto, CA 94302
Bell and Howell Company
 7100 McCormick Road
 Chicago, IL 60645
Benefic Press
 1900 North Narragansett Avenue
 Chicago, IL 60639
The Bobbs-Merrill Co., Inc.
 4300 West 62 Street
 Indianapolis, IN 46268
Borg-Warner Educational Systems
 7450 North Natchez Avenue
 Niles, IL 60648
R. R. Bowker Company
 1180 Avenue of the Americas
 New York, NY 10036
Bowmar/Noble Publishers, Inc.
 4563 Colorado Boulevard
 Los Angeles, CA 90039
Boy Scouts of America
 National Office
 Box 61030 Dallas
 Fort Worth Airport, TX 75261
Bradbury Press, Inc.
 2 Overhill Road
 Scarsdale, NY 10583
Wm. C. Brown Company
 2460 Kerper Boulevard
 Dubuque, IA 52001
Burgess Publishing Company
 7108 Ohms Lane
 Minneapolis, MN 55435
California Test Bureau
 Div. of McGraw-Hill Book Co.
 Del Monte Research Park
 Monterey, CA 93940

Cambridge Book Company
888 Seventh Avenue
New York, NY 10019

Cambridge University Press
32 East 57 Street
New York, NY 10022

Center for Applied Research
in Education, Inc.
Subs. of Prentice-Hall
Englewood Cliffs, NJ 07632

Chandler Publishing Co.
124 Spear Street
San Francisco, CA 94105

Changing Times Education Service
1729 H Street NW
Washington, DC 20006

Childcraft Education Corporation
20 Kilmer Road
Edison Township, NJ 08817

Children's Art Foundation
P. O. Box 83
Santa Cruz, CA 95063

Childrens Press
1224 West Van Buren Street
Chicago, IL 60607

Children's Television Workshop
1 Lincoln Plaza
New York, NY 10023

Chilton Book Company
Chilton Way
Radnor, PA 19089

Citation Press
Scholastic Book Services
50 West 44 Street
New York, NY 10036

Clapper Publishing Co.
14 Main St.
Park Ridge, IL 60068

William Collins Publishers, Inc.
2080 West 117 Street
Cleveland, OH 44111

Continental Press, Inc.
520 East Bainbridge Street
Elizabethtown, PA 17022

Coronet, The Multimedia Company
65 Southeast Water Street
Chicago, IL 60601

Coward, McCann & Geoghegan, Inc.
200 Madison Avenue
New York, NY 10016

Creative Education, Inc.
123 South Broad Street
Mankato, MN 56001.

Creative Playthings Division
Box 306, Route 407
Herndon, PA 17830

Crestwood House, Inc.
P. O. Box 3427
Highway 66 S
Mankato, MN 56001

Croft Educational Services
100 Garfield Avenue
New London, CT 06320

Thomas Y. Crowell Company, Publishers
201 Park Avenue S
New York, NY 10003

Crown Publishers, Inc.
1 Park Avenue
New York, NY 10016

Curriculum Associates, Inc.
5 Esquire Road
North Billerica, MA 01862

Curriculum Innovations, Inc.
3500 Western Avenue
Highland Park, IL 60035

Delacorte Press
c/o Dell Publishing Co., Inc.
1 Dag Hammarskjold Plaza
New York, NY 10017

Dell Publishing Co., Inc.
1 Dag Hammarskjold Plaza
New York, NY 10017

Developmental Learning Materials
7440 Natchez Avenue
Niles, IL 60648

Dexter & Westbrook, Ltd.
958 Church Street
Baldwin, NY 11510

The Dial Press
1 Dag Hammarskjold Plaza
New York, NY 10017

Dodd, Mead & Company
79 Madison Avenue
New York, NY 10016

Doubleday & Co., Inc.
  45 Park Avenue
  New York, NY 10017
Dreier Educational Systems, Inc.
  25 S. 5th Avenue
  Highland Park, NJ 08904
d₃ learning
  H-103 Norwich Court
  Columbia, SC 29206
E. P. Dutton
  2 Park Avenue
  New York NY 10016
The Economy Company
  1901 North Walnut Street
  Oklahoma City, OK 73125
Educational Activities, Inc.
  1937 Grand Avenue
  Baldwin, NY 11510
Educational Developmental
  Laboratories, Inc.
  Div. of McGraw-Hill Book Co.
  1221 Avenue of the Americas
  New York, NY 10020
Educational Teaching Aids
  3905 Bohannon Drive
  Menlo Park, CA 94025
Encyclopedia Britannica Educational
  Corporation
  425 North Michigan Avenue
  Chicago, IL 60611
Farrar, Straus & Giroux, Inc.
  19 Union Square W
  New York, NY 10003
Fearon•Pitman Publishers, Inc.
  6 Davis Drive
  Belmont, CA 94002
Follett Publishing Company
  1010 West Washington Boulevard
  Chicago, IL 60607
Four Winds Press
  50 West 44 Street
  New York, NY 10036
Garrard Publishing Company
  1607 North Market Street
  Champaign, IL 61820
General Learning Corp.
  Silver Burdett, Inc.
  2450 Embarcadero Way
  Palo Alto, CA 94303

Ginn & Company
  191 Spring Street
  Lexington, MA 02173
Girl Scouts of the U.S.A.
  830 Third Avenue
  New York, NY 10022
Globe Book Co., Inc.
  50 West 23 Street
  New York, NY 10010
Golden Gate Junior Books
  1224 West Van Buren Street
  Chicago, IL 60607
Goodyear Publishing Co., Inc.
  1640 Fifth Street
  Santa Monica, CA 90401
Greenwillow Books
  105 Madison Avenue
  New York, NY 10016
Grolier Educational Corporation
  Sherman Turnpike
  Danbury, CT 06816
Grosset & Dunlap, Inc.
  51 Madison Avenue
  New York, NY 10010
Grune & Stratton, Inc.
  111 Fifth Avenue
  New York, NY 10003
E. M. Hale & Co.
  128 West River Street
  Chippewa Falls, WI 54729
Harcourt Brace Jovanovich, Inc.
  757 Third Avenue
  New York, NY 10017
Harper & Row, Publishers, Inc.
  10 East 53 Street
  New York, NY 10022
Harvey House, Publishers
  20 Waterside Plaza
  New York, NY 10010
Hastings House, Publishers, Inc.
  10 East 40 Street
  New York, NY 10016
D. C. Heath & Company
  125 Spring Street
  Lexington, MA 02173
Highlights for Children, Inc.
  2300 West Fifth Avenue
  Columbus, OH 43216

Hoffman Information Systems
  4423 Arden Drive
  El Monte, CA 91734
Holiday House, Inc.
  18 East 53 Street
  New York, NY 10022
Holt, Rinehart & Winston
  383 Madison Avenue
  New York, NY 10017
Houghton Mifflin Company
  1 Beacon Street
  Boston, MA 02107
Ideal School Supply Company
  11000 South Lavergne
  Oak Lawn, IL 60453
Instructo Corporation
  200 Cedar Hollow and Matthews Rds.
  Paoli, PA 19301
International Reading Association
  P. O. Box 8139
  800 Barksdale Road
  Newark, DE 19711
Jamestown Publishers
  Box 6743
  Providence, RI 02940
Jastak Associates, Inc.
  1526 Gilpin Ave.
  Wilmington, DE 19806
Johnson Publishing Co., Inc.
  820 South Michigan Avenue
  Chicago, IL 60605
Judy Publishing Co.
  Box 5270
  Chicago, IL 60608
Kendall/Hunt Publishing Company
  2460 Kerper Boulevard
  Dubuque, IA 52001
Kenworthy Educational Service, Inc.
  Post Office Box 60
  Buffalo, NY 14205
Keystone View
  2210 East 12th Street
  Davenport, IA 52803
Klamath Publishing Company
  1301 Esplande
  Klamath Falls, OR 97601
Alfred A. Knopf, Inc.
  201 East 50 Street
  New York, NY 10022

Laidlaw Brothers
  Thatcher & Madison Streets
  River Forest, IL 60305
Language Research Associates, Inc.
  Post Office Box 2085
  Palm Springs, CA 92262
Larousse & Co., Inc.
  572 Fifth Avenue
  New York, NY 10036
Learning Research Associates
  1501 Broadway
  New York, NY 10036
Learning Systems Corporation
  60 Connolly Parkway
  Hamden, CT 06514
Learning Through Seeing, Inc.
  8138 Foothill Blvd.
  Sunland, CA 91040
Learning Tree Filmstrips
  7108 S. Alton Way
  Inglewood, CA 90306
Leswing Press, Inc.
  750 Adrian Way
  San Rafael, CA 94903
J. B. Lippincott Company
  East Washington Square
  Philadelphia, PA 19105
Little Brown Bear
  Learning Associates, Inc.
  P. O. Box 561167
  Miami, FL 33156
Little, Brown & Company
  34 Beacon Street
  Boston, MA 02106
Liveright Publishing Corp.
  Subs. of W. W. Norton Co., Inc.
  500 Fifth Ave.
  New York, NY 10036
Longman, Inc.
  19 West 42 Street
  New York, NY 10036
Lothrop, Lee & Shepard Books
  105 Madison Avenue
  New York, NY 10016
Lyons & Carnahan Educational
  Publishers
  Rand McNally & Company
  Post Office Box 7600
  Chicago, IL 60680

Macmillan, Inc.
  866 Third Avenue
  New York, NY 10022
Mafex Associates, Inc.
  90 Cherry Street
  Johnstown, PA 15902
Marvel Comic Group
  Cadence Industries Corporation
  21 Henderson Drive
  West Caldwell, NJ 07006
McCormick-Mathers Publishing Company
  135 West 50 Street
  New York, NY 10020
McGraw-Hill Book Company
  1221 Avenue of the Americas
  New York, NY 10020
David McKay Co., Inc.
  2 Park Avenue
  New York, NY 10016
Meredith Corporation
  1716 Locust Street
  Des Moines, IA 50336
G. & C. Merriam Company
  47 Federal Street
  Springfield, MA 01101
Charles E. Merrill Publishing Company
  1300 Alum Creek Drive
  Columbus, OH 43216
Julian Messner
  The Simon & Schuster Building
  1230 Avenue of the Americas
  New York, NY 10020
Miller-Brody Productions, Inc.
  342 Madison Avenue
  New York, NY 10017
Milton Bradley Company
  1500 Main Street
  Springfield, MA 01115
Modern Curriculum Press, Inc.
  13900 Prospect Road
  Cleveland, OH 44136
William Morrow & Co., Inc.
  105 Madison Avenue
  New York, NY 10016
National Geographic Society
  Educational Services
  Dept. 01075
  17th & M Streets NW
  Washington, DC 20036

National Wildlife Federation
  1412 16 Street NW
  Washington, DC 20036
Thomas Nelson, Inc.
  405 Seventh Avenue S
  Nashville, TN 37203
New American Library, Inc.
  1633 Broadway
  New York, NY 10019
Open Court Publishing Company
  1058 Eighth Street
  La Salle, IL 61301
The Overlook Press
  667 Madison Avenue
  New York, NY 10021
Oxford University Press, Inc.
  200 Madison Avenue
  New York, NY 10016
Pantheon Books, Inc.
  201 East 50 Street
  New York, NY 10022
Parents' Magazine Press
  52 Vanderbilt Avenue
  New York, NY 10017
Parnassus Press
  P. O. Box 8443
  Emeryville, CA 94608
Penguin Books
  625 Madison Avenue
  New York, NY 10022
Personnel Press, Inc.
  Division, Ginn & Company
  191 Spring Street
  Lexington, MA 02173
Phonovisual Products, Inc.
  Post Office Box 2007
  Rockville, MD 20852
Plays, Inc.
  8 Arlington Street
  Boston, MA 02116
Prentice-Hall, Inc.
  Englewood Cliffs, NJ 07632
Psychological Corporation
  304 East 45 Street
  New York, NY 10017
G. P. Putnam's Sons
  200 Madison Avenue
  New York, NY 10016

Raintree Publishers Group
205 West Highland Avenue
Milwaukee, WI 53203

Rand McNally & Company
Box 7600
Chicago, IL 60680

Random House, Inc.
201 East 50 Street
New York, NY 10022

Reader's Digest Services, Inc.
Educational Division
Pleasantville, NY 10570

Reading is Fun-Damental
1833 S. Burdick
Kalamazoo, MI 49001

Reading Joy, Inc.
2210 Wellington Court
Lisle, IL 60532

Reading Laboratory, Inc.
Post Office Box 681
South Norwalk, CT 06854

The Riverside Publishing Company
1919 South Highland Avenue
Lombard, IL 60148

Saturday Evening Post Book Division
P. O. Box 528B
1100 Waterway Boulevard
Indianapolis, IN 46206

Scholastic Book Services
50 West 44 Street
New York, NY 10036

Scholastic Testing Service, Inc.
480 Meyer Road
Bensenville, IL 60106

Science Research Associates, Inc.
155 North Wacker Drive
Chicago, IL 60606

Scott, Foresman & Company
1900 East Lake Avenue
Glenview, IL 60025

The Scribner Book Companies, Inc.
597 Fifth Avenue
New York, NY 10017

Silver Burdett Company
250 James Street
Morristown, NJ 07960

Singer School Division
Random House
201 East 50 Street
New York, NY 10022

Slosson Educational Publications
140 Pike Street
East Aurora, NY 14052

Steck-Vaughn Company
P. O. Box 2028
Austin, TX 78768

Strawberry Books
572 Fifth Avenue
New York, NY 10036

Teachers College Press
Teachers College
Columbia University
1234 Amsterdam Avenue
New York, NY 10027

Teaching Resources Corporation
100 Boylston Street
Boston, MA 02116

Troll Associates
320 Route 17
Mahwah, NJ 07430

United Learning Corp.
Box 5351
Eugene, OR 97405

U.S. Government Printing Office
North Capitol & H Streets, NW
Washington, DC 20401

The Viking Press
625 Madison Avenue
New York, NY 10022

Henry Z. Walck, Inc.
2 Park Avenue
New York, NY 10016

Walker Publishing Co., Inc.
720 Fifth Avenue
New York, NY 10019

Frederick Warne & Co., Inc.
2 Park Avenue
New York, NY 10016

Franklin Watts, Inc.
730 Fifth Avenue
New York, NY 10019

Webster Division
McGraw-Hill, Inc.
1221 Avenue of the Americas
New York, NY 10020

Weekly Reader
Xerox Corporation
1250 Fairwood Avenue
Columbus, OH 43206

Western Publishing Co., Inc.
  1220 Mound Avenue
  Racine, WI 53404
The Westminster Press
  925 Chestnut Street
  Philadelphia, PA 19107
Weston Woods Studios, Inc.
  389 Newtown Turnpike
  Weston, CT 06883
Albert Whitman & Company
  560 West Lake Street
  Chicago, IL 60606

John Wiley & Sons, Inc.
  605 Third Avenue
  New York, NY 10016
Windmill Books, Inc.
  1230 Avenue of the Americas
  New York, NY 10020
Xerox Education Publications
  245 Long Hill Road
  Middletown, CT 06457

Index

Accommodation, 219, 234, 238, 239
Achievement-level grouping, 195, 200-201
Activities that promote sharing of literature, 187-190
    arts and crafts, 189
    miscellaneous, 189-190
    oral language, 188-189
    written language, 187-188
Acuity, 105
    auditory, 21, 238
    visual, 21, 234-235
Administrators, 260-262
Affixes, 50
Allen, R. V., 82, 102, 415
Allington, R., 284
American Optometric Association, 235, 240
Analogies, 56
Analytical method (Fernald technique), 201-202
Annotation, 171
Appreciation of reading, 75-76
Approaches to reading, 81-102

Arbuthnot, M. H., 178, 192
Artley, A. S., 3, 18
Arts and crafts activities, 189
Ashton-Warner, S., 106, 107, 127
Assessment:
    of children's hearing, 238-239
    of children's interests, 173-174
    of children's vision, 234-235
    of reading and reading-related abilities, 151-169
        formal, 151-154
        informal, 151, 154-155
        specific reading abilities, 162-168
Attitudes toward reading, 175-177
Auditory, definition of, 219
Auditory acuity, 21, 238-239
Auditory discrimination, 21, 238-239
Auditory Discrimination Test, 239
Aukerman, R. C., 415

Baaman, H. A., 149
Bader, L. A., 165, 168, 216

Baldwin, R. S., 149, 396
Barbe, W. B., 15, 18
Barrett, T. C., 10, 19, 65, 79
Basal readers, 81
Basal reading programs, 81, 85-89
Basal reading series, 271-278
Bateman, B., 221, 241
Bauer, C. F., 183, 191
Becking, M. F., 192
Beginning sounds, 33-34
Best Books for Children, 178
Betts, E. A., 165, 169
Bibliotherapy, 171, 186, 382
    intermediate grades,
        386-390
    young children, 383-385
Bingham, A., 79
Blair, T. R., 204, 216, 241
Bloom's taxonomy, 64, 79
Boehm Test of Basic Concepts,
    160, 169
Bond, G. L., 9, 19, 27, 37, 228,
    240, 248, 265
Book Finder, The, 186, 192
Books:
    binding, 284-286
    (*See also* Interests)
Bormuth, J. R., 169
Botel Reading Inventory, 186
Braam, L. S., 144, 149
Broman, B. L., 149
Brophy, J. E., 198, 200, 216
*Bulletin of the Center for
    Children's Books,* 179
Burg, L. A., 265
Burmeister, L. E., 54, 60
Burns, P. C., 149, 265
Buros, O. K., 37, 169
Buros' *Mental Measurement
    Yearbook,* 28, 37, 152, 169

Caldecott Award books, 102, 178,
    184, 303-305
Calendar, The, 179
Campbell, P., 176
Categorizing, 31
Catterson, J. H., 169
Chall, J., 94

Checklists:
    classroom observation, 270-271
    for evaluating games, 284
    of instructional needs, 288-289
    materials, 206-214
    parent, for encouraging
        reading, 420-421
    readiness, 28-29
    vision, 235-237
Chester, R., 44, 60, 61
Chisholm, M., 260, 265
Cianciolo, P., 178, 191
Cinquain, 133, 184
Classroom library, 182
*Classroom Questions: What
    Kinds?,* 64, 79
Classroom Reading Inventory,
    169, 186
Cleland, D. L., 9, 19, 232, 241
Cloer, T., 284
Cloze procedure, 96-97, 163
*Clymer-Barrett Prereading
    Battery,* 28
Co-basal, 105
Compound words, 49
Comprehension, 63-79, 111,
    124-125
    creative, 63, 65
    critical, 63, 65
    interpretative, 63, 65, 69-72
    limitations to, 77-78
    literal, 63, 65-69
Concepts, language, 159-162
Conceptual background, 151,
    159-162
Conferences, parent-teacher, 420
Configuration, 41, 46, 48-49
Content-area reading, 121-126
    comprehension, 124-125
    materials, 93-100
    requirements for, 99
    study skills, 125-126
    vocabulary, 124
Context, 41, 46, 50-51
Coody, B., 192
Copperman, P., 2, 19
Corboy, M., 393, 400, 403, 421
Creative comprehension, 63, 65
Creative reading, 75, 77

Creative writing, 129
Criscuolo, N., 270
Criteria for book selection, 177-178
Criterion-referenced tests, 151-153
Critical comprehension, 63, 65
Critical reading, 72-75
Critical Reading Develops Early, 72, 79
Cruickshank, W. C., 226, 240
Cultural and linguistic diversity, 228-230
  instruction, 229-230
Cultural factors, 21, 25-26
Cursive writing, 129, 136-137
Cushenberry, D. C., 196, 216
Cutts, N. E., 230, 240

Dale, E., 43, 61, 94
Dale-Chall formula, 94
Dallman, M., 265
Davis, F. B., 64, 65, 79
Dawson, M., 149
Dechant, E., 226, 241, 260, 265
deHirsch, K., 27, 38
Deighton, L. C., 54, 61
Developmental reading program, 81
Dewey, J., 22
Dialect, 219
Dictionaries, 46, 51-52
  elementary school, 282-283
  picture, 283
Directed reading activity (DRA), 105, 109, 110-119, 123
Directed reading-thinking activity (DR-TA), 105, 109, 119-121, 123
Directionality, 32
Directions, following, 31
Discrimination, 105
  auditory, 21, 238-239
  visual, 21, 234
Dolch, E. W., 45, 61
Dolch word list, 44-46, 55, 60, 61
Downing, J., 23, 37

DRA (*see* Directed reading activity)
Dreyer, S. S., 186, 192
DR-TA (*see* Directed reading-thinking activity)
Drummond, H., 149
Durkin, D. D., 22, 37, 49, 61, 65, 79, 149, 196, 197, 216, 415
Durrell, D. D., 27, 37, 169, 289
Dykstra, R., 27, 37

Early, M. J., 75, 79
Eberhart, N. A., 265
Ekwall, E. E., 169, 415
Evaluation:
  of DRA, 112
  program, 245-255
Expectancy, reading, 245, 247-249
  Bond and Tinker formula, 248

Farr, R., 2, 19
Feely, T. M., Jr., 102
Fernald, Grace M., 216
Fernald technique, 201-202
Filbeck, R., 224, 241
First Grade Studies, National, 2, 65
Five-finger technique, 94
Flesch, R., 2, 19, 88, 94
  reading ease formula, 94
Flexibility, 129, 141, 144-145
Flood, J., 48, 61, 192, 241, 265
Fluency, 129, 141-142
Forgan, H. W., 38
Francis, W. N., 44, 60, 61
Free reading, 172
Frustration level, 151, 165
Fry, E. B., 137, 153, 169, 216
  readability formula, 95

Games, 101
  checklist for evaluating, 284
Gates-MacGinitie Readiness Skills Test, 28

Gifted children, 230–233
  characteristics of, 231
  instruction for, 231–233
Grade placement, 245, 247
Greene, F. P., 133, 149
Greene, H. Λ., 140, 149
Grouping:
  achievement-level, 195,
    200–201
  heterogeneous, 1, 15, 195
  homogeneous, 1, 15, 195
  interclass, 195–198
  skill-needs, 195, 201–202
  special-interest, 195, 202–203
Guidance counselor, 258–259
Guided reading procedure (GRP),
  106, 123–125
Guided reading techniques,
  109–121
Guszak, F. J., 15, 19, 50, 61,
  66, 79, 156, 169, 415

Haiku, 133–134, 183–184
Handwriting, 134–138
  cursive, 129, 136–137
  left-handedness, 137–138
  manuscript, 129, 136–137
  readiness, 135–136
Handwriting lesson, 136
Hansen, L., 196, 216
Hardin, V. B., 3, 18
Harker, W. J., 10, 19
Harris, A. J., 61, 94, 139,
  141, 149, 153, 169, 196,
  199, 216, 415
Harris, L. A., 49, 61
Harris-Jacobson formulas, 94
*Harrison-Stroud Reading
  Readiness Profiles*, 28, 234
Hearing, 238–239
Hearing (listening) vocabulary,
  41, 43
Heckleman, R. G., 201, 216
Heilman, A. W., 415
Heimberger, M. J., 187, 192
Herber, H. L., 10, 19, 65, 79,
  102, 123, 124, 127, 232, 241

Heterogeneous grouping, 1, 15,
  195
High-interest, low-vocabulary,
  books, 101, 278–282
High-interest, low-vocabulary
  magazines, 391
Hill, W. R., 44, 61
Hillerich, R. L., 46–47, 60, 61
Homogenous grouping, 1, 15, 195,
Horn Book, The, 179
Houston, S. H., 241
Huck, C. S., 178, 192, 259, 265
Huey, E. B., 22, 38
Huus, H., 172, 192

Impress method, 201, 202
Independent learning, 195,
  198–200
Independent level, 151, 171
Individualized reading programs,
  81, 89–93, 182
Informal reading inventory (IRI),
  152, 162–168
Ingram, R., 418
Instructional level, 152, 165
Interclass grouping, 195–198
Interests:
  active, 171, 173
  assessing, 173–174
  and attitudes, 175–177
  children's choices, 305–382
  incomplete sentences, 401–402
  inventory, 400
  potential, 171, 173
Interpretive comprehension, 63,
  65, 69–72
Interpretive reading, 70–72
*Inventory of Teacher Knowledge
  of Reading,* 3, 18

Jacobs, L. B., 89, 102
Jacobson, L., 26, 38
Jacobson, M. D., 94, 139, 149
Jansky, J., 27, 38
Jensen, J. M., 44, 61
Johnson, D. D., 44, 49, 54, 61
Johnson, G. O., 226, 240

Johnson, M. S., 164, 169
Johnson, T. D., 79
Joplin plan, 196, 197
Junior Great Book Clubs, 185

Kaluger, G., 221, 239, 241
Karlin, R., 42, 61
Kaufman, R. K., 396
Kennedy, E. C., 60, 61
Kephart, N. C., 226, 241
Keystone Visual Survey Tests,
    24, 235
Kinesthetic approach to reading
    instruction, 1
Kinesthetic sense in Fernald
    technique, 201
Kirk, S. A., 221, 241
Koch, K., 184, 192
Koenke, K. A., 415
Kolson, C. J., 221, 239, 241
Kress, R. A., 164, 169
Kucera, H., 44, 60, 61
Kuhn, D. Y., 259, 265

Labeling, 34
Lamkin, F. D., 75, 79
Language and cultural diversity,
    228-230
    instruction, 229-230
Language development, 155-159
Language-experience approach,
    22, 82-85, 106-109
Lapp, D., 48, 61, 192, 241, 265
Larrick, N., 178, 192
Learning disabilities, 220-226
    definition of, 221-222
    implications of, 222-223
    instruction and, 223-226
Lee, D. M., 79, 82, 102
Lee, J. M., 231, 233, 241
Left-handedness, 137-138
Letter matching, 32
Letter names, 33
Levels, 162-163
    frustration, 151, 165
    independent, 151, 165, 171
    instructional, 152, 165
Lewis, N., 54, 61

Librarian, 259-260
Linguistic and cultural diversity,
    228-230
    instruction, 229-230
Literal comprehension, 63, 65-69
Literature in elementary
    curriculum, 182-186
Locational skills, 129

McCracken, M., 93, 102, 415
McCracken, R., 93, 102, 415
McCullough, C. M., 50, 51, 61,
    233, 234, 242, 263, 266
McGuffey Readers, 85
McLaughlin, G. H., 96
McMenemy, R., 230, 241
Macmillan Reading Readiness
    Test, 28
Magazines for children, 179-180,
    391-393
Management:
    classroom, 195-216
    of materials, 206-214
Mangieri, J. N., 44, 61, 149,
    258, 260, 265
Manuscript writing, 129, 136-137
Manzo, A. V., 110, 123, 127
Materials:
    content area, 93-100
    high-interest, low vocabulary,
        101, 391-393
    locating and selecting,
        177-180
    management of, 206-214
    supplementary, 82, 100-101
    teacher-made, 98-100
Maze technique, 96-97
Media, use of, 184
Metropolitan Readiness Tests, 28
Miller, W. H., 196, 216
Moe, A. J., 44, 60, 61
Monroe, M., 27, 38
Morphett, M. V., 22, 38
Moseley, N., 230, 240
Motivation, 286-287
    activities, 92-93
Murphy-Durrell Reading
    Readiness Analysis, 28, 234

Musgrave, G. R., 220, 241

National First and Second Grade
    Studies, 2, 65
Nelson, J. B., 232, 241
Newbery Award books, 102, 178,
    184
    grade equivalents, 302-303
Newport, J. F., 196, 216
Newspapers for children, 180

Objectives, developmental
    program, 245, 249-250,
    290-299
Olson, W. C., 90, 102
Oral expression, 130-132
Oral language:
    activities, 188-189
    development, 30-31
    expression, 158
Oral reading, 111-112, 156-157,
    163, 183
Organic reading, 106-107
Organization, classroom, 200-203
Organizations for reading
    professionals, 414
Orthorater, 24
Otto, W., 44, 60, 61, 196, 216,
    225, 230, 241

Parents, 262-264
    materials and suggestions for
    dealing with, 417-421
Patterns of organization:
    in content-area comprehension,
    125
    of signal words, 67
Pearson, P. D., 44, 49, 54, 61
Peterson, R. I., 261, 265
Petty, D. C., 192
Petty, W. T., 44, 61, 140,
    149, 192
Phonics, 41, 46, 48
Physical limitations, 233-239
    assessment and accommodation,
    234-235, 238-239

Physical limitations (*Cont.*):
    auditory, 238-239
    visual, 233-239
Picture clues in context usage, 50
Planning and materials, 206-214
Plays for Reading, 92
Poetry, teaching of, 183-184
Polette, N., 192
Potential, testing and, 247-249
Pottorff, D., 23, 38
Prefixes, 50
Prereading activities, 30-36
Principals, 260-262
Professional organizations, 414
Professional Vision Tester, 24
Program development, 245-264
    evaluation, 246-255
    improvement, 255-257
Propaganda techniques, 73-74
Publishers, names and addresses
    of, 423-430
Purposes for reading, 143-144

Quandt, I., 225, 241
Questionnaires for program
    evaluation, 250-255

Raths, L., 200, 216
Raygor, A., 94
    readability formula, 94,
    396-397
Read-a-Thon, 112
Readability, 1
Readability formulas, 17, 94-96,
    396-397
Readiness, 21, 22-30, 36
    for handwriting, 135-136
    for spelling, 138
    for study skills, 145-146
Readiness checklists, 28-29
Readiness tests, 27, 28, 406
Reading, recreational (*see*
    Recreational reading)
Reading Attitude Inventory, 176
Reading expectancy, 245, 247-249
Reading Interest/Attitude Scale,
    The, 176

Reading inventory, 1
Reading Is FUNdamental (RIF), 112, 119, 181
Reading journal, 174-176
Reading models, 171
Reading rates, 141-145
Reading record, 174-176
Reading specialist, 257-258
Recall, delayed, 46-52
Recreational reading, 172, 301-382
  children's choices, 305-382
  magazines, 391-393
  survey of, 402-403
Reger, R., 228, 241
Rhyming words, 35
RIF (Reading Is FUNdamental), 112, 119, 181
Rinsland, H., 44, 60, 61
Robinson, H. A., 51, 61
Roe, B. D., 265
Root words, 49-50
Rosenthal, R., 26, 38
Ross, R. R., 92, 102
Ruddell, R. B., 26, 38, 415
Rupley, W. H., 204, 216, 241
Russell, D. H., 65, 79, 102

Sanders, N., 79
Sartain, H. W., 241, 250, 266
Sartain Attitudes Toward Reading Inventory, 176
Sawyer, J., 230, 241
Sawyer, R., 92, 102
Scanning, 129, 143
Scheduling in classroom organization, 203
School Vision Tester, 235
Self-concept, 219
Sequencing, 31-32
Sex differences and maturity, 23
Shrodes, C., 102
Sight vocabulary, 41, 44-46
Silent reading, 111
Silvaroli, N. J., 169, 415
Singer, H., 22, 38, 397

Singer Eyeball Estimate of Readability (SEER), 94, 397
Sipay, E. R., 61, 94, 141, 149, 169, 196, 199, 216, 415
Skill-needs grouping, 195, 201-202
Skimming, 129, 143
Slow learning rates, 226-228
  instruction, 227-228
  reading, 226-227
Smith, C. B., 49, 61
Smith, F., 415
Smith, H. A., 266
Smith, J. A., 192
Smith, N. B., 65, 79, 106, 127
Smith, R. J., 196, 197, 216, 230, 241
Smith, S. L., 222, 241
SMOG formula, 96
Snellen Chart, 234
Socher, E. E., 98, 102
Social and psychological factors, 21, 25
Spache, E. B., 24, 38, 102, 198, 216, 229, 242, 415
Spache, G. D., 24, 38, 102, 198, 199, 216, 229, 233, 242, 415
  readability formula, 94
Spache Binocular Reading Test, 24, 235
Special-interest grouping, 195, 202-203
Special services, 245, 257, 260
Speech difficulties, 157-158
Speech sounds, 157
Spelling, 138-141
  content of, 139
  objectives of, 138
  readiness for, 138
  and reading, 141
Spelling demons, 140-141
Spelling lesson, 139-140
Spelling rules, 139-140
SQ3R, 146
Stanton, P. E., 241, 259, 266
Stauffer, R. G., 109-110, 127, 415
Stereotests, 24

Storytelling, 92–93, 183
Strain, L. B., 192
Strang, R., 233, 234, 242, 263, 266, 401
Strange, M., 284
Strickland, D. S., 26, 38
Strickland, R., 106, 127
Structural analysis, 41, 46, 49–50
  compound words, 49
  prefixes and suffixes, 50
  root words, 49–50
  variants, 49
Study skills, 145–148
  readiness, 145–146
  teaching, 147–148
Suffixes, 50
Sustained silent reading (SSR), 93
Sutherland, Z., 178, 192
Synthetic method approach to remediation, 201–202

Taba, H., 61, 65, 79
TABA lesson, 55–56
Teacher, 106
Teacher-made materials, 98–100
Testing, word-list, 163–164
Tests:
  diagnostic: group, 410
    individual, 408–409
  informal reading inventories, individual, 406
  intelligence: group, 412
    individual, 411
  readiness, group, 406
  reading achievement, group, 407
  standardized, 152
Thompson, R., 228, 242
Thorndike's Word List, 50, 56
Tinker, M. A., 9, 19, 50, 61, 228, 240, 248, 263, 265, 266
Titmus School Vision Tester, 235
Tracking, 1, 15, 195
Trade books, 171
Traxler, A. E., 233, 234, 242, 263, 266
Tyler, R. W., 249, 266

Typing Course for Children, 137

VAKT senses in Fernald technique, 201
Variants of words, 49
Veatch, J., 89, 90, 102, 199, 216
Vision problems, 233–238
Visual acuity, 21, 234
Visual discrimination, 21, 234
Visual tests, 24, 235
Vocabulary:
  content-area, 124
  expressive, 151, 155–156
  hearing (listening), 41, 43
  reading, 41, 43
  receptive, 152, 155–156
  speaking, 41, 43
  writing, 41, 43
Vocabulary acquisition, 52–54
Vocabulary activities, 54–59
Vocabulary retention, 52–54

Wallach, L., 24, 38
Wallach, M., 24, 38
Washburn, C., 22, 38
Wasson, B. B., 9, 19, 228, 240, 265
Wepman, J., 239
Whitehead, R., 149
Why Johnny Can't Read, 75, 88
Wilson, R. M., 233, 238, 242
Witty, P. A., 231, 242
Woelfel, S., 79
Word bank, 106
Word recognition, 46
Writing, 129
  activities emphasizing, 187–188
  (*See also* Creative writing; Cursive writing; Manuscript writing)
Written expression, 132–134, 158–159

Zintz, M. V., 203, 216, 242, 415